A Book of Evidence

A Book of Evidence

The Trials and Execution of Jesus

NANCY L. KUEHL

RESOURCE *Publications* · Eugene, Oregon

A BOOK OF EVIDENCE
The Trials and Execution of Jesus

Copyright © 2013 Nancy L. Kuehl. All rights reserved. Except for brief quotations in critical publications or reviews, no part of this book may be reproduced in any manner without prior written permission from the publisher. Write: Permissions, Wipf and Stock Publishers, 199 W. 8th Ave., Suite 3, Eugene, OR 97401.

Scripture quotations marked (NIV) are taken from the Holy Bible, New International Version®, NIV®. Copyright © 1973, 1978, 1984, 2011 by Biblica, Inc.™ Used by permission of Zondervan. All rights reserved worldwide. www.zondervan.com The "NIV" and "New International Version" are trademarks registered in the United States Patent and Trademark Office by Biblica, Inc.™

JPS TANAKH 1985 (English). The TANAKH, a new translation (into contemporary English) of The Holy Scriptures according to the traditional Hebrew text (Masoretic). The Jewish Bible: Torah, Nevi'im, Kethuvim. Copyright © 1985 by The Jewish Publication Society. All rights reserved. This fresh translation began work in 1955. Used by permission.

A Book of Evidence: The Trials and Execution of Jesus. Nancy L. Kuehl. Copyright © 2012. Wipf and Stock Publishers, 199 West 8th Avenue, Suite 3, Eugene, OR 97401 USA.

Resource Publications
An Imprint of Wipf and Stock Publishers
199 W. 8th Ave., Suite 3
Eugene, OR 97401

www.wipfandstock.com

ISBN 13: 978-71-62032-497-4

Manufactured in the U.S.A.

For Mom who never stopped believing;
For my three children: Rob, Kris, and Kerry
whose constant love and patience have kept me dedicated to my purpose;
and
For my grandchildren: Julian, Bianca, and Zac

Contents

List of Illustrations | viii
List of Tables | viii
Foreword by DeLinda Goodman Osteen | ix
Preface | xi
Acknowledgments | xiii
List of Abbreviations | xv
Prologue | xvii
Introduction: Jesus: The Hebrew Messiah or The Christian Christ? | xxi

1 The Crime: Apostasy from the Law | 1

2 The Night of Watching | 53

3 The Jewish Trial | 99

4 The Roman Pseudo-Trial | 126

5 Beth Pagi: The Place of the Crux | 151

6 The Execution | 187

7 The Lamp of the World | 206

Epilogue | 223
Appendix A | 225
Appendix B | 226
Bibliography | 227

ILLUSTRATIONS

Figure 1 Quadrate
Figure 2 The Three Encampments of Jerusalem
Figure 3 Olive Tree in the Garden of Gethsemane
Figure 4 Rolling Stone Tomb at Bethphage
Figure 5 Graffiti on Tomb at Bethphage
Figure 6 Layout of Tomb #21 at Bethphage

TABLES

Table 1 Comparison of Greek word *plateia* in Bible versions
Table 2 Comparison of Greek word *topos* in Bible versions
Table 3 Comparison of Hebrew words *rechob* and *charuts* in Bible versions

Foreword

THE AUTHOR OF *A Book of Evidence* is among a growing number of people who are seeking to better know Jesus in the context of his Jewish roots. Ms. Kuehl has chosen to use the laws of both the Jews and Romans as the tool with which to diligently search and dig through to the light. The supremacy of the Roman laws over all the lands it dominated as a cruel overlord, coupled with ensuing arrogance, provided researchers with myriad amounts of documentation. The "splitting of hairs" by the religious and powerful aristocracy was recorded with equal fervor. Thus, a great benefit was handed down in time for the day when scholarly researchers would uncover "nuggets of truth" that would take the wraps of obscure statements and individual words of special context. This now exposes the readers to details and intimations that allow us to glean for ourselves a more authentic look at Jesus. We begin to see Jesus in a different light . . . the light of a Hebrew Messiah! There is an additional blessing in that as this new light enters, the burdens and barriers created by misconceptions and false ideation that arise from seeing Jesus as a Greek Christ—vanishes! It is much like taking a glass of clouded water and running tap water into it until the clouded water is displaced. All that then remains is the sparkling, clear, delicious, and healthful water. The great beauty of this is that the glass is never made empty!

    Someone might say, why the fuss over achieving a Hebrew perspective, the grid or mindset that all the New Covenant writings should be seen through. It is because the perspective held becomes the driving force behind the perception received. In other words, be careful *how* you hear! It is that point of reference that becomes one's point of contact with the word being perceived. For example, here is just one event in Jesus' life that truly needs to be viewed from a Hebrew perspective: Jesus went down to the Jordan where John was at ministry. All who knew Jesus were aware of his love for the God of Abraham, his dedication to the law of Moses, and the sweetness of his pious daily life. But on this day, a gripping need in his soul hit him, to draw closer to the God of Israel and seek out what God really wanted for his life. The fact is that he, himself, could not truly articulate in words the desires of his heart. As he was being immersed, there under the waters it seemed that the world with all its noise and bluster was made dead to him! As Jesus came up out of those waters of obscurity and womb-like covering . . . it happened! He came forth into God's marvelous light—heavenly light. It was as if his very own eyes had just opened to a heaven that had just then been opened to him. He heard the fiery words of grandeur—Beloved Son—this day have I begotten thee. The vibrating sound of the Voice of those words rolled through him in torrents of transforming glory. The regenerating power in that utterance

Foreword

took hold of his inner being and completely redirected his entire view of reality. Old things had passed away. Behold indeed, all things had become new. This was that which was so consistently referred to by the prophets. This experience was, in fact, the glorious entrance that was being made for him into the Kingdom of God. The sacred silence within him rested in an awareness of unity with he who had begotten him by his word. His life had now been meshed into and within that very source of Life itself. He had been brought into perfect union with the God of Israel and as such he had now become the Hebrew Messiah foretold of in the Scriptures that he so dearly loved.

This author of this book has "turned the faucet tap on" more fully for us and, thus we see Jesus—the author and finisher of our faith—more clearly.

DeLinda Goodman Osteen

Preface

THE FOCAL POINT OF this book is the legal process of the trials and execution of Jesus. Over the years I have read and studied numerous books on the Passion event but found they did not fully answer my questions. I began the research for this book in 1994. It has gone through several revisions from that period of time until the present. Due to personal responsibilities I was unable to spend the time necessary to prepare the book for publication. My time, too, was spent writing other commentaries on Bible books and in historical studies. It was only in January of 2012 that I was able to give focused attention to its preparation. Had it not been for the encouragement of loved ones the book would still be in the depths of my computer.

A Book of Evidence is unique in that it is written from a Jewish *legal* standpoint. Although the Tosefta and Mishnah were not codified until about 200 CE, the laws in those volumes arose from Jewish customs and Scripture, some existing from the time of Moses, and many were in effect at the time of Jesus. The Talmuds that followed are compilations of discussions about those laws, some arising from unique events that had occurred centuries earlier. The New Covenant gospels and other ancient writings give us a basic outline for the trials and execution, but they can hardly be considered completely historical. Even though they are theological documents, they do describe the basic tenets of the overall history of the death of Jesus. Although I have used the King James Version of the Bible for most Scriptural quotations, in some instances I have used other editions like Rotherham's Emphasized Bible, the JPS Tanach, the Companion Bible, and numerous others to clarify the wording of important phrases. I have also reviewed extraneous material such as the Hebrew Gospel of Matthew found in the Jewish document, *Evan Bohan* by Shem Tov and translated by George Howard. I, also, found of some value the *Slavonic Josephus* in its three forms and discussed by Hugh Schonfield, a scholar of the earliest Jesus Movement. Much of the material in the book pertaining to the aristocratic priesthood and the Herodian dynasty has been supplied by the Jewish historian, Josephus and has clarified statements made in the Mishnah and the Babylonian Talmud. The Dead Sea Scrolls and other early writings have also been utilized. Various sources have been compared as evidence to arrive at my conclusions.

My purpose in writing the book, at first, was my own sense of curiosity and for my own understanding. I knew the Jesus I had learned of in Sunday school and church, but I had a burning desire to experience a personal relationship with him that I simply could not find there. I felt I wasn't getting the entire story and had important questions that I needed to answer for myself. The more I read and studied about the earliest days of Christianity as it existed during the first sixty years, the more I realized there was much more to the movement than I had ever imagined. I set out on a journey to truly know Jesus as a Jew in his own setting and culture and to know him as *my Jewish* Messiah on a personal level. What I learned was of such importance that I believe the entire religious community should become aware of the ultimate conclusions of my research. Since that time, I have learned there are others who have had the same questions as myself. I hope this book will be enlightening to those who have those questions and provide them with some of the answers they have sought.

Acknowledgments

THIS BOOK WAS WRITTEN and re-written over a period of almost fifteen years. Hundreds of hours have gone into the research for it. Librarians and staff at numerous libraries need to be acknowledged for their time and dedication, among them: Bates Law Library at the University of Houston; the Sterling Evans Library at Texas A&M; Steen Library at Stephen F. Austin State University; the Texas Christian University Library; and the Grapevine Public Library for the City of Grapevine, Texas.

I owe a debt of gratitude to my dear friend Dr. John W. Stewart, former professor in Hebrew and Old Testament Studies at Texas Christian University, and my pastor for many years, from whom I learned biblical Hebrew and Greek.

I also especially appreciate the love and support of my friends and study partners, Bill and Delinda Osteen, Gayle Zientek, and Sheila Saunders, without whose eagerness to share their faith this book could not have been written.

Gratitude goes to all those who went before, the scholars and colleagues from whose books and studies have assisted and influenced my life and education. Without the research of men like E. P. Sanders, John Lightfoot, Hugh Schonfield, William Winston, John Crossan, Bart Erhman, Benjamin Mazar, Jacob Neusner, Ernest Martin, Richard Rubenstein, and numerous others, the list too lengthy to name individually, this book would not have been possible.

Special thanks to all my friends and correspondents who have influenced and supported me in my theological endeavors: Daniella Whelchel, Rebecca Bergeron, Ian Mune, Lambert Dolphin, Mike Sanders, Moza, Daniel Dror, Mike Richardson, Michael Devolin, Dennis Jump, and many others.

Abbreviations

ABD	Anchor Bible Dictionary
Ant.	*Antiquities of the Jews*
b.	Babylonian Talmud
BAR	Biblical Archaeology Review
BCE	Before the Common Era
Ber.	*Berakoth*
b.m.	*Baba Mezi'a*
CBN	Companion Bible
CE	Common Era
EBR	Rotherham's Emphasized Bible
Eccl.	*Hist. Ecclesiastical History*
ISR	The Scriptures
JE	Jerusalem Encyclopedia
JPS	The Hebrew Tanakh
Kel.	*Kelim*
KJV	King James Bible
m.	*Mishnah*
Macc.	*Maccabees*
Men.	*Menahot*
Mid.	*Middot*
NIV	New International Version
NRM	Netzarim Reconstruction of Matthew
Nah.	*Pesh. Nahum Pesher*
Neg.	*Nega'im*
Par.	*Parah*
Pes.	*Pesahim*
R. H.	*Rosh Hashanah*
ROSN	Restoration of the Sacred Name Bible
Sanh.	*Sanhedrin*
Shab.	*Shabbat*
Shebu.	*Shebuot*
Sot.	*Sotah*
Ta'an.	*Ta'anit*

xv

Abbreviations

Tam.	*Tamid*
Toh.	*Tohoroth*
Tosef.	Tosefta
y.	Jerusalem or Palestinian Talmud
Yeb.	Yebamoth
YLT	Young's Literal Translation
Yom.	*Yoma*

Prologue

It is Passover—Racham, a lone Galilean pilgrim approaches the final leg of his journey to Jerusalem. He wonders if it is the anticipation of the festivities or the chill of the spring morning breeze causing goosebumps to prickle on his skin. Faltering in his steps, he rubs his arms roughly, shrugs, and hastens on. A few moments more and he can pause for rest on the "prospect" overlooking the magnificent splendor of Jerusalem. He rushes along, drawing in the crisp spring air, letting his eyes linger here and there on patches of wildly brilliant spring flowers. The world seems alive with carnival color after what seemed like so long a winter. At last he tops the ridge and leans against a lone olive tree to survey the gleaming city below with its white limestone and marble structures, now golden, reflecting the rays of the early morning sun. The beloved Temple captures his attention at once. Rising majestically above the Kidron Valley below, it too, seems to loom from utter darkness into the *Shekinah*, itself. On either side of the stony road descending into the valley below, the northwestern slope is speckled with gnarled fig trees rising from rocky soil, and olives with their silver and dark green leaves swaying in the breeze. Also here are sparse clusters of palms, myrtles, pines, and cedars. His eyes scan the Temple Mount, mesmerized by the breathtaking size of it. A carpet of tents, resembling the colorful flowers he had earlier passed dot the northern landscape of the western slopes of Olivet, stretching as far as the eye can see. It is here Racham's family would be gathering. He wondered if they would be awaiting him in their usual campsite. He lets his gaze wander southward toward the Red Heifer bridge spanning the Kidron Valley below. Near the public square Racham could trace the outline of the administrative temple buildings, where he must report to the Chamber of the Census to be counted for the season. In Beth Pagi were the numerous other executive offices, like the chamber where the witnesses for the New Moon gathered, and the Arch of Accounts where the ledgers were kept. Near the Plaza was also the altar *Miphkad* where the Red Heifer was slain and the *Bet HaDeshen*, the pit for burning the sin-offering. Its sacred ashes were to be used in purifying Passover pilgrims for entrance into the Temple. Near the Plaza, itself, were the four Bazaars of Annas and the two famous cypress trees under which the dovecotes were located. Today Racham would not have to purchase a dove; he would make enough profit from this season's crops to offer, instead, a lamb for his peace-offering. It was an honor that he could do this for his God.

But something didn't seem quite right with the scene before him this year. He found it unsettling. Ordinarily, the booths would be crowded and chaotic. Racham's

Prologue

eyes darted toward the double-arched bridge where pilgrims often gathered to exchange their Roman coins for the half-pieces of silver required for the Temple tax. It, too, was almost devoid of people. His eyes followed the path of the bridge back to the Plaza of *Gulgoleth*. Now he knew what he found so disturbing. A throng was gathered around the *Bet HaSeqilah*, the execution site! How was it possible that an execution could take place on this day? This was Passover! Impossible! From this far distance, Racham saw only that there appeared to be three naked criminals suspended on the ancient olive tree in the center of the Plaza. The scene troubled him greatly. It always distressed him to participate in an execution, yet as a citizen of Israel he would be required by law to do so. His parents had often told him he was too compassionate for his own good. They had chosen his name well at his circumcision: Racham, "compassionate". The sight of the Roman-type crucifixion, adopted and modified by the Babylonian-Alexandrian priesthood, was appalling! They, like the High Priest Alexander Jannaeus before them, had begun to execute criminals by hanging them *alive* on the tree. Never in all Israel's history had such atrocities been committed!

Racham had begun to slowly descend the mount and to make his way along the southern Jericho Road, passing by Gethsemane on his way to the Plaza, but now he hastened his steps, partly walking, sometimes running, until at long last, gasping for breath he reached the public square. He pushed his way through to the edge of the droning din crowded around the tree. His vision was hindered by the closeness of the masses, and he was unable to see the man suspended on the front. As he sought to even his breathing, Racham edged his way westward for a better view. It was not the other two but the man facing westward that seemed to be the object of the crowd's derision. Hushed insults hissed from lips of pilgrims passing through the Plaza on their own journeys to the Temple. Only when they had passed out of the square and separated themselves from the midst of the rustling horde did their voices grow bolder and louder. It had been unlawful for them to speak while stoning a man. The only sounds to be heard came from the criminals, themselves, crying out for mercy. The two criminals on back slipped into merciful unconsciousness, and the crowd's attention riveted to the man on front. There appeared, at first, some apprehension on the part of some within the group to cast their stones at this quiet, meek man. Mingled together as they were, the whispered words of the crowd were difficult for Racham to distinguish: something about a king, he thought. It was not until the aristocratic priests urged the crowd that the pilgrims began hurtling stones at the naked man on front, sending their silent curses to bite sharply into the man's already bloody flesh, peeling away tiny hunks of skin and leaving it flapping from his exposed and whitened bones. Racham, too, would soon be required to curse the *mesith*, excommunicating him forever from the congregation of Israel. He stooped to pick up one of the loose limestone fragments from the rock-strewn ground nearby and drew closer to the tree. It was all he could do to fight his nausea as he pushed his way through the, by now, frenzied hive of human chaos. Agitated, Racham fidgeted with the stone, now clasped tightly in his fist. He watched as the man braced himself against the onslaught of pelting stones, noting his sharp gasps and soft murmuring groans as the sharp-edged stones nipped at his face. Suddenly, Racham's eyes were caught by those of the man on the front of the tree. Shock-waves rolled violently through him. His breath caught. Those eyes reflected agony so intense that it pierced Racham's very soul, and in an instant he recognized Jesus of Nazareth! Although he did not know him well, Racham had heard him speaking to a multitude near the shores of Tiberius. He had given some thought to the man's powerful words and had often thought of him. There was something special about this man. Never had Racham known such a tender God-fearing man nor such an exquisite teacher. It was preposterous to think that such a kind, gentle man who had done so much for the people was now being repaid evil for good. Although many of the rulers had believed his teachings were politically dangerous, Racham rejected such a notion. He stood frozen in time and space, still gazing compassionately into the anguished eyes of Jesus. He thought he saw a glimmer of something more than anguish, though. Strangely, there was a hint of confidence and quiet victory in his eyes, even amidst the whispered taunts of rancor and piercing insults he was yet enduring. Tears slowly welled in Racham's eyes until they could no longer be confined to such a limited space, and the first, a solitary tear, rolled down his cheek. Transfixed, he slowly opened the fist at his side. The limestone rock he had held in his sweating fist dropped to the ground. In Racham's ears the stone clapped like thunder. The rock's impact on the perforated surface of the execution floor continued to resound loudly. The sound was strikingly contradictory to the thudding of stones impacting tender flesh and the ghoulish screams emitted by the two Zealots on the back side of the tree. They had now regained consciousness and returned to their living Hell. The man Jesus gazed intently at Racham for a moment more, then in a convulsion of pain, he sought to lift himself from his *sedile* for a breath, then dropped his head in quiet dignity. The spikes that pinned his wrists to the yoke prevented him from catching a complete breath. Racham stood glued to the spot, horrified at the man's reaction to his agony. When he could bear the torturous scene no longer, Racham turned quietly aside and began to slip away. He pushed his way through the crowd, revolted, fighting the darkness that threatened to engulf him. He made it as far as the Miphkad Gate and leaned against it for a moment to regain his balance. The tumultuous sounds of the multitude now congregating on the bridge seemed far away, overcome by the ongoing reverberation made by the stone's impact with the ground. He would never forget the clapping thunder of the dropped stone, nor the forgiveness so evident in the man's eyes. Racham escaped the execution site and the Plaza, but he did not escape the brutality. It would be written in the annals of his mind for years to come. It was not with the anticipation he had experienced earlier that morning that he entered the narrow gate leading to the Eastern Cloister, but with a sad emptiness and a revolting visage that would, in future years, become for him the seed of life.

Introduction
Jesus: The Hebrew Messiah or The Christian Christ?

THE PRECEDING STORY IS not the traditional rendering of the execution of Jesus. It is not the comfortable story of Easter that has been polished by Christian tradition. It is, however, more in line with the indignation and the true sufferings of that Hebrew Passion Passover. It is within the scope of this story that Jesus is revealed as the Hebrew Messiah of Israel.

The historicity attached to the evidence, arrest, trials, and execution of Jesus is paramount to any significant spiritual understanding of the man and his mission. While the focus of this book is the passion event, it is essential to entertain some notion of first century religious thought, both Jewish and Gentile, in order to give the events meaning. Some earnest attempt is made within the totality of this book to show who Jesus is through the eyes of his first century contemporaries; that is, through the eyes of 1) the ruling class Jew in Israel; 2) the general mass of Jewish population; 3) the Herodian Dynasty; 4) the Roman authorities garrisoned in the land; and 5) the remainder of pagan Gentiles living in and near Judea. Was Jesus the Hebrew Messiah, or was he the Gentile Christ? As we shall soon learn, there is a world of difference.

The historical Jesus has, in recent years, been the subject of intense scholarly debate. The following investigation also searches for the humanity of Jesus but not in isolation from his spiritual side. This search is made in a manner that conflicts neither with Scripture nor history but actually complements it. Even through the use of many of the same tools and resources that the "Jesus historians" utilize, his humanity actually verifies that he was and is the Son of God, the promised Hebrew Messiah of Israel: the very person he claimed to be! This is not to say the findings are based on a totally *emotional* bias. Every attempt has been made to present the evidence in as objective a manner as possible to arrive at the "truth". Since New Covenant writings have remained virtually silent, lending themselves only to scant verifiable data concerning the trials and execution, we must approach the problem caused by such lack of evidence through use of peripheral documentation. Without *some* empirical attempt to draw logical and reasonable conclusions about these matters Jesus and his execution remains for us an enigma. When *traditions*, whether Christian or Judaic, are removed from such an analysis, however, the facts can be chronicled in such a way as to view the man as he really was. It then becomes entirely unnecessary to invent plausible theories regarding seemingly contradictory statements made by the four gospel narrators. Once the historical data is meticulously gathered, it remains only to organize and compile them into a natural order that will lead to a single, definite conclusion, that Jesus was, and is, the promised Hebrew Messiah of Israel. One will be able to discern both the human *and* spiritual character of Jesus, of what he intended to accomplish, and how the events of his life meshed into a religious *tradition* that has become one of the most powerful forces in the world.

An investigation into Hebrew Scriptures, Mosaic legislation, rabbinic law, and historical data renders a reasonable, real, logical, and true conclusion about that fateful week almost two thousand years ago. The human Jesus cannot be separated from the spiritual Jesus. His whole character must be studied in order to determine who he is. It must be stated that such investigation is long overdue. Unless the conclusions of the "historical Jesus" researchers lead to some spiritual truth, they are of little consequence to anyone. It becomes necessary to strike some equilibrium. The equilibrium is to be found, not in "mystical spirituality", but in balancing Jesus' humanity with his devotion and unity with God. The results of such a study are astounding. Without employing the use of *biblical* logic, the truth becomes impossible to attain. The methods of research used to arrive at some semblance of the truth did not require the emotional "blind faith" on which some would rely in embarking on such a study. Such faith is, indeed, "blind", because "faith cometh by *hearing,* and *hearing by the word of God"* (Rom. 10:17). Unless we *hear* what God says in the patterns he gives us in Scripture, we cannot possibly know and understand, nor might we identify the person and character of Jesus. Jesus said, "And if the blind lead the blind, both shall fall into the ditch" (Matt. 15:14). Such a study does not require adherence to the bland humanism of "historical Jesus" research. Since Jesus was both human *and* spiritual, such research requires us to examine *both* qualities of his person. This is not to say that such spirituality is in any way equal to the "mystical" qualities assigned to Jesus by a first century populace associated with the pagan "mystic" religions of the East. He, instead, exhibits the human quality assigned to the Son of David, receiving his title Son of God through his spiritual union with YHWH.

Hebrew idiom, custom, usage, and history play a great part in any such investigation. There is simply no getting around the fact that Jesus was a Jewish man who lived in a Jewish (albeit somewhat Hellenized) culture and was certainly influenced by the Judaic religion as it existed during the early first century. Judaism, too, was multifaceted, laden with its *own* contemporary traditions, practices, and belief structures. All these things affected the way Jesus thought. To step backward from the Christian-Hellenic world into the world of Jesus requires a transition to a foreign culture which many individuals are either unaware of or are unwilling to make. Unless this step is taken, however, it is impossible to learn even a scintilla of truth. Not only have our present translations with their vague Greek definitions deluded the Gentile population, they have, in effect, turned the Jewish world against Jesus. It is, therefore, imperative that terminology should play a part in the unfolding of the truth. In order to understand the meanings of certain words, we must define them from the perspective of what they would have meant to Jews living during that period of time. We must also consider that while Hebrew is a specific language, often using a single word to describe a definite set of terms, in Greek and/or English those words are ambiguous. These languages often have only one vague and inadequate term to serve in translation. For example, the word "man", which

Introduction

is simply "man" in English, can be defined in Greek as "any man", "no man", or "some man", not a descriptive but a limited term. In Hebrew, however, there are a number of words for "man". There are, to name a few, *adam*, mankind; *ish*, an extant, mortal man; *geber*, a valiant or mighty man; *zakar*, a esteemed man; *elem*, a young man; and *enosh*, a consecrated man. Besides these, there are also specific designations for a wicked man, an unrepentant man, *et cetera*. Each Hebrew term thus specifies not only that the man is a living male but it also describes the *kind* of man he is. The exactness of the language is also specific when in spoken form. An example of just how precise the Hebrew language becomes is discussed in the Jewish Talmud.

> The Judeans were particular about their use of language. For example, a Judean once announced that he had a cloak to sell. He was asked, "What is the color of your cloak?" He replied, "Like that of beets on the ground." The Galileans were not particular about their use of language. For example: A certain Galilean went around asking, "Who has *amar*?" [Note 7—Since he did not pronounce some sounds distinctly, it was not clear whether he meant *hamar* ("an ass"), *hamar* ("wine"), *amar* ("wool"), or *immar* ("a lamb").] "Which do you mean, O foolish Galilean?" he was asked. "An ass for riding, wine to drink, wool for clothing, or a lamb for slaughtering?"[1]

If such precision is required in the spoken language, it is easy to determine that much is lost in written translation from Hebrew to Greek, and from Greek to Latin, and even more when the Greek and Latin are translated into English. This is just one reason our translations of the New Covenant are somewhat vague and misunderstood. The philology of the Hebrew and Greek languages, then, becomes instrumental in determining the real method and manner of Jesus' death. By utilizing key words, we are able to determine and identify specific linguistic elements within the Scriptures and New Covenant writings that logically and spiritually fit the purpose and mission of Jesus. This will become increasingly important in the pages that follow.

The patterns within the pages of the Old Covenant provide us with the answers we seek. These patterns point out initial clues as to the location of the true execution site, as well as evidentiary features important in establishing procedures and motives for the Jewish trial. Once these patterns are properly connected, the events take on an entirely new and logical perspective, one that "makes sense" of many confusing passages in the New Covenant writings. These, then, correspond most succinctly to the Mosaic precepts, aiding in the clarification and explanation of what would seem to be a series of disconnected episodes that, in our present translations of the New Covenant, both contradict and misinterpret the events. Furthermore, once these patterns are identified, the fulfillment of Old Covenant prophecies are more clearly defined. Consideration is also given to the *nature* of the writings of the New Covenant. The gospels must be viewed as finite, that is, mere outlines. In order to cram so much history within a limited space, only the slightest details would have been revealed. The Pesach meal, for example, would have occurred over a period of several hours but is abbreviated within each of the synoptic gospels, shortened to less than a page. On the other hand, the discourse having occurred during the meal, as narrated in the Gospel of John, is several chapters (13–17) in length. The author of

1. Bialik and Ravnitzky, *Legends*, 376:23.

Introduction

John, while covering the Pesach to some greater extent, places little emphasis on topics narrated by other gospel writers. Other incidents found within the gospel narratives are simply chronicled in such a way as to facilitate a general understanding while giving the least number of details. Since the gospels were written as theological documents rather than historical ones, and since they were written primarily for an Israelite audience living within the timeframe in which the events occurred, little attention would have been given to circumstances with which their Jewish readers certainly would have been fully aware. The majority population to whom the earliest gospels were written would have been well acquainted with Israel's current political and religious agenda, with legislation, with the Dual Torah, and with traditions and customs *in situ* at the time.

While Jesus is sure to have spoken a Semitic language, there can be little doubt that he did know at least a smattering of Greek. It is possible he knew several other languages as well. His religious wisdom and apparent knowledge of the Jewish law make it unlikely he was less skilled than those members of the Sanhedrin who were to judge him. It is a little known fact that near the village of Nazareth, where Jesus lived early on, was one of the priestly stations (*ha-amadot*) located in Galilee. Furthermore, the main East-West highway passed near it. As a result, Jesus would have received his training and education from several fronts. He surely would have been exposed to a plethora of languages through contact with pilgrims traversing the highway and having come from all parts of the known world. He, also, would have been exposed to the Temple Cult and the existing law because of the priestly station situated there. The point is that Jesus would have been deeply influenced in his earliest years by the religious institution and probably began to prepare himself for the priesthood and, perhaps, membership as a scribe in the Sanhedrin itself. Since the Roman soldiery spoke Latin as their common language, Jesus would have been able to speak that language as well. Members of the Sanhedrin are known to have had a passable knowledge of it, too. Besides the host of other requirements one needed to demonstrate in order to apply for membership in the Sanhedrin, "he must have been an accomplished linguist, familiar with all the languages of the surrounding nations".[2] Jesus is commonly called "Rabbi", "Teacher", "Master", and "Rabboni" (that is, scribe) at different times throughout the gospels, and for this reason we must contemplate his abilities in linguistics. The scribes and Pharisees of the early first century were certainly well versed in many languages. While *they* were forbidden to study Greek, the Hellenic priesthood, the aristocratic class, certainly did. It must also be remembered that while the rabbis certainly used occasional Greek terms in the later Talmudic writings, these records were first written in Hebrew and Aramaic. The general language of the masters (certainly in Galilee) is proven to have been Aramaic. Debates between the rabbis or "masters" themselves were in Mishnaic Hebrew. It must be pointed out, though, that the term "rabbi" was not in use during the early part of the first century at all and is a New Covenant anomaly. The term "Master" or "Lord" was, instead, the predominant form of address for teachers of the Torah. We often find Jesus referred to as "Rabbi" or "Lord" in the Greek translations, a gloss not found in Hebrew manuscripts. It is apparent that Jesus exhibited his authority as being from God alone. He cited no precedents of the "scribes" but used only Scripture as law. One of the major accusations against Jesus was,

2. Aiyar, *Legality*, p. 50.

Introduction

in modern terminology, that he practiced law, so to speak, without a license. He began to do this at a young age, which prompted these rulers to rebuke him as one rebelling against the nation's government. It is not only suspected but well known among biblical scholars that the earliest narratives were, indeed, written in both Hebrew and Aramaic for a Hebrew Nazaraean audience. The so-called Gospel of the Hebrews (not to be confused with the Epistle to the Hebrews in our present canon) is believed to be the original text of the later Greek Matthew. "Papias says that Matthew, the disciple, 'put together the oracles of the Lord *in the Hebrew language, and each one interpreted them as best he could*."[3] In other words, since the "oracles" were written in the Hebrew language for a Hebrew audience, the Gentiles had to interpret them, not in the Hebrew sense in which they were intended, but as their own culture and society dictated. Gentiles reading the gospel could not have known the context in which the traditions were intended. Since the Hebrew race was monotheistic and quite distinct from its surrounding neighbors, few of their laws and customs would have been understood by the Gentiles, who were polytheistic and cosmopolitan in both their religions and their societies. It was not until the Antiochan period that the followers of Jesus became known as "Christians". The latter church also first became known as "catholic" or "universal" at Antioch. As John Romer states in *Testament*, "this was the first indication of the church's ambitions to penetrate the gentile, imperial world".[4] By the time the religion reached Antioch, it no longer bore the "purity" of early intent, nor any resemblance to the original movement. It was fast becoming a socio-political rather than a theological phenomenon.

Antioch was founded near the end of the fourth century BCE by Selecus Nicator. It became the new Babylonian capital. What Selecus had done was to invite Babylonian priests to become the foremost of Antioch's citizens. Syria was, therefore, saturated with Babylonian teaching, religion, and philosophies long before 70 CE when the "church" became known as "Christians". By that time, Nazaraean messianism was replaced by a "universal" religion that conformed to the pagan religions then in Antioch, so that its religious intent was lost sometime between 66 and 70 CE. It is certainly clear that Jesus' earliest followers, the Nazaraeans, differed little from the many factions of Judaism at the time. There is stark contrast between theologies situated in Jerusalem and in Antioch.

Any careful Bible student cannot fail to notice thousands of mistranslations, many of them "wilful falsifications". Over 14,500 alterations had been made to the *Codex Sinaiticus* by the time of Eusebius. This particular manuscript is thought to have been none other than one of the fifty Bibles prepared on vellum and ordered by Constantine himself. It is clear that the early church fathers held in contempt the Aramaic-Hebrew Gospels, probably because these texts did not deify Jesus. But there is no doubt the original Semitic texts did not ascribe "divinity" to him (as Gentiles understand that term) until after his resurrection. The authors of these Aramaic and Hebrew Gospels believed Jesus was the Messiah, a "man", divinely inspired, but not "divine" in the pagan sense.

The messianic movement was at first an inner-Jewish phenomenon. Neither "baptism" (immersion) nor missionary efforts, even among Gentiles, caused the original splintering from Judaism. These activities were both recognized and encouraged within

3. Fosdick, *The Man*, p. 36; op. cit., Roberts and Donaldson, I, 155.
4. Romer, *Testament*, p. 188.

the earliest movement. Even Paul's belief in freedom from the law was not inconsistent with basic Jewish thought in his day. The belief in Jesus as Messiah was in no way contested. It fully fell into the accepted milieu of Jewish messianism. It is not until after the destruction of Jerusalem that we find ostracism of the Christian *minim* (heretics) by the Jewish sages. Furthermore, these comments were not aimed at the Jewish Nazaraean community at all but to this later "Gentile" church. These opinions about the "Christian Jesus" were not written until the second or third century and beyond. They did *not* reflect early first century Jewish thought. The anti-Semitism exhibited by Hellenistic leaders of the Gentile church had done much to alter their original beliefs about Jesus and his followers. The conflict eventually came between the Jerusalem community and the pagan Gentile population (and Hellenistic Jews of the Diaspora) when these latter found in Jesus a type of Hellenistic "hero". The major conflict over circumcision and dietary laws that the Jerusalem sect adhered to became the catalyst over which they clashed. It is also true that the original gospels written by Jews within the Holy Land were not easily adapted to the Hellenistic model of the savior-god that the later universal church held so dear. The Jewish Nazaraeans never used the Septuagint. It had been prepared by a group of Hellenistic Jews in Alexandria, Egypt, whose common language was Greek. It has become clear from the scrolls found in the Qumran caves and from the histories of Josephus that the most faithful and pious Jews did not use the Greek translation of the Tanach (Old Covenant), but instead used a text from an archaic form of Hebrew. The Jewish population in Jerusalem never used it. They believed it was an "abomination", thinking it the worst thing that could have ever happened to their precious Holy Scriptures. Our present translations are based primarily on the Hellenistic Septuagint. It is important to note that neither Jesus nor his first century contemporaries, used the Septuagint. It was through the dominance of Constantine's influence that our present canon emerged, some three centuries after Jesus. It is within this context that I present the historical and theological evidence that follows. As a result of early Greek mistranslations we have texts that no longer bear the stamp of original intent borne by their writers. The chronicle of events in the gospels, already condensed and abbreviated, is now only confounded by errors in translation and both supposed and determined lengthy interpolations.

The sequence of events concerning the trials and execution of Jesus are the somewhat longer narratives of the gospels, and various evidence regarding the crimes he is said to have committed is scattered throughout each. This allows the careful scholar to take apart these pieces of evidence and compare them with Jewish law in order to determine their validity. Unfortunately, the gospels fail to include any necessary elements that would make them understandable from a *Gentile* point of view, and this society is left to "interpret" the gospels in the best way it can. It necessarily follows that any Gentile wanting to discover the nature of the crimes and events as they really occurred would be required to "fill in the blanks", so to speak, through use of other historical sources and through our present Greek translations of the Aramaic or Hebrew Gospels. By the time the Gentile world had "taken over" and supplanted the Primitive Assembly first established within the bounds of Palestine (40s-50s, as attested by Eusebius), the gospels and other New Covenant writings had become *objective* documents, having lost much in translation. It is fact that few Gentiles would have thought of them in Hebrew terms, because they had little concept of Hebrew culture and laws. We need only take notice of the works of various ancient pagan authors in their descriptions of the Jewish people to learn that they considered them "odd". Division within the legitimate Primitive Assembly had already begun to take place as early as 50 CE when Paul wrote his epistles to the Galatians, Corinthians, and Thessalonians. These epistles were written in defense of the true faith against Greek philosophy within the communities. Clement, the disciple of Peter, when he wrote his own epistle to the Corinthians (before the destruction of the Temple in Jerusalem; 1 Clem. 18:20) had already experienced some of the changes within the primitive movement. He was quite explicit in his instructions.

> Seeing then these things are manifest unto us, it will behoove us, to take care that looking into the depths of the divine knowledge, we do all things in order, whatsoever our Lord [Master] has commanded us to do. *And particularly, that we perform our offerings and service to God [YHWH], at their appointed seasons: for these he [YHWH] has commanded to be done, not rashly and disorderly, but at certain determinate times and hours.*[5]

Any reasonable person is able to understand Clement's words: there were obvious attempts being made by those in the pagan world to infiltrate the earliest Hebrew communities with their own religious agendas. This is evidenced also within the Epistle of I John (2:18–19), where the author claims "antichrists" have gone out from the congregation itself: "They went out *from us*, but they were not *of us*". He could be speaking of nothing more than a change in the structure of the earliest assembly of Messiah. These earlier followers had been commanded by Jesus not to abandon the Hebrew "appointments" that YHWH had commanded Israel to keep (that is, Passover, the Feast of Weeks, and Tabernacles). The universal church leaders, who introduced a religious hierarchy of bishops and priests in direct defiance of 1 Peter 2:8–9, accepted a compromise. They accepted Jesus' teachings, but only insofar as they could weave those teachings into a pagan world.

Should any Christian doubt the veracity of the pagan origins of the institutional church, he only needs to review the *order* in which the New Covenant books have been placed by early leaders of organized religion. It is blatantly obvious that Paul's Epistle to the Romans gave supreme authority to the Roman church. We cannot help but notice that the earlier so-called general epistles (the *Hebrew* ones) were appended only to the *end* of Paul's letters. The reason is that Paul's epistles were more easily *adaptable* for use by the Roman church. The current arrangement, therefore, favored the universal Gentile "Roman" church. The idealized "Christ" of Christianity is markedly different from the "Messiah" of the earliest Jewish followers of Jesus. The Gentile concept of "Christ" was, in a nutshell, simply the pagan belief in a worldwide "savior-god". To some, it was Osiris; to others it was Bacchus; to some it was Mithras; and to some it became "Christ". Every polytheistic religion existing during the first century had its "resurrected god". "Christ", to many of them, was merely Jesus' second name—Jesus Christ—another god to add to their pantheon of worship. The gospels themselves were written as a tribute to the disciples' master. They differ little from the writings of other disciples at that time who wrote about their own teachers.

---

5. I Clem. 18:13–14 in *Lost Books*, p. 131.

Introduction

> Those who teach Torah are given the status of a parent and their pupils are then called their "children"... The Master was attended by his disciples who traveled with him, tended to his needs, and later transmitted his words and the incidents of his life. The obligations of the disciple to his Master were at least as great as those due a parent.[6]

Jesus, who taught Torah, was the Master (a Jewish sage), his disciples attended him, and they wrote about him after his death and resurrection. The term "master" identified in Hebrew as *ba'al* is a term that most specifically means "lord", "master", or "husband" and is used in the rabbinical sense "to marry". The rabbi "marries" or becomes one with his God. His followers or disciples are thus the children (or sons) of God. That the Pharisees and scribes believed Jesus exemplified immoral living is not to be denied. They accused him of rebelliousness against his parents, of wine-drinking, of associating with sinners and tax-collectors who collaborated with the Roman government (the "unclean"); they accused him and his disciples of not washing before meals, not obeying the Pharisaic "law", and numerous other offenses against "scribal" interpretations. While it is not the intent and focus of this work to dispute doctrinal matters in-depth, an essential understanding of the unity/trinity hypothesis becomes necessary in arriving at the true meaning of the Hebrew Messiah's sufferings. It is because the early universal church elevated Jesus to deity and dejudaized him, that the Hebrew population refused to see him as their Messiah. They have never been able to see the *Jew* in him! It is unfortunate that the Jews of today have spent lifetimes finding it necessary to counteract the deification of Jesus, *one of their own*, and this has had great influence on how they now interpret the prophecies of Isaiah 52–53.

Something must now be said about the place where Jesus was executed, because that, too, must follow biblical logic. The "Holy Sites" that Christian *tradition* erroneously champion have illogical pagan beginnings. The superstitious nature of third and fourth century citizens, in particular, gave rise to "visions" and pagan images. The alleged execution sites now contradicted are located on the *northern* and *western* side of the Temple Mount and pose a problem to biblical logic. All Hebrews know that judgment and execution, whether human or animal, were to be carried out only in the "face" (Presence) of YHWH. *That* would have been on the *eastern* side of the Temple Mount near where the Atonement Goat, bulls that were wholly burned (referred to as "sinners") and the Red Heifer were burned; to wit, the *Mount of Olives*! While the Temple stood, the Jewish people always prayed toward the west, that is, toward YHWH's face. The reason is given that to pray to the east would have been construed as worship of the "sun". The Sanhedrin Tractate of the Talmud, in fact, tells us exactly where the execution site was located.

> And was the place of stoning only just outside the court and no further? Has it not been taught: The place of stoning was outside the three encampments?... It is here stated, Without the camp; *and in reference to the bulls that were [wholly] burned*, it is also said, without the camp; Just as there [it means] without the three camps, so here too... On the contrary, *it should rather be deduced from the sacrifices slaughtered without [for instance, the Red Heifer, the Atonement Goat, and the Bullock bearing sin]*, since they have the following in common; [i] human

---

6. Hammer, *Classic Midrash*, p. 319.

being; [ii] sinners; [iii] life is taken; and [iv] *piggul?* ... [note] "in ... these cases, the leading 'without the camp' was in order to take life—*that of the blasphemer and the sacrifice yet to be slaughtered.*[7]

The execution site was located in a position outside the camp near where the sin-offerings were burned and near the place of ashes (where all "fat" ashes from the altar of burnt offering were dumped). The "bullock bearing sin", the Red Heifer, and the Atonement Goat were all burned on the Mount of Olives in the Presence of YHWH (as the Talmud clearly states); therefore, blasphemers, who were similarly classified, were to be executed in the same general area as "sinners" (sin-bearers).

The Scriptural patterns within the following pages leave little room for doubt concerning these matters if the reader is willing to accept *God's Word* rather than *man's tradition*. We must bear in mind that God created from *chaos* all things in an *orderly* fashion: "For [YHWH] is not a God of confusion [commotion, disorder] but of peace [rest, not chaos] (1 Cor. 14:33).

Because He is a God of order, he has left behind a blueprint in Scripture, as it were, for us to follow. This blueprint allows us to trace the pertinent facts concerning the execution of Jesus. Once we realize the Old Covenant is a pattern for the New, we are enabled to learn how Jesus came to "fill up" or "complete" (illuminate) the instruction [Torah]. In order to follow these patterns, it first becomes necessary to understand the translation of the Hebrew word *torah*. It has consistently been mistranslated in the New Covenant writings as "law", thus we have an incomplete understanding of its purpose. "The title 'Law', however, is of *Greek, not Hebrew*, origin and derives from the word *nomos*, 'law' ... [B]ut the word *torah* itself means "instruction" or "teaching".[8]

Although there were certain statutes laid down by YHWH for Israel, we must understand that the "instruction" was given to them so that they might lead orderly and uncomplicated lives. Jesus admitted that he came not to abolish the instruction given to the Israelites by YHWH through Moses but to illuminate it (Matt. 5:17). That he and his followers "kept" the instruction, there can be no doubt. Even after the resurrection of Jesus, his earliest followers *continued to do so*. The Greek word for "fulfill" (in KJV) is *pleroo*. It means "to complete", "to cram a net", "level up a hollow", "to explain", or "to instruct". As all Hebrews know, this is the ultimate mission of Messiah. Jesus rebelled against the irreligious rulers, the aristocratic priests, of the Jews and their hypocritical "theocracy". As a result, he suffered "outside the camp".

Jesus' instruction, however brief in the land of Israel, was powerful, so powerful he was considered a danger and a threat to the nation by the theo-political element. Jesus, as a scribe, a teacher and interpreter of law, sought to bring truth to the backslidden theocracy. Government envoys repeatedly spied upon him, seeking to bring him to trial and put him to death. He was named an outlaw, a rebel, and seldom came to Jerusalem in the three and a half years of his ministry. The majority of his travels were in northern Israel, where the officials in Jerusalem hardly dared to wander. They would have feared the necessity of crossing through Samaria where their enemies, armed bands of Galilean

---

7. *b. Sanh.* 42b.
8. Holtz, ed. *Sources*, p. 84.

Introduction

Zealots and Samaritan heathens, often lay in wait for travelers. It was from this northern vicinity that the "Lost Sheep of the House of Israel" had been scattered and dispersed. Many of the "Lost Sheep" were still in that location. Jesus traveled to Jerusalem only at the festive seasons: Passover, Pentecost, and Tabernacles (as well as to the Feast of Dedication). It was mandatory by law for all Jewish males to present themselves in the Temple during these times.

It was only during the last week prior to his execution that Jesus openly announced his message to the populace of Jerusalem. The New Covenant writings, over and again, state the reason the government did not openly seize him: they were afraid of the people! It was not until Jesus was alone that Judas was able to lead the officials to arrest him, at a time when the populace was engaged in celebration of the busy Passover night and did not accompany him. It was a prime opportunity for the Sanhedrin and Herodians (who had sought him for some forty days) to arrest him on an outstanding warrant.

While Jesus was accused of several crimes resulting in capital punishment, the underlying reason for his arrest is to be ultimately found in his upsetting the financial balance of the powerful priestly oligarchy and the wealthy family of Annas, the *ab bet din* (vice-president and "father of the court"). This man had been a former high priest of the twenty-three-member *judicial* Sanhedrin (the criminal court). It was Annas who made the initial accusation. The charge *masking* the true personal "offense" was "leading the nation astray". It might be noted that Annas, in his examination of Jesus, asked him only of "his followers" and "his teachings". The inference is that by his doctrine Jesus was "leading the nation astray" from the teachings of the scribes. This particular charge consisted of the collective complaints lodged against Jesus and was considered the most blasphemous in the corpus of Mosaic legislation. It had been for "leading the town" of Nazareth "astray" that the good citizens of that city led Jesus to the cliff to "throw him down headlong" in order to stone him. The usage of these very words indicate that it was the Temple Cult and the Pharisaic element among the people that determined the attempted method of stoning. The Saducean penalty for stoning was executed in a markedly different manner. The actions of the good people of Nazareth were in response to what in Jewish law is referred to as a "collective crime". If they had allowed Jesus' "errant" teachings to go unchallenged, the entire town would have not only been held accountable but implicated in his "crime". These people feared for their homes and lives because such an act was well-defined by Mosaic legislation. The city would be put to ruin: goods would be plundered, the population killed, and the city burned, utterly destroyed. It is clear they wanted only to protect their homes and families from such complete disaster.

Nor when the verdict of guilty was pronounced by Caiaphas (who simply rubber-stamped the verdict of his more powerful colleague) was it even necessary to be tried before the Roman prefect, although they would have to seek his approval for execution. The first- century court legally found Jesus guilty of "blasphemy", not a crime we would understand today, but a crime recognized by the government of Israel during the early first century. His "crime" was one that was believed so terrible that it would bring God's wrath against the *entire nation of Israel*.

The evidence is irrefutable that Pilate was blackmailed into verifying the Sanhedrin's verdict as the facts will reveal. This does not excuse his behavior. He was a ruthless politician, self-seeking and full of bitterness and hatred for the Jewish people. The execution, however, was administered by the wealthy aristocratic Sadducean leadership—the Hanan family, in particular—and Pilate was coerced into sending a four-man execution detail to "oversee" the execution.

It was not the general population of Israel who executed him. It was the wealthy caste. Let it be known that it was prophesied of Messiah that it was *YHWH'S will and purpose to "bruise" him*, and he, also, who chose to hold *both* Gentiles and Jews responsible for the death of Jesus. The patterns found within Scripture point us toward the logical execution site and tomb. It is not the "hill of vision" and burial cave under the Church of the Holy Sepulchre established by Helena in the fourth century, nor is it Gordon's anti-Semitic "Calvary" and the corresponding "Garden Tomb". Both are whimsical traditions based, not on God's Word, but on man's rationality. The discussion in the pages that follow will provide proof beyond any reasonable doubt that Jesus was tried at the Stone House in the Temple precincts where the high priest had been required to purify himself and his garments for seven days prior to Passover, then on to the village of Bethphage where he was flogged, returned to the Stone House for sentencing and, finally, led out to the Plaza of Gulgoleth on the Mount of Olives for execution, buried in a garden tomb at Bethphage, and ascended, as Luke states, at "Bethany" (*Beth Hini*).

We are prepared to tediously examine the various crimes of which Jesus was accused, the accusation and charge, the legal Jewish trial, the pseudo-Roman trial, the execution site, the mode of execution, the burial site, and the resurrection event. We shall discover that Jesus was judged and executed by the Sadducean priesthood, hanged on a real living tree, and that he was excommunicated from society by *the whole congregation of Israel*, as prescribed by Mosaic law. While ordinarily criminals might be hanged only *after* death, we shall learn that this did not apply in the case of Jesus.

The beauty of the Messiah and the glory of YHWH can only be imagined without understanding God's patterns, plan, and purpose. In the following pages we shall attempt to uncover the Hebrew Messiah instead of the Greek Christ. There are those who might believe there is no difference in the two terms. The old adage "a rose by any other name will smell as sweet" is simply not true. In Hebrew, the name is everything! How we view the Messiah determines what we know of him. Thorough research borne by Scripture, canonical and non-canonical New Covenant books, Pesharim, Midrashim, Mishnah, Tosefta, Talmud, history, and language provides a logical, not emotional, basis for our belief. The result of our conclusions provides a foundation for spiritual rebirth to the individual seeking to enter the Kingdom of God. It is the ultimate adventure for both scholar and layman.

The evidence is overwhelming that it was, in fact, the Epicurean government, *not* the Jewish populace, who put Jesus to death. Haim Cohn says it well:

> It is quite true, as other available sources indicate, that the "chief priests" and ruling classes did not see eye to eye with the general populace, and it is highly probable that while the "chief priests" would have been very happy to get rid of Jesus, the masses of the people were attracted by him and loved him, not only because he was one of their own, but also because of his reputation as a worker of miracles, a healer and consoler of the poor, a fighter against corruption and a

Introduction

sworn enemy—like themselves—of the rich and mighty. The idea that the masses of the people in Jerusalem in those days could be brought to deliver a man like Jesus into the hands of the Romans or to demand his crucifixion at their hands, is so unhistorical and so unrealistic as to verge on the absurd.[9]

So it is that we must *all* accept responsibility for the death of Jesus, not because any one particular race of individuals (whether Jew or Gentile) took it upon themselves to put him to death, but because God, himself, willed it. There must be no division among ourselves. Whether Jew or Gentile, we must be united into one body. We *all* long for truth; we *all* long for salvation; we *all* long for peace. The entire world is straining expectantly in anticipation of the coming of the Hebrew Messiah and the revealing of the Sons of God (Rom. 8:19). Let us, with one voice, proclaim: Blessed is he who comes in the name of Yahweh (Ps. 118:25).

---

9. Cohn, *Jewish Law*, p. 91.

1

The Crime: Apostasy from the Law

IT IS GENERALLY ADMITTED that Jesus was tried for blasphemy, although theologians and scholars are hard-pressed to explain just how the blasphemy occurred. The following excerpt from the Anchor Bible Dictionary sums up the perplexity of Christendom:

> The grounds on which Jesus is found guilty of blasphemy is a vexed question, since no profanation of the divine name appears to be involved (Lev. 24:15; Sanh. 7:5) But Caiaphas' tearing his garments in 26:65 (again, cf. Sanh. 7:5) supports the reading that a judicial finding is involved.[1]

It has been suggested that Jesus spoke the ineffable name, but the Christian concept of *Ani Hu* (I am) is not any part of Jewish theology. There is no evidence in the primary source material (New Covenant gospels) to indicate Jesus ever spoke the Name at all, especially during his trial. In fact, every distinction is made to contradict it. In an allusion to Scriptures found in the books of Daniel (Dan. 7:13) and the Psalms (Ps. 110:1) Jesus was quite specific in using the self-appellation *Son of Man*, that is, the Hebrew *Ben Adam*, in answer to the high priest's query of whether or not he was the messiah. Jesus' response "thou hast said" implied that he *was* the messiah, not the nationalistic one expected by most first century Jews, but the biblical messiah of the Old Covenant prophecies. To prove that it was the biblical and not the nationalistic figure Jesus referred to he stated that he would, in fact, sit down on the right hand of "Power" and come in the clouds of Heaven. Caiaphas took Jesus' admission to mean he *was* a serious threat to national security. But claiming to be a messiah of any kind was still not a crime. How this fits into the general verdict of blasphemy will be investigated a bit later. For now, let us turn to the specific words that Jesus used. We note that Jesus had used a circumlocution for the name of God in his response, and it is this that we need to first explore. The substitution of the euphemism "Power" for the name of God would have ordinarily been inoffensive to the rulers. This device, and numerous others like it, was often employed by Jews to prevent them from accidentally speaking the ineffable name. Other similar

---

1. Chilton, "Caiaphas", ABD, v. 1, p. 803.

terms were in use at the time, including "Heaven" and "Adonai", and Jesus' use of the term "Power" was entirely acceptable in Jewish theology. While in itself the term was not considered "blasphemous", if the utterance were made while under *oath* and that oath determined to be false by the judges, it carried with it the penalty of "forty stripes save one". As the evidence will show, Jesus did receive the prescribed penalty. The rulers had believed his statement was a "vain oath".

> What is a vain oath? [If] one has taken an oath to differ from what is well known to people . . . *If one has taken an oath concerning something which is impossible*—". . . if I did not see a camel flying in the air . . ." [*M. Shebu* 3.8 Ia–b, IIf–g] . . . "I impose an oath on you," "I command you," "I bind you,"—lo these are liable. By "heaven and earth," lo, these are exempt. (1) "By [the name of] Alef-dalet [Adonai]" or (2) "Yud-he [Yahweh]," (3) "By the Almighty," (4) "By Hosts," (5) "By him who is merciful and gracious," (6) "By him who is long-suffering and abundant in mercy," *or by any other euphemism—lo, these are liable*. "He who curses [i.e., swears by the euphemism to something the rulers believed impossible to perform] making use of any one of these is liable," the words of R. Meir . . . [The law governing] a vain oath applies to men and women, to those who are not related and to those who are related, to those who are suitable [to bear witness] and to those who are not suitable [to bear witness], before a court and not before a court. *[But it must be stated] by a man out of his own mouth. And they are liable for deliberately taking such an oath to flogging . . .*[2]

We are specifically told in Matt. 26:63 that Caiaphas did, in fact, put Jesus under oath in order to question him concerning the charges made against him. Prior to that moment, Jesus had remained silent. Why? Christian theology teaches it was in response to Isaiah's prophecy ("and he opened not his mouth"), but this is not the case. That prophecy was fulfilled in another way as we shall learn in the chapter, "The Execution". So why did Jesus remain silent? The answer is to be found in the corpus of Jewish legal procedure: "*Testimony as to the admissions of the accused is inadmissible*; for even if they were made in open court, the judges would not listen to them, nor be influenced by them in their decision."[3] Since it was established Jewish law that an accused might not speak and thus condemn himself, Jesus did not attempt to speak in his own behalf until he was placed on oath and directly asked to do so. The silence of the accused is based on the legal principle that "no man can make himself out guilty" (*b. Sanh.* 9b).

> The basic assumption in *halakhah* is that a man does not belong only to himself; just as he has no right to cause physical harm to others, so he has no right to inflict injury on himself. This is why it was determined that the confession of the defendant had no legal validity and should not be taken into consideration . . . Not only can no man be forced to incriminate himself through his own testimony, but self-incrimination has no significance and is unacceptable as evidence in court.[4]

There is, of course, one exception to this rule. In the case of a *mesith*, an extracted confession can be obtained by the high priest by placing the accused under oath. The

---

2. *m. Shebu.* 3:8:Ia; 3:8:IIb–c; 3:8:IIf–h; 3:11Iia–c; 4:13a–Ie.
3. "Accusatory", J.E., p. 163.
4. Steinsaltz and Galais, *Esential Talmud*, pp. 167–168.

The Crime: Apostasy from the Law

entire trial procedure in such a matter is then reversed on every point, even to the extent of allowing the high priest greater leverage in the way he conducts the trial against the accused. This reversal process will be discussed in "The Jewish Trial". There is little doubt that Jesus was brought before the *Beth Din* as a *mesith*, which is both a religious *and* political crime (one to be discussed in a future chapter). At least one scholar agrees with this assessment. "The description of the interrogation undergone by Jesus before the Sanhedrin conforms to the procedure, which is confirmed by the Talmud, adopted against a political agitator (*mesith*). The members of the Sanhedrin began by asking the accused for details of his activities and purposes."[5]

When placed on oath by Caiaphas, Jesus was freed from restraint. There can be no question that Jesus deliberately used the euphemism to indicate his biblical messianism: "But Jesus was silent [as the law requires]. And the High-priest said unto him: *I put thee on oath by the living God*, that to us thou say whether thou are the [Messiah], the Son of God" (Matt. 26:63). As the "speaker of the court", it was entirely proper and legal for Caiaphas to have administered the oath. Since no two witnesses had agreed in their testimonies about Jesus, he decided something had to be done in order to extract a confession. Caiaphas simply took it upon himself to end the matter. The Tosefta is clear that if the "matter is too obvious", that is, a "commonplace in law unworthy of debate, or of any further investigation", the high priest has the right to place the defendant under oath in order to extract a confession by self-condemnation (especially when the charge was the enticement of Israel to apostasy). Since none of the witnesses agreed in their testimonies, the high priest, Caiaphas, had the right to put Jesus on oath. The law states: "But when it is a case of deciding between two members of the court, or two disciples, or two ignorant men, or two *halakoth*, or two questions, or two answers, or two precedents, *the authority for the decision at such point lies with the speaker of the court.*"[6] We are told in the Gospel of Matthew that after Jesus' admission Caiaphas, as the "speaker of the court" (the *nasi*, or Prince of the *judicial* Sanhedrin), exercised the decision not to call forth more witnesses as was his legal prerogative. There was no need for further testimony: "He hath spoken blasphemy; what further need have we of witnesses? behold, now ye have heard his blasphemy?" (Matt. 26:65). This profanity or "cursing" of God is not blasphemy in the sense that Christians generally recognize. The Gentile world has become all too dependent upon its own moral understanding of how blasphemy might be defined, having failed to take into consideration how first century Jews would have interpreted that term. From a Jewish standpoint, the making of such a statement of "impossibility" *after being placed on oath* is tantamount to a "cursing of God."

> You shall not swear falsely by my name. (Lev. 19:12). Why is this stated? Since it says You shall not swear falsely by the name of the Lord your God (Ex. 20:7) we might have thought that one is guilty of this only if one uses the Unique Name. What indicates that all of the various designations of God are to be included [in this prohibition]? The verse says *by my name* (Lev. 19:12)—*any name that I have. This teaches that a false oath profanes the Name of God.*[7]

---

5. Craveri, *The Life*, p. 396.
6. Danby, *Sanhedrin Tractate*, p. 74; *Tosef. Sanh.* 7.7.
7. Hammer, *Classic Midrash*, p. 435; *Mid. Lev.* 19:11-12, *Sifra Weiss* 88b.

A Book of Evidence

One explanation from the Talmud declares that a vain oath brings God's wrath not only upon the accused individual but also upon the nation. The reasoning is that an Israelite's individual conduct reflects upon society as a whole; therefore, he does not belong only to himself but to the entire nation. Society's evils, indeed, were believed to have been caused by the negligence of the people in making vain oaths.

> *Evil beasts come upon the world: For the sin of false swearing and false testimony and profaning the Name* there is a letting loose of evil beasts upon the world; the cattle perish and human population dwindles and the highways are made desolate, as it is said, And I will send the beast of the field among you, which shall rob you of your children, and destroy your cattle, and make you few in number; and your ways shall become desolate (Leviticus 26:22) (ARNB).[8]

There is also a *baraitha* (extraneous *mishnah*) in the Tosefta that gives clarity to the meaning of how God is "cursed" by such behavior and why it is considered a "blasphemy".

> It is as though there were two brothers, twins, who were like one another in appearance; one became king of the world, while the other went off and consorted with thieves. After a time the latter was captured and *crucified on a cross*, and all who came and went said, *"It is like as though the king were crucified."* Therefore it is said: *For that which is hanged is a curse of God* [Tosef. Sanh. IX 6b]. "The illustrative parable in Tosefta *implies the interpretation of a cause of cursing against God, something which brings God in disrepute*".[9]

The taking of a "vain oath" resulted in *niddui* ("to cut off", "cast out", "anathematize") and specifically involved *hillul ha-Shem*, the desecration of the Holy Name, that is, bringing God into disrepute. A rendering by the court of "blasphemy" does not necessarily include the pronunciation of the sacred Name, itself.

> *Niddui* was also pronounced upon the following: *a person who publicly despised the teachings of the rabbis* (Mishnah 'Eduy. v. 6); or who was summoned to attend court and showed disrespect by appearing late, or by non-attendance (B.K. 1112b); who did not obey an order of, or did not comply with the terms of a verdict pronounced by, the bet din (ib. 113a) . . . who desecrated the festal seasons by labor, even the second days, though the latter were founded on custom only (Pes. 52a); *who pronounced God's Name in vain, or who, in taking an oath, made exaggerated protestations . . . Ned. 7b), or whose conduct created hillul ha-Shem (desecration of the holy Name), that is to say, any misconduct or scandal that reflected upon or endangered the morality and religious character of the community (Yer. M. K. l.c.).* Niddui was also pronounced upon *one who was guilty of "putting a stumbling-block before the blind . . . who interfered with public exercise of religious duty (Yer. M. K. l.c.); who was guilty of the distribution of unclean food (Sanh. 25a) . . . [and] upon a rabbi who had fallen into evil repute (M. K. l.c.)* . . . It was not hastily pronounced. The transgressor was repeatedly warned to mend his ways, to repent, or to make restitution.[10]

---

8. Goldin, *Mishnah Avot,*, p. 128.
9. Danby, *Sanhedrin Tractate*, p. 92; *Tosef. Sanh.* IX 6b, IX 7.
10. "Anathema", J.E., p. 561.

The Crime: Apostasy from the Law

The rulers believed that Jesus had desecrated the Name because of his public behavior. There can be little doubt that he publicly denounced the teachings of the scribes. He had taken the vain oath, which the rulers would have felt was an exaggerated protestation. He had also interfered with public exercise of religious duty by cleansing the Temple precincts of the sacrificial booths and moneychangers, and his teachings would have been considered a "stumbling-block" placed in the path of otherwise observant *ammei ha-aretz* (uneducated population, literally "people of the land"). He had also been accused of "burning his food" like pagans do.

> For Rab Hisda said that Rab Jeremiah bar Abba said, 'What is that which is written: There shall no evil befall thee, neither shall any plague come nigh thy dwelling [Ps. xci. 10] . . . Another explanation: There shall no evil befall thee, 'that evil dreams and evil thoughts may tempt thee not,' and neither shall any plague come nigh thy dwelling *'that thou mayst not have a son or a disciple who burns his food in public like Jeshu the Nazarene.*[11]

But this does not mean the obvious. Figuratively, the phrase "burns his food" means to bring dishonor upon himself. The scribes would have used that phrase to convey and imply that Jesus was suspected of sorcery. He had repeatedly been warned, although subtly, about his teachings and was believed to have fallen into evil repute. The Gospels consistently record instances wherein it is evident the rulers believed he had committed many of the offenses listed above. Craig Blomberg states:

> "In the fifth-century Babylonian Talmud a rebellious disciple is compared to one 'who publicly burns his food like Jesus of Nazareth', using a metaphor which refers to the distortion of Jewish teaching (b. Sanh. 103a). A few columns further on, the claim is made that 'Jesus the Nazarene practised magic and led Israel astray' (b. Sanh. 107b). Both of these traditions reflect Jesus' disputes with the prevailing Jewish interpretations of the Law.[12]

Certainly, he had little respect for the *beth din* and the Temple Cult. As a follower of John, he would have already placed himself in a precarious position and in dangerous opposition to that cult. John, as both Josephus and the New Covenant tell us, had assuredly crossed the line in arousing popular resentment against the Temple and the government of Israel.

> . . . John seems to preside over a convocation of otherworldly saints who, having already achieved spiritual perfection by themselves, come to John just for physical purification. But Josephus's apologetic insistence on what John was not doing lets us see exactly what he was doing: *He was offering a free and populist alternative to the temple's purification process for sin.* This is the first point that Josephus, himself a Temple priest before its destruction, wishes to obscure about John's program. In that second paragraph, the tone changes completely. We now hear about *crowds aroused to the highest degree by John's sermons* and about eloquence potentially *leading to some form of sedition, uprising, or upheaveal.*[13]

---

11. *b. Sanh.* 103a.; Epstein (1981 ed.; not found in 1994 ed.).
12. Blomberg, *Historical Reliability*, p. 198.
13. Crossan, *Who Killed Jesus?*, p. 43.

John was eventually put to death for interfering with the activities of the Temple Cult. Evidence is scattered throughout the gospels that Jesus' behavior, like John's, was being watched by the Epicurean government, and like John, Jesus too would be executed. What is clear, however, is that the "vain oath" in and of itself did not determine the final verdict resulting in Jesus' execution. We must seek for some *other* underlying crime to serve as the basis for the charge of "blasphemy" and the subsequent *niddui*, which would not have been *permanent* in the case of a "vain oath". Jesus was merely flogged as a *result* of the vain oath (the prescribed penalty). It was for this *other* charge that the final verdict was pronounced and for which he was "cast away" (that is, excommunicated) from the Congregation of Israel, and ultimately "cut off" (executed). The "vain oath" simply served as the catalyst for the determinate conviction of a far greater blasphemy. The "vain oath", in the end, proved to be the *lesser* of the combined "blasphemies" allegedly committed by Jesus. While it was "injurious" (blasphemous) to speak any euphemism of the Name while under oath, we shall soon learn that it was not this "transgression" but a "sin unto death" (in Jewish law, sin is classified into categories) that caused Caiaphas (and all the other judges as well) to rend his robes. This custom of grief and mourning is only performed at the pronunciation of a verdict of blasphemy: "And the judges stand on their feet and tear their clothing, and never sew them back up."[14] Scholars have often objected to the historicity of the rending of the high priest's holy garments on the basis that such "holy" robes would never be profaned. Fortunately, we have the Jewish records to reveal it was not his priestly attire at all that was damaged but merely the robes of justice.

> (Deut. 1:13). "They should be well known to you, for when someone *wraps himself in his cloak [Hammer's note: The judge wore a cloak when trying a case]* and comes and sits before me, I do not know what tribe he comes from, but you recognize him for you grew up amongst them".[15]

Excommunication from the nation of Israel logically follows the rending of the "cloak" or robes of justice. Anathema is then followed by the penalties to be inflicted upon the accused. In the case of Jesus, the penalties included a flogging of thirty-nine stripes for the "vain oath" and execution for the endmost crime of blasphemy. That Jesus employed such euphemism as "Power" in his own defense in presence of the high priest and before the court of the Sanhedrin is evidence only that he was found guilty of the *lesser* crime. The members of the court simply believed the *performance* implied by his statement was clearly impossible. Nor was the phrase "Son of Man" a blasphemous offense under Jewish law, whether a messianic declaration or not. The prophets, too, had called themselves by that colloquialism in deference to their humble situations, and during the tumultuous early first century, there had been other similar messianic claims. There was absolutely no claim to divinity evident in such a self-appellation.

> In some instances at least he seems to have used the phrase in the normal Aramaic idiom—"son of man" = man (cf. Ps 8:4), though with something of a self-reference (the polite English style of referring to oneself by the general "one" is a useful parallel). "[Even] [i]n Dan. 7:13 it is not a title: the manlike figure

---

14. *m. Sanh.* 7:5e.
15. Hammer, *Classic Midrash*, p. 295 and 295n.

represents Israel over against the beastlike figures which represent Israel's enemies in a creative reuse of the familiar creation mythology".[16]

The phrase "Son of Man" is evidence of nothing more than a declaration of Jesus' own first century Jewish concept of messianism and did not require the "supernatural" qualities inherent within the prophecies; however, Jesus' use of the Scripture in Daniel, clearly reflected that *he* believed himself to be the *biblical* Messiah of God. There were those, to be sure, who looked for a supernatural messiah (e.g., the Essenes), but the majority of the Jewish population merely sought a nationalistic messianic figure who would give them freedom from Roman oppression. "On one point the rabbis were unanimous, viz. he *would be just a human being divinely appointed to carry out an allotted task*. The Talmud nowhere indicates a belief in a superhuman Deliverer as the Messiah."[17] There were certain Pharisees, however, who *did* expect a superhuman Messiah. Clearly, such expectations are found in Rabbi Akiva's sponsorship of Kosiba (bar Kochba) as Messiah in the early second century (*Y Ta'an.* 68d; *b. Shab.* 93b). Prior to that, there had been a number of others; for instance, the "Egyptian" introduced by Josephus. The high priests also thought that, perhaps, John the Immerser was the expected Messiah (John 1:19–27).

And while the Talmud might not have indicated to the Jews a belief in such a superhuman deliverer, it is quite clear from other pre-first century writings that such belief did, in fact, exist among various segments of the population. The Messianic Scroll found among the scrolls in the caves at Qumran and the first century CE apocalyptic literature provide evidence that these sects expected such a superhuman. Most Jews, however, especially the religious Zealots (who were simply a splinter group of Pharisees), still expected a common man, alternating between Davidic and Levitical descent, or both, to arrive on the scene (like, perhaps, one of the Maccabees) and wrest the nation of Israel from the grasp of the Romans.

> The pressure was on him, and it must have grown as, during the early months of his ministry, the multitudes flocked about him. When the rumor ran among the crowds that perhaps this was he who should redeem Israel, *the militant spirits there were thinking, not of an apocalyptic Son of Man from heaven, but of the rebel against Rome who would lead them to triumph in a messianic war.*[18]

The Saducean priesthood feared finding such a man. There had already been several such revolutionaries (for instance, Judas the Galilean) who had attempted to take away their important "positions" and "national status", which the Romans had appointed for them. It must be remembered that the Saducean priesthood as it existed in the early first century did not descend from Aaron and had little knowledge of Scripture. They were, in a word, *secular* and *practical* when it came to running the government. Out of all segments of the Israelite population, theirs was the most secure.

> The Sadducees stressed man's power of choice and saw the nation's future depending on the uncertainties of that, rather than on the predestinating providence of God. The messianic hope, as the Pharisees held it, they could not find

16. Dunn, "Christology", ABD, pp. 981–982.
17. Cohen, *Everyman's Talmud*, p. 347.
18. Fosdick, *The Man*, p. 193.

in the Torah and, being rich, powerful, on co-operative terms with Rome, they felt no flaming desire for a change in the status quo such as was setting the Jewish people, as a whole, afire.[19]

This illegitimate Sadducean priesthood would not have believed in the concept of an "everlasting" Messiah and would have viewed Jesus as an itinerant "trouble-maker" stirring up the people of Israel to revolt. The Sadducean agenda had long since become political power and financial gain. They had been appointed to office (many for a substantial bribe) by the Roman government through the influence and consent of the Herodian dynasty with whom they were allied. During the last phase of the Jewish War, the Zealots would finally rebel against them, taking both their positions and their "nation", the very thing they had feared the *Romans* might do.

> As there was only one God, so there was only one Temple, and one high priest. These individuals had been chosen from one single family, that of Zadok, *from at least the time of Solomon until the early decades of the second century b.c.e.* but when the Jewish dynasty of the Hasmoneans restored national control over their homeland in the 160s, they themselves assumed the high priesthood, although they were not of Zadokite lineage. It was probably legitimate Zadokite priests who withdrew in protest to Qumran where, among the Dead Sea Scrolls, their Community Rule decrees that 'the lot shall come forth . . . [on] all matters concerning the Law or property or justice' (5:3). Thereafter, under the Herodians and the Romans, *high priests were chosen from four main families, not of legitimate Zadokite lineage, and were appointed and fired almost like servants.* What the peasant Zealots are doing is quite logical, coherent, and traditional against that background. They are ousting the aristocratic government of their country and replacing it with a peasant leadership chosen from legitimate Zadokite stock by the ancient method of lottery. That action, of course, was intended to leave the ultimate decision up to God. Because all of that lineage are legitimate, let God choose. They would not choose the smartest, or the tallest, or the richest, or the most powerful. Lottery was their radical egalitarianism in action. They also killed their chief opponents, Ananus II and Jesus, former high priests of 62 to 63 and 63 to 64 CE, respectively.[20]

To those first century rulers, then, *Ben Adam* (Son of Man) would have meant little more than that, a descendant of the first sinful man, *a human being*. Jesus' claim of messianism would have been viewed more in the light of political dissidence than as a supernatural savior of the nation. His claim would have seemed to the rulers little different than the many others who had come before him, and perhaps, even more so since he was a Galilean, an area known for its "trouble-makers".

> Parkes, *op. cit.*, p. 22, writes that "a flood of messiahs sprang up in the first half of the first century A.D. The causes of emergence of so much messianic unrest have often been missed. It was not merely a reaction against the loss of national sovereignty. It was brought about by the fact that according to the calendar in use

---

19. Fosdick, pp. 66–67.
20. Crossan, *Who Killed Jesus?* p. 53.

among the Jews at that time, the coming of the Messianic age was expected about the middle of the first century".[21]

In Aramaic, *ben adam*, used in Hebrew Scriptures as a poetic synonym for "man", is *bar nasha*, which simply means "human being". While the phrase "son of man" had previously been used as a polite way of speaking of oneself in the third person, by the time of Jesus' trial, it had, among the Essenes (another splinter group) and other divisions of Pharisees, come to imply a *supernatural* messianic figure. In the book of Daniel the "coming" of the "son of man" was interpreted as the Messiah ushering in the kingdom of Heaven. In one Pseudo-Danielic Aramaic writing (4Q246) found at Qumran there is a phrase that refers to the supernatural messiah as the son of God. "He shall be called son of God, and they shall designate him son of the Most High."[22]

In another scroll (4Q174) a connection is made between the Son of God with the Son of David.

> The Lord declares to you that He will build you a House (2 Sam. vii, 11C). I will raise up your seed after you (2 Sam. vii, 12). I will establish his throne [for ever] (2 Sam. vii, 13). I [will be] his father and he shall be my son (2 Sam. vii, 14). He is the Branch of David who shall arise with the Interpreter of the Law [to rule] in Zion [at the end] of time. As it is written, I will raise up the tent of David that is fallen (Amos ix, 11). That is to say, the fallen tent of David is he who shall arise to save Israel.[23]

Even while these two titles are somewhat connected, the title "Son of God" alone could never have been offensive to any Jew. All Jews believed they were Sons of God. Furthermore, a younger contemporary of Jesus, Hanina ben Dosa, had also been titled Son of God because of his own religious acumen.

> All Jews, then, are Sons of God. But as time went on—and this was already apparent in Old Testament days—the idea was narrowed down to a special kind of distinctive sonship by eminent people, for example pious and righteous individuals, and, in particular, the monarchs of Israel ... Yet these relationships had not generally been conceived in physical terms, since they were a matter not of birth but of election. Between the Testaments this concept of an ethical, metaphorical Sonship gained in strength ... Jesus himself fully accepted the ancient Jewish doctrine that God was the father of the entire community.[24]

Jesus had more often than not stressed the fact that he was simply a human tool for God, suffering the physical and emotional trials that all men do. He *learned obedience through what things he suffered* (Heb. 5:8) in the same manner as any other Jew striving for spiritual union with God.

> The problem of evil was attacked from another angle, by the denial that sufferings endured in this life were intended by God as punishment, or that they were

---

21. Cohn, *Trial and Death*, p. 353 n.43.
22. Vermes, *Dead Sea Scrolls*, p. 275.
23. Vermes, p. 294.
24. Grant, *An Historian's Review*, p. 106.

> evidence of His disapproval. On the contrary, they were indicative of His love and served a beneficient purpose. The declaration, 'Behold it was very good' (Gen. i.31), was referred to suffering. 'Is then suffering good? Yes, because through its means human beings attain to the World to Come' (Gen. R. ix. 8). 'Which is the way that leads a man to the World to Come? The answer is, the way of suffering' (Mech. to xx. 23; 73a). 'Whoever rejoices in the sufferings that come upon him in this life brings salvation to the world' (Taan. 8a).[25]

Jesus, like other *hasidim*, believed he must suffer in order to attain entrance into the World to Come. He was not "mystically" endowed with perfection, and only attained that perfection at his death. He sought and learned blamelessness (the more exact translation of perfection) only as he *grew* into his ministry. Even in the supposed spurious chapters of Luke a kernel of truth is conceded. He was not, in the beginning, *full* of wisdom but was "becoming filled with wisdom" as he grew in age. "And the child [Jesus] went on growing and waxing strong, *becoming filled with wisdom*; and the favour of God was upon it" (Luke 2:40). This passage bears little resemblance to those of the "miracle child" in the later infancy gospels, and in the other elaborations of Matthew and Luke. Little distinction is made between his growth and development and that of his alleged cousin, John the Immerser: "And the child [John] went on growing *and being strengthened in spirit*" (Luke 1:80). Even though he called himself "Son of Man", Jesus believed he was the Israelite Messiah, the *Son* of the Living God. First and foremost, his mission was as an agent of righteousness.

> Sonship to God, in Jewish thought, was not a metaphysical category; *it involved no such thinking as Hellenistic Christianity later put into the Nicene Creed*; it was a matter of spiritual quality and divine vocation, involving in its supreme exhibition a unique commission to fulfill it. *That*[,] the first disciples clearly perceived in Jesus ... Messiahship is a category of vocation and mission. It is not primarily metaphysical but instrumental. The Messiah, human or superhuman, is a doer of deeds, a divinely appointed agent of salvation to his people.[26]

So whether Jesus saw himself in the natural or the supernatural, he did see himself as the divinely appointed agent who would usher in the kingdom. He truly believed YHWH would resurrect his human body from the dead; he also believed he was the "prophet like unto Moses".

When Gentile Christians replaced the early Jewish assembly, Jews would view him as the thing worshipped—that is, an "idol". It is one thing to honor him as God's Son, but it is quite another to worship him as a god. The earliest followers of Jesus understood his purpose and mission as that of reintroducing the Jewish people to their God. Even Jesus' name (Joshua) means "Yah has Liberated". To explain exactly how important it was that he receive that specific name, we must look a bit deeper." To the Oriental, a name is not merely a label as with us. It was thought of as indicating the *nature of the person or object by whom it was borne*."[27] Even the large contingent of pious Pharisaic Jews during the first century would not have expected God to raise a "human being" from the dead

---

25. Cohen, *Everyman's Talmud*, pp. 118–119.
26. Fosdick, *The Man*, pp. 179–181.
27. Cohen, *Everyman's Talmud*, p. 24.

The Crime: Apostasy from the Law

until the "last day". For an example of this mode of thought we might look at Martha's statement when Jesus was about to raise Lazarus (Eleazar) from the dead: "Jesus saith unto her thy brother shall rise again. Martha saith unto him, I know that he shall arise again in the resurrection *at the last day*" (John 11:23–24). To raise a "human being" from the dead would be *the greatest testimony of YHWH's word and existence* to a nation that had lost sight of God! The "testimony of Jesus" is not the testimony *about* Jesus; it is the *testimony that Jesus gave about his father: YHWH*. When we begin to view Jesus as a *fully* human being, a Jew, indoctrinated in Jewish culture and philosophy, the resurrection event becomes a more true witness of Jesus' messiahship and of YHWH's omnipotence. It had not been until his immersion by John that the fullness of the Holy Spirit had dwelt wholly within him, and even then he had remained a human being but now *filled* with Holy Spirit and a desire to commit himself entirely to God. If this were not so, the prophecy of Psalm 2 would not have been fulfilled in Jesus: "I will declare the decree: the LORD hath said unto me, Thou art my Son; *this day I have begotten thee* (Ps. 2:7). The day referred to in the Psalm is the day of Jesus' immersion by John when the full fount of the Sevenfold Holy Spirit descended upon him. It is within the earliest gospels that we find the true nature of Jesus as the human Hebrew Messiah.

> There were in the early years of Christianity several Jewish-Christian sects, such as the Ebionites, reported in Epiphanius *Against Heresies* .30, in which Epiphanius states that the Ebionites took Matthew as a teacher of his Gospel in Hebrew, and he shows how this vegetarian sect accepted Jesus as *"begotten of the seed of man"* but was the choice of God and called the Son of God. Christ [i.e., Messiah] came into Jesus from above in the likeness of a dove.[28]

Marcello Craveri states further:

> From the beginning, believers in Christ [Messiah] sought to find in his baptism [immersion] a sign of divine consecration. The Ebionites, the Ophites, the Adoptianists, Cerinthus the heretic, Basilides, the first Apostles themselves, regarded that ceremony as the first moment of the Messiahship of Jesus: *only then (and not, as came to be believed later, from the time of his birth) had God endowed him, like the Biblical prophets and seers, with his own illumination and adopted him as his son.*[29]

Of course, this is just one more area in which the universal church sought to change the original teachings of Jesus.

> As early as the end of the second century, those little groups of Christians [Nazaraeans] who looked to the kingdom as the end of the misery of the humble (in Hebrew, *ebionim*) *were proclaimed heretics*, and, in order to buttress the argument that the social content of their preaching could not be traced to Jesus, the Church invented a presumptive leader for them and called him Ebion. Alterations were made in the Gospel of Matthew to weaken the two Beatitudes that explicitly envisage the abolition of want and hunger.[30]

---

28. Barnstone, *Other Bible*, p. 203 n.1.
29. Craveri, *The Life*, p. 80.
30. Craveri, p. 173.

A Book of Evidence

Note the similarities in the following gospels:

> And it came to pass when the Lord [Master] was come up out of the water, the whole fount of the Holy Spirit descended upon him and rested on him and said to him: My son, *in all the prophets I was waiting for you that you should come and I might rest in you.* For you are my rest [the Hebrew name of Messiah - Menachem, Comfort]; *you are my first begotten Son* that reigns forever.[31]

> When the people were baptized [immersed], Jesus also came and was baptized [immersed] by John. And as he came up from the water, the heavens were opened and he saw *the Holy Spirit in the form of a dove that descended and entered into him. And a voice sounded from Heaven that said: You are my beloved Son, in you I am well pleased.* And again: *I have this day begotten you.* And immediately a great light shone round about the place. When John saw this, it is said, he said unto him: Who are you Lord? And again a voice [*bath kol*] from Heaven rang out to him: *This is my beloved son in whom I am well pleased.*[32]

> Luke 3:23 cf. *Gospel of the Ebionites*, (in Epiphanius, *Against Heresies XXX.13.2*)—"There was a certain man named Jesus, about thirty years old, who chose us" Also cf. Justin, *Dialogue 88:3*—When Jesus went down in the water, fire was kindled in the Jordan; and *when he came up from the water, the Holy Spirit came upon him.* The apostles of our Christ [Messiah] wrote this.[33]

As further evidence that Jesus was "on that day" confirmed by YHWH as Messiah, he was "led by the Spirit" into the wilderness to be *physically* and *mentally* tempted by the Accuser (and YHWH cannot be tempted by evil—Jas. 1:13), where his worthiness might become finalized.

Within these illustrative events the title "Son of Man" might be more clearly seen as a device used by him to reveal his humanity. The earliest followers of Jesus had accepted him as fully human, a man like themselves, albeit someone they had recognized as a "holy" teacher (a Master of Israel) and, finally, as Messiah. They never questioned the divinity of the One God, YHWH, and while they did accept Jesus as the Son of God and Messiah (Son of David), they never accepted Jesus as "divine" until after his resurrection.

Regardless of the relevance attached to these terms, the fact is Jesus *was* accused, charged, and legally tried for the crime of blasphemy, not for biblical nor nationalistic messianism, but for the more subtle crime of leading the nation astray. As stated earlier, it was not a blasphemy in the sense most Christians would recognize today.

In the corpus of Mosaic legislation, there were numerous crimes termed "blasphemous". Jesus had also been accused of injurious conduct against the Pharisaic scribes, and this was "blasphemy" in itself. Because the verdict is so clearly implied in the gospels, it becomes necessary to make an investigation into all the crimes of which Jesus was accused in order to arrive at a reasonable hypothesis and conclusion concerning what his "blasphemy" was. Since the Sanhedrin's viewpoint was that Jesus was a human, and ours must be as well, it will be necessary to look at the pertinent points of law in light

---

31. Barnstone, *Other Bible*, p. 335.
32. [32] Barnstone, p. 338.
33. Throckmorton, *Gospel Parallels*, p. 11.

The Crime: Apostasy from the Law

of the government's behavior toward any other man. If Jesus *did* commit the crime of blasphemy in their eyes, the facts will reveal it. Jesus *was* an apostate from the law, that is, from the *authoritative scribal interpretations* of the intricate Jewish law. He was accused of numerous blasphemies as they are defined in Jewish legislation.

A thorough search into the gospel narratives and into Jewish law will provide proof beyond doubt that Jesus did, in fact, commit blasphemy in the eyes of the legalistic rulers. While a host of other offenses might have been asserted, the crime for which he was ultimately executed was "leading the nation astray", an even graver crime than uttering the ineffable name. The numerous accusations against Jesus were simply combined into a *single* allegation, and this made the charge of "leading the nation astray" the most serious and worst type of blasphemy in all Israel. It was this charge made by the priestly family of Annas that was used to mask the *personal* crime against them: the cleansing of the Temple precincts. The revenues collected by the infamous Bazaars of Annas, where "acceptable" sacrificial animals and birds could be bought for offerings, and where "qualified" moneychangers made exorbitant profits for exchanging national coins for Temple tax, provided that family with most of their wealth.

> It has been suggested that all these creatures and commodities had to be "officially inspected" so as to exclude "any doubt of ritual purity"; that the pilgrims had no choice but to pay well and even exorbitantly for the certainty that their offerings would not be rejected for some flaw; and that the priests, to whom inspection fees went, were so interested in their "perquisite" that they must have fumed against any meddling with the traders and moneychangers as a brazen trespass on their own revenue.[34]

Mr. Cohn believes these suggestions are unrealistic, but there is sufficient evidence within both history and ancient Jewish writings in their defense. Considering the corruption of the priestly families, it is not farfetched to think they would use their private interests to extort a price for "purity". Further, Jesus was not the only Jew to object to the graft system within the Temple precincts. It is referenced within the Talmud that other pious Jews objected to their profaning presence (*b. Yeb* 6b; *b. Ber.* 54a). Even Gentiles had set up booths in the area for secular trade.

> Solomon's Portico had three colonnades, and here was the so-called merchants' quarter (*hanuyoth*). The vendors were especially busy on days of religious observance, when they were thronged with crowds that commingled Jewish pilgrims, Eastern merchants (especially Phrygians), Roman soldiers, tourists, and curious locals. Here one could buy or sell everything needed for sacrifices: sheep, doves, salt, grain, wine, incense, oil. In addition, there was a thriving trade in secular goods.[35]

There are so many clues within the gospels pointing to the true "blasphemy" of Jesus that it is amazing no tally has ever been made of them. A discussion of each of the alleged crimes that Jesus was purported to have committed will enlighten the reader as to the true nature of the "blasphemy".

---

34. Cohn, *Trial and Death*, p. 56.
35. Craveri, *The Life*, p. 298.

BREAKING THE SABBATH

There are only *seven* incidents in New Covenant writings in which it is alleged that Jesus profaned the Sabbath. Most often it appears that Jesus is accused of breaking the Sabbath by his healing activities. While the Mishnaic law (compiled somewhat later) is quite explicit regarding the rabbinic laws of Sabbath breaking, healing is not listed among them. Although the Mishnah was not compiled until around 200 CE, there were traditions among the various groups of Pharisees, and although the law was yet unsettled, we often find that instances became encoded at that date. Each instance in which Jesus had healed an individual on the Sabbath is found to have been perfectly legal. It is not within the healings that we find the true crime; it is within the *methods* he used.

> Nobody could reproach such a one for breaking the law: *the law was not yet settled, and his conception of what it was, or ought to be, would be as valid, and carry as much force, as that of the next man.* In an indeterminate legal situation such as this, the Pharisaic rule is that each may act as he thinks right; and in the formation of Jewish law a particular rule is crystallized time and again by virtue of a scholar's behaving in practice as if it were already operative. There could, therefore, have been no objection or protests on the part of the Pharisees to Jesus' healing the sick on the Sabbath, even if the rule making it lawful had not yet been codified; there could have been legitimate differences of opinion, but no rancorous exception could have been taken to one divergent opinion among several being propounded and demonstrated.[36]

It is only to the careful eye that the actual crime becomes apparent in these cases. No one having knowledge of Mishnaic law can fail to notice that it was not Jesus' acts of healing that were objectionable. In these instances, however, are hints of far worse crimes. They are simply masked by debates between Jesus and the scribes concerning the legality of "healing" on the Sabbath, an everyday occurrence between scholars. Subtle hidden "crimes" form the backdrop for the basic charge against him, a greater all-encompassing crime in Jewish eyes: leading the nation astray.

We might note one of these examples in John 5:8–12. Jesus had healed the man on the couch; "Jesus saith unto him, Rise take up thy bed, and walk." While the legality of the healing activity itself is not in question, the fact that Jesus told the man to *carry a burden* on the Sabbath is. The healing activity, itself, was not inappropriate. By telling the man to act in the prescribed manner, Jesus was effectively breaking the Sabbath, not by healing the man, which any scribe *might* have done legally even on a Sabbath, but by "leading one astray" from the teachings of the scribal leaders. While the scribes themselves might have healed on the Sabbath, individual situations were always taken into consideration. If it could be determined that the man had been in need of emergency aid, the scribes would have had no problem in attempting to heal him. On the other hand, if the man had been in the same condition for some time (which seems likely in our present case), they might have preferred to wait until after the Sabbath. Jesus' argument would have been that the man has suffered long enough; why prolong his suffering? This would

---

36. Cohn, *Trial and Death*, p. 43.

The Crime: Apostasy from the Law

have been a breach in scribal interpretation, something he had *not* heard from his own Master. The Talmud is quite clear about such legal breaches.

> R. Eliezer said: He who utters something he has not heard from his teacher causes the Presence to depart from Israel.[37]

From the scribal perspective, Jesus was causing the man to sin by directing him to act in a manner inconsistent with their own Sabbath regulations. They would have viewed Jesus as argumentative and arrogant, contemptuous of the (Oral) Torah. He would have "shown them up" in public, so to speak.

> A person who despises the Torah or *despises those who devote themselves to it, that is to say, the scholars—if he is guilty of either of these—is called "contemptuous toward the Torah"* (Aknin) . . . A man should sooner fling himself into a fiery furnace than disgrace his fellow in public. (Vitry) The Tanna taught (*Baba Mezia* 58b) in the presence of Rab Nahman bar Isaac: *If one disgraces his fellow in public, it is though he sheds blood.* (Aknin).[38]

Certainly, they would have found Jesus' manner insulting and disrespectful; furthermore, Jesus was not teaching Torah in accordance with contemporary *halakah* (law). Since he was only about thirty years of age, an individual unordained by the Sanhedrin, the scribes would have believed he was inexperienced in such matters.

> *Teach the Torah not in accordance with Halakah*: That is, not rendering a proper decision . . . for example, *a disciple not yet qualified to render decisions doing so.* (Vitry) . . . to teach the Torah not in accordance with the Halakah is to say of the forbidden that it is permitted and of the permitted that it is forbidden (Rabbi Jonah).[39]

Because he *was* so young, when Jesus healed the man with the withered hand (Matt. 12:10; Mark 3:2; Luke 6:6), the synagogue rulers made a point of testing his knowledge of scribal law in order to entrap him in his own words: "Is it lawful to heal on the sabbath days?" (Matt. 12:10). Jesus, however, responded to their question in the proper way by countering their query with a question of his own. This was not an unusual practice in rabbinical debate. It is designed to cause one to think deeply about the subject. Sometimes, a riddle (what in the New Covenant is called a parable) is added to the discussion for just this purpose.

> The rabbi embodies his lesson in a story, whether parable or allegory or seeming historical narrative; and the last thing he and his disciples would think of is to ask whether the selected persons, events and circumstances which so vividly suggest the doctrine are in themselves real or fictitious. The doctrine is everything; the mode of presentation has no independent value. To make the story the first consideration, and the doctrine it was intended to convey an afterthought as we, with our dry Western literalness, are predisposed to do, is to reverse the

---

37. Bialik and Ravnitzky, *Legends*, 428:254; *op. cit., b. Ber.* 27b.
38. Goldin, *Mishnah Avot*, p. 74.
39. Goldin, p. 128.

A Book of Evidence

Jewish order of thinking, and to do unconscious injustice to the authors of many edifying narratives of antiquity.[40]

Jesus often used the "riddle" or parable, though, to indict the rulers of Israel without truly saying what was on his mind. This made it difficult for the rulers to openly accuse him of a legal crime. Without some training in Torah interpretation and Mishnaic debate, his inexperience might have rendered him unable to spar with the Pharisees and scribes. The debate, however, did not alter Jesus' intentions. After the scholarly discourse between Jesus and the rulers had ended, he restored the man's hand. It is important to note *that they made no further accusation or comment regarding the legality of healing on the Sabbath!* They had recognized his intelligence and his acute ability to debate with them on their own grounds. The question might have simply been rhetorical had they not been trying to entrap him as an inexperienced scribe on a point of unsettled law. If the subject of their query was not the healing activity, then what exactly was it they *did* question? Quite simply, it was objectionable to them that he had dared to usurp their authority.

> Teaching as one who has "authority" cannot merely mean that his speeches were powerful and his doctrines impressive (cf. Luke 4:32); it is that his authoritative teaching is, ostensibly, differentiated in a particular way from the teachings of the scribes, which might be impressive and powerful as well. For everybody knew that Jesus had no "authority"—hence the astonishment that he taught as if he had; not as the scribes, who would, like all ordinary preachers, describe and explain to you in intelligible form what the laws required of you and how best to observe them if you wished reward and not punishment, but rather as one who had the "authority" to lay down the law and determine it for you and prescribe new rules of conduct. *Such "authority" no man might take himself: it had to be conferred by a person already in "authority," in a formal act of ordination, a scholar already ordained "authorizing" a second. In the time of Jesus such ordinations were very rare, so that everybody knew who was and who was not ordained.*[41]

The scribal method of interpretation is through tradition. While Jesus *used* many of the traditions of the elders (very often his parables are echoed in the Talmud), he did not cite verbatim the dictums of the ancient sages, nor did he begin with a precedent to give authority to his own words.

> Some authority must confirm the dictum of every teacher, the authority, viz., of some previous teacher, or else the authority of the Torah interpreted according to some recognized rule. No teacher could base his teaching merely on his own authority; and the fact that Jesus did this, was no doubt one of the grievances against him on the part of the Jews. *Ye have heard that it was said to them of old time . . . but I say unto you, etc.* (Matt. v. 21, 22), implies the disavowal of the Rabbinical method; and the statement (Matt. vii. 28, 29) that Jesus *taught them as one having authority and not as their scribes*, was certainly cause sufficient that the people should be *astonished at his teaching*, and that the scribes should be incensed and alarmed.[42]

40. Grant, *An Historian's Review*, p. 38.
41. Cohn, *Trial and Death*, pp. 59–60.
42. Herford, *Christianity*, p. 9.

The Crime: Apostasy from the Law

The scribes saw themselves as God's agents in the world, the nation's "healers". It was *their* jurisdiction Jesus had invaded. To act in the capacity of a scribe in those days without ordination by the Sanhedrin would be similar to one practicing law today without a license. Jesus, however, having grown up and studied in the priestly station at Nazareth or else in an Egyptian Jewish school, *knew* the law and the teachings of the scribes. He had studied the current oral *halakah* (law) of the, as yet, unwritten Mishnah and the ancient Midrash. An uninformed individual would have certainly fallen into their trap.

In Mark 3:4 (concerning the incident of the withered hand), it is plainly stated "they remained silent". Jesus' question had visibly thrown their own hypocrisy in their faces. Their silent reaction hints at their disapproval of his making them a spectacle in public, and indicates their jealousy of Jesus' "talents". Healing had been one of their specific callings, and the scribes believed themselves to be the only "authorities" in these matters. From that moment they went out "straightway with the Herodians" and were "giving counsel against him, that they should destroy him" (Mark 3:6). Had Jesus' actions on the Sabbath been illegal, there would have surely followed an envenomed accusation and a warning by at least two witnesses. Any lawbreaker found a *second* time engaged in the same type of activity would have been arrested immediately, brought before the *beth din* (the judicial branch of the Sanhedrin), and tried for the offense. It was not necessary, however, for an individual to belong to the Sanhedrin in order to bring such accusations. Any ordinary citizen might have brought the charges against him. Since Jesus continued his healing activities over the three and a half years in which he ministered to Israel, it can safely be determined that he was not arrested for Sabbath-breaking. Luke's account of the same incident reveals the rulers' frustration of being unable to entrap him on some point of law: "And they were filled with madness, and communed one with another what they might do to Jesus (Luke 6:11)." The word "madness" is the Greek *anoia* and more precisely means "rage". The scribes were more than just annoyed that they were unable to argue with the reasoning of one so "inexperienced". They were *enraged* that Jesus had shown them such disrespect.

In the healing of the woman with the issue of blood (Luke 13:10), Jesus had again been upbraided and scorned by the local synagogue ruler. Again, he had *not* been accused of a crime. No warning was given in this instance, either; the ruler had merely made a pious objection. The ruler was, however, "shamed" for his false piety while the "multitude rejoiced." Why did they rejoice? It was because this Jewish audience, both educated and uneducated, disliked and disapproved of the Temple Cult and the government. Any victory over the "rulers" was a victory for the people.

> What did the Jewish peasantry think about the Temple (Theissen 1992:95–114)? Were they for it, or against it? Was it the place of prayers and sacrifices, or the place of tithes and taxes? Was it divine dwelling, or central bank? Was it the link between God and themselves, between heaven and earth, or the link between religion and politics, between Jewish collaboration and Roman occupation? It was clearly both, and peasant attitudes were correspondingly ambiguous.[43]

---

43. Crossan, *Who Killed Jesus?* p. 50.

A Book of Evidence

It would be well to note that in all three instances where Jesus healed with a "word" or "command", he was *not* accused of having broken the Sabbath (Matt. 12:10; Mark 3:2; Luke 6:6; Luke 13:10; Luke 14:1). The scribes might have disliked it, but they gave no warning, nor made any accusation against him. Sickness and malformations were believed to have been conditions imposed by God for some sin committed, whether by the person himself, or by his ancestors. For this reason, those persons who might be healed with a "word" were believed to have been healed through divine intervention of the Holy Spirit, whether the agent was Jesus or some other scribe. The population was well-accustomed to these types of healings, as we have been told in the Talmud, and there would have been little amazement that Jesus had been empowered as an agent of God to effect such healings. The Jewish writings are packed with examples of divine healings performed by the sages themselves. They *did*, however, disapprove of using Scriptural citations in curing disease or wounds (even though the practice was widespread). These they termed "incantations".

> It will also be seen that incantations not infrequently formed part of the treatment, these sometimes including Biblical verses. This practice was severely condemned by the Rabbinic authorities. 'It is forbidden to cure oneself by means of Scriptural citations (*Shebuoth* 15b), they urged. Among those who will have no share in the World to Come is the person who utters an incantation over a wound which includes the quotation: 'I will put none of the diseases upon thee that I have put upon the Egyptians, for I am the Lord that healeth thee' (Exod. xv.26) (Sanh. x.i.).[44]

The real conflict came, however, when the scribes, who believed themselves to be the *only* authorized "healers", were confronted with someone not from within their exclusive circle who exhibited the same abilities (and even more pronounced than they). They opposed him as one who had come from "outside the camp". We might wonder why, since Jesus was well-versed in the "law", these scribal leaders might have objected so strenuously to his teachings. The answer lies in the fact that he had come from Galilee, where "Masters" were more relaxed in their religious beliefs.

> For in spite of their reputed religious unsoundness the Jews of Galilee retained all the ardour characteristic of converts; and this produced a rich crop of Galilean sages, before, during and after the lifetime of Jesus. *These saintly figures, often known as Hasidim* or 'the pious' (after a group of strict believers of the second century BC), were alien to the Jewish leadership at Jerusalem because they cared little for Law or for ritual, but instead confidently claimed an intimate, informal direct familiarity with God,* operating as exorcists, healers and miracle workers.[45]

This phenomenon also explains Jesus' use of *Abba*, the familiar term for God as Father. In this he was not alone. It appears that many of the *hasidim* of Galilee were accustomed to the term. For example, Rabbi Hanina ben Dosa, also a Galilean, was known to have used that affectionate term in referring to YHWH. The political priesthood in Jerusalem objected to the conservatism of these Galileans because the teachings of the

---

44. Cohen, *Everyman's Talmud*, p. 251.
45. Grant, *An Historian's Review*, p. 75.

The Crime: Apostasy from the Law

hasidim were in direct conflict with the practices of the Temple Cult. The scribes had also objected to the fact that Jesus did not use prayer as a method of healing in these instances. It is worthy of note that in the one instance where Jesus did use prayer to heal a "lunatic" (an epileptic who was believed to have had demons) (Matt. 17:14–20), not one scathing word is heard from the rulers. In Mark 2:7 the Gospel records the scribes' belief that he spoke "blasphemies" [*blasphemia*]; that is, they believed he was speaking blasphemies (injuries) *against them*. They believed that only God himself had the power to forgive sins, and that he did so only through his "government". Jesus' statement cannot be taken to have meant that *he* forgave the man his sins. Marcello Craveri explains.

> First of all, *the statement "thy sins be forgiven thee"* is (since disease was considered a divine punishment that could be canceled by repentance and prayer) *the equivalent of "God hath pardoned thee."* This was the formula ordinarily used by the priests in such circumstances, speaking as the interpreters of God. Hence it means, not that Jesus had arrogated a supernatural power to himself, but only that he had claimed priestly power. Even in the Old Testament there are instances of priests and prophets who made the same statement. Jesus did not say: "I forgive thy sins," but he did say, in effect: "Thy sins be forgiven [and I will stand warranty for it]." The outrage of the Scribes arose only from this pretension of Jesus to a priestly authority that they refused to recognize in him.[46]

To have healed any individual without first having asked God's blessing in prayer was, in the scribes' eyes, enough, but to add insult to injury by claiming to possess an *unordained* priesthood was just too much. Jesus *was* able to heal the man without prayer, thus verifying his claim, and because of that they sought to accuse him of using sorcery to usurp the authority of YHWH (and themselves). Yet they *still* did not openly accuse him of a crime; they merely *warned* him that his activities were going to get him into trouble. For Jesus to have made statements like "forgiven are thy sins" and "by the power of my *tallit* arise" (*Talitha Koum*) was to them an outrage. No Jewish priest would have allowed a woman to touch him at all, and certainly not the powerful *tallit* in which was said to dwell the holiness of God. There is a special reason for this. It might be useful to digress from our discussion to explain the significance of such an event. The *tallit*, a four-cornered robe, on which are *tzitzit*, or tassels, is commonly called the prayer shawl. It is the holiest garment a Jew can wear and expresses his monotheism; the garment was so holy, in fact, that the tassels must have been cut off before it might be sold. The tassels are said to be the *pe'er* (glory) of God. What makes it holy are the four *tzitzit*, which are said to represent the 613 commandments of written law outlined in the book of Deuteronomy, which is Torah, the Power of God's *Word*! Each tassel is tied in exactly 613 knots. In Jewish gematria (numerical equivalents of Hebrew letters) the sum of these knots equals YHWH Echad, meaning *God is one*. The symbolic significance of the *tzitzit* is that the Power of the Holy Spirit resides in the tassels of the garments. The woman with the issue of blood (Luke 8:43–44) understood that the power would make her whole if she could but touch it. In restoring the dead child to life, Jesus used the words (*Talitha Koum*) "by the power of the *tallit* arise!" That is, he was, in effect, saying by the power of the Holy Spirit of the One God, YHWH, arise. The "unclean" woman who had recently

---

46. Craveri, *The Life*, p. 105.

touched his *tzitzit* rendered him defiled. Since he was no longer in a state of "purity", he dared not physically touch another individual imparting to her his "uncleanness". Jesus merely used the power of the *tzitzit* (which was representative of the Holy Spirit) to raise the child from the dead, possibly by touching her dead body with one of the tassels. For Jesus to have raised the child through the use of the *tzitzit* while in a state of "uncleanness" would have greatly offended the Jewish rulers, whose purity regulations were, to them, of utmost importance.

It was only when some hidden *mishnaic* law came into play that Jesus was actually accused of Sabbath breaking. One of two examples is the incident in which the disciples were walking through the corn field, plucking the "ears of corn" and "rubbing them together with their hands" (Matt. 12:1; Mark 2:23; Luke 6:1). Again, the law was not yet codified and was much disputed, but to these extreme Pharisees to reap any amount of grain on the Sabbath was sin. Their laws were, in their own eyes, the valid ones, and it was, in their opinions, their duty to "judge" offenders. It is to be noted that it was only after the Sadducees began to wane in power (i.e., just prior to 70 CE) that the Pharisaic interpretations of the Dual Torah gained dominance.

> During the First Roman War the Temple of Jerusalem was burned to the ground as it fell to Titus's troops in the year 70 CE the Jewish aristocratic class of priests, or Sadducees, was destroyed forever, and it was the scribal class of legal experts, or Pharisees, who inherited that vacuum in Jewish leadership. They met at Yavneh, west of Jerusalem near the Mediterranean coast, to save Judaism. They not only advocated religious fidelity and moral integrity, but also extended the lost Temple's ritual purity into every Jewish home. The home and its regular meals would be observed as once was the Temple and its sacrificial meals.[47]

There is much evidence in New Covenant writings, in the Talmud, and in the histories of Josephus to indicate their bitter battle. It was a battle between not only the two opposing brotherhoods (Pharisees and Sadducees) of the Sanhedrin but among other groups as well. Besides parties of Zealots and Essenes (who were also Pharisees), there were numerous other divergent splinter groups in the Pharisaic branch, itself, and many times they did not agree with each other. One might note that not all Pharisees were hostile to Jesus. It is clear, however, that the ruling Pharisees (later called rabbis) did win the battle, because when the law was codified the Mishnah clearly sets into place a law that specifically states "He who takes out a quantity of . . . ears of grain (corn) sufficient for a lamb's mouthful . . . he is liable [for breaking the Sabbath]" (*m. Shab* 7:4 a,b). It was, perhaps, the incident with Jesus and his disciples that provided the precedent for the codification of such a law. If the disciples, who surely must have had healthy appetites, managed to allay their hunger, it is likely they reaped quite a bit more corn than was necessary for a "lamb's mouthful." The rulers' objection, however, had little to do with the fact that the disciples had "reaped" their food on the Sabbath. It was disapproval of the disciples' laxity in observing the Pharisaic purity laws that prompted their criticism. The disciples had not washed before eating. Galileans, in particular, seemed to care little for the Jerusalem sect's numerous cleanliness and purification laws. The rulers would

---

47. Crossan, *Who Killed Jesus?* pp. 16–17.

have, of course, held Jesus responsible for his disciples' behavior. So vehement was their rejection of this type of behavior among disciples that we read of special scribal condemnation against sloth among disciples some years afterward.

> A disciple of the wise should be modest at eating, at drinking, at bathing, at anointing himself, at putting on his sandals; in his walking, in dress, in the sound of his voice, in the disposal of his spittle, even in his good deeds. A bride, while still in her father's house, acts so modestly that when she leaves it her very presence proclaims: "Whoever knows of anything to be testified against me, let him come and testify." Likewise, *a disciple of the wise should be so modest in his actions that his ways proclaim what he is.*[48]

For the Pharisaic scribes, their purification laws were of utmost importance. They surely would have viewed the disciples' behavior as immodest, immoral, and most importantly, a failure to conform to their own values.

> To take but one example of a social code that caused contention, the Pharisaic laws of purity were so important in some early social groups that they occasioned vociferous debate, realignments of traditional loyalties, and the redrawing of group boundaries. Families were split apart and the structure of village authorities was rearranged by taking sides on the definition of purity. Why? Because social relations were in the process of being reconsidered and realigned in light of the novel social vision they called the kingdom of God.[49]

The cosmopolitan world in which various ethnic groups of the first century had found themselves required them to seek solutions for some type of self-government, even if those solutions were only moral ones. The rulers of the Temple Cult sought to bypass the absolute authority and control of the Roman government by exhibiting their own power in the *religious* sphere. These phenomena gave them a sense of national identity while keeping them separate from the pagans that surrounded them. They did this by promulgating moral rules that in the Diaspora became the laws of the Jewish nation.

> [T]he concept of purity was basic to the Jewish system of social and practical propriety. From a large system of legal, ethical, and sacrificial law that had been developed during the second-temple period, Pharisees had succeeded in isolating a small list of ritual practices they could perform at home. These would count, they said, as full observance of the Jewish law and tradition. The list included tithing (or offering one-tenth of one's agricultural production to the priests), giving to charity (alms), sabbath observance (including daily prayers and a fast day during the week), cleanliness (or washing after activities that made one unclean), and rules that governed the selection of foods, the preparation of foods, and the people with whom one ate (or "table fellowship"). These rules should not be thought of as laws, for the Pharisees had no official authority over any Jewish institution. They were signs of piety for a progressive sect engaged in redefining what it meant to be Jewish in the shadow of the temple's end. They were, however, extremely important

---

48. Bialik and Ravnitzkey, *Legends*, 434:30.
49. Mack, *Who Wrote the New Testament?* p. 12.

rules for the recognition of any Jew who wanted to be "pure," that is to be recognized in the Jewish community as loyal to Jewish traditions.⁵⁰

Even though the purity regulations were not yet enacted into a law code, Mr. Mack's statement should make it clear that there could have been only disapproval for the behavior of Jesus and his disciples.

Another incident in which the Pharisees concluded that Jesus had broken the Sabbath was when he had made clay from earth and spittle in order to anoint the eyes of the blind man. Had the law been codified during the early first century, he would have, indeed, broken the Mishnaic authority making it illegal on the Sabbath to take "earth for clay enough to make . . . a seal for a letter" (*m. Shab* 8:5 a,b). Since the quantity used by Jesus to cover two eyes would have exceeded the amount it would take to make a seal for a letter, he would have surely exceeded the Sabbath limit. Once again, the actions of Jesus might have set the precedent. Implicit within the mixture of the two properties, however, is an illegality far more serious in the eyes of the Jews, as we shall discuss later. Again, while the law might have been in existence during that early first century, it was not yet strictly enforced. While this and many other laws of the Mishnah had been traditionally set for centuries, they were not yet legally engraved in stone, so to speak. It was not until the second century that the Pharisaic (rabbinical) law would become acceptable by the Jewish nation and canonized into law. During the time of Jesus, disputes arose on a daily basis between scribes concerning just what the law was. At that time, the Saducean rulers stood in complete opposition to the Pharisees, and even though they, themselves, knew little Scripture, they controlled the priesthood and were autonomous in both government and religious matters. There were, in the land of Israel, other more fundamental Saducees, as well as any other number of groups (for instance, the Essenes) for whom the priesthood found it necessary to put up a facade of the biblical observance of law.

> From what we know of [popular] Saducean tenets, we might be right in assuming that the Saducees would demand rigid observance of the Old Testament precepts, whilst Pharisaic instruments of law represented a more flexible interpretation of the Torah, adjusted to contemporary needs and conforming with current ways of thought . . . Saducean penal practice [for instance] was carried out rather in the manner indicated in Acts 7 58.59 than in Mishnah Sanh. vii 4.⁵¹

The Saducean rulers, at least on the face of things, set priority on the *written* law of Moses, while the Pharisees claimed Moses had also handed down an "oral" tradition, and that *it*, not the written, was the more sacred law. These "oral" traditions made it quite convenient for them to set legal precedents at any whim. With such a wide range of legal principles espoused by them, it is little wonder that Jesus remonstrated the ruling Pharisees: "Blind guides! Straining out the gnat, but the camel swallowing (Matt, 23:24). With a plethora of burdens later placed on the Sabbath, it is easy to understand his apostasy from the existing legalism and their concern for his splintering off from the rulers' precepts. Even though some of the traditions of the Midrash had begun as early as

---

50. Mack, pp. 57–58.
51. Winter, *On the Trial*, p. 68.

the time of Ezra, they were not as yet solidified as "law". The Oral Torah, in the early first century, was believed to hold an equal status of "holiness" as the written.

> The nature of these commentaries is unique in that the commentaries themselves are seen as part of the work on which they comment . . . Just as the rain comes down upon fruit trees and gives each one its own flavour according to its nature . . . so it is with words of Torah. Although they are basically one, they contain Scripture, Mishna, Talmud, *halakhot* in some manuscripts "midrash") and *haggadot* . . . One may be Written Torah, the other Oral Torah but both are Torah—Divine Teaching.[52]

Since Jesus adhered to a more ancient rendering of the Tanach (Old Covenant) than did the Sadducees, (who for the most part had become less religious and more political), and he had almost completely denounced the "oral law" of the Pharisees), he could hardly have broken the Mosaic Sabbath. The scribes, who had their own interpretations, are certain to have disagreed. It is likely the *methods* Jesus used in his healings might have been called into question and misconstrued by them as sorcery. Mishnaic law is quite specific in that it required that "exact paraphernalia works through demons" and "he who does not [use prayer] works by pure enchantment," (*b. Sanh.* 67b). Exact paraphernalia was that "demanding particular properties for different kinds of magic".[53] Jesus had healed one blind man with "earth" and "spittle", two properties which, when mixed together, might have been construed as "paraphernalia". While this mixture might have been legal for making clay seals, it would have been highly illegal for use in a divine healing. Spittle alone would have posed no problem at all. "For eye-trouble spittle was commonly used, but we are told 'there is a tradition that the spittle of the first-born son of a father has healing powers, but not of the first-born son of a mother' (B.B. 126b)".[54]

There were many "fine lines" between acceptable and unacceptable healing practices. Apparently, Jesus used methods entirely unacceptable to them. Since sorcery was the handmaid of a *mesith* (an enticer who leads the nation of Israel astray from the scribal teachings), it is reasonable to imagine that Jesus' actions might have been defined as sorcery.

Jesus is known, also, to have talked with impure spirits and demons (Mark 1:21–27; Luke 4:31–37), who in response called him the "Holy One of God". While he expelled the spirits with a word of command, the crowd in the synagogue was sure to have suspected him of sorcery. They were "astonished at his doctrine because for his word was with power" (Luke 4:32). The crowd would have believed Jesus was usurping God's authority: a blasphemy in their own eyes. To be certain of this, we must look to a more expanded definition of the word "astonishment". The Greek word *ekstasis* not only means "amazement", but it also means "to strike with fear or panic". This type of healing would have been most uncommon and would have certainly struck them with fear and panic.

> Casting out devils was a different process from winning God's mercy and forgiveness. We know from the Talmud that "whispering," for instance, was a recognized mode of treatment, but there was a dissentient view that no whispering

---

52. Hammer, *Classic Midrash*, p. 191.
53. Hammer, p. 19.
54. Cohen, *Everyman's Talmud*, p. 253.

> ought to be allowed "in respect of demons," which seems to imply that for demoniac states other cures were prescribed, and that whispering was good only for natural, that is, divinely sent, illnesses.[55]

For Jesus to have spoken to impure spirits and demons was, in itself, improper in the eyes of the crowd. It was popular Jewish belief that to speak to such a "demon" was to invite him into your own spirit. Commentary on Deuteronomy 18:12 found in the *Sifre B.* 107 explains: "He who joins himself to uncleanness, on him rests the spirit of uncleanness; but he who cleaves to the Shechinah, it is meet that the Holy Spirit should rest on him." Likewise, the commentary on Deuteronomy 17:16 states: "What is the way of a 'demon'? He enters into a man and subjects him (*Sifre b*:136). At least as early as Honi, the Circle Drawer (that is, the "rainmaker") [before the first century CE] demonology had pervaded Jewish society. It is ironic that Jesus would have been accused of demonology in light of the ridiculous superstitious beliefs and practices to which the scribes and Pharisees themselves adhered; they were known to have often practiced "whisperings" and "magic".

> Since the human being was so exposed to the harmful activities of evil spirits, means had to be devised to circumvent their mischievous designs. Some of these have already been indicated, such as *incantations and amulets*. Formulas have been quoted for the purpose of banishing demons in special circumstances; but the general rule is given: 'To exorcise a demon say, "Be split, be accursed, broken, and banned, son of mud, son of an unclean one, son of clay, like Shamgaz, Merigaz, and Istemaah' (Shab. 67a).[56]

"Whisperers" are defined in the sources as any number of evil personalities, from sorcerers, to Egyptians and pagans, and even to our infamous High-Priest, Annas, and his family. Josephus, rather than using the Talmudic term for this family of "whisperers", uses the word "hissers" to define their personalities as "serpents". Even John the Immerser had called them a "brood of vipers" (Matt. 3:7; Luke 3:7), and Jesus, himself, referred to them as "serpents" and "vipers" (Matt. 12:34; 23:33). History records that both Josephus and the *Tannaim* viewed the family of Hanan (and their partners) as corrupt governmental officials in league with the Roman government, an oligarchy not above accepting and offering bribes to get their own ways. The plain fact is the rulers of Israel were willing to accuse Jesus of anything in order to keep him from "leading the nation astray" from the teachings of the scribal authorities.

It follows that the aforementioned exorcism by Jesus' "words" and the fact that the demons, themselves, spoke to him would have suggested to Israel's rulers that Jesus was practicing a form of sorcery. While they might, at any other time, have overlooked the offense (after all, they themselves practiced such exorcisms), the fact that it occurred during the Sabbath was offensive to them. Simply put, they could claim that Jesus was "leading astray", enticing Israel to follow his own example, even though a select few of other preventive measures against evil spirits *were* allowed on that day. These were held to a bare minimum. For example:

---

55. Cohn, *Trial and Death*, p. 52; *T. Shab.* VII 23; *m. Sanh.* X 1.
56. Cohen, *Everyman's Talmud*, p. 267.

The Crime: Apostasy from the Law

> The use of a root inside a signet-ring as an amulet is mentioned in the Rabbinic sources. 'A person may not walk out on the Sabbath wearing an amulet unless it had been written by an expert' (Shab. VI.2). 'Which is the amulet of an expert? Such as had effected a cure a second and a third time, whether it be *an amulet in writing or one consisting of roots. With such he may go out on the Sabbath*; obviously so if he had not yet been attacked by a demon, but also if he had not yet been attacked; obviously so if it is in a circumstance where there is danger, but also if there is no danger. One may tie it and untie it during the Sabbath, provided he does not insert it in a necklace or signet-ring and carry it about, because of appearances' sake' (Tosifta Shab. IV.9). The law with regard to written amulets is: 'Even though they contain the divine Name, they may not be rescued from fire on the Sabbath, but must be allowed to burn' (Shab. 115b).[57]

To teach Israel, by example, that to practice such exorcisms on the Sabbath was an acceptable practice would have been highly offensive to the rulers. They had declared such activities unlawful and would have seen it as a form of enticement. Mr. Haim Cohn, a leading legal scholar and Chief Justice of Israel from 1948–54 explains its significance.

> Apart from sorcery, Jesus is said to have been charged with enticing Israel and leading them astray. This is a grave offense, if not the very gravest known to Jewish law: it means enticing another to "serve other gods, which thou hast not known, thou, nor thy fathers; namely, the gods of the peoples which are round about you" (Deut. 13:6–7), idols of wood or stone, as the heathen worship.[58]

While Mr. Cohn never makes any personal assertion that Jesus was an idolater nor a sorcerer, we must, nevertheless, consider the impact of his words. Since Jesus had been given "all authority" to act in behalf of YHWH, and since his words were essentially those of his Father, he simply found it unnecessary to do more than speak a "word", something the rulers simply could not comprehend.

Suffice it to say that, while Jesus' healing activities were not the focus of the accusations of Sabbath-breaking, his presumptuous manner and methods of healing were found by the scribes to be extremely blasphemous (injurious) to God, Israel, and, most importantly, to themselves. They believed he was guilty of the more serious crime of "leading the nation astray" and because of their intense jealousy, they were willing to do anything to bring him to trial. Such an accusation would legally carry the death penalty; that is, execution by stoning.

SORCERY

We have already mentioned one incident wherein Jesus might have been accused of sorcery through his healing activities. The methods by which Jesus cast out demons and made clay for the blind man's eyes are only two examples that might be misinterpreted as sorcery. But there is an even more blatant accusal of this crime. Jesus was said to have had a familiar spirit, that is, Beelzebub (or Baal-Zebub, the Lord of the Flies, or excrement) through which he was able to cast out demons (Mark 3:22–30; Luke 11:14–25; John 8:488–49). In

---

57. Cohen, pp. 268–269.
58. Cohn, *Trial and Death*, p. 299.

order to understand the significant danger of this accusation, it becomes necessary to digress into a discussion of pagan religion as it existed in Israel during the first century. Since Jesus was accused of "having a demon" (perhaps even meaning he was mad) and healing through "Beelzebub", we ought to know the scope of that accusation.

> Beelzebub (in Hebrew, *Ba'al zebub*), a Philistine deity worshipped in antiquity by the Israelites as well, was the god of the flies, whom it was necessary to propitiate in order to be safe from those dangerous carriers of infectious germs. The Greek text of the Gospels uses (βεειεβούλ Beezeboul), which is a transcription of Ba'al zebul, the god of excrement. Whatever the attribute, he was a god of evil, an enemy of Yahweh, a "prince of devils," who may well be identified with Satan. Jesus uses both names in his answers to the Pharisees' insinuations: "Every kingdom divided against itself is brought to desolation; and a house divided against a house falleth. If Satan also be divided against himself, how shall his kingdom stand? . . . And if I by Beelzebub cast out devils, by whom do your sons cast them out?"[59]

The serpent, or python (Asclepius in the Greek) was worshipped throughout northern Israel, Egypt, and Asia Minor as Isis (sometimes Semiramis) during the time of Jesus, but was known by the Jews as *Ba'al Ob*, the necromancer or "conjurer of the dead". He was accused of having a "devil" (or "demon", "familiar spirit"; John 7:20; 8:52; 10:20). That designation is connected with Ba'al Ob and the Python. There are references to this Python in both the Mishnah and the Tosefta: "He who has a familiar spirit [M. 7:4D4] (Lev. 20:27)—this is one who has a Python which speaks from his armpits."[60]

> The *Ba'al 'Ob, that is the Python* who speaks from between his joints and elbows, and the Yidd'oni, who has the bone of a Yidd'oni in his mouth, are to be stoned; and he who inquires of them offends against an explicit warning [*Tosef. Sanh.* X 6] . . . *He who inquires of the dead*;—that is, one who conjures up the dead by witchcraft . . . When one conjures up the dead by witchcraft it (the ghost) does not come up in the proper way, nor will it come up on the Sabbath.[61]

Zebub (in Hebrew) is a stinging fly; the definition is meant to convey the stinging nature of the serpent's poisonous bite. *Baal* means Lord, Master, or god. The term *Baal-Zebub* then is the Master of the Serpent and refers to the worship of Osiris (Nimrod), the "god" and Isis (Semiramis), the "healing serpent" (Asclepius) of the Egyptian pagan Cult of the Dead. Being connected with the *Ba'al Ob* was a dangerous accusation for it implied one effected miracles through other "gods".

The Talmud goes so far as to connect the miracles of Jesus to magic, which he was said to have learned during his stay in Egypt (*b. Shab.* 104b). We have no evidence for his whereabouts during the period of time between ages twelve and thirty. It might be surmised that since Jesus was so well informed in both Torah and scribal interpretation, he might have been enrolled in either a Jewish school in Egypt or in the school at Nazareth. There was, at least, a rumor that Jesus had spent time in Egypt. If he did, it could be that this fact is the reason he was accused of sorcery. As a young child he would have

---

59. Craveri, *The Life*, p. 141.
60. *m. Sanh.* 7:7b.
61. Danby, *Tractate Sanhedrin*; *Tosef. Sanh.* X 7.

learned Torah from his father; however, it is certain he had spent at least some period of time in the teaching facility near Nazareth. Nazareth was one of the priestly stations (*ma amadot*) located in Galilee. The priestly centers are referred to as *ma amadot* and are described by Rabbi Hayim Donin:

> What were the *ma'amadot*? They made up a network by which the public-at-large was represented at the Temple during the offering of the daily sacrifices. Since the Torah states (Num. 28:1) that the sacrifices were brought by the people, it was necessary that the people be represented at the ritual even though they were not permitted to perform any of the priestly or levitical duties ... The priests and Levites were divided into twenty-four watches or shifts of duty (*mishmarot*), each of which took its turn in officiating at the Temple sacrifices. Each *mishmar* was responsible for one week's tour of duty every six months. The country, likewise, was divided into twenty-four districts. Each district appointed a delegation of distinguished Israelites known for their piety to represent it at the public offerings ... The prayer gatherings of these delegations, both in the Temple and in their respective villages, were called *ma'amadot* (s. *ma'amad*) (Maim. Hil. Klei Hamikdash 6:1-6).[62]

These priestly stations are thought to have been the earliest synagogues and teaching centers (*ha mikdash*). If Jesus had attended one of these, he would have learned Torah, Midrash, and the scribal interpretations of the Mishnah from the scribal authorities and priests assisting in the priestly station at Nazareth, even though the laws and customs were not yet codified and written down. Every word would have been memorized. His education would have begun in his hometown synagogue and would have been completed at the priestly *beth hamidrash* (house of interpretation).

> In the synagogue, the hazzan, aside from directing choirs, was also charged with teaching the elements of learning to the children. The Oriental didactic method (still employed today in many Asiatic countries) consisted of making all the students continually repeat in chorus, in a loud voice, the various verses and sentences they were to learn by heart. Consequently the verb *shanah* ("to repeat") finally came to have the colloquial meaning of both "to teach" and "to learn". Besides, it would have been virtually impossible to learn directly by reading the scrolls. In Hebrew, words are (or were) all run together, and only their consonants were written".[63]

It is also interesting that Jesus was probably not the "poor" carpenter Christian tradition makes him to be. The Greek word *ho tekton* is probably used figuratively for the Aramaic *naggar*, meaning either a "craftsman" or scholar.

> The Greek *ho tekton* is trying to render a word of Semitic origin. In the old Jewish writings, the word 'craftsman' or 'carpenter' had a metaphorical meaning: in the language which Joseph and Jesus would have spoken, Aramaic, the word is *naggar* and it could either mean a craftsman or a scholar, a learned man. There is no reason to suppose that Mark believed Joseph to have been a wood-worker or joiner.[64]

---

62. Donin, *To Pray*, pp. 12–13.
63. Craveri, *The Life*, p. 59.
64. Wilson, *Jesus, A Life*, p. 83.

A Book of Evidence

The Hebrew word translated "carpenter" as used in Zechariah 1:20 is *charash* and means an "engraver"; i.e., a scribal lawyer, and it is in this sense that Jesus was called a "carpenter". He was a "builder" of the stones of Torah. The fourth century *Toldoth Jeshu* was written by Jews who have understood the word "carpenter" in a symbolic sense. In it Mary is betrothed to a pious sage descended from the House of David, a *scribe*.

Jesus has often been connected with "the Egyptian magician" or "false prophet" in the *Talmud*, but this is clearly not our Jesus of Nazareth. Josephus narrates the advent of an Egyptian magician (also named Jesus) who was said to have appeared in Israel during the turbulent years after Jesus' resurrection, during the time of Agrippa.

> But there was an Egyptian false prophet that did the Jews more mischief than the former [that is the Sicarii or Zealots]; for he was a cheat, and pretended to be a prophet also, and got together thirty thousand men that were deluded by him; these he led round about from the wilderness to the mount which was called the Mount of Olives, and was ready to break into Jerusalem by force from that place; and if he could but once conquer the Roman garrison and the people, he intended to domineer over them by the assistance of those guards of his that were to break into the city with him, but Felix prevented his attempt, and met him with his Roman soldiers, while all the people assisted him in his attack upon them, insomuch that, when it came to a battle, the Egyptian ran away, with a few others, while the greatest part of those that were with him were either destroyed or taken alive; but the rest of the multitude were dispersed every one to their own homes and there concealed themselves.[65]

The later Talmudic sages simply connected Jesus of Nazareth with the Egyptian false prophet because oral traditions from the first century had either become confused by the time the accounts were written, or because they simply resented Christianity's deification of him. The later sages knew the tradition of the accusations made against the Nazaraean during his trial, and as they often do, the sages simply connected him with this Egyptian "Jesus".

With the foregoing background information we might now begin to understand the seriousness of the accusations against Jesus. Such dangerous charges brought against him would certainly have foreshadowed the events of his future trial and execution. One who "leads the nation astray" is also said to be an idolater or sorcerer. The definition of an idolater did not necessarily involve worshipping other gods. The simple fact that they believed he was not "divinely inspired" was enough to accuse him of that crime.

> ... and *that prophet which shall presume to speak a word in my name, which I have not commanded him to speak, or that shall speak in the name of other gods, even that prophet shall die. And thou shalt put away the evil from among you* (Deuteronomy 18:20 – 19:19) (T.J., 3:5).

We now begin to see the fabric of elite society working against Jesus, and how he might have been accused of the gravest of crimes. Alan Watson explains:

> It remains to mention in this brief historical survey that in the hellenistic world the belief in magic, in the efficacy of spells for good or evil, was extremely

---

65. Josephus, *War*, 2:13:5.

The Crime: Apostasy from the Law

common and was found everywhere. Miracle workers and magicians were often regarded as having particular connections with a deity or devil, or it was thought that the deity or devil worked through them. One example may stand for all. Vespasian, under whom the Temple was destroyed in A.D. 70, was in Alexandria in 69. He had just become emperor: Suetonius, *Divus Vespasianus* 7.2. He as yet lacked prestige and something akin to divine qualities because he was a new and unexpected emperor. But these were given to him. *A man of the people who was blind and another who was lame* together approached him as he was sitting on the tribunal begging for the help with their health which *Serapis [Osiris Apis in the Egyptian pantheon; that is, the sun god] had promised in a dream. The god declared Vespasian would restore the eyes if he spat in them; and would strengthen the leg if he would deign to touch it with his heel.* 3. Though he had scarcely any faith that this would succeed in any way and therefore did not dare to make the attempt, he did try both things at the end because of the exhortation of his friends, before a very large crowd. *And he had success* . . . [t]hus, the emperor who destroyed the Jewish nation publicly performed miracles similar to Jesus' greatest. And in this he was not alone.[66]

The method of healing that Vespasian used was "spitting in the eye", and this *appears* to be the same method used by Jesus. As mentioned earlier, it was quite common to use "spittle" as a cure for eye problems. There were any number of "miracle workers" roaming the land of Israel during the first century. Much of the populace that followed Jesus around Galilee consisted of selfish hangers-on. They had found someone who could heal their various maladies; some believed he was sent from God as Messiah; others simply took advantage of his miracles, caring little for his message.

> Jesus repeatedly declared that he was able to heal the crippled and the sick, that is, those possessed by demons, only through their belief in *him and his power* (e.g., Mark 10:51-2). This, evidently, was enough to provoke the accusation that his work was done by Beelzebul. As Morton Smith has remarked, *these accusations reflect a real difference between his methods and those of the scribes, a difference 'that led to his being charged with magic'*. It was alleged 'that Jesus "had" a demon and did his exorcisms by this indwelling demonic power. Since this charge was not brought against the other exorcists they must have been thought to effect their exorcisms by other means, presumably prayer to God.[67]

But as we have found earlier, the Scribes had often used "whisperings" and enchantments, rather than prayer, to effect their own healings. The difference is more to be found in that Jesus believed he was authorized by the Holy Spirit that dwelt within him, and that he spoke his words in the name of YHWH. The rulers simply believed he was not authorized by God to do so. They, therefore, accused him of healing through the demons of pagan religion. It is a certainty that in the Sanhedrin Tractate of the Talmud Jesus is called a *"Mesith"* (an enticer), "concerning whom Scripture says, Neither shalt thou spare, neither shalt thou conceal him." It is stated he had "practised sorcery and enticed Israel to apostasy" (*Sanh.* 43a). For this reason, scholars recognize that Jesus is

---

66. Watson, *The Trial*, pp. 18–19.
67. Zeitlin, *Jesus and the Judaism*, pp. 63–64.

often associated with Balaam in the Talmudic writings. The following extract is one such example where that conclusion might seem valid.

> A soothsayer? But he was a prophet!—R. Johanan said: At first he was a prophet, but subsequently a soothsayer. R. Papa observed: This is what men say, "She [Mary] who was the descendant of princes and governors [a reference to the Davidic line], played the harlot with carpenters [a reference to Joseph] . . . A certain min [heretic] said to R. Hanina: Hast thou heard how old Balaam [Jesus] was?—He replied: It is not actually stated, but since it is written, Bloody and deceitful men shall not live out half their days, [it follows that] he was thirty-three or thirty-four years old [thus corresponding to the date of 31 CE when Jesus was executed as will be discussed in "The Roman Pseudo-Trial"]. He rejoined: Thou hast said correctly; I personally have seen Balaam's Chronicle [one of the gospels], in which it is stated, 'Balaam [Jesus] the lame was thirty-three years old when Phinehas the Robber [a reference not to Pilate but to Annas, the *ab bet din*] killed him'.[68]

The name Phinehas in Hebrew means "mouth of a serpent". It is derived from a variant of the word *nachash* meaning "to hiss or whisper". A case might be made for Annas, whose family members were called "hissers" and "whisperers" by their contemporaries. Since Annas was responsible for bringing the accusation against Jesus, it is likely that the reference is made to imply he was the instigator of the charges. The Talmudic scholars were merciless in their descriptions of Annas' family.

The Jews consider Balaam to have been the most wicked of all Old Covenant prophets. Early Talmudic writings used his name as an alias for Jesus in order to protect their commentaries from censorship by Christian authorities. Similar literary devices were often employed by the sages when they wanted to debate issues in which Jesus played a part. By using the device "play on words", they were able to avoid detection by the universal church. Once we look at the evidence from a Jewish perspective, we can easily see how the rulers might have believed Jesus was a "sorcerer" and an enticer who was leading the nation astray from the usual scribal teachings into idolatry. Since Jesus radically opposed the teachings of the Pharisaic scribes, and since his healing methods were somewhat suspect, they would have believed he was perverting the Jewish populace, leading them into the idolatrous religious practices of the nations surrounding them. Such behavior was a national crime because it was believed to have caused God's wrath to descend upon the entire nation of Israel.

FALSE PROPHECY

A third companion to sorcery and idolatry is false prophecy. The three are inexplicably tied together as parts of the gravest crime of all in ancient Israel. That the rulers of the government of Israel believed Jesus was a false prophet, there can be little doubt. At the end of the trial before the Sanhedrin we learn their innermost thoughts about his crime. He is blindfolded and told to *prophesy* as to who struck him (Matt. 26:68; Mark 14:65; Luke 22:64). He had made a prophecy that the Temple would be destroyed and that he would rebuild it in three days. His words were, of course, misunderstood (Jesus, too, was

---

68. *b. Sanh.* 106a–b.; Epstein (1987 ed.).

adept with the "play on words" device). The practice of beating (flogging) the accused was known to have taken place after any verdict of blasphemy. Again, though, it was for the vain oath that Jesus received his beating. Mosaic legislation requires the beating of a "lawless man" with not more than forty stripes (Deut. 25:2-3). When a verdict of blasphemy is rendered through an accusation of false prophecy, it also includes spitting and the plucking out of the facial hair (the beard). One who had been shaved or had his beard cropped was believed to be accursed. It was a sign of shame.

> The beard was regarded as a symbol of manly beauty and virility, as an adornment of the face . . . Beards have always been highly symbolic for Jews. In the ancient Near East, the priests of pagan cults shaved certain areas of their faces to designate their sacred status. As a way of differentiating Israel from these cults, the *Torah prohibited shaving the *corners of the beard, as well as practicing divination and mutilating the face, other common pagan practices.[69]

That they would pluck his facial hair, his beard, goes to show that they planned to execute him as an object of shame, that is, as one associated with idolatry. Furthermore, it enabled them to make a subtle statement about his messianic claims. Isaiah had prophesied that though the Suffering Servant was to be cut off from the land of the living, he would *yet see his seed* (Isa. 53:10)! The rulers, who had only a vague concept of messianism, plainly wanted to prove to the population that Jesus was not Messiah. How were they to do this? The answer is simple: by executing him before he was able to have physical children. The plucking of the beard was a symbolic gesture designed to indicate that the accused had no virility and would not see his "generations". The author of *Toldoth Jeshu* (a Jewish document in which an attempt is made to justify the actions of the rulers against Jesus) relates a scene in which Jesus' dead body is taken from the tomb and dragged through the streets of Jerusalem (5:21) in order to ensure there would be no mistaking his "future generations". It must be stated here, though, that this would appear to be an interpolation of an event occurring sometime near the fourth century.

> v, 21. "*They bound cords to the feet of Jesus, and dragged him round the streets of Jerusalem.*" Sozomen relates in his *Ecclesiastical History* (Bk. V, xxi) that in the reign of the Emperor Julian (A.D. 362) there was a celebrated statue of Christ [this statue is mentioned by Eusebius] at Paneas (Caesarea Philippi), which was taken down by the Pagans "and dragged round the city and mutilated." If this incident was familiar to the Jews, as is likely, it affords further evidence for the compilation of the *Toldoth* in the fourth century in Palestine.[70]

In the canonical gospels, the judges were striving to denigrate Jesus to the status of a mere pagan by "mutilating" his face and "plucking" his beard. Isaiah prophesied this event quite succinctly: "I gave my back to the smiters [that is, the thirty-nine stripes], and my cheeks to them that plucked off the hair [the beard] I hid not my face from shame and spitting (Isa. 50:6).

The author of the Gospel of John records the profession of the "rulers and Pharisees", in response to Nicodemus: they simply did not believe that a prophet could come

---

69. Frankel and Teutsch, *Encyclopedia*, p. 18.
70. Schonfield, *According*, pp. 224-225.

A Book of Evidence

from Galilee (John 7:52). There are several reasons for their belief. First of all, the Roman pagans inhabited the Herodian-built cities of Galilee. No pious (nor especially pseudo-pious) Jew would set foot within one of these cities where temples of idols were located. Secondly, and most importantly, this northern region was the location in which their enemies thrived. The Zealots, under Judas the Galilean, had revolted against the Jewish authorities in Jerusalem for their patronage to the Romans inhabiting the region. It was this Zealot segment of the population that would divide the nation during the Jewish War. They became known contemptuously as *sicarii*, those who carried curved swords. Josephus tells us they hated the rulers of the priesthood so much that they made it their especial duty to assassinate them on a regular basis.

> When the country was purged of these, there sprang up another sort of robbers in Jerusalem, which were called Sicarii, who slew men in the day-time and in the midst of the city; this they did chiefly at the festivals, when they mingled themselves among the multitude, and concealed daggers under their garments, with which they stabbed those that were their enemies; and when any fell down dead, the murderers became a part of those that had indignation against them; by which means they appeared persons of such reputation, that they could by no means be discovered. *The first man who was slain by them was Jonathan [a member of the family of Annas] the high-priest, after whose death many were slain every day.*[71]

It should be well known that these rulers were deeply concerned that the multitude believed Jesus was a prophet. We are told by the author of Matthew that "seeking to secure him they feared the multitudes; since for a prophet were they holding him" (Matt. 21:45-46). Jesus, himself, claims to be a prophet (Luke 13:33; Matt. 13:57; Mark 6:4) and is called by others a "great" prophet" (Matt. 21:11; Mark 6:15-17; Luke 4:24, 7:16, 7:26–28; John 4:19, 4:44, 6:14, 7:40, 9:17–34). When he stated to the rulers that his Father is greater than their father (who we know he said was really the devil), it must have infuriated them. While they believed he was speaking disrespectfully of Abraham, Jesus was, instead, referring to the evil impulse within them. In the Mishnah there is a statement of great resentment for these words and for other sayings known to have been from the mouth of Jesus.

> And (2) it was also for the sake of peace among people, so that someone should not say to his fellow, *"My father is greater than your father."* And (3) [it was also on account of the *minim*] [heretics] so that the *minim* should not say, *"There are many domains in Heaven".*[72]

One might note that it was for the "sake of peace among people" that these things were not to be said. The statement would seem to imply that Jesus, while not militant himself, had caused certain militant factions within the nation of Israel to revolt against the government and its leaders. The passage would also indicate that Jesus was partially responsible for the increasing Zealot population that Josephus claims caused the destruction of Jerusalem in 70 CE. This, of course, would be tantamount to "leading the

---

71. Josephus, *War*, 2.13.3.
72. *m. Sanh.* 4:5 l-m; John 38-44; John 14:2.

The Crime: Apostasy from the Law

nation astray". The topic of any relationship he might have had with the Galilean Zealot movement will be discussed in a future chapter.

But was Jesus *accused* of false prophecy? The answer is decidedly no. While the rulers *believed* him to be guilty of false prophecy, it is clear from the narratives of the trial that he was *not* specifically accused of that offense. They did, however, seek for someone who would *testify* that he was a false prophet in order to prosecute him as a *revolutionary*! The single word translated as "false witness" in Mark 14:56–57 is the Greek *pseudomartureo*, that is, "to offer falsehood in evidence". The word is found in contradistinction to a similar word *pseudomarturia*, an "untrue testimony". Though many bore *pseudomartureo* (that is contrived testimony) against Jesus, their untrue testimonies did not agree. Apparently, these were the spies that had been sent to entrap him, and this does not surprise us. Jesus had said (Mark 10:19; Luke 18:20), "do not be an untrue testifer" i.e., offer falsehood in evidence. But in Matthew 26:59 where it is stated that they "*sought false witness against him*" *false witness* is defined by *two* Greek words: *pseudocristos* [that is, spurious messiah or false messiah] and *pseudomartia* [untrue testimony]. Although many bore *pseudomartureo* [falsehood in evidence], nobody was willing to give *pseudocristos pseudomartia* [false messiah untrue testimony]. They were searching for someone who would claim Jesus was not the Messiah, and they could find *no one who would give that testimony*! That this is exactly what is meant, we have an example in the words of Jesus (Matt. 24:24; Mark 13:22) where the words "false christs" are rendered by the same single word *pseudochristos*. The implications of this are astounding; no one from among the Jewish people would deny he was the Messiah, not even the envoys who had been sent to spy upon him! On top of that, no "untrue testimony" was found to incriminate him. This meant that the rulers must take responsibility for the execution, themselves, and this they did not want to do because they feared the people.

> Jesus' Jewish enemies did not wish to assume the responsibility of executing him, and the Gospels make plain the reason. He was too popular. They "feared the people." Let the Romans bear the burden of resentment against his liquidation! If the Romans would execute him as a disturber of the peace, that would gain the desired end at minimum cost.[73]

The rulers sought to place the blame on the Roman government, but as we shall learn in a future chapter they were entirely unsuccessful. They would eventually attend to the execution themselves and accept the responsibility for their actions, not something they originally *wanted* to do but something they felt absolutely *necessary* to secure their own power.

CLAIMING EQUALITY WITH GOD

What exactly does "equality with God" mean? The word "equal" (the Greek *isos*) in John 5:18 does not mean "equal with" but "resemblance" or "similarity to". The rulers were not accusing Jesus of making himself God. They merely resented the purity and familiarity of his relationship with God. In that respect, he was "like" God. Again, it must be stressed

---

73. Fosdick, *The Man*, p. 209.

that it was the Hebrew race who themselves fully developed the concept of union with God, that is, to be in complete agreement and harmony with his Word and Spirit, and it was this very quality in Jesus that caused them to resent him.

> If you have carried out the commandments of the Torah and acquired wisdom—know in truth that God exists, *walk in His ways so that you may be like Him*—and if you have delighted in and yearned for these just as you yearn for the fulfillment of your bodily needs and pleasures; then the Holy One, blessed be He, will grant you your wishes and desires, He will carry them out as you have carried out His will. And if you have bestirred yourself and cancelled your will for the sake of His will—engaged in divine occupation and abandoned the pleasures of this world which you naturally desire, and yearned instead to cleave to the ways of the Lord—then the Holy One, blessed be He, will reward you in accordance with what you have done, and He will undo the will of others who wish to harm you, He will destroy their counsels against you. Measure for Measure! (Aknin).[74]

They were, quite simply, jealous that Jesus, an unordained scribe, might have a closer relationship to God than they. There are at least two instances in the Gospel of John in which he was accused of claiming equality with God. The first refers to the affectionate term *Abba* that he often employed: "Therefore the Jews sought the more to kill him, because he not only had broken the sabbath, but said also that God was his Father, making himself equal with God" (John 5:18). The incident of Sabbath-breaking was that earlier described in which Jesus had told the man to pick up his couch and walk. Not only was this a violation of Sabbath law in the eyes of the rulers (John 5:10), but Jesus used the words "My *Abba*" in response to their questioning. For Jesus to have used such a term to show his union with YHWH was entirely offensive to the rulers in Jerusalem. As mentioned earlier, the Galilean holy men did not approve of the Temple Cult and maintained a familiarity with God that the rulers in Jerusalem did not.

> Jesus not only referred to God as *my Father*, he used an Aramaic term of endearment in addressing God. Edward Schillebeeckx and other scholars have called this the '*Abba*' experience. *Abba* implies 'father dear', it is the word that young children, in particular, used in Jesus' time to address their fathers; and it is still used in Israel today. The word *Abba* appears in its Aramaic form in the Greek text of Mark's Gospel; and as the Greek texts are the earliest we possess, the transliteration in them of Aramaic words is highly significant.[75]

Nothing within the concept of the Jewish Fatherhood of God would seem to indicate that Jesus had made himself equal with God. What, in Galilee, would not have seemed offensive was hypocritically grievous and irreverent to the Jerusalem authorities. The familiarity that Jesus exhibited to God merely brought God into the realm of personal human affairs; it did not conflict with true Jewish theology. Fatherhood was, and still is, the ultimate concept of God.

> Throughout the utterances of the Talmudic Sages, the relationship which exists between the Creator and His creatures is conceived under the image of Father

---

74. Goldin, *Mishnah Avot*, pp. 36–37.
75. Zeitlin, *Jesus and the Judaism*, pp. 61–62.

and children. God is constantly addressed, or referred to, as 'Father Who is in heaven'... And it was considered a mark of exceptional grace on His part that this intimate relationship exists and was revealed to man. 'Beloved are Israel, for they were called children of the All-present'; but it was by special love that it was made known to them that they were called children of the All-present; as it is said, "Ye are children of the Lord your God" (Deut. xiv.1)' (Aboth iii.18). Although this dictum specifies Israel, it being based on a Biblical passage, the doctrine of Fatherhood was not restricted to one people and was extended to all human beings"... The Fatherhood of God is synonymous with His love for the human family.[76]

Not only would the fact that Jesus called YHWH his own parent seem offensive and irreverent to the governmental Pharisees and scribes, it brought God into the realm of personal human affairs, which the rulers obviously did not believe was entirely possible. They had conveniently forgotten that Moses had instructed them to attend the *Ohel Moed*, Tent of Mutual Appointment "outside the camp" when they wanted to speak to YHWH as a "friend" (Exod. 19:17; 33:7–12). The rulers, instead, preferred bondage for the people of Israel, preferring worship in a Temple made by their own hands, making sacrifices of animals that enriched the priesthood that sold and approved them, and generally doing things their own way. This was a political and financial move by the rulers. God had made it clear that he did not dwell in temples made by human hands (2 Sam 7:5–6), because the pagan gods were worshipped in such places. He would build His own spiritual house (2 Sam 7:11). Even at Mount Sinai, they had refused to listen to his voice, asking Moses to intercede for them (Exod. 20:18–19). To bring God to such a personal level, for the scribes, was considered irreverent, but more than that, it disrupted the contents of their own pocketbooks. What they really objected to was Jesus' comparison of himself to Moses. The implication was that Jesus was the "prophet like unto Moses" (Deut. 15–18).

But the charge is clarified in John 10:30–33. It was not his "works" (that is, healing on the Sabbath) but, again, his "arrogance" (bringing God into "disrepute" on a personal level) that was called into question.

> I and the Father are one. Then the Jews took up stones again that they might stone him. Jesus answered them, Many good works have I shewed you from my Father; for which of those works do you stone me? The Jews answered him, saying *For a good work we stone thee not; but for blasphemy; and because that thou, being a man, makest thyself God [that is, elohim, a judge or magistrate]* (John 10:32).

The profane speech was not that he claimed equality with God, nor even that he had dared to call YHWH by the affectionate term *Abba*. What was really behind their statement was that Jesus, an unordained layman, dared to make himself a judge (*elohim*) of Israel, placing himself on their own level. Furthermore, they were concerned that he was deciding *halakhah* (law), a distinct duty they reserved for themselves.

Nor was this the only occasion in which Jesus was accused of making himself equal with God. Other examples might be found in Mark 14:62, Luke 4:21, John 7:28–29, and John 8:58. The form of speech (the euphemism *Abba*) that Jesus used to refer to God was

76. Cohen, *Everyman's Talmud*, pp. 20; 22.

simply not within the rulers' milieu of acceptability. They would have considered Jesus' allusions to himself as Messiah and the "prophet like unto Moses" as blasphemous and, indeed, idolatrous by Mosaic and Mishnaic law. Furthermore, he was teaching others that they, too, might have a personal relationship with God. The Mishnaic law states: "He who *beguiles* others to idolatry (M7:4H)—this refers to an ordinary fellow who beguiles some other ordinary fellow (*m. Sanh.* 7:10a–n)." As mentioned earlier, idolatry did not necessarily mean the worship of a foreign "god". Salvation had never been personalized before. It was the nation of Israel as a whole, rather than the individual, who was to receive salvation. Jesus taught that we might all become prophets and sons of God.

ALLOWING OTHERS TO HONOR HIM AS MESSIAH:

While Jesus only admitted to the disciples, his family, and a couple of other individuals (Bar Timaeous and the Samaritan woman) that he, indeed, was the Hebrew Messiah, the title was often conferred upon him by the multitudes. Even the demons cast out by him early on had called him by name and title. Although Jesus never definitively called himself Messiah, he encouraged an open proclamation of his person (Matt. 21:15; Mark 11:9–10; John 12:18; Luke 19:38–40). To the leaders of Israel, accepting the accolades of others was the height of rebellion, idolatry, and false prophecy. While Jesus was not a militant, it is clear Israel's leaders identified him with the faction of Zealots (formed by Judas of Galilee in 6–7 CE) who, in turn, were identified with the nationalistic messianic figure. The government naturally *assumed* Jesus was himself a Zealot, perhaps because of the company he kept. In order to understand the significance of this, we might note the words of Irving M. Zeitlin.

> The Zealots as a social and religious movement were committed to the fundamental principle that God was the sole ruler of the Holy Land, and that the Jews had only one master. It followed that they could never reconcile themselves to foreign domination. Freedom was their overriding concern. The adage, 'God helps those who help themselves', accurately describes the outlook of the Zealots, who believed that the people cannot expect God to aid them in the attainment of freedom if they will not endeavour to help themselves. The Zealots, then, may be seen as a splinter group within the broad Pharisaic movement, which contained other significant divisions such as the schools of Hillel and Shammai.[77]

These Zealots, who were called *lestai* by Josephus are identified as thieves in the gospels. The two "thieves" or "robbers" (*lestai*) who were hanged on the tree with Jesus were Zealots executed as *mesith* for "leading the nation astray", both a political *and* a religious charge. As we shall learn in "The Pseudo-Roman Trial", Jesus was *not* a Zealot; he was a pacifist. He had resisted all attempts to "make him king". And though he, himself, was not, it might well be that several of his apostles were. Zealots were often *called* Galileans like their leader, Judas.

Militant or not, the government plainly viewed Jesus as a national troublemaker. The political leaders of Israel attempted to balance their powerful religio-political

---

77. Zeitlin, *Jesus and the Judaism*, p. 31.

leadership between the Jewish populace (who intensely disliked them) and the Roman government (with whom they had allied themselves). They feared losing control over both. More evidence will be presented later on this subject. Suffice it to say that the leadership was frustrated by the popularity of Jesus and jealous of his "talents". Messianic claims often caused civil unrest, whether nationalistic or supernatural. Both would have the same effect upon the population of Israel.

> The term "Messiah," however, in Jesus' day, connoted no such clear-cut idea as we moderns commonly assume. The Messiah might be a man, rising from among the people—"A man shall arise ... like the sun of righteousness"; "a man working righteousness and working mercy." Or he might be a military leader fomenting revolt against Rome, and more than one such violent rebel was greeted as the Expected One. Peaceable or militant, such a Messiah was human—"Nor shall he do all these things by his own will, but in obedience to the good ordinance of the mighty God." The Messiah might spring from the house of David—that idea is prominent in our Gospels—but there was another tradition also, that he would come from the house of Levi. In conceiving the Messiah's mission, nationalistic victory might be stressed—"he shall make war against Beliar, and execute an everlasting vengeance on our enemies," or in the center of attention might be the whole world's welfare—"Neither shall there be any sword throughout the land nor battle din ... No war shall there be any more," and "there shall be peace in all the earth." The Messiah, however, in some circles, took on superhuman aspects. He was pre-existent, at least in the sense that his name was known to God from all eternity. So Moses is represented in saying of himself: "He designed and devised me, and he prepared me before the foundation of the world, that I should be a mediator of his covenant." In time, however, this Viceregent of God was pictured by some as personally present in the heavens, ready to come in glory at God's appointed time to usher in the kingdom.[78]

The rulers thus thought to dispel his popularity by claiming Jesus was a revolutionary or a sorcerer (or perhaps both) and that he was leading the nation of Israel astray.

THE CRIME OF THE REBELLIOUS SON

While it is true that Jesus could not be charged with this crime after the age of thirteen, it is clear the rulers thought Jesus had been allowed too much liberty as a child. The entire purpose in stoning a "rebellious son" was to keep him from growing into idolatry and indolence. The crime illustrates a breakdown in the effectiveness of Jewish family life. Much is to be said in behalf of the Jewish family. The entire Hebrew concept of Unity with God is, in fact, focused in family life and worship. From the time a child is able to utter its first word, the teaching of Torah is begun. By the age of twelve he is well versed in the instruction preparatory for his way of life. It is for this reason we cannot accept the accuracy of Luke's description of Jesus at the age of twelve sitting among the teachers in the Temple precincts, amazing them with his understanding of Scripture. While the passage was meant to impress upon us that he was a "wonder" child, we must look more closely at the incident. First and foremost, the *bar mitzvah* or a boy's entrance

---

78. Fosdick, *The Man*, pp. 180–181.

into adulthood took place during the second day of Passover in Jerusalem at the age of *thirteen*. Luke leads us to believe that Jesus was then twelve, the age for a female's entrance into the adult community. But what should strike us instantly is that Jesus had stubbornly resisted his parents' instructions. It is certain his parents had informed him when they would be leaving Jerusalem—yet he chose to remain behind. That he would have retorted in the way he did (Luke 2:49) shows (to Jews at least) a lack of respect for his parents. Of course, we understand the lesson the passage is designed to teach, that he would devote his life to God above everything else, but Jews would not have viewed it in that manner. Mary's use of the Greek word for "son" is revealing.

> When Mary had recovered her lost son after so much anguish, she could not restrain herself from angrily reproaching him for having, with typical boyish thoughtlessness, disappeared without a word to his parents: "Son, why has thou thus dealt with us? [B]ehold thy father and I have sought thee sorrowing." In the Greek text, it should be noted, Mary says, not "son" (which appears in a great many translations, including the King James), but, in obvious censure, "boy" (τέκνον *teknon*), rejecting the more affectionate term (υἱός *hyos*). Jesus, excited by the arguments he had been having with the teachers, was not even aware of his impertinence in replying to his mother: "And why did ye seek me? Knew ye not that only here, in the house of God our Father, could I be found?"[79]

It might be worthwhile to note that the words "in the house of God our Father" are not to be found in the Greek. Instead, the word used here is *en tois*; "among these people"; that is, Jesus is sitting among the rulers of Jerusalem in the Chamber of the Bridge (which was also a house of study).

It was, at that time, situated in the precincts of the Temple near the southern exit of the Temple platform. One thing is certain: had Jesus retorted in that way in the presence of the rulers, he would certainly have been cast "outside the camp" and immediately stoned as a "rebellious son". It is because of widespread early education and the great attention given to religious study that a rebellious son *is* cast out. Any individual, having learned so much at an early age, was believed to have known better than to dishonor his parents. The Talmud gives numerous examples in which a son goes to extremes to honor his parents, even to the point of carrying one's mother in order to keep her feet from touching the ground. There is a great deal of Mishnaic law regarding the rebellious son. Jesus was believed to have disregarded the law in several respects, and there are hints in the gospels as to the leaders' feelings about his actions. They knew he consorted with tax collectors (or publicans) who were hired by the Romans. A pious Jew would never have associated with them socially, and certainly not in "table fellowship". While the publicans might not have been members of the commonest stratum of society (*ammei ha-aretz*), these tax collectors were nevertheless considered lower than *mamzers* (bastards).

> According to the Gospels of Matthew and Luke, Jesus once or twice accepted an invitation to the home of a Jewish tax collector, a "publican," who, as we have said, by entering into Roman service had, in the eyes of the people, forfeited the right to mix in good Jewish society: no Jew would sit at table with him. As distinguished from the disqualification of such men as witnesses, this was not a

---

79. Craveri, *The Life*, p. 66.

The Crime: Apostasy from the Law

rule of Pharisaic law, but a widespread custom which may have grown out of an instinctive rejection and boycott of Roman hirelings.[80]

Scholars are agreed that tax collectors were considered outcasts from Jewish society for a number of reasons.

> Today, tax collectors are regarded as regrettable, but not necessarily degraded or evil; the readers of the New Testament are often puzzled to find them so specifically and persistently ranked among sinners. But in Roman Judaea and the adjoining Jewish princedoms of Herod Antipas and Philip . . . the two categories of officials grouped under this heading—general tax collectors (*Gabbai*) and customs-house functionaries (*Mokhes* or *Mokhsa*)—were so ill-regarded that they even lacked ordinary basic civil rights. This was not only because they shared the evil reputation habitually attached to such functionaries in the near east (and especially in the desperately impoverished Jewish homeland) but also because in these Jewish lands, serving pagan or pagan-influenced superiors or masters, they could not help mixing with ritually unclean persons, so that it was impossible for them to keep the Law. In Jewish literature, therefore, they rank as sinners.[81]

Neither might a Jew be a glutton and a winebibber, and he must never disregard his widowed mother. All these were the characteristics of the "rebellious son". The rulers believed Jesus had erred in all these ways. While they did not accuse him of the crime of the rebellious son, there is at least one clue in the gospels that they believed he had more liberty as a child than was lawful. Jesus is quoted as having said "The Son of Man is come eating and drinking, and ye say, Behold, gluttonous man, and a winebibber, a friend of publicans [tax-collectors] and "sinners"! (Luke 7:34). The Mishnaic law states:

> He is not declared a rebellious and incorrigible son—unless *he eats meat and drinks wine, since it is said, A glutton and a drunkard* (Dt. 21:20). And even though there is no clear proof for the proposition, there is at least a hint for it, for it is said, Do not be among the wine-drinkers, among gluttonous meateaters (Prov. 23:20).[82]

The penalty for such behavior is death by stoning. While the sentence seems a bit stiff to those of us accustomed to the freedoms of child-rearing in modern society, it kept Jewish society in unity. The reasoning assigned for such a harsh death penalty for the accused of this crime is expressed by Mishnaic law:

> A rebellious and incorrigible son is tried *on account of [what he may] end up to be*. Let him die while yet innocent, and let him not die when he is guilty. For when the evil folk die, it is a benefit to them and a benefit to the world. But [when the] righteous folk [die], it is bad for them and bad for the world.[83]

The leaders might have looked upon still another incident as the irresponsible act of a "rebellious son".

---

80. Cohn, *Trial and Death*, p. 39.
81. Grant, *An Historian's Review*, p. 55.
82. *m. Sanh.* 8:2k–o.
83. *m. Sanh.* 8:5a–b; 1c–d.

A Book of Evidence

> There came then his brethren and his mother, and, standing without, sent unto him, calling him. And the multitude sat about him, and they said unto him, Behold, thy mother and thy brethren without seek for thee! And he answered them, saying, Who is my mother or my brethren? And he looked round about him, and said, Behold my mother and my brethren! For whosoever shall do the will of God, the same is my brother, and my sister, and mother (Mark 3:31–55).

While it was not Jesus' intent to dishonor his mother nor his family, the governmental leaders would have believed such a statement reflected the act of one who openly rebels against not only his parents and family but *all* authority, including their own. His actions were those of one who was destined to become a *mesith*. As a rebellious son, Jesus would have been held legally responsible for the actions that would, in Jewish opinion, lead to the more serious crime. It is, in fact, noted in the gospels that his family and friends, as well as the rulers believed he was "mad" (Mark 3:21; John 10:20). Not even his family believed he was the Messiah until after the resurrection event. A Jew hearing Jesus' reply would necessarily believe Jesus was dishonoring his parents, acting in the manner of a rebellious son. They would have suspected no fatherly guidance, which would have naturally resulted in his mother and siblings being unable to "control him". Taken in conjunction with the other crimes he allegedly committed, the incident might be said to lead to "blasphemy", but this was still not the crime of which he was accused.

DESECRATING THE TEMPLE

Crimes against the Temple were also legally defined as blasphemous. We know of at least three instances in which Jesus is said to have desecrated the Temple. First of all, he was thought to have been speaking (or prophesying) against the Temple, which was also by law a "false" prophecy. It was, perhaps, the rulers' own paranoia that their Temple might indeed be destroyed by Roman instigation that made the issue so sensitive. The two witnesses brought to testify about the tearing down of the Temple had no spiritual understanding; they thought only of their Temple buildings (Matt. 26:61; Mark 11:15–16; Luke 19:45). The incident angered the priesthood because they were the recipients of the revenues of trade and usury in that district. Jesus became a nuisance to them. One important point should be made here. The site of the "cleansing" was the Temple precincts, and not the Sanctuary building on the Temple Mount. Like other Galileans, Jesus did not approve of the political and financial graft carried on in the name of God.

> We are dealing, rather, with a demonstrative condemnation of their trade, a condemnation which was directed at the same time against the ruling temple aristocracy, which derived profit from it . . . Such an episode did not call forth intervention on the part of the occupation forces, but it did make the hierarchy the deadly foes of Jesus.[84]

He was not the only pious Jew to disapprove of the Temple cult's trading activities. It just so happened that Jesus became a "thorn" in the sides of the priestly functions at

---

84. Hengel, *Was Jesus a Revolutionist?*, pp. 17–18.

The Crime: Apostasy from the Law

the Bazaars of Annas. To those who held the most fundamental of beliefs regarding the precincts of God's house, the practice amounted to profanation.

> Citing the rabbinic literature pertaining to the temple, I. Abrahams points out that in this instance Jesus 'sided with those who ordained that *the temple must not be made a public thoroughfare*' (TB Yebamoth 6b). Others went further and *forbade frivolous behaviour outside the temple precincts and in the neighborhood of the Eastern Gate* (Berachot 54a).[85]

The act of "cleansing the Temple" of the merchants (many of them foreign secular traders) and moneychangers lined along the *chel* (the rampart) was sure to have infuriated the Sadducean priesthood who were, themselves, profiteering from the sale of sacrificial items and from the usury charged by the moneychangers.

> Profane history has clearly and minutely described the crafty and serpent-like cunning by which Annas had been enabled to retain this coveted dignity within the control of himself and his family; and has also described the rise and nature of the Temple Bazaars, that infamous system of traffic in the sacrificial offerings of the Temple, and the Temple Tribute, established and controlled by the sons of Annas, which was a source of immense wealth to that family, and which had grown to such proportions in the time of Jesus as to make the Temple, in very truth, a 'den of thieves'.[86]

Jesus had cleansed the Temple precincts, twice during a three and a half year period (John 2:15; Mark 11:15). His actions did not go unnoticed by those who stood to profit in the trade regularly pursued there prior to and during festival days, i.e., the four families [Hanan, Boethus, Kimchit (Kathros, Kithros, Caiphas), Phiabi] who comprised the priestly oligarchy.

> The scene of Jesus' exploit was the huge, splendidly paved and colonnaded courtyard extending over thirty-five acres round the Temple [that is, on the Mount of Olives] . . . But in their own court they had set up a Merchants' Quarter (Hanuyoth) [Bazaars of Annas], housing money-changers and sellers of sacrificial animals and birds. These activities were fully authorized by the Temple authorities, and performed an obvious practical service to the pilgrims who thronged to the shrine for its solemn festivals.[87]

The rulers of Israel had "narrowly watched" Jesus after the first Temple cleansing, and for three and a half years they had sought to entrap him, perhaps, legally or either on trumped-up charges, masking the *real* offense: interfering with the trade revenues of the wealthy priestly caste. The gathering of evidence would result in the final charge being leveled against Jesus.

---

85. Zeitlin, *Jesus and the Judaism*, p. 149.
86. Richards, *Illegality*, pp. 6–7.
87. Grant, *An Historian's Review*, p. 148.

A Book of Evidence

LEADING THE NATION ASTRAY

To this point, we have investigated a series of accusations which, taken as a whole, were simply indicators pointing to the crime for which Jesus was ultimately tried. There can be no doubt the leaders of Israel brought him to trial for the more subtle of the blasphemies, that of leading the nation astray. As such a perpetrator, Jesus would also be known as "one who leads a whole town astray" (*m. Sanh.* 10:4h) (for instance, in Nazareth). There will be little argument that Jesus was a teacher, a Master, and that he explained and *added to* certain of the Torah precepts. A teacher or Master in those days was simply a scribe (*grammateus*), an interpreter of Torah. The word *grammateus* in the Greek derives from the root *grapho* meaning "to describe", but more specifically it means "in the Bible, *a man learned in the Mosaic law and in the sacred writings, an interpreter, [or] teacher*" (Thayers, p. 121). While Jesus is never called a *scribe* in New Covenant writings he is often called Rabbi, Rabboni, Master, or Teacher (depending on which version is consulted), and all these terms are *synonymous* with the word scribe. As further evidence that Jesus was, in fact, a Jewish Master, the words used to induct his disciples—shortened in the canonical gospels to "follow me"—were simply the rabbinical formula inviting individuals to become pupils of the Master's teachings.

> The curt sentence of the Gospels, (Δεύγε οπίσω μου *Deute opiso mou*), "Come ye after me," was the traditional formal rabbinical invitation to become a master's pupil and to follow him wherever he went.[88]

As a scribe, whether as an ordained member of the Sanhedrin or not he, legally, would have been more strictly dealt with than others.

> A more strict rule applies to the teachings of scribes . . . [if one] add[s] to what the scribes have taught, he is liable. *They put him to death* not in the court in his own town or in the court which is in Yabneh, *but they bring him up to the high court in Jerusalem.* "And they keep him until the festival [Passover], as it is said, And all the people shall hear and fear and no more do presumptuously (Dt. 17:13)" . . . "They do not delay the judgment of this one, but they put him to death at once . . ." "And they write messages and send them with messengers to every place: "Mr. So-and-so, son of Mr. So-and-so, has been declared liable to the death penalty by the court.'"[89]

Jesus *knew* he would be arrested in Jerusalem because of the outstanding warrant he had ignored. It might be noted above that "they put him to death on the festival" and "do not delay judgment of this one, but they put him to death at once." It is, indeed, true that Jesus was "put to death" at the festival of Passover, and that his trial was speedy, what is called in rabbinic terms "a decision for the hour" (*horaat sh'ah*). There is overwhelming evidence in New Covenant writings that Jesus was eventually brought to trial for "leading the nation astray", which was by far the worst crime of which he had been accused, because it embodied *all* other capital crime. The criminal court, the Lesser Sanhedrin (called the *Sanhedrin Ketana*) had sent spies throughout Israel in order to entrap Jesus

---

88. Craveri, *The Life*, p. 90.
89. *m. Sanh.* 11:3a–c; 11:4a–f.

The Crime: Apostasy from the Law

in his "blasphemy". As the Mishnah records, it is only for this crime that spies are, in fact, employed.

> [A]gainst all those who are liable to the death penalty in the Torah they do not hide witnesses [for the purposes of entrapment] except for this one [that is, leading the nation astray].[90]

Examples of this having been done by the judiciary are found in at least forty-six verses in all four gospels (see Appendix A). In the passages that follow, it is quite specifically stated.

> And when from thence he came out the Scribes and Pharisees began with vehemence *to be hemming him in, and trying to make him speak off-hand* concerning many things,—*lying in wait for him, to catch something out of his mouth* (Luke 11:53-54).
>
> Then went the Pharisees and took counsel, *that they might ensnare him in discourse. And they sent forth to him their disciples with the Herodians* saying, Teacher! we know that true thou art . . . (Matt. 22:15-16).
>
> Then were gathered together the High-Priests [Annas and Caiaphas] and the Elders [one chamber of the Sanhedrin tribunal] of the people, into the court of the High-priest who was called Caiaphas; and they took counsel together in order that Jesus, *by guile, they might secure and slay* (Matt. 26:3-4).
>
> And watching narrowly they sent forth suborned men [spies], feigning themselves to be righteous, that they might lay hold of a word of his so as to deliver him up unto the rule and authority of the governor [Herod, not Pilate] (Luke 20:20).

The "governor" here mentioned is none other than Herod Antipas (this is explored more thoroughly in a later portion of this book). Although, as royalty of Israel, he was called "king", and his official position in Rome was that of "tetrarch", Herod Antipas was more commonly referred to as "governor" or "king" by the Jewish population. There is evidence in the canonical gospels (and in the non-canonical Gospel of Peter as well as Toldoth Jeshu where Queen Helene is a pseudonym for Antipas) that it was Herod before whom Jesus was to appear.

> The same day there came certain of the Pharisees, saying unto him, Get thee out, and depart hence: for Herod will kill thee. And he said unto them, Go ye, and tell that fox, Behold, I cast out devils, and I do cures to day and to morrow, and the third day I shall be perfected (Luke 13:31-32).

Herod, at the time, was in Galilee from whence he ruled. That Sabbath evening [Friday-Saturday] Jesus entered a house belonging to a ruler of the Pharisees and abode there until after the Sabbath (Luke 14:1) (thus proving there were splinter groups among this brotherhood). Near the end of the three days (on Tuesday morning) Jesus is quoted as saying: "Behold, we go up to Jerusalem, and all things that are written by the prophets concerning the Son of man shall be accomplished" (Luke 18:31). It was also a three-day journey to Jerusalem from that location. He arrived in Bethany on 10 Nisan [Friday evening to Saturday evening; John 12:1], "6 days before the passover", where he would become the perfect, unblemished Passover lamb. Mary of Bethany anointed him that

---

90. *m. Sanh.* 7:10c.

A Book of Evidence

Sabbath (Friday) evening. On Saturday evening, 11 Nisan, after the evening sacrifice and after 6:00 P.M., he first entered Jerusalem (John 12:12).

Jesus had been traveling with other Galileans, perhaps members of the *ma amadot* from Nazareth, and those who would have traveled in a large group for reasons of safety. The diaspora pilgrims were also making their journeys to the festival of Passover in Jerusalem. The Galilean pilgrims were known to have customarily encamped on the northern extremity of the Mount of Olives (i.e., Mount Scopus) for the festival. If they had suffered Levitical defilement (for instance, at a funeral), it became necessary to be purified prior to entrance into the Temple.

> And the Jews' passover was nigh at hand: and many went out of the country up to Jerusalem before the passover, to purify themselves" (John 11:55).

It is well known that the Jewish populace began to study the multitudinous Passover laws and prepare for the festival some thirty days before, beginning at Purim on 14–15 Adar.

> Due to the complexity of Passover laws, the rabbis recommended that people begin to inquire about them thirty days before the holiday . . . [t]hus the early version of the beraita in *Sanhedrin* (12b) and *Megillah* (29b) reads: "They [the people] inquire [*shoalin*] about the laws of Passover thirty days before Passover."[91]

The reason for inquiring *early* is given in the Talmud.

> Raba said to R. Nahman: Let us consider! Between Purim and the Passover there are thirty days, and from Purim we begin to lecture on the laws of Passover, as has been taught: People must begin to inquire into the Passover laws thirty days before the Festival. R. Simeon b. Gamaliel said: A fortnight before. If, then, it [sc. Passover] is postponed at the beginning of the month [of Nisan], people will be liable to disregard the law regarding leaven [on Passover]—He [R. Nahman] answered him: It is well-known that the intercalation of a year depends on [minute] calculations, hence they would say that [the declaration was not made until the thirtieth day] because the Rabbis had not completed their calculation until then.[92]

During the days of the Passion Passover there are thought to have been nearly three million pilgrims from the countries and regions nearby vying for the precious space afforded by the twin villages of Bethphage and Bethany, within the Temple precincts but outside the city of Jerusalem. Many of the pilgrims making the journey into Jerusalem that Passover week were the multitude who "were amazed; and as they followed they were afraid" (Mark 10:32). It would become for Jesus his final journey to Jerusalem. The crowd was amazed that a man wanted by the government of Israel would dare to make the trip into the capitol at all. They feared not only for him but for themselves.

By the time they arrived, many had become convinced he was, indeed, Messiah. Prior to entering Jericho, Jesus had not allowed anyone to call him Son of God, not even Legion whom he had cast out earlier in his ministry. In an effort to keep from drawing attention to himself before his ministry was completed, he had repeatedly warned

---

91. Bloch, *Biblical*, p. 214.
92. *b. Sanh.* 12b.; Epstein (1987 ed.).

The Crime: Apostasy from the Law

individuals he had healed not to "tell anyone". But in Jericho, blind Bar-Timaeus had called him Son of David, the first open proclamation to the Jews that he was their long-awaited Messiah, and Jesus did not rebuke him. He had accepted his fate; his ministry was completed. It was this multitude who surrounded him and prevented the Sanhedrin from seizing Jesus in Jerusalem during the first days of Passover. Because Jesus had so evidentially proven himself to the people, the Sanhedrin was afraid to arrest him. They greatly feared an uprising of the population! Even after the second cleansing of the Temple precincts, they could do no more than await an opportunity to seize him.

> And the chief priests [Annas and Caiaphas] and scribes [the second chamber of the Sanhedrin tribunal] sought how they might kill him; for they feared the people" (Luke 22:2).

Some of the rulers were afraid to follow the prescribed law (that he should be executed during the festival) for fear of the riot his execution might incite, but the opposing political priesthood would have its own way.

> After two days was the feast of the passover, and of unleavened bread: and the chief priests and the scribes sought how thy might take him by craft, and put him to death. But they said, Not on the feast day, *lest there be an uproar of the people*" (Mark: 14:1-2).

However, the legal requirement for the execution of one who is found to be "leading the nation astray" is that he be put to death at once during *the* festival (Passover) in order to deter others.

> They put him to death not in the court in his own town or in the court which is in Yabneh, but they bring him up to the high court in Jerusalem. And they keep him until *the festival*, and they put him to death on *the festival*, as it is said, And all the people shall hear and fear and no more do presumptuously (Dt. 17:13).[93]

"The festival" in relation to such a crime is always Passover, since it is that festival which commemorates YHWH's redemption of Israel from Egypt and from *idolatry*. Such is the evidence found in both the Tosefta (quoted below) and in the Temple Scroll.

> A stubborn and rebellious son, a defiant elder, a beguiler to idolatry, one who leads a town astray, a false prophet, and perjurers, are not killed at once but brought up to the great court at Jerusalem and kept in prison till a feast and *killed at a feast*, for it is written: *And all the people shall hear and fear, and do no more presumptuously* ... Then why should they postpone such a one's death? Therefore they kill him at once, and write and send everywhere, saying "The trial of N. has been completed in such and such a court, and N. and N. are his witnesses; such and such has been done to him".[94]

But we have evidence that this law had been followed centuries before the trial of Jesus. The Essenes were well-acquainted with it, and its Mishnaic counterpart (end of the second century) had changed little during the time of Jesus. Within the Temple Scroll (11QT) discovered at the cave complex at Qumran we read the following:

---

93. *m. Sanh.* 11:4a–c.
94. Danby, *Tractate Sanhedrin*, p. 87; *Tosef.* XI, 6.

> If a prophet or a dreamer appears among you and presents you with a sign or a portent, even if the sign or the portent comes true, when he says, 'Let us go and worship other gods whom you have not known!', do not listen to the words of that prophet or that dreamer, for I test you to discover whether you love YHWH, the God of your fathers, with all your heart and soul . . . That prophet or dreamer shall be put to death for he has preached rebellion against YHWH, your God, who brought you out of the land of Egypt and redeemed you from the house of bondage, *to lead you astray from the path that I have commanded you to follow. You shall rid yourself of this evil* . . . If among you, in one of your towns that I give you, there is found a man or a woman who does that which is wrong in my eyes by *transgressing my covenant*, and goes and worships other gods, and bows down before them, or before the sun or the moon, or all the host of heaven, *if you are told about it, and you hear about this matter, you shall search and investigate it carefully. If the matter is proven true that such an abomination has been done in Israel, you shall lead out that man or that woman and stone him (to death) with stones* . . . Do not stray from the law which they proclaim to you to the right or to the left. The man who does not listen but *acts arrogantly without obeying the priest who is posted there to minister before me, or to the judge, that man shall die*. You shall rid Israel of evil. All the people shall hear of it and shall be awe-stricken, and none shall ever again be arrogant in Israel . . . If a man slanders his people and delivers his people to a foreign nation and does evil to his people, *you shall hang him on a tree and he shall die* . . . *For he who is hanged on the tree is accursed of God and men.*[95]

In the passage from the Tosefta, the sages might well have been referring to Jesus, himself, since there is a tradition that the Sanhedrin had suspected him of all of the crimes listed there. The Sanhedrin and their allies, the Herodians had been seeking to "destroy him" for a number of months, they had investigated the rumors, and they ultimately issued an arrest warrant some forty days prior to the festival. The Sanhedrin Tractate of the Talmud records this information:

> And a herald precedes him etc. This implies, only immediately before [the execution], but [also, apparently,] previous thereto [that is, anytime previous thereto, because] [*In contradiction to this*] *it was taught: On the eve of the Passover Yeshu was hanged. For forty days before the execution took place, a herald went forth and cried, 'He is going forth to be stoned because he has practiced sorcery and enticed Israel to apostacy. Any one who can say anything in his favour, let him come forward and plead on his behalf.*' But since nothing was brought forward in his favour *he was hanged on the eve of Passover!* [hanging was part of the sentence of stoning]—'Ulla retorted: Do you suppose that he was one for whom a defence could be made? Was he not a *Mesith* [enticer], concerning whom Scripture says, *Neither shalt thou spare, neither shalt thou conceal him? With Yeshu however it was different, for he was connected with the government [or royalty, i.e., influential][malkhut; in other words, the kingdom, royalty].*[96]

Please note that the punishment for these crimes was stoning *and* hanging the criminal *alive* on a tree. These phenomena will be quite thoroughly discussed in "The

---

95. Vermes, *Dead Sea Scrolls*, pp. 149–156.
96. *b. Sanh.* 43a.

The Crime: Apostasy from the Law

Execution". For over forty days they had summoned witnesses to come forward in behalf of Jesus. Of course, the Sanhedrin was certain there would be none forthcoming, because to do so would necessarily implicate the individual as a conspirator in Jesus' crime. Not one witness was willing to risk his own life for Jesus, not even his closest disciples. It should be noted, however, that the tribunal had already taken counsel to ensnare him at the time they learned Jesus had raised Lazarus (Eleazar) from the dead.

> *Then from that day forth* [that is, the day they learned Jesus raised Lazarus] *they took counsel together for to put him to death.* Jesus, therefore, walked no more openly among the Jews, but went thence to a country near the wilderness, into a city called Ephraim; and there continued with his disciples (John 11:53-54).

The word "counsel" is *sunbouleuo*, "to determine" or "deliberate". The word derives from two roots: *sun*, "complete unity" and *bouleou*, "resolve". In other words, a meeting of the Sanhedrin took place in which they determined his guilt. Jesus' presence would not actually be required since his own testimony would be invalid in any case. The city of Ephraim where Jesus and his disciples hid was located in the territory of Benjamin. It is believed to be the Old Testament Ephron and Ophrah and is located north of Jerusalem, near the spot where Abraham bought with silver a field from the Hitite Ephron. Few travelers would have strayed into this territory (and certainly not the rulers) for fear of brigands and marauding bands of heathens. The rulers, in fact, had been searching for informers during the Passover festival to relate to them his whereabouts. No attempt had ever been made to capture him outside the Jerusalem area. The city, during the festival, would have been overrun with pilgrims. Josephus gives us an early estimate of nearly three million. It would not be easy to isolate him from the crowd following him.

> Now both the chief priests and the Pharisees had given a commandment, that, if any man knew where he were, he should shew it, that they might take him" (John 11:57).

At this point, Jesus was an apostate of the law, an outlaw in hiding. To be more exact, he might be said to have been "standing against the scribal interpretations of the law"; that is, he renounced the hypocritical government and became a defector from the scribal interpretations. After all, he had said he did not come to bring peace, but division (Matt. 10:34). But at long last, the rulers' guile and patience paid off. One of Jesus' own disciples would betray his whereabouts during the early morning hours (about 3:00 A.M.) in the sleepy little garden orchard of Gethsemane, where no crowd would be near to hinder them. The multitude would be in their homes or in the Temple precincts "watching" for redemption on the "Night of the Vigils of YHWH." Little did they know their redemption had already arrived! It is entirely logical that the Sanhedrin would use this opportunity to "destroy" him, since it was during this same time period that the "Destroyer" slew the idolaters in Egypt.

The major crime for which Jesus was brought to trial, that of "leading the nation astray", is specifically mentioned in the New Covenant numerous times. We might note just one example here. For other examples, see Appendix B.

> And there was much murmuring among the people concerning him: for some said, He is a good man: others said, Nay; but he deceiveth the people [*leading the people astray*] (John 7:12).

It is, in fact, this same charge that was recounted to Pilate during the Roman pseudo-trial:

> We found this fellow perverting the nation (Luke 23:2).
>
> He stirreth up the people, throughout all Jewry [Judaea], beginning from Galilee to this place (Luke 23:5).
>
> Ye have brought this man unto me, as *one that perverteth the people* (Luke 23:14).

The most specific evidence in the gospels is noticeable in detail to anyone having studied the law of the Sanhedrin. Jesus was accused by his own hometown of teaching extraneous doctrine. It is for this reason that the townsfolk led him to the cliff.

> And all they in the synagogue, when they heard these things, were filled with wrath. And rose up, and thrust him out of the city, and led him unto the brow of the hill whereon their city was built, that they might cast him down headlong. (Luke 4:28–29).

Now, the purpose of leading him to the hill was to "throw him down headlong". These are the words describing the process of the *Pharisaic* method of stoning a victim who is thought to be "leading a whole town astray" (*b. Sanh.* 45a) "And whence do we know that both stoning and hurling down (were employed)? From the verse, He shall surely be stoned or thrown down"]. The Nazareth example is evidence of the penalty exacted by the sect of Pharisaic scribes residing at that priestly station (*ma-amadot*).

> The place of stoning was twice the height of a man. One of the witnesses pushes him over from the hips, [so hard] that he turned upward [in his fall]. He turns him over on his hips again [to see whether he had died]. [If] he had died thereby, that sufficed. If not, the second [witness] takes a stone and puts it on his heart. If he died thereby, it sufficed. And if not, stoning him is [the duty] of all Israelites, as it is said, *The hand of the witnesses shall be first upon him to put him to death, and afterward the hand of all the people* (Dt. 17:7).[97]

The incident that occurred in Nazareth is what is termed by the Tosefta as "irregular justice". "Zealous people may attack them".[98]

> To these are added: they who break the yoke and violate the covenant, or misinterpret the [Pharisaic] Law.[99]

The teachings Jesus expounded in that synagogue in Nazareth would have offended the townspeople as a misinterpretation of the law and a violation of the covenant. Their fear and anger were not unfounded in light of the consequences. The penalty for allowing

---

97. *m. Sanh.* 6:4a–g.
98. Danby, *Sanhedrin Tractate*, p. 119; *M. Sanh.* IX 6.
99. Danby, p. 120; *Tosef. Sanh.* XII 9.

The Crime: Apostasy from the Law

one to beguile and lead astray a town through "misinterpretation" or breaking away from the yoke of scribal interpretations was the utter destruction of the entire town.

> The members of a beguiled city,—as it is written: *There shall go forth from thy midst men, sons of Belial, and they shall beguile the inhabitants of their town* . . . Thou shalt smite the people of that city with the sword; but an ass or camel caravan passing through from place to place—such are to be set free. *Utterly destroy it, and all that is in it, and its beasts, with the sword . . . all the spoil thereof thou shalt gather into the midst of the marketplace . . . and thou shalt burn the whole city and all its spoil with fire . . . and it shall be a perpetual heap and shall never again be built upon . . .*[100]

The citizens, however, might be spared if they took it upon themselves (as "zealous people") to stone the individual believed to be breaking the law. The townspeople of Nazareth had no desire to be legally indicted as a "town led astray" by a *mesith*. They thought to rid themselves of any such trouble immediately. It is for such a "dangerous" person that spies were sent for the purposes of entrapment. For the careful reader, it is possible to see that this was done on any number of occasions with Jesus (for exact references, see Appendix A). It is certainly apparent that Jesus was outlawed and in hiding. The disciples, themselves, hid in the wilderness with him. Each gospel makes mention of this fact: Matt. 20;17–19; Mark 10:32–34; Luke 18:31–34; and John 11:4–8. From the Feast of Dedication (24/25 Kislev) onward (for three and a half months) Jesus was known to be in hiding. We might, at this point, wonder why Jesus went to the Feast of Dedication. As a Jew, he was only required to present himself for the three annual feasts of Pesach, Weeks, and Tabernacles. Yet the gospels specifically state Jesus also attended the Feast of Dedication, a recently reinstituted festival resurrected by the Maccabeans the century before. My suggestion is that Jesus understood the significance of the feast far greater than the other Jews attending. For him it was a time of "marriage" and for dedication of himself to YHWH. Furthermore, it was a "sign" for the coming "new creation" of the Kingdom of God. Anciently, it had been a time for the ordination of the priesthood and a time for symbolically "purifying" the house of God and for being anointed by the Sevenfold Holy Spirit. The Maccabeans had celebrated this feast, not as the secular Feast of Dedication that it later became but, as the sacred Feast of Tabernacles, which they had missed while hiding in the wilderness during the Revolt. For most religious leaders, however, it was a time of rededication.

> The story of the dedication of the Sanctuary is one of both triumph and tragedy. The Midrash enhances both. It depicts the day of the dedication as being as great as that of creation itself. It is as if the Sanctuary and its successor the Temple represent the universe in miniature and serve as the basis for the world's existence. Once again the Song of Songs is utilized to create a wedding picture. *This time the wedding takes place at the ceremony of dedication where once again God is the groom and Israel the bride.*[101]

Here we find the dedication of the future priesthood symbolically enacted by Jesus. It must be emphasized: Jesus is *not* the Bridegroom of the New Covenant. In the parable

---

100. *m. Sanh.* 10:4a–0; 5; 6a–b.
101. Hammer, *Classic Midrash*, pp. 180–181.

of the ten virgins, we find lacking the word "bride" (again, a convenient device for the church). Eight of the original manuscripts of the gospel add "and the bride" *after Matthew 25:1*. The original "virgin mother" of the Christian religion was, in fact, not Mary but *the body of assembly (or church), itself* (the Mother Jerusalem as born from above)! As the Virgin, it was often described as the Bride. The emphasis placed on oil in the Parable of the Ten Virgins cannot be missed. It is also associated with the Feast of Dedication (or Lights) in which that commodity plays no small part. Without oil, no lamps (vessels) can be lighted in order to greet the Bridegroom and Bride. The analogies are quite apparent. With these facts now in place, it becomes possible to trace the last three and a half months of Jesus' life.

The Gospel of John gives us the detail we need and provides a starting point for our narrative. After the Feast of Dedication the rulers had sought to stone him (John 10:31) and were "seeking to take him" (John 10:39-40). Therefore, he and his disciples went into hiding at the edge of the wilderness in Ophrah. At some point shortly after his visit to Jerusalem and during this period of time Lazarus was said to be sick. The disciples were quite concerned that Jesus was considering a trip into Bethany of Judea (less than two miles from the seat of government) to visit Lazarus. They knew to do so was quite dangerous for them. They said to him, "Master [that is, Teacher], the Jews of late *sought to stone thee*; and goest thou thither again?" (John 11:8). They were utterly astounded that Jesus would again put himself into danger. But Jesus would not be deterred from his purpose. He knew the end was drawing near. Ironically, Doubting Thomas was the disciple who favored the journey when Jesus had determined to return to Bethany, so near Jerusalem. Thomas knew to go to Jerusalem was to die: "Then said Thomas, which is called Didymus, unto his fellow disciples, Let us also go, *that we may die with him*" (John 11:16). There is no doubt they knew Jesus was a fugitive from the law, and that their own allegiance to him and the fact that they were his followers would necessarily implicate them in his "crime". Apparently, while Jesus was in Bethany, the aristocratic mourners present that day informed the government in Jerusalem about Lazarus: "Then many of *the Jews [the rulers]* which came to Mary and had seen the things which Jesus did, believed on him. But *some of them went their ways to the Pharisees, and told them what things Jesus had done*" (John 11:45-46). The reason for their final decision was because this incident, to the Jews, was nothing short of necromancy, and for them, the proverbial last straw. While many of the rulers that day "believed on him", there were some, at least, who believed he had raised Lazarus from the dead through *Baal Ob*, that he was an idolatrous "conjurer of the dead". This high council would have occurred somewhere near forty days prior to Passover. "Then from that day forth [the day of the high council], they took counsel together for to put him to death" (John 11:53). As indicated earlier, the Greek *sunbouleuo* indicates that some action was determined. "Determined" as defined by Webster means "to decide by judicial sentence" and/or "to fix the form, position, or character of beforehand." In order to bring Jesus to trial, it was first necessary to deliberate among themselves, form a consensus of guilt, and formally issue a warrant of arrest. This is in accord with what we know about the issuance of arrest and death warrants during that time. Paul, too, had sought such arrest warrants from the Sanhedrin in Jerusalem against the followers of Jesus prior to his own conversion to messianic belief in Jesus.

> And Saul, yet breathing out threatenings and slaughter against the disciples of the Lord [Master] *went unto the high priest, and desired of him letters* to Damascus, to the synagogues; *that if he found any of this way [The Way], whether they were men or women, he might bring them bound unto Jerusalem* (Acts 9:1–2).

The author of the Gospel of John tells us that "Jesus, therefore, no longer was openly walking among the Jews (the rulers) but departed thence into the country near the desert, unto a city called Ephraim; and there abode with his disciples (John 11:54). This must certainly have been about forty days prior to Passover because he goes on to say that "the passover of the Jews was *at hand*, and many went up unto Jerusalem out of the country before the passover, that they might purify themselves". Since this pilgrimage normally began thirty days before Passover on 14-15 Adar we might determine that Lazarus was raised some forty days before the Passover. The gospel states that "Then sought they for Jesus, and spake among themselves, as they stood in the temple. What think ye, that he will not come to the feast?" (John 11:56). The arrest of Jesus must have been a topic of daily conversation among the rulers during the forty days prior to Passover. "Informers" were now called upon to advise the Sanhedrin of Jesus' whereabouts (if they knew where to find him) so that the authorities might seize him. It was, however, the multitude that learned of his whereabouts before the government of Israel did, and the government was afraid to arrest him in their presence for fear of a riot. The general Jewish population despised this aristocratic Babylonian-Alexandrian government almost as much as it did the Romans. The priests were plainly afraid that the people would "stone" them, and even considered waiting until Passover was completed before taking Jesus into custody. They deemed it more politically advantageous, however, to make a spectacle of Jesus at Passover because of the number of pilgrims streaming into Jerusalem, so the original plan proceeded. The population might then "hear and fear and do no more presumptiously". The execution of Jesus would be a strong deterrent for those aspiring to revolutionary causes (for example, the Zealots) to hold their peace. The great press of people, though, had surrounded Jesus during the early days of the festival. The Sanhedrin and the Herodians would bide their time until an opportunity arose for them to make their move. Such fortune came their way through one of Jesus' own disciples, one who would know his exact whereabouts on the Eve of Passover, none other than Judas Iscariot. The accusations against Jesus were many and varied, but the crime of blasphemy was not the "vain oath" or the utterance of the ineffable name. It was not the breaking of the Sabbath, claiming equality with God, nor the crime of the rebellious son; neither was it false prophesy or "desecration" of the Temple which formed the specific accusation. But each of these charges played a role in the final verdict. Jesus was, instead, sentenced for blasphemy as one leading the nation of Israel away from the large body of pseudo-pious Pharisaical scribal interpretations of the Oral Torah, and from the economic and political aspirations of the Sadducees. Furthermore, Jesus had interpreted the Torah in an innovative manner that conflicted with their own self-serving interpretations. This radical "new instruction" was not the kind of instruction with which they might convincingly argue. It became politically and socially expedient to them to bring him to trial and execution in order to secure their positions and status within the government of Israel. The following summary written by S. Srinivasa Aiyar contains several of Jesus' activities that were perceived as illegal and immoral by the rulers of Israel.

> It was charged that he was a preacher of turbulence and faction, that he flattered the poor and condemned the rich, that he denounced whole cities, that he gathered about him a rabble of harlots and drunkards under the pretense of reforming them; that he subverted the laws and institution of the Mosaic commonwealth, and in their place built up an unauthorized legislation of his own liking; that he had no regard for society, nor of religion, but commended the idolatrous Samaritan while he damned the holy priest and pious Levite. That he tore down the solemn sanctions of holy religion, did eat with publicans and sinners without washing his hands, disregarded all obligations of the Sabbath . . . These and many other charges were doubtless presented to the members of the Sanhedrin during the course of the trial.[102]

These charges are all true. The fact is they were combined into a single accusation, one that would seal his fate. Everything about Jesus was repugnant to the ruling class in Israel. For the wealthy Sadducean priesthood, he was a political dissident. For the Pharisaic scribes his teachings were thorns of contention and disrespect. For the aristocratic Elders he was the epitome of immoral living. The tribunal found little in him to commend. Even the Zealot movement, who had at first tried to "make him king" had abandoned the mild-mannered Jesus. He was not their militant leader. It was only the general Jewish population that clung to his words, and it was by those very words that he would be convicted.

Jesus was legally accused of "leading the nation astray", the gravest crime and the worst form of blasphemy with which Israel might charge an individual. He was deemed a *mesith*, a revolutionary, a sorcerer, and a false prophet; he would be tried in a Jewish court for Jewish crimes and it just might be possible that he would pay the ultimate Jewish penalty for his apostasy through Jewish execution.

---

102. Aiyar, *Legality*, p. 42.

2

The Night of Watching

IN ORDER TO FOLLOW the events of the arrest and accusation of Jesus it first becomes necessary to provide an exposition of the events occurring earlier in the evening of the 14th of Nisan. Without some knowledge of the "Night of Watching" and the "Last Supper", the cohesiveness of the gospel narratives is not readily apparent. Sometime during the afternoon of the 13th of Nisan (the first Day of Unleavened Bread) Jesus had given instructions to two of the disciples for preparation of the Passover meal (to occur later that evening after dark, the 14th of Nisan). The 13th of Nisan historically became the day set aside for *ushering in* the feast known as Unleavened Bread. During ancient days Unleavened Bread was a separate and distinct feast from Passover. It would have occurred during the days of Moses on the 13th of Nisan. At the time of Jesus, the two festivals had been merged into one day, the 14th. The problem presented by the contradiction of the Gospel of John and the synoptics is resolved quite simply.

The Jewish tradition of the search for leaven marked the Passover season. It was on 13 Nisan (after dark, in the evening, which was when the 13th began) that the "search" for leaven was to begin. This was the First Day of Unleavened Bread in ancient days. It was the day on which leaven was purged from the home and the day on which unleavened bread was prepared for the following evening (14 Nisan), the Passover. It was to precede the Fast of the Firstborn at midnight on 14 Nisan.

> The night preceding the 14th of Nisan [i.e., the night of the 13th of Nisan] was especially set apart for this inspection by candle-light or lamplight, not by moonlight, though it was not necessary to examine by candle-light places that were open to sunlight . . . As soon as night (on the 13th) had completely set in, the father of the household ("*ba'al ha-bayit*") lighted a plain wax taper, took a spoon and a brush, or three or four entire feathers, and, after having deposited a piece of bread in some noticeable place, as on a window-sill, to mark the beginning of the search, made the complete round of the house and gathered up all the leavened bread that was in it . . . *This "investigation" was transferred to the eve of the Sabbath when the 14th of Nisan coincided with Sabbath* . . . The Fast of the

First-Born, in commemoration of the escape of the Hebrew first-born in Egypt, occurs on the 14th of Nisan [that is, the early morning hours of 14 Nisan, from Midnight until about 3:00 a.m.].[1]

The lamb to be consumed at the "Last Supper" would have been slain about 3:00 p.m. on the 13th (the First Day of Unleavened Bread) at the time of the daily sacrifice. It was, at that time, called the "peace offering". Although it was sometimes *called* the "Passover", it was not the regular "Passover" lamb which would be slain the *next* day (the 14th). In order to understand the sequence of events, it is requisite the reader acquaint himself with the Hebrew soli-lunar calendar. The Hebrew day was established in the book of Genesis: it was reckoned as the creation day, i.e., "evening and morning". The Jewish day then begins at sunset (about 6:00 p.m. in the evening or dusk) and ends the following evening at the same time. This practice of intercalating the day (beginning at dusk) in the Hebrew calendar is to be substituted for the "solar day" of our present calendar, which begins the day at midnight. Much of the confusion in the study of biblical writings has occurred because of this important difference in the reckoning of time. Another quite interesting difference in the calendars is that, in the Jewish calendar, if an event carries forward past dusk into the next "day", even for a few minutes, those few minutes *are counted as an entire day*. This fact will become increasingly important in determining the "three days and nights" in the tomb. The "Night of the Vigils of YHWH" (called the Night of Watching), would not begin until midnight on the 14th of Nisan. It was at midnight on the 14th of Nisan that the doors to the Temple were opened to Passover pilgrims (similar to the customs of Shavuot or "Pentecost" and Tabernacles where we also find a "night of watching" and where the doors are again opened at midnight). The time sequence involved here is quite important, since it points us to the exact time of Jesus' arrest. It was during the afternoon of the 13th (shortly before 3:00 p.m. "when they killed the passover" (Mark 14:12) that Jesus had instructed his disciples to prepare the Passover.

The "Eve of Passover" on which Jesus was executed as referenced by the author of John was actually on the 14th of Nisan, a Friday. The day before Passover (in this case the 14th), even though it were fully daylight, is always referred to as the "Eve of Passover". The synoptics, however, written by "Galileans" who were strict in their biblical observance of Passover would, as is to be expected, have referred to the 14th (the day on which Jesus was executed) as Passover. The 13th of Nisan (Thursday until 6:00 p.m.) had marked the day of the "sacrifice" (3:00 p.m., Thursday) of the first "passover" lamb (or "peace offering"). When evening came (still Thursday to us, but an entirely "new day" in Hebrew time, the 14th), Jesus and the disciples would have gathered into the third-story guest room of one of his presumed followers for what is called by Christians the "Last Supper". No less than ten nor more than twenty individuals could be called an "association" or "company" (*haburah*); nor was it confined only to males. It is almost certain more than the twelve disciples were present. For example, Lazarus (Eleazar), whom Jesus was known to have raised from the dead, his sisters Mary and Martha, and perhaps even his own family (which seems likely) might have been present for the supper. There is evidence in the non-canonical Gospel of the Hebrews and in other early

---

1. "Passover", J.E., pp. 551–552.

Christian writings that his brother James had been a guest at that Passover meal. At the time of Jesus' resurrection, in fact, it is said that James had not tasted food nor drink since the "Last Supper". This reference to James having been present would seem to infer the twelve disciples were not the only celebrants of the Pesach meal.

> Cf. Gospel according to the Hebrews (in Jerome, *On Illustrious Men*, 2—Also the gospel called according to the Hebrews, recently translated by me into Greek and Latin, which Origen often uses, says, after the resurrection of the Savior: "Now the Lord [Master], when he had given the linen cloth to the servant of the priest, *went to James and appeared to him (for James had sworn that he would not eat bread from that hour in which he had drunk the Lord's [Master's] cup until he should see him risen from among them that sleep)*." And a little further on the Lord [Master] says, *"Bring a table and bread."* And immediately it is added, *"He took bread and blessed and broke and gave it to James the Just and said to him 'My brother, eat your bread, for the Son of man is risen from among them that sleep'"*.[2]

That Jesus appeared to James appears to be, also, recorded in Paul's writings.

> For I delivered unto you first of all that which I also received, how that Christ [Messiah] died for our sins according to the scriptures; And that he was buried, and that he rose again the third day, according to the scriptures: And that he was seen of Cephas, then of the twelve: After that, he was seen of above five hundred brethren at once; of whom the greater part remain unto this present, but some are fallen asleep. *After that, he was seen of James*, then of all the apostles. And last of all he was seen of me also, as of one born out of due time (1 Cor. 15:3–8).

The appearance of Jesus must have had a profound effect on James, who had not believed in Jesus' messiahship when he was in the height of his ministry. James, greatly revered as a "just" or "righteous" man, was highly esteemed by the Ebionites (or Nazaraeans). He was to preside over the Jerusalem Nazaraean community until his death in 62 CE at the hands of Ananus II, a son of the very high priest Annas, who had formed the accusation against Jesus.

Certain restrictions applied to individuals who were to participate in the Passover celebration. Each member of the "company" was required to eat at least a *ke-zayit* (the equivalent of an olive); the sexes were kept apart; an individual must have been circumcised to partake of the meal; and, most importantly, he must not have had contact with a corpse, thus becoming Levitically defiled. For this reason, the graves were whitened during the month preceding Passover. This is why Jesus mentions the whitening of the graves in the gospel narratives.

THE PASSOVER

As confusing as it is to understand the Passover Day as it existed during the first century, there is even more confusion when it comes to the *seder* meal. There were not one but *two seders* during the Passover celebration. The event of the "Last Supper" was, in fact, the first *seder* of the Passover Festival, at which the peace offering would have been eaten.

---

2. Throckmorton, *Gospel Parallels*, p. 190.

A Book of Evidence

Since the end of the earliest dispersion of the nation of Israel, the Jewish people had held the festival for two days (14/15 Nisan), holding two *seders* if Passover fell on a Sabbath. Two *chagigah* (sacrificial lambs) were thus offered, one as a peace offering and the other as the "real" Passover lamb. This was because the Jewish population still residing in Babylon depended upon the Palestinian Jews for intercalating the day of Passover. Since some distance separated the two groups, the Babylonian Jews feared they might miss the actual Passover date intercalated in Jerusalem. The first *seder* (the peace offering or biblical Passover lamb) would actually have been the more scriptural of the two.

To add to the confusion, there were also two "Passovers" held one month apart (Num. 9:2–14) (the second was called Lesser Passover), and these two events should not be confused with the two *seder* meals of the *first* Passover. *Seder* simply means "order" and refers to the formality of the two dinners held during the *first* Passover. This first *seder* would have begun about 6:00 p.m., continuing from "after dark" (on the 14th of Nisan) until about midnight when the last portion of the Hallel (which as a whole includes Psalms 113-118) was sung. The Great Hallel (Ps. 136) would have been sung at midnight. A great deal of emphasis was placed on this hour since it was at "midnight" that YHWH had "passed over" the children of Israel in Egypt. It was also believed that David had been accustomed to rise at midnight to praise YHWH. The Talmudists determined that it was at that hour that YHWH would have entered into the Garden of Eden to converse with the righteous. In commemoration of these events, the Temple doors would have been opened to accommodate the Passover pilgrims. Because the Great Hallel is sung at midnight we know the "Last Supper" can be identified with the "Eve of Passover" and not simply a last meal. We are told that after a "hymn" or "praise" was sung that Jesus and his disciples went across the Kidron brook to Gethsemane on the Mount of Olives (Mark 14:26). That specific hymn would have been the praise psalm called the Great Hallel (Ps. 136). The psalms were always a part of the *seder* ceremony.

> The first Passover [14 Nisan] *requires the recitation of the Hallel psalms* when it is eaten, but the second Passover [14 Iyar, one month later] does not require the recitation of the *Hallel* Psalms when it is eaten.[3]

It is this first *seder* that can be more correctly identified with the Exodus event and the one which Jesus surely would have observed. Suffice it to say that the representations of the meal as narrated by the gospel writers are greatly condensed. In order to understand just how condensed they actually are and to timely follow the later events of the evening, it would be well to present a summary of the meal, itself. The head of the company or the head of the table (in this case, Jesus), commenced the Pesach meal. Since four cups of wine are prescribed for the *seder*, it is necessary to distinguish that the *pouring* (only) of the first cup, along with a special blessing called the *Kiddush*, began the ceremony. The first part of the prayer is begun thus: "Blessed art thou, YHWH our Elohim, creator of the fruit of the vine." This first portion of the *Kiddush* is quite lengthy and is recited in response to the wine used in the *Seder* ceremony. The next portion then follows; it is the thanksgiving recited in response to the *bread* of the Seder. While the prayer is recited the participants remain standing. At the conclusion of the *Kiddush*, the

---

3. *m. Pes.* 9.3d.

company then reclines at the *Seder* table and the cup of wine (which had only previously been poured at the beginning of the ceremony) is now drunk. Since the thanksgiving precedes this cup of wine, it can be identified as the cup alluded to in Luke 22:17–18. This has been mistaken for the "cup of blessing" in Christianity's "communion". Luke is quite exact in his description of the "cup of thanksgiving".

> And he took the cup and gave thanks [therefore, it is the "cup of thanksgiving"], and said, Take this, and divide it among yourselves.

The cup is first poured; prayer is recited *afterward*. The preliminary dish, one of a select group of vegetables and salt water (called *karpas*), is then brought forward. The head of the company (Jesus) dips the sop into the salt water and passes the bowl to his left for the other members. It was during this portion of the ritual that Jesus passed the sop to Judas Iscariot.

> And he answered and said, He that dippeth his hand with me in the dish, the same shall betray me (Matt. 26:23).

While Judas partook of the "cup of thanksgiving", he did *not* partake of the "communion" cup offered later by Messiah. After the preliminary *karpas* (similar to our present appetizer), the dishes are removed from the table and each celebrant is required to wash his hands. It was at this point that Jesus made the first alteration in the *Seder* meal. Such alterations were entirely legal and allowable. Instead of the hand-washing ceremony, Jesus washes the disciples' feet.

> After that he poureth water into a bason, and began to wash the disciples' feet, and to wipe them with the towel wherewith he was girded (John 13:5).

The "linen cloth" is known as a *kittel*. It was the same as the type of white cloth worn by a high priest. Only the head of the company (in our case, Jesus) would be required to wear it; however, as we shall learn later in this chapter, another individual donned the garment this night as well. It was worn to remind the Israelites of their redemption from Egypt by YHWH.

> It is customary for the leader of the Seder to put on a white robe (*kittel*) in honor of the festive occasion. In Aramaic, the word *chor* ("free") is akin to *chavar* ("white").[4]

After the washing ceremony was complete, the traditional questions about the history of the Passover were asked by the youngest member present at the *Seder* meal, perhaps Lazarus (Eleazar), "a youth". The head of the company (again, Jesus) would then begin to narrate the entire history of the Exodus tradition, beginning with Abraham's father, Terah: "A Syrian, ready to perish was my father . . ." until the narration had reached the present. The Mishnah is quite explicit in describing this portion of the Passover.

---

4. Bloch, *Biblical*, p. 229.

> He begins [answering the questions] with disgrace and concludes with glory, and explains [the Scriptures from], *A wandering Aramean was my father* . . . (Dt. 26:5ff) until he completes the entire section.[5]

It is important to note that this narration *could last an hour or more*. While the *haggadah* became a rote ritual after 70 CE, at the time of Jesus its purpose was likely to bring to mind the family genealogies of various individuals. These genealogies had been of utmost importance after the Babylonian Captivity. With the final dispersal of Israel, many Jews would forget their family ancestry. History confirms that the Romans burned the genealogical scrolls stored within the Temple during their siege of Jerusalem. The gospel writers do not attempt to follow the narration because this portion of the *Seder* ceremony would be generally well known and understood by the Hebrew audience for whom they were writing.

At the end of the narration, the dishes were again replaced on the table and the reasons for including the three required items of Passover (the lamb, or *Pesach*, the bitter herbs, and the unleavened bread) were singularly explained. Afterward, the *second cup* was poured and the first portion (Pss. 113-114) of the Hallel was sung. The second cup was then drunk, and hands were again washed while reciting a brief benediction. Only now was the meal or supper portion commenced. One of the two loaves of unleavened bread was now broken. In this particular part of the supper the thanksgiving *did not precede* the breaking of the bread but *followed* it. The bread was broken into small pieces called the "bread of poverty" or "affliction". The reason for this was to show that the poor did not have whole cakes but only broken pieces when they left Egypt. We know this was *not* the bread symbolic of the "body" of Jesus. In any event, he would not have offered them bread of affliction as a promise. No Hebrew would have celebrated the Passover by giving "thanks" to YHWH for the poverty or affliction of their ancestors. The bread Jesus used to symbolize his body was broken only *after* thanksgiving. Paul reaffirms this.

> For I have received of the Lord [Master] that which also I delivered unto you, That the Lord [Master] Jesus the same night in which he was betrayed took bread: And when he had given thanks, he brake it . . . (1 Cor. 11:23–24).

Since Jesus gave thanks *preceding* the breaking of the loaf that became symbolic of his body, it requires that communion loaf is broken later during the supper. Pieces of the "bread of poverty", however, were dipped into the bitter herbs and the bowl *again* passed to the left. The third cup was poured at the same time the second loaf was broken. This is the "cup of blessing" and became what Jesus called the cup of the "new covenant" (1 Cor. 11:25). "New" is the Greek *kainos* and does not mean new at all but "refreshed". This particular cup is of such importance that it is distinguished from all others in the Talmud as possessing ten peculiarities (*b. Ber.* 51.1). Jesus, again, uses the specifically Jewish significance of this cup to allude to the covenant.

> *The cup of blessing* which we bless, is it not the communion of the blood of Christ [Messiah]? (1 Cor. 10:16)

---

5. *m. Pes.* 10:4j.

After the meal, Jesus introduced and instituted the second alteration to the present *Seder* meal: the "afikoman" or *third loaf*, an after-dish. It was this dessert item which became the bread symbolic of his body. It was prior to this that he, "And when he had given thanks, he brake it, and said, this is my body which is broken for you: this do in remembrance of me (1 Cor. 11:24). Appropriately, *Afikoman* is the Greek word meaning "the coming one" or "he comes". It represents the appearance of YHWH and his vice-regent, the Messiah. By breaking this loaf Jesus was announcing his identity to the disciples, showing them that only by the breaking of his body (i.e., his death) could the Kingdom of YHWH be established. Today this loaf is broken at the beginning of the Passover *Seder*. The two halves of the loaf are symbolic of his two advents: the half to be consumed was representative of his sufferings; the last half, not eaten but hidden for a later time, was representative of the victory of his return and of the resurrection of the dead. Paul, again, properly placed the breaking of this loaf in the correct order, *after* the cup of blessing had been consumed (note the second part of verse 16): "The bread which we break, is it not the communion of the body of Christ [Messiah]?"(1 Cor. 10:16). The order in which these items were offered was to become quite important in taking communion. The ceremony, now altered to partaking of the "body" first, *is exactly opposite of what was originally intended*! Unless one first partakes of the "blood", his sufferings, by following him in the regeneration (refinement and purification), he can have no part or share in the "body". In fact, the apostle Paul warned that it is this order that is required. One must first partake of the sufferings of Jesus if he is to enter into the body of the Messiah. Not to do so is to call down judgment upon oneself.

> Wherefore whosoever shall eat this bread, and drink this cup of the Lord [Master], and drink this cup of the Lord [Master], unworthily, shall be guilty of the body and blood of the Lord [Master]. But let a man examine himself, and so let him eat of that bread, and drink of that cup. For he that eateth and drinketh unworthily, eateth and drinketh damnation to himself, not discerning the Lord's [Master's] body (1 Cor. 11:27–29).

The man who would first eat of the body without partaking of Messiah's sufferings is like the false shepherd who enters the sheepfold through "another gate".

> Verily verily I say unto you, He that entereth not by the door [Messiah's sufferings] into the sheepfold [the congregation], but climbeth up some other way, the same is a thief and a robber (John 10:1).

The New Covenant informs us that there is only one gate that leads to redemption. Spiritually that gate is through the blood of Jesus (the true *Ohel Moed;* Heb. 8:2). Prior to any entrance into the Kingdom, one is required to follow him, bearing his own sufferings ("cross", or "burden"; "cross" was not a Hebrew term), refinements, and purifications through the pattern he left. This is called the process of "regeneration". The word regeneration in the Greek (*paliggenesia*) derives from a root meaning "oscillating". To oscillate is to go from one extreme to the other; i.e., in Jewish terms, to go to the right or left, not following the middle, balanced way. In other words, it is the process of honing and refinement (spoken of in Dan. 12:10), trying to stay in the narrow way, learning truth by wavering to the right or left on occasion. Through this "honing" process, one is to finally present himself blameless. This refinement process is required of each individual. One must refine himself even as Jesus did. He opened the *way* of salvation; i.e., he *delivered* or *freed* from bondage those willing to do so in order that when he reappears one might have "salvation". This is the pattern Jesus gave to follow.

> For even hereunto were ye called: because Christ [Messiah] also suffered for us, *leaving us an example* [a pattern] *that ye should follow in his steps* (1 Pet. 2:21).

It is a difficult journey to follow the one narrow way. Both Torah and Talmud warn the individual not to go to the right or to the left, yet we as humans, often misstep. When one does, he must always strive to get back in the "way", the strait and narrow path. This process of regeneration or refinement leads to the spiritual blamelessness Jesus referred to when he said "Become ye perfect [blameless], even as your Father in Heaven is perfect." It is similar to the honing process used in the refinement of silver and gold. Note that Jesus did not say "my Father" in this instance; he said "your Father". All who follow him are to become sons of YHWH as well (Gal. 3:26; Rom. 8:14–17).

The conversation occurring during the *Seder* meal (and not on the way to Gethsemane) is recounted by the author of John in chapters 13:33 – 17:26. The service concludes then with a fourth cup of wine over which the second portion of the Hallel was sung. This second portion included Psalms 115–118. Two brief prayers then followed. The word for these praise psalms (known as the Hallel-yah, "Praise ye Yah") is the derivative for the word Hallelujah. Mark and Matthew tell us "having sung praise (Ps. 136, the "Great Hallel") they went forth unto the Mount of Olives" (Matt. 26:30; Mark 14:26). Luke and John designate a specific "place" on the Mount of Olives as one in which Jesus and his disciples often met. This place will be explored more thoroughly in the next section. The hour is easily assigned to midnight in that the praise psalm (136, the "Great Hallel") is always sung at midnight on 14 Nisan. The doors to the Temple were customarily thrown open for worshippers at that time, after which the Passover offering could no longer be eaten (*m., Pes* 10.9).

> But in the Paschal Night, when the great Temple-gates were opened at midnight to begin early preparations for the offering of the *Chagigah* [the second lamb], or festive sacrifice, which was not voluntary but of due, and the remainder of which was afterwards eaten at a festive meal [the second and considered by the priesthood the most important seder on 15 Nisan], such preparations would be quite natural.[6]

This follows the pattern of the original Exodus tradition where the Destroyer was expected to "pass over" the children of Israel at midnight (Exod. 12:29).

IN THE GARDEN

So it was that "When Jesus had spoken these words, he went forth with his disciples over the brook Cedron [Kidron], where there was a garden (*kepos*)" (John 18:1). That the Garden of Gethsemane was more than a garden orchard is clear. It would seem that this place is where Jesus and his disciples abode while they were in Jerusalem for the

---

6. Edersheim, *Life and Times*, v. 2, p. 508.

Passover. In that event it would be necessary for the spot to provide some shelter from the cold weather of the Passover season. It was, indeed, cold that night because we note that later Peter sat warming his hands by a fire in the "courtyard" of the high priest. There is every indication that within this garden (Latin *campus*) was a cave. The Greek word *kepos* translated here as "garden" is derived from *chao* a "cavern" or "abyss", a "hollow rock". Joan E. Taylor, in a recent article, has successfully researched this probability.[7] She is not the first to suspect that Jesus was arrested in the cave.

> It was not so much a structure as a *natural cave*, well protected against the weather, which even in autumn retained the high temperatures best suited to the squeezing of olives.[8]

So it was into this cave that Jesus and his disciples retired on the "Night of Watching."

THE NIGHT OF THE VIGILS OF YHWH

The ensuing events of 14 Nisan are patterned by the tradition of the original Exodus of the Jews from Egypt. The night is referred to as the "Night of the Vigils of YHWH" and commemorates the "passing over" and "deliverance" (or "redemption") of the children of Israel. It derives its common name from Scripture.

> It is a night to be much observed unto the LORD [YHWH] for bringing them out from the land of Egypt: *this is that night of the LORD [YHWH] to be observed of all the children of Israel in their generations* (Exod. 12:42).

The deliverance theme is alluded to in the book of Esther (3:12–13) when the scribes of the king (on behalf of Haman) gathered on the 13th of Nisan (First Day of Unleavened Bread) to produce an edict to destroy the Jewish people. The custom of prohibiting the partaking of the Passover offering after midnight is a tradition now called the "Fast of the Firstborn." Originally, it occurred the day preceding "Passover" (i.e., 13 Nisan) to commemorate thanksgiving for being spared. It *later* came to denote the fear and reverence observed during the three-hour period beginning at midnight in which YHWH *preserved* the firstborn of Israel. Jesus, as Firstborn, would have observed the vigil.

> This custom, of biblical origin, is based on the account presented in Exodus 12:21–28, in which all Egyptian firstborn were slain and the firstborn of Israel were spared. The word "Passover" (Pesach in Hebrew) is from the verb *pasach*, meaning "to spare, to pass over." To commemorate and express gratitude for the sparing of the firstborn of Israel, *the day preceding passover became a fast day* of the firstborn male in each family.[9]

The Passover Festival was originally linked to the rites of circumcision, or *brit*, and even in present times it is customary to conduct a *Wachnacht* (the German word for "night of watching") the night before circumcision is performed.

---

7. Taylor, "Garden", BAR, v. 21, n. 4, pp. 26–35.
8. Craveri, *The Life*, p. 391.
9. Kolatch, *The Jewish Book of Why*, p. 186.

> The eve of circumcision itself was disguised under the term "shabua' ha-ben" (week of the son: Sanh. 32b, and Rashi *ad loc*).[10]

It is mentioned in the Talmud (*b. B. K.* 80a) as Yeshua Haben ("the salvation of the son").

> Rashi identified this celebration with Pidyon Haben (the redemption of the firstborn) . . .[11]

This, too, is logical in our pattern since Jesus was "circumcised" by death to the flesh on the Eve of Passover (Friday). The Hebrew word for circumcision meaning "to cut off flesh" is associated with the covenant between YHWH and Abraham; i.e., the *brit* (or *berith*), which also means "to cut pieces of flesh as a compact".

> He who takes his leave of the foreskin is as if he *took leave of the grave* [and must be sprinkled on the third and seventh day after circumcision as if he had suffered corpse uncleanness].[12]

Circumcision was regarded as death to the "flesh" of a man, thereby separating him from the "world" and giving him a fresh spiritual life. It is also connected with sacrifice because of the *akedah* (the binding and sacrifice of Isaac). The "circumcision" of Jesus, that is, his death (in which his flesh was "cut off") symbolically "safeguarded" *his entire body* of followers, the "assembly" of the firstborn, by "cutting" what Christians now call a "New" Covenant, the *brit*. Actually, the word "new" (as mentioned earlier) does not mean "new" at all. The Greek *kainos* means, instead, "to freshen" or "renew". Jesus was not making a "new" covenant but was freshening and renewing the original one. As he himself admitted, he did not come to abolish the Torah, but to completely explain it. The "head" of the fleshly body was cut off by death, just as the flesh of the male genital organ is cut away. It is on the occasion of circumcision that Hebrew children receive their new spiritual *names*.

> By cutting off the foreskin and ritually offering it to God, the Jew symbolically *safeguards the whole body by sacrificing a part of it*. The baby thus marks his transition from a purely natural state into the social community. *Only at the circumcision does he formally receive his Hebrew name.*[13]

For this reason Jesus not only received *his* new name but promised a new name to those "separated" from Mystery Babylon in the book of Revelation (2:17). Within Jesus' circumcision of death we then find the [natural] human suffering servant Jesus receiving his new name: Emmanuel [his social and political position in the Kingdom society], prince (or literally, high priest) of Israel, the triumphant Messiah who will "head the truncated body" of the spiritual and physical Kingdom of YHWH. In Luke the messenger rightly says: "And, behold, thou shalt conceive in thy womb, and bring forth a [natural] son, and shalt call his name Jesus" (1:31). In Luke Jesus is a man like any other and receives his *natural* name at birth. But he is destined as the Messiah of Israel to

---

10. "Wachnacht", J.E., p. 454.
11. Bloch, *Biblical*, p. 3.
12. *m. Pes.* 8:8f.
13. Frankel and Teutsch, *Encyclopedia*, p. 26.

receive a new name at his death by circumcision, one that reflects his social status as Prince [High Priest or *nasi*] in YHWH's Kingdom. In Matthew he receives his *new spiritual name*: "Behold, a virgin [Israel] shall be with child [Messiah], and shall bring forth a [natural] son [Jesus], and *they* [Israel] shall call his [spiritual] name Emmanuel; which being interpreted [translated], God [YHWH] with us" (Matt. 1:23; Isa. 7:14); that is, YHWH with us through the agency of his King-Priest Messiah. Mary gives birth to the human son, Jesus, and Israel gives birth to the spiritual Messiah, who ruling by the Holy Spirit of the Father dwelling within him [YHWH with us] is to be the representative Emmanuel, Prince (High-Priest, *nasi*) of the peaceful kingdom of YHWH. The process of receiving a new name through the circumcision of death institutes the "Kingdom of YHWH". In other words, during the Night of Watching, "the first-born of the flock (and even of men) was offered that the lives of those born later might be safe".

> Hence the ceremony came naturally to be associated with the intention of "saving," and then with the fact of having "spared," . . . the Hebrews' first-born had been "spared" in Egypt, God "passing over" their houses. The sprinkling of the blood points in the same direction. This was a feature accompanying every propitiatory slaughtering (see Samuel Ives Curtis, "Ursemitische Religion," p. 259, Leipsic, 1903). It is suggested that when later the tendency became dominant to give old festivals historical associations — a tendency clearly traceable in the evolution of the Biblical holy days—*this very primitive practice was explained by a reference to the occurrence in Egypt during the "night of watching"—another expression which plainly refers to the night preceding the day of the flock's departure, and which, as such, as marked by a proper ritual.* It has been urged that the term "night of watching" points to a custom similar to that which prevails in Germany, where the night before Easter is set apart for seeing the sun "jump" or "dance," as it is called; *it is more likely, however, that the phrase has reference to the moon's phases.*[14]

The concept is fully Hebraic. Pesach, during ancient days, was, in fact, the festival of the circumcision for all that had attained the proper age during the previous year. In the book of Revelation (12:1-6) we read that the Woman [the "old creation" Israel] gave birth to Messiah [Jesus] and he was "snatched up" [or resurrected] to YHWH, while the Woman [the "new creation" Israel] was dispersed into the "wilderness"; that is, into the world. It is important to remember that the "passing over" of those firstborn Israelites in Egypt was the birth of the nation. A new nation (consisting of Jews and Gentiles, both the natural and wild olive trees) would be born on the Passion Passover.

The Fast of the Firstborn (*Taanit Bechorim*) did not become formalized in Judaism until about the eighth century, but it was a tradition to which some Jews informally adhered from the time of the Exodus forward. The practice of the "head" of the company wearing a *kittel* probably derived from the fact that the firstborn Egyptians who had been killed during that plague served as the priests of their families. The Fast, therefore, became a fast of gratitude since firstborn Jews, who deserved the same fate as their Egyptian counterparts, acted in the same capacity. The "company" thus became participants in the fast, the "assembly" or "congregation" of YHWH.

---

14. "Passover", J.E., 554.

Individuals who participated in the *brit* were known to gather into a "circle of protection" to ward off the Destroyer by their prayers and vigils. The practice has now become superstition, substituting "Evil One" for Destroyer, but the original concept is derived from the first Pesach narrated in the book of Exodus where the Destroyer was allowed by YHWH to enter in (Exod. 11:5). This, too, is paralleled in the death of Jesus. It was YHWH who "purposed to bruise him" (Isa. 53:10). The Israelites had been told to eat the Passover in haste with sandals on their feet, staff in hand, because this was the night YHWH executed judgment on the *firstborn* of both man and animal. It was an austere appointment, because YHWH, Himself was to pass over *at midnight* for judgment. The theme for Passover thus evolved into a time of waiting and watching in a "circle of protection" of the firstborn. Jesus was the "firstborn" of "many sons" (Rom. 8:29). This "circle of protection" during the time of the Exodus included those members of the Passover ceremony, huddled fearfully within their homes, praying and watching, lest the Destroyer enter and slay the firstborn. The firstborn was to be the priest or religious leader of the family. This is also true of the Egyptians. The event occurred on the evening of the 14th of Nisan (Eve of Passover beginning about midnight, but still Thursday night). Jesus, too, on the night of the 14th *at midnight* began to watch and pray for he, as the "firstborn" of the Father would be delivered up (by YHWH, Himself) to become the "firstborn of the dead" (Col. 1:18). His "circle of protection" consisted of his disciples and, more specifically, Peter, James, and John. He had directed them to "watch" with him: "Tarry ye here and *watch* with me" (Matt. 26:38). It was at this time Jesus asked that the "cup" of YHWH's wrath be removed from him. It must be mentioned here that the "agony" in the garden where Jesus "sweated blood" is a later interpolation into the text. It is well known among scholars that Marcion, Clement, and Origin added verses 43–44 into the text: "And there appeared to him an angel from heaven strengthening him. And being in an agony he prayed more earnestly; and his sweat became like great drops of blood falling down upon the ground".[15] Similar descriptions have been found describing the suffering of pagan gods worshipped by the nations surrounding Israel. The true text explains that after one hour (about 1:00 a.m.), Jesus returned to find the disciples asleep.

> Could ye not *watch* with me *one hour* to watch with me? *Watch and pray, that ye enter not into temptation* (Matt. 26:41).

After that "one hour" he again returned to his place of prayer, repeating the same prayer.

> He went away again *the second time*, and prayed (Matt. 26:42).

When he returned from the second hour of praying (about 2:00 a.m.), he once again found them sleeping.

> And he left them, and went away *again*, and *prayed the third time saying the same word* (Matt. 26:44).

For *three hours* the terrified Jesus (for this is the meaning of the Greek word describing his anguish) had prayed. Each time he uttered the same prayer, but the "circle of

---

15. Throckmorton, *Gospel Parallels*, p. 170.

protection" had been broken. The disciples had found themselves incapable of "watching" and "praying" and had fallen asleep. Thus YHWH allowed the Adversary his momentary triumph, allowing the "bruising" of the Messiah in order to provide mankind with a "substitutionary" sacrifice, patterned after those sacrificial firstborn animals and children of Egypt. The arrest takes place near 3:00 a.m. in the morning (after three hours of prayer) and is also patterned after the original Exodus.

> And Pharaoh rose up *in the night*, he and all his servants, and all the Egyptians; and there was a great cry in Egypt; for there was not a house where there was not one dead. *And he called for Moses and Aaron by night* and said, Rise up, and get you forth from among my people, both ye, and the children of Israel, and go serve the LORD [YHWH] as ye have said. Also take your flocks and your herds, as ye have said, and be gone; and bless me also (Exod. 12:30–32).

The common misconception that the Exodus event occurred during full daylight hours is unfounded. It was, in fact, still dark when Pharaoh called Moses and Aaron. Since the Destroyer had passed through all Egypt at *midnight*, and this had been a time of vigilant watching, waiting, and praying for redemption, it can be assumed that the command for the Exodus event to begin did not occur until shortly before 3:00 a.m., while it was still dark. Note how similar to the Exodus command are the words of Jesus to his disciples at the end of his third hour of prayer.

> Ye are sleeping what time remaineth and taking your rest: *Lo! The hour hath drawn near*, and the Son of Man is being delivered up into the hands of sinners, *Arise! Let us be going*,—Lo he that delivereth me up hath drawn near (Matt. 26:46).

It is true that the darkest part of the day is that hour just before dawn, and that would certainly account for the use of "torches and lamps" used by the arresting officers. The arresting party was fully expecting armed resistance for the participants carried with them weapons: swords and clubs. The word here used for sword is the Greek *machaira* identified as a "short sword". For this reason, some have thought it was the weapon of the Roman soldier. The Septuagint, however, uses the Hebrew word *chereb* to identify this sword. The *chereb* was the usual "knife" or "short sword" used by *the Temple guards*. It was also the kind of sword that Peter carried under his cloak that night and used to injure Malchus.

THE ARREST PARTY

A warrant for Jesus' arrest had been issued some forty days prior to his execution. His purpose in hiding in the wilderness was to escape detection by the population of Israel, since postings had been made by that time throughout Israel on the "bulletin boards" in town squares. Certainly, the herald—mentioned in the Talmud (*b. Sanh* 43a)— posted them. Edersheim has noted the Talmudic references to the postal service and communications of importance to the public domain.

> For the Jerusalemites had friends and correspondents in the most distant parts of the world, and letters were carried by special messengers [*Shabbat* x.4], in a kind of post-bag. Nay, there seem to have been some sort of receiving-offices in towns, and

even something resembling our parcel-post. And, strange as it may sound, even a species *of newspapers, or broadsheets*, appears to have been circulating (*Mikhtabhin*), not allowed, however, on the Sabbath, unless they treated of public affair.[16]

Now that the groundwork for the arrest is established, let us begin with a description of the arresting party. Since the Gospel of John provides some scholars with the only so-called evidence for the belief that Romans were included within the arresting party, we must first begin by ridding ourselves of such notion. The Greek word *chiliarchos* has been translated as "captain of a thousand men". On that basis, it has been generally assumed that it was a Roman tribune who led a *cohort*, or arrest party. But this rendering is highly deceiving. The word is used to denote *any* "high captain" (and in our case, the Captain or "Man" of the Temple). One piece of evidence that would dispel the Roman myth is found in the population of Roman soldiers garrisoned in all the Near East at the time. History is quite clear that during the time of Jesus only one-half a legion occupied the whole of the tetrarchy. Since a legion has been variously defined as anywhere from three thousand to six thousand men (a more accurate estimate would be four thousand eight hundred), we must assume that, at best, only fifteen hundred to three thousand (probably twenty-four hundred) Roman soldiers might have possibly constituted the total occupying force of Rome *in the entire near East*, this under not only Pilate's weak rule but also under the rule of the Syrian governor to whom Pilate answered, who also had his own hand in the affairs of Judea and Galilee. This means there could have been only one or two tribunes stationed within the *entire* region. Furthermore, these fifteen hundred to three thousand soldiers (twenty-four hundred) were permanently stationed, not in Jerusalem but in Caesarea Philippi in northern Palestine. Pilate removed a portion of these men each winter from Caesarea to Jerusalem, but the bulk of the soldiers would have remained in the northern region (a trouble spot).

> To commit a people so conditioned to separatism and nationalism to the comparatively weak rule of procurators, small men, *armed with no more than half a legion almost confined to barracks at Caesarea*, was a risk which the Empire took. It failed, and one reason is that the procurators, court favourites, diplomats by profession, senior civil servants, were ill-equipped for a task so subtly difficult, and were perhaps under orders to hide, where possible, the mailed fist.[17]

As a point of interest, the Mekilta (Midrash on the Torah) notes that *only one hundred men were located in Jerusalem* at the time.[18] Historically, this would indicate that a century (or eighty men, ten squads) was assigned to the capitol. This would mean it was most probable that only *one centurion* might have been stationed in Jerusalem. This centurion was allegedly Longinus (who, according to church legend, later became the first bishop of Cappadocia and a Christian martyr). If he was present, however, it was only as a member of the four-man Roman execution detail sent by Pilate to oversee the execution and was not present at the arrest. From the emphasis placed on the Roman

---

16. Edersheim, *Life and Times*, v. 1, p. 131; *b. Shab.* x. 4, *Shab.* 19a; *b. R.H.*; *Tosef. Shab.* xviii.
17. Blaiklock, *Compact Handbook*, p. 64.
18. Mahan, *Archaeological*, p. 4.

occupation of Palestine by the church, one might think there were hundreds of thousands of soldiers posted there. One recent scholar even suggests that a *thousand soldiers* were sent to arrest Jesus! This would, of course, be an improbability. In any event, it is highly unlikely Pilate would have taken the much needed tribunes (if, indeed, there were actually more than one) from Caesarea for the Passover in Jerusalem. They would have been needed to control the flow of pilgrims in and out of the northernmost and southernmost regions of Palestine then known to be "trouble spots". Furthermore, it is well known that the Romans *used Jewish Temple guards to effect arrests of non-citizens of Rome*. The Jewish Sanhedrin also acted independently of Rome to effect their own law: "It administered the criminal law, and *had independent powers of police, and hence the right to make arrests through its own officers of justice*."[19]

It is, further, illogical that Pilate would have had Jesus arrested by a "tribune" and then have sent only a "centurion" to oversee the execution. Parallel with this logic lies more collaborating evidence: the word "band" is used in the gospels to denote the "cohort of soldiers" (i.e., four hundred and eighty men), and simply means a *tribunal guard*. While it is misused to indicate that Roman soldiers were present, it is rendered in the Septuagint as the Hebrew *shalosh*, "officers of the third rank". The word for band here is, in fact, rendered in Strong's Concordance as "a squad of Levitical janitors" (or attendants). Luke called them the "captains" of the Temple; i.e., the Temple police. Again, we must look to the Jews for a reasonable explanation. When we do, we learn that a band is only five men (certainly not the "multitude" of later translations).

> Rabbi Halafta of Kefar Hananiah says: *When ten sit studying the Torah, the Shekinah resides in their midst, as it is said*, God standeth in the congregation of God (Psalm 82:1). *How do we know that the same is true of five? For it is said*, This band of His He hath established on the earth (Amos 9:6). *Ten . . . Congregation*: The word "congregation" is applied to a group of ten. (Vitry) *Five . . . Band: The word "band" (agudah) is related to the verb agad, as in the expression "what a man gathers into one of his hands." Now the hand has five fingers . . . and the sum of these five fingers may be called "band."* (Maimonides).[20]

The "high captain" was known as the "Man of the Temple Mount"; i.e., the Captain of the Temple Guard. He was a man of *first* rank; the three priests belonging to the Temple captains were of the *second* rank; and the officers (or attendants, known as captains) were of the *third* rank. Each squad or patrol consisted of ten guards. Since we now have five officers of the third rank (the "band"), three priests of the second rank, and the Captain of the Temple, only one more individual is needed to complete the party of ten (a squad). That individual is "Malchus", the high priest's servant, probably a Herodian spy/ally (see below). His kinsmen were to be found awaiting the outcome of the trial with Peter in the "porch". The Herodians were kin to much of the Saducean priesthood through the marriage of Mariamne I, the granddaughter of the high priest Hyrcanus II, and Mariamne II, the daughter of the high priest, Simon Boethus. By his marriages to two Jewish priestesses, Herod the Great sought to secure a political advantage over the

---

19. "Sanhedrin", J.E., p. 42.
20. Goldin, *Mishnah Avot*, p. 67.

religious institution of Israel. He attempted to endear both Pharisees and Sadducees to him by dangling religious "carrots" before them. The scheme proved to have had both political and religious implications for connections between his own royal government and the supposed theocracy of Israel.

> *In an effort to legitimize his kingship [Herod the Great], married Mariamne, the granddaughter of the high priest Hyrcanus II,* and though he eventually ordered her killed he insisted that any prince marrying a daughter of the Herodian family must be circumcised. He paid for the relocation in Jerusalem of many important Jewish religious leaders and their families living in Mesopotamia and Egypt, including the family of Hillel from which would come important Torah scholars. Despite their opposition to him, *he provided funds for the scriptural study centers of the Pharisees. And he won the enthusiastic support of the Sadducees* when he ordered the beginning of reconstruction of Jerusalem's Temple, insisting again with ritual correctness that the actual work of building would be carried out only by priests themselves.[21]

Herod Antipas married his own niece, Herodias (a granddaughter of Mariamne I), who had also been married to his brother (and her uncle), Herod Philip I, the son of Mariamne II, the daughter of Simon Boethus. Since Herodias was a descendant of both priestly families, and Herod Antipas sought to please her, he would have been inclined to favor the Sadducean priesthood in charge of the Sanhedrin. It is small wonder that Malchus might have been among the arrest squad. The Temple duties and functions of the spy Malchus cannot be determined within the structure of the Temple government. Since he was said to have been a "servant" to the high priest, we might well suppose he was a representative of the Herodian royal house and was placed as a secular emissary over the proceedings. As the "servant" to Annas, it is possible he directed these "captains" of the Temple, and even the "Man of the Temple" himself. It is to be noted that the word "captains" in Luke 22:4 is rendered as "Levitical Temple wardens" or janitors. One authority explains:

> The real identity of the Jewish participants in the arrest is deducible from the reference in Luke to "the captains of the temple" (22:52). The term here translated into English as "captains" is the Greek *strategoi*, military commanders. It has been suggested that these "temple commanders" are the vice-priests (*seganei kohanim*), of whose functions we have some knowledge in the Jewish sources: wherever *seganim* occurs in the Bible (e.g., Jer. 51:23, 28, 57; Ezek. 23:6, 12, 23), it is rendered in the Septuagint as *strategoi*. These vice-priests were charged, *inter alia*, with the public relations of the temple administration: they had to proceed to the gates of the city and there welcome the people arriving from other parts of the country with the first fruits of their fields and vineyards as a gift to the temple. There is a list of precedence of temple officers, in which *seganim* rank after officiating priests and before the commanders of the temple police, from which it would appear that police commanders were their immediate subordinates. Since, in the verse quoted from Luke, the "captains of the temple" are mentioned as present together with the "chief priests" it has been argued that the *seganim* represent the "chief priests," whereas the commanders of the temple police are the "captains of the temple," suggesting that the police commanders

---

21. Idinopulos, *Jerusalem*, pp. 77-78.

and their immediate superiors might both have been present. But it seems clear, on any view, that the term *strategoi* can refer only to a commanding officer of military or quasi-military character and, in the context of the temple, to none but officers of the temple police.[22]

It is also interesting that the "high captain" or so-called "Man of the Temple Mount" might also be referred to as a "tribune" since he was the chief officer of the Sanhedrin, the body of which was, in fact, a *tribunal*! The Sanhedrin consisted of three separate and individual chambers with specific duties prescribed for each: The Chamber of the Priests, The Chamber of the Elders, and The Chamber of the Scribes. This subject will be discussed in greater detail in the next chapter. There is also an indication that a few of this "multitude" (which should simply be translated "company of men") were elders (Mark 13:43). These "elders" or "counsellors" were known to have been the "standing council" who regulated completely the affairs and services of the Temple; they also regulated the Temple captains or police guard. Some of them were probably members of the Temple police. They did not generally participate in the sitting of the judicatory criminal process. In a case of one "leading the nation astray" their involvement might have, perhaps, become necessary. It is imperative, however, that they become involved in the arrest of Jesus since their duties were to regulate the Temple police. This, however, does not mean that the presence of the entire seventy-one-member religious Sanhedrin (some call it the Supreme Court of Israel) was required for the Jewish trial of Jesus. As one last proof that the arrest party was the Captain and the members of the Temple police, it might be noted that all four canonical gospels concur that they were sent by the judicial Sanhedrin, *not* by the Roman prefect, to wit:

> Judas, then, having received a band of men and officers *from the chief priests and Pharisees*, cometh thither with lanterns and torches and weapons (John 18:3).
> And immediately while he spake, cometh Judas, one of the twelve, and with him a multitude [company] with swords and staves, *from the chief priests and the scribes and the elders* [that is, from the Sanhedrin tribunal] (Mark 14:43).
> Then Jesus said unto the *chief priests, and captains of the temple, and the elders* which were come to him . . . *I was daily with you in the temple* . . . (Luke 22:52–53).
> And while yet he spake, lo, Judas, one of the twelve, came, and with him a great multitude [company] with swords and staves, *from the chief priests and elders* of the people (Matt. 26:47).

Malchus, the *servant* (an apparent kinsman) of the high priest, as mentioned above, was specifically named in the narration. The Hebrew name "Malchus" is derived from the Hebrew word for king [*melek*], but the word can mean either the government (of Israel), or royalty. It is probably a simple play on words (of which the Hebrew race is so fond) to indicate that it was Herod Antipas who lurked behind the scenes, using the authority of the priesthood to bring Jesus to trial. That Malchus might have been a member of the Herodian "secret police" first instituted by Herod the Great and, therefore, a member of the royal government seems entirely plausible. This man then would complete the ten individuals who formed the arrest party, or squad, sent to apprehend Jesus. Certainly, Herod would have wanted a representative present at the arrest.

22. Cohn, *Trial and Death*, p. 73–74.

> *The Herodians*, mentioned three times in the story of Easter Week (Matt. 22:16; Mark 3:6 and 12:13), *were probably a sub-group of the Sadducees [linking them with the Sadducean appointed priesthood]*. They were such a society as any modern country can show, committed to the promotion of some special common interest, or pledging loyalty to one political figure. *Their attachment was to the royal house.* Augustus enjoyed the support of a similar group in Rome. Perhaps the Herodians were an activist group among the Sadducees, who saw the political stability of the royal house and its policies as the ground of their own safety and stability in a dangerously exclusive society, and therefore combined to support it.[23]

It is certain that Herod's son, Antipas (the Herod of the New Covenant), like his father before him, continued the practice of sending spies in to entrap people suspected of crimes against the State of Israel. In fact, there is some evidence for it in New Covenant writings.

> And the Pharisees went forth and straightway took counsel *with the Herodians* against him, how they might destroy him (Mark 3:6).

Already Herod Antipas had made it plain that he was bent on destroying Jesus as he had destroyed John the Immerser, Jesus' mentor. Jesus was warned of this shortly before his last journey to Jerusalem.

> That same day there came certain of the Pharisees, saying unto him; Get thee out, and depart hence: *for Herod will kill thee* (Luke 13:31).

In the non-canonical Gospel of Peter, there is further evidence that it was by Herod's command that Jesus was arrested and put to death.

> And then *Herod the king* commandeth that the Lord [Master] be taken saying to them, *what things soever I commanded you to do unto him, do*.[24]

This scenario conforms to the Targum *Toldoth Jeshu* wherein Herod is figuratively personified as the "queen" Helene (Queen of Adiabene), a first century Palmyran convert to Judaism. Herod Antipas was not Jewish at all (he was an Edomite) but also a "proselyte" to Judaism like Helene.

> [ii, I.] *"Now the rule of all Israel was in the hand of a woman."* The woman, called Queen Helene, whose name has already been explained, represents the authority, actual or delegated of Rome. There is an important parallel in the *Sibylline Oracles* (Bk. III, 75), where we find, "Then shall the world be ruled beneath a woman's hand, and obey her in all things" (cf. Rev. xvii, 3). *We believe that Herod the tetrarch [i.e., Antipas] was the name that stood in the source.*[25]

This statement is clarified upon examination of the text.

> [iii.12] Jesus went forth to Upper Galilee. And the wise men [judicial Sanhedrin] assembled and came before the queen [figurative for Herod Antipas], and said unto her [him] . . . he practiseth sorcery and therewith he leadeth the world astray . . . [iv.10–11] And when the wise men [Sanhedrin] had entered into the

---

23. Blaiklock, *Compact Handbook*, p. 144.
24. Gosp. Pet.; *Lost Books*, p. 283.
25. Schonfield, *According*, p. 222.

temple where those were that came from Antioch, and the wicked one [Jesus] also with them; then entered Ga'isa [Judas Iscariot as the "prideful man"] with them, left the whole congregation and made obeisance to the wicked Jesus. Immediately the wise men [Sanhedrin] perceived this, they rose up against him, and seized him [an account of the trial follows] . . . [iv. 16] Forthwith they held him, and his three hundred and ten disciples were unable to deliver him.[26]

Objection is sometimes made to the excess of twelve disciples. Jesus is known to have had at least one hundred twenty disciples during Shavuot alone (Acts 1:15). We learn in the book of Acts that Judas Iscariot's replacement should be "of these men which have companied with us all the time that the Lord [Master] Jesus went in and out among us. Beginning from the baptism [immersion] of John unto the same day he was taken up from us, must one be ordained to be a witness with us of his resurrection" (Acts 1:21). Jesus had also sent out "seventy" other disciples, two by two, "into every city and place, whither he himself would come" (Luke 10:1). It is also necessary to consider that many of his disciples were still in Galilee where he had preached in the beginning of his ministry, perhaps unaware of the events taking shape in Jerusalem. There were also disciples of the disciples; for instance, we know Mark and Clement were disciples of Peter but were still disciples of Jesus as well.

That the execution was a Jewish affair, we have verification in Acts 4:9, where the rulers of Israel are confronted with the execution of Jesus. There is just no getting around the fact that the entire process was a Jewish affair from beginning to end, and it is the only conclusion we can draw from the Talmudic writings, which speak nothing of the Romans. The passage in the Babylonian Talmud is proof of that.

> On the eve of the Passover Yeshu [Jesus] was hanged. For forty days before the execution took place, a herald went forth and cried, "He is going forth to be stoned because he has practised sorcery and enticed Israel to apostasy . . . he was hanged on the eve of the Passover! [14 Nisan]"[27]

The Slavonic Josephus (which will be discussed in some detail later) agrees in content and character with this assessment, even pointing out to the reader that the rulers of Israel "bribed" Pilate. This would certainly conform to what we know of the rulers of Israel during the time of Jesus.

> And when thereafter news of it was brought to the Jewish leaders, they assembled together with the high priest and said, "We are powerless and (too) weak to resist the Romans [at which time they communicate their desires to Pilate who] . . . pronounced (this) judgment: "He is (a benefactor, but not) a malefactor (nor) a rebel (nor) coveteous of king(ship)". . . The scribes (therefore) being stung with envy gave Pilate thirty talents to kill him. And he took (it) and *gave them liberty to carry out their will (themselves). And they took him and crucified him [i.e., hanged him on a tree alive] contrary to the law of (their) fathers.*[28]

---

26. Schonfield, pp. 42; 48–49.
27. *b. Sanh.* 43a.
28. Schonfield, p. 162.

A Book of Evidence

All these documents were written *by Jews*. There is no reason for them to have contrived such "fantasies" concerning Israel's involvement in the arrest and execution of Jesus, especially in light of the tendency toward anti-Semitic persecution of Jews by the universal church of the latter first century and onward. Quite simply, the arrest (and execution) was entirely a Jewish affair. There is little doubt that both Herod (as reigning royal ruler) and the Sanhedrin (the legislative body of Israel) had already identified Jesus as a wanted man and were only awaiting their opportunity to seize him in Jerusalem.

The arrest party arrived at the Garden of Gethsemane shortly before 3:00 a.m. on the 14th of Nisan. Jesus "went out" of the cave to meet them (John 18:4), at which time he inquired who it was they were seeking. These men, already expecting an armed resistance and still unable to see clearly within the recesses of the cave, although they carried torches, then stated their command: "Jesus the Nazarean." When Jesus responded that he was the man they sought and knowing he had numerous disciples, many from the party of the Zealots, they all "went backward, and fell to the ground" (John 18:6) in anticipation of an ambush. There is nothing in the statement that would indicate the police were overwhelmed by the "mystical" power of Jesus. Jesus then asked again "whom seek ye?" and they again, emboldened and noting an ambush was no longer imminent, repeated their command. It was at this time that Jesus made a plea for his disciples. Peter, who was certainly armed, rash, and with his customary lack of understanding, "smote the Highpriest's servant (Malchus), and cut off his right ear." Angered by Peter's behavior, Jesus healed the man's ear. This momentary distraction allowed the disciples an opportunity to flee, and an opportunity for the Temple guard to apprehend Jesus and bind him. Their focus was on Jesus, *not* his disciples. The primary duty of the ten-man arrest squad was to apprehend Jesus, nothing more. The disciples, if need be, could be dealt with later. The reason for Jesus' anger when Peter lashed out at Malchus was surely because he did not want the authorities to perceive him as a militant "Zealot". In fact, he is noted to have remarked, "Are you come out against a thief (*lestes,* insurgent, Zealot) with swords and staves for to take me?" (Matt. 26:55) (Josephus uses the word *lestes* to refer to the *sicari,* a later title for Zealot). The officers then led Jesus to the illustrious Annas, former high priest and vice president of the judicial Sanhedrin. Although he was no longer *high* priest, he was still a priest in the Temple and retained the dignity of the title *high priest.*

THE ACCUSATION

It was Annas' duty as the *ab bet din* [father of the court] to interrogate the accused and form an accusation.

> In the Accusatory method, a representative of the commonwealth, perhaps of the injured party, frames a written accusation, in which it is set forth that the accused, at a specified time and place, committed a certain offense. This accusation being denied by the accused, or standing controverted by operation of the law, the prosecutor brings his witnesses and other proofs . . .[29]

---

29. "Accusatory", J.E., p. 163.

The accusation, however, was not always "written," especially if the case was one that involved a mesith (religious and political insurgent). That necessarily would have been deemed a "decision for the hour" (horaat sh'ah).

> This short method of dealing with a man who has by his misdeed brought God's wrath down upon his people was deemed "a decision for the hour" (horaat sha'ah), not to be taken as a precedent in the affairs of life in later days.[30]

As established in the last chapter, Jesus was accused of the crime of "leading the nation astray," a crime that would be considered as one bringing "YHWH's wrath down upon his people" (a desecration of the Name). Since it was the gravest crime for which a man might be tried, there would not necessarily have been a written accusation. Such criminals were often accused spontaneously and promptly executed, as has been previously demonstrated. Furthermore, the basic deliberations in the case of Jesus had already been made some forty days previous. It must be stated here that Annas, as the supreme authority of the criminal court, would have been the high priest to which the author of John refers. There were actually *two* high priests that ruled over the government of Israel at the time.

> Two persons were at the head of the bet din [Lesser Sanhedrin]: one, the actual president [Caiaphas] with the title "nasi" [prince, high priest]; the other, the second president or vice-president [Annas], who bore the title "ab bet din" (father of the court).[31]

While this phenomenon had been in practice for at least since the days of the Hasmonians, it continued until the Sanhedrin was abolished by the Romans in the centuries following the destruction of Jerusalem. The fact that two high priests are mentioned in the New Covenant are indications of that.

> *Yose ben Joezer . . . and Yose ben Johanan*: All the Sages listed in this chapter from this point through Hillel and Shammai are known as the Pairs (Duran), and they were the heads of the Sanhedrin . . . one serving as Nasi and the other as Ab Bet Din. (Vitry)".[32]

Annas, as the *ab bet din*, was simply the more powerful of the two priests. As proof of his power, his family would serve the priesthood for the next forty years (until 70 CE). It might be noted that his kinsmen were also present at the trials of Peter and John (Acts 4:5–6), Stephen (Acts 6:15), Paul (Acts 23:2) and James (Josephus, *Ant.* 20.9.1). The powerful position Annas held as vice-president of the *beth din* would require him to make such formal accusation. The high priest, the president of the assembly of Sanhedrin (Caiaphas), was merely a figurehead who rubber-stamped the decisions of the higher authority.

> It appears that even while Caiaphas performed the duties of the office, *the power of high priest lay in the hands of Annas* . . . [t]he actual trial took place on the next

---

30. "Accusatory", J.E., p. 163.
31. "Sanhedrin", J.E., p. 44.
32. Goldin, *Mishnah Avot*, p. 9.

day, the eve of Passover, before the twenty-three members of the Sanhedrin over whom Caiaphas presided (Matt. xxvi 57).[33]

Although the Gospel of John claims that Annas (Ananus) was the father-in-law of Caiaphas (John 18:13), little else is known of the latter. It is Annas who looms large in history. No other historical source mentions any particular kinship between the two. We know Caiaphas is linguistically connected with ha Kof or (Kithros) and that the Kithros family were involved in the incense trade in Jerusalem. His name is also connected with Cantheras, which we believe to be a variant of the name. This would seem to indicate that Simon Cantheras, son of Boethus, was also a son of a female named Caipahas.

It is suggested here that it might have been the *title* of Annas to which the author of John referred as "father-in-law". As "father of the court" of law, he would have been the "father-in-law" of the high priest. No mention of Caiaphas is ever made as *son-in-law* in the gospels. It should also be mentioned that the term "in-law" had not yet fully come into customary family use. When someone married a woman in those days, her father became his father as well. It was not until the latter first century that the term "in-law" was used in such a prolific manner (for example, in the writings of Josephus). If Caiaphas is a corruption of Kithros, then his family was a partner in the Bazaars of Hanan.

Annas, makes no charge of treason against Rome; instead, he asked Jesus *about his disciples and his doctrines* (John 18:19). The inquiry would seem to imply that there is something peculiar about these two subjects that he found contrary to *Jewish* law. The fact that he did so indicates that the ultimate charge concerned *only* the Jewish nation, *not* the Roman administration. Treason against Rome forms no part in the accusation, as we shall learn in a future chapter. The interrogation focuses only on the teachings and followers of Jesus as if to imply that "leading the nation astray" is the *only* charge listed in the accusation, the crime of insurgency against both the political *and* religious establishments.

ANNAS

It becomes, once more, necessary to digress from the narrative in order to better understand the nature and personality of this *ab bet din* or "father-in-law" who was ultimately responsible for the formal accusation of Jesus. The ancient Jewish authorities as well as contemporary scholars are in agreement concerning the character of Annas. The Talmud and Tosefta describe him and his family as "whisperers" (*Tosef. Sot.* XIV). They were known to have bribed Roman officials whenever they found it necessary and also known to have paid them a "tribute" for the honor of governmental position and status. Josephus gives the following description.

> [B]ut the king deprived Joseph [Caiaphas] of the high-priesthood, and bestowed the succession to that dignity on the son of Ananus [Annas], who was also himself called Ananus. Now the report goes, that this elder Ananus [Annas] proved a most fortunate man; for he had five sons, who had all performed the office of a high-priest to God, and he had himself enjoyed that dignity a long time formerly, which had never happened to any other of our high-priests; but this younger Ananus,

---

33. "Caiaphas, Joseph–Caiaphas", J.E., p. 493.

who, as we have told you already, took the high-priesthood, was a bold man in his temper, and very insolent; he was also of the sect of the Sadducees, who are very rigid in judging offenders, above all the rest of the Jews, as we have already observed; when, therefore, Ananus was of this disposition, he thought he had now a proper opportunity [to exercise his authority]. Festus was now dead, and Albinus was but upon the road; so he assembled the sanhedrin of judges, and brought before them the brother of Jesus, who was called Christ, whose name was James, and some others [or, some of his companions]; and when he had formed an accusation against them as breakers of the law, he delivered them to be stoned.[34]

Note that here, too, an accusation was formed against James and other Nazaraeans by another ab bet din, in this case, Annas II. Four families, in particular, must be counted as constituting this priestly oligarchy: the House of Chanan (Annas); the House of Boethus; the House of Cathrus [Cantheras, Kithros, Caiaphas, or Kimchit]; and the House of Phabus [Phiabi/Fabus]. The Talmudic sages were quite explicit in their criticism of this group of priests.

> Woe is me because of the house of *Boethos*, Woe is me because of their staves; Woe is me because of the house of *Hanin* [Hanan or Annas], Woe is me because of their whippings; Woe is me because of the house of *Kathros* [Cathrus, Kithros, Caiaphas], woe is me because of their pens; Woe is me because of the house of Ishmael the son of *Phiabi*, Woe is me because of their fists! *For they are high priests; and their sons are treasurers; and their sons-in-law are overseers; and their servants come and beat us with staves.*[35]

The Boethus family, especially, was connected with the Herodian dynasty through the marriage of Herod the Great with the two Mariamnes, one a granddaughter of Hyrcanus II (a Hasmonean high priest), the other a daughter of Simon Boethus (an Alexandrian Jewish high priest). As mentioned earlier, it was in this manner that Herod assured himself of both the political and religious reins of government.

> There was one Simon, a citizen of Jerusalem, the son of one Boethus, a citizen of Alexandria, and a priest of great note there: This man had a daughter, who was esteemed the most beautiful woman of that time; and when the people of Jerusalem began to speak much in her commendation, it happened that Herod [the Great] was much affected with what was said of her; and when he saw the damsel, he was smitten by her beauty, yet did he entirely reject the thoughts of using his authority to abuse her; as believing, what was the truth, that by doing so he should be stigmatized for violence and tyranny; so he thought it best to take the damsel to wife. And while Simon was of a dignity too inferior to be allied to him, but still too considerable to be despised, he governed his inclinations after the most prudent manner, by augmenting the dignity of the family, and making them more honorable; so he immediately deprived Jesus the son of Phabet [Phabi] of the high-priesthood, and conferred that dignity on Simon, and so joined in affinity with him [by marrying his daughter].[36]

---

34. Josephus, *Ant.*, XX, 9, 1.
35. b. Pes. 57a; *Tosef. Men.* XIII 21.
36. Josephus, *Ant.*, XX.9.3.

A Book of Evidence

Once the linkage between these two families is known, one is able to better perceive the political connections between the Sadducean priesthood and the Herodians. The history of the Family of Boethus is said to have "reflected all the characteristics of social development of Palestine in those days . . ."

> The Boethos family formed part of the stratum that had achieved prominence together with Herod, and its interests were intertwined with those of the Herodians. Like many of the great families of those days, the house of Boethos was not of Palestinian origin but came from the Diaspora—*from Alexandria in Egypt*—and several of its members later became *High Priests*. Its chief rival was the house of Hanan [Annas], which produced some of the most important statesmen and personalities of Judea in the last decades before the Great Revolt. Outstanding among them were Jonathan ben Hanan and Hanan ben Hanan [Ananus, son of Annas of New Covenant infamy]. The latter was a militant Sadducee and the acknowledged leader of the Jewish upper classes during the revolt. The greatness of the third priestly family, the house of Phiabi, which also seems to have *come from Egypt*, is reflected in the fact that it supplied three High Priests: the first, Joshua ben Phiabi, held office under Herod himself; the second, Ishmael ben Phiabi I functioned as High Priest under the early Roman governors; the third, Ishmael ben Phiabi II, was appointed by Agrippa II. The High Priest was assisted by a staff of high Temple officers. The most important of them is known in the Greek sources as the 'strategos of the Temple'. Other important functionaries were the *amarcalim* ('overseers') and treasurers.[37]

Several members of the Boethus family were known to have been among the judges of Jesus. They, along with the Hanan family, would later gather to condemn Peter (Acts 4:5–6). Of these and the Sadducean families ruling the Sanhedrin at the time a great deal more is known.

> In Roman times the high priesthood was confined to a few families; identical names recur again and again. It was not that qualified candidates could not be found in other circles, but that these were the only Jerusalem clans that could afford the costs involved . . . [a]ll the families belonged to the Sadducean aristocracy, so that the mass of the people found itself faced by *an apparent alliance between the hateful alien overlord [Rome] and the rich and wealthy Jews* . . . [t]hey knew not only how intensely the Romans were hated, but also that their own collaboration with the Romans and their dependence on them were popularly viewed with scorn and disgust. And the fact that it was by their wealth alone that the high priests had qualified for the holy office, and had procured and went on holding it, did nothing to enhance their standing or give them added goodwill.[38]

Investigations into the personalities and circumstances of these families have been made by numerous scholars. Alfred Edersheim, who has written voluminous material on the Hebrew customs and the Temple cult has this to say about Annas:

> The Sadducean Annas was an eminently safe churchman, not troubled with any special convictions nor with Jewish fanaticism, a pleasant and a useful man also, *who was able to funish his friends in the praetorium with large sums of money*. We

---

37. Ben-Sasson, *A History*, p. 266.
38. Cohn, *Trial and Death*, pp. 22–23.

have seen what immense revenues the family of Annas must have derived from the *Temple-booths*, and how nefarious and unpopular was the traffic . . . [the reason he dealt with Jesus in such a curt manner was that] Annas might [be able to continue to] have the conduct of the business [provided by the booths].[39]

It is, perhaps, S. Srinivasa Aiyar, however, who gives the best summary of the character of Annas and his family.

> In the year 7 A.D. Coponius, the Procurator, appointed one Ananos, or Annas, the son of Seth, an Alexandrian Sadducee, to be the High Priest at Jerusalem, and thus laid the foundations of the House or High Priestly family of Annas, which, with brief and occasional interruptions in the terms of that office, held sway in and about the Temple for the next fifty years. Five sons of Annas were High Priests during that period, and his son-in-law, Caiaphas, was in possession of that office at the time of the trial of Jesus. Profane history has clearly and minutely described the *crafty and serpent-like cunning by which Annas has been enabled to retain this coveted dignity within the control of himself and his family*; and has also described the rise and nature of the *temple bazaars, that infamous system of traffic in the sacrificial offerings of the temple, and in the temple tribute, established and controlled by the sons of Annas*, which was a source of immense wealth to that family, and which had grown to such proportions in the time of Jesus as to make the Temple, in very truth, a "den of thieves" . . . With the rise of the House of Annas it had come to be completely under the control of that family and of their associates, including those who, at intervals, had also held the High Priestly office and were thus entitled to seats in the Sanhedrin. *These, together with a few others of its membership who were allied in interest with the family of Annas, were of sufficient number to constitute at least a quorum of the Sanhedrin, which was fixed at 23*".[40]

One might provide the reader with endless lists of quotations concerning these priestly families and their connections with the Herodian dynasty. Considering the conditions existing in Jerusalem at the time we find something similar to the "boss" system of the larger United States cities during the earlier part of the twentieth century. Annas was the chief leader of just such a system; he and his priestly cult, through an "unholy" alliance with the Roman rulers, controlled not only the political and jurisdictional aspects of the Temple and the government but the financial arrangements as well. Furthermore, he and his family netted huge revenues from the sales of sacrificial items at the Temple booths and the usury of the moneychangers.

> He [Annas] enjoyed all the dignity of the office, and all its influence also, since he was able to promote to it those most closely connected with him. And, while they acted publicly, *he really directed affairs*, without either the responsibility or the restraints which the office imposed. *His influence with the Romans he owed to the religious views which he professed, to his open partisanship of the foreigner, and to his enormous wealth.*[41]

---

39. Edersheim, *Life and Times*, v. 2, p. 547.
40. Aiyar, *Legality*, pp. 6–7.
41. Edersheim, *Life and Times*, v. 2, p. 547.

A Book of Evidence

By the time of Jesus, the Temple had effectively become a national bank for Israel's citizens, bearing little resemblance to its original purpose. The practice of wealthy Israelites depositing their money within the Temple treasury had come into existence through distrust of Greek-run banks that had been established by the Ptolemies in 188 BCE.[42]

> In Jesus' day the Temple was not only the central religious shrine, *it was also the major industrial and banking facility of the nation.* It received the annual Temple tax payed by Jews throughout the world. Great sums of money were deposited at the Temple by wealthy families and by the hundreds of elderly Jews who had come to retire in the Holy City. The daily sale of sacrificial animals was routinely conducted in *the temple area*. At the Passover, with the city's population bloated by pilgrims . . . one can imagine the congestion of pilgrims, priests, beasts, blood, and money. Conduits carried blood drained from the sacrificed animals down the southern side of the Temple into the Kidron Valley, where it was used as fertilizer for vegetable gardens. The Temple itself gleamed from the sheer amount of gold, marble, and bronze used in its construction. And *outside the walls of the temple were artisan shops of gold and silver, and other shops of incense and shewbread catering directly to temple needs*. One need not have had so lofty a view of religion as Jesus to have found himself nauseated by such sights in a city whose ritual purity was promptly restored at sunrise each morning by an army of street cleaners. It was Jesus' preaching of the coming kingdom at the Temple [precincts] that drew the adverse reaction of Temple officials.[43]

It was the priestly partnership among the most prominent families that controlled the secular Temple trade. The trade became known as *Beth Hanuyoth*, the Bazaars of Annas, and was situated at the public square in *Beth Pagi*. It was what the rabbis referred to as *Beth-Hanioth* or *Beth-Hini*, from which the twin villages might have derived their New Covenant names. Certainly, there is a linguistic connection between the House (*Beth*) of Hanan (*Hanin, Hanioth, Hini*) and Bethany. The Greek *Bethania* has been defined as meaning "date-house". Bethphage and Bethany are sometimes linked together in the Talmud and appear to have been (for administrative and festive purposes) considered a single part of Jerusalem, yet outside its original city limits. Some years prior to the destruction of the Temple these Bazaars (near the Temple) (*b., RH* 31a, b; *Jer. Taan.* iv. 8) were destroyed (*Siphre* on Deut. 105; *y. Peah.* 1.6), at which time the *beth din* completely removed to Beth Pagi on the Mount of Olives, where they sat until they were again removed to the City of Jerusalem proper. It was here "While going forth to Beyt-Khanan (House of Annas), Y'hoshua was hungry".[44]

> The name in Talmud Y'rushalmiy is Beyt-Khanan; House of Khanan. Hanan was the family name of a priestly family (above) mentioned in Yirmiyahu 35:4. This seems the most likely original name of the village that was also known for the Khanan family dove aviary. [It] may have become corrupted . . . Ms. Or. Rome #53 reads Beyt Tana; House of the Tanna. This seems to be the only reference to

---

42. Idinopulos, *Jerusalem*, p. 68.
43. Idinopulos, p. 134.
44. Ben-David, NRM, v. I, 21.2.

The Night of Watching

Beyt Tanna as a precursor of the Beyt Miydrash. It also implies that Y'hoshua was more closely related to the P'rushim (Pharisees).[45]

Yirmiyahu Ben-David also calls this Beyt Pagah (or Beth Pagi - House of meeting, from *pegeeshah* - "to meet"; i.e., the Place of Meeting). The House of Tanna (Tannaim or Sages) is where most of the Sanhedrin resided. The ancient Bethany, too, must have been destroyed by the Roman tenth legion during the last siege of Jerusalem. A new village (in a different site) later appeared called *El-'Aziriyeh* (the Arabic name for Lazarus, the village founded by third century Christianity). As will be shown in a later chapter, Bethphage was likely the ancient priestly city of Nob. Please note that in the *Toldoth Jeshu* (written by Jews) Nob is identified as the place where Jesus asks for the ass on which to ride into Jerusalem, and in the New Covenant that site is Bethphage.

> They send messengers to him, Annani and Ahaziah, feigning to be his disciples, and bidding him on behalf of the leading citizens of Jerusalem to come to them. Jesus agrees on condition that the members of the Sanhedrin come out to receive him and acknowledge him as their lord. The elders decide to humour him, and Jesus sets forth immediately. *On arriving at Nob, he asks for an ass, and rides into Jerusalem proclaiming his act as a fulfilment of Zechariah's prophecy.*[46]

The New Covenant gospels identify the village of Bethphage as the same site. Other evidence equating Nob and Bethphage is that David ate the Bread of the Presence when the Tabernacle had been erected at "Nob". This is also where he prayed on the Mount of Olives when leaving Jerusalem.

The three priestly villages Anathoth (about two miles north of Jerusalem in the territory of Benjamin), Nob, (Bethphage on the Mount of Olives) and Ananiah (Bethany, 500 yards south of the limit of Bethphage) lie in a North-South path, within 5 miles of each other near Jerusalem. Early claims place these three villages within the territory of Judah, having been removed from the region of Benjamin during the days of Nehemiah. The Bordeaux pilgrim (333 CE) locates Bethany 1500 paces east of the Mount of Olives. But *Beth Hini* (or Beth Pagi) was probably the original suburb and might well have been confused with Bethany. It was at *Beth Hini* that Jesus ascended (Luke 24:50) into a "cloud" (Acts 1:9-10) ("a Sabbath Day's Journey"). Since the present "Bethany" lies much more than a "Sabbath's Journey", it is likely this should have been translated "Beth Hini", at the Bazaars of Annas in the Plaza on the Mount of Olives. A number of sources, including the Talmud and Josephus, are known to have made numerous complaints against this Saducean family. Alfred Edersheim again states succinctly:

> It deserves notice, that the special sin with which the house of Annas is charged is that of 'whispering'—or hissing like vipers—*which seems to refer to private influence on judges in their administration of justice*, whereby 'morals were corrupted, judgment perverted, and the Shekinah withdrawn from Israel.'[47]

---

45. Ben-David, NRM, v. II, 21.17.1.
46. Schonfield, *According*, p. 41, n.4.
47. Edersheim, *Life and Times*, v. 1, p. 263; *Tosef. Set.* xiv.

A Book of Evidence

There is little doubt that the Saducean oligarchy headed by Annas had an ulterior motive for bringing Jesus to trial and execution. Not only had Jesus twice attempted to rid the Temple precincts of the merchants who reported to Annas, the Chief Merchant, he had spoken out against the Temple Cult (as had his predecessor, John the Immerser) in an attempt to lead the nation into a more pure worship of YHWH. Annas and his partners stood to lose enormous amounts of profits if Jesus succeeded in turning the population against the Temple Cult. Already hated by the populace and envied by their Roman overlord, Annas and his priestly clique feared the loss of the family wealth, its powerful position and its status as leaders in the government of Israel.

> If we let him thus alone, all men will believe on him: and the Romans shall come and take away both our place [office] and our nation [destruction of the political power base] (John 11:48).

The Greek word *topos*, while ordinarily understood to refer to the Temple precincts, in this case is used to imply the position or office within the governmental structure, itself. Paul Winter states:

> The word τόπος topos can imply "office", "position" (the German Stellung) and was used in this sense in particular of the positions filled by holders of priestly offices . . . in Acts 1 52 we read of the τόπος topos (= office) "of deaconship and apostleship" . . . The Romans could hardly "take away" αίρειν the Temple from where it stood, but they could take away the rights of individual members of the Sanhedrin to sit in an assembly which was authorized to legislate, administer, and judge in matters of local or internal interest.[48]

It would seem the greedy and malicious Annas had a covert motive in bringing an accusation against Jesus that would ensure his execution. Jesus was not only interfering with his *personal* economic welfare but was turning the populace away from the more favorable scribal interpretations of the law, from the trade monopoly, and from the interests of the priestly cult in general. This logical conclusion seems to be verified in that the Sanhedrin during the time of Jesus is consistently identified as an institution corrupted by Annas, his family, and his wealthy friends and associates. But there is even more. This priestly oligarchy consisting of Babylonian-Alexandrian Jews were deeply influenced by their Hellenistic culture. They had, after all, been imported from Babylon and Egypt by Herod the Great!

> To understand how the Sadducees became more of a party in the political sense, we need to recall that already in the Persian, but especially in the Hellenistic period, the priestly upper classes were in charge of political affairs. The high-priest served as head of state, and he together with other leading priests directed the *Gerousia*, the high council which eventually became the *Synedrion* (Sanhedrin). In time, political interests so profoundly affected their lives that such interests often took precedence over those of religion. This tendency became especially pronounced in the Hellenistic period, then worldly, political success largely depended on one's attitude toward the Hellenistic rulers and culture. Thus, even the leading priests of Jerusalem, as we have seen, had made such far-reaching concessions to the pagan

---

48. Winter, *On the Trial*, pp. 39–40.

culture, and had so alienated themselves from the pious masses, that they provoked the Maccabean uprising and the Pharisaic revolution.[49]

THE "HOUSE" OF THE HIGH PRIEST

The location of the *two* houses of the "high priests" where the accusation and trial procedures took place might seem trivial to those accepting traditional views of such events; however, it will become increasingly important as our narrative continues. The house of the high priest is traditionally believed to be within the present southwestern quadrant of the "western" Upper City of Jerusalem, but this is quite a distance from both the Garden of Gethsemane and the accusation site. Like other Christian traditions this, too, is misleading. As we shall learn, the so-called "house" of the high priest was not his home but his "private residence" during Passover. This was not the first "house" where Jesus was taken. He was first led to Bethphage to the "district house" where the high priest Annas was situated for the initial accusation. An investigation into the historical records will at once prove our case.

First of all, the high priest (Caiaphas) would have taken up residence (as was required of him) in a chamber (the Parwah Chamber, also known as the "Stone House") within the Temple precincts (often referred to simply as the Temple) seven days prior to the Passover and other festival days.

> Seven days before the Day of Atonement [and Passover] the high-priest left his own house [his residence] in Jerusalem, and took up his abode in his chambers [called the Stone House] in the Temple [precincts].[50]

The "Stone House" is more specifically defined as the "councillors' chamber" in the Mishnah.

> Seven days before the Day of Atonement they set apart the high priest from his house [residence] to the councillors' chamber [Stone House].[51]

This Stone House was not the same as the Lishkat Hagazit (Chamber of Hewn Stone) which was located southeasterly of the Holy House and where the Great Sanhedrin (religious Sanhedrin) met. This was, instead, the location of the office of the High Priest, who was required to remain there for seven full days to avoid being contaminated and in study.

> Those in the south: the office made of wood, the office for the Exile, the office made of *hewn stone*. The office made of wood—said R. Eliezer b. Jacob, "I forgot what purpose it served"—Abba Saul says, *"It is the office of the high priest, and it was behind the other two* [A] [that is, behind the offices of Exile and Hewn Stone], and the roof of *all three of them was on the same level."* The office for the exile: there was a permanent cistern, and a wheel was placed on it, and from there did they draw water for the *whole courtyard*. The office made of *hewn stone*:

---

49. Zeitlin, *Jesus and the Judaism*, p. 22.
50. Edersheim, *The Temple*, p. 307.
51. *m. Yom.* 1:1a.

> there the Great Sanhedrin [seventy-one member religious Sanhedrin] of Israel was in session, and it judged the priesthood.[52]

As a matter of fact, the seat of the Sanhedrin was moved to the Bazaar's of Hanan on the Mount of Olives about the time of Jesus' execution. This area will be discussed in-depth in "Beth Pagi, the Place of the Crux".

> John's statement (2:20) is supported by Talmudic references (Sanhedrin 41:2, Aboda-Zara 8:2) which state that the seat of the Sanhedrin was transferred from the Lishkat Hagazit, "chamber of hewn stone" . . . to the place called the Hanuyot in the temple precincts . . . forty years before the destruction of the Lishkat Hagazit, i.e., about A.D. 30. This is very probably the time when the monumental Hanuyot colonnade was completed.[53]

But by the time Jesus was brought to trial, this Hall of Hewn Stone had been abandoned! The Sanhedrin had removed from that site in 30 CE to the Mount of Olives where the Bazaars of Annas were situated.

> A piece of stone fragment found in front of these gates was identified as belonging to another piece found over one hundred years ago near the Triple Gate. The two pieces preserve part of an inscription that includes the word "elders" in Hebrew. This may refer to the elders of the Sanhedrin who met, among other places, "at the entrance to the temple mount" (*Sanhedrin* 11. 2), probably at a place near the Triple Gate.[54]

But, again, the Hall of Hewn Stone was the meeting place of the *religious* Sanhedrin who were not qualified to judge criminal cases. It was *not* the seat of the *criminal beth din*. The criminal court had, at that time, sat at the "*entrance* to the Temple mount" in Beth Pagi near a public Plaza where the Bazaars of Annas were also located. This *beth din* met at Bethphage where accusations were made, sentences were usually formally pronounced,[55] and where accused individuals were flogged. The latter is the site of Jesus' triumphal entrance into Jerusalem.

The reason for the high priest having to reside in a "private" administrative residence was due to a Levitical purification requirement. He would not have been allowed to trek back and forth to his usual residence believed to have been in the Western part of the City of Jerusalem during that time. He and the vestments were to undergo an extensive seven-day purification ritual during the three major festivals and on the Day of Atonement. At the time the vestments of the high priest were kept in the custody of the Romans in the Fortress of Antonia.

> But Vitellius came into Judea, and went up to Jerusalem; it was at the time of that festival which is called the Passover. Vitellius was there magnificently received, and released the inhabitants of Jerusalem from all the taxes upon the fruits that

---

52. *m. Mid.* 5:4 a–g.
53. Mazar, *Mountain*, p. 112.
54. Mare, *Archaeology*, p. 155.
55. In the case of Jesus this was not possible. It was mandatory that sentence be pronounced in the "Stone House" due to the fact that the high priest was unable to leave the Temple office during that seven-day purification period.

The Night of Watching

> were bought and sold, and *gave them leave to have the care of the high-priest's vestments, with all their ornaments, and to have them under the custody of the priests in the temple; which power they used to have formerly, although at this time they were laid up in the tower of Antonia, the citadel so called.* [Note by translator William Whiston: *This mention of the high-priest's sacred garments received seven days before a festival, and purified in those days against a festival, as having been polluted by being in the custody of heathens,* in Josephus, agrees with the traditions of the Talmudists, as Reland here observes. *Nor is there any question but the three feasts here mentioned, were the Passover, Pentecost, and Feast of Tabernacles; and the Fast,* so called by way of distinction (as Acts xxvii, 9), *was the great day of* expiation [Day of Atonement].[56]

> *It was here [at Antonia] that the high priests' vestments were kept* [*ib.* xviii.4, § 3], if the tower "built" by the high priest Hyrcanus is to be identified with Antonia, as is done by Josephus.[57]

The reason for the secreting of the priestly garments seems to be connected with the fact that Herod the Great, at an early date, began the practice of "sealing" these vestments in order to prevent the influential priestly families from gaining *too much* control within the political and religious arenas. The purification ceremonies of these vestments were known to have taken seven full days to complete.

Further, the high priest was required to spend time in the Temple residence for seven days in prayer, meditation, and study of the duties he would be required to perform on the festival day, itself.

> Above some of these chambers were other apartments, such as those in which the high-priest spent the week before the Day of Atonement in study and meditation.[58]

Therefore, it would have been impossible for the high priest to have been resident in his own home in Jerusalem because of the purification requirements. Jesus was taken, instead, to the Temple office of the high priest, the Stone House. It was situated near the "Wing" of the Temple and near the Gabbatha, or "The Pavement" of Raised Stone surrounding the Hall of Moqed (Hearth) and the Antonia, whose "smooth pieces of stone" formed a court. This Wing *was* in the "Outer Court" or ecclesiastical district (*hieron*). Sylvester Saller and Emmanuel Testa excavated the region of Beth Pagi. It is near the *Gulgoleth* (or "ridge", "skull", or "crux") of the Mount of Olives.

> According to the Talmud *Bethphage consisted of some buildings* and the space of ground extending from the wall of Jerusalem about a mile (or half-way) *toward the town of Bethany (now el 'Azariyeh)* (CBN, p. 1355).

> This is known also from Talmudic references, where it is given as the Sabbath distance limit (Neubauer, "G. T.", p. 147) . . . Yet it is referred to as surrounded by a wall (Pes. 63b, 91a; Men. 78b), which description does not exactly correspond

---

56. Josephus, *Ant.*, XVIII 4.3.
57. "Jerusalem", J.E., p. 123.
58. Edersheim, *The Temple*, p. 52.

A Book of Evidence

to any known locality in the immediate neighborhood of Jerusalem. The exact location, however, has not been determined.[59]

The reason it has not been located is because the Holy walled region of Beth Pagi (which included the twin villages of Bethphage and Bethany on the Mount of Olives) was utterly destroyed. It is to be noted that Luke, a Hellenist proselyte, used the only Greek word he believed to be the equivalent of the "private Temple residence" (house) of the High Priest. He used the word *oikos*. Jesus had used the feminine of that root, *oikodome*, to refer to these "buildings" of the Temple. The other gospel narrators, who were Jewish, used an entirely different Greek word, *aule* (translated as palace), which, as we shall soon learn, is also translated "hall" and referred to the Place of Trumpeting at the Pinnacle of the Temple.

The village of Bethphage played a large role in ecclesiastical affairs during the early first century. It is within the ecclesiastical district of the Mount of Olives near the southern summit (the unnamed third mountain in the Olivet chain) that we find the *Beth HaDeshen* [Place of Fat Ashes] where the Red Heifer and Atonement Goat were burned. The Septuagint designates it "The Place (or Plaza) of the Rosh (Golgotha)". Sometimes, it is referred to as Asahel and Asael (the place of the appointment of YHWH), the Hebrew *asah* meaning to govern, execute, sacrifice, or appoint; that is, the place of YHWH's government on earth. Haim Cohn, Justice of the Supreme Court in Israel, gives us further information.

> The Gospel translations, which render it as "the temple," are inaccurate: *The locality mentioned in the gospels is the mount of the temple* [the Mount of Olives is often called the "Mount of the House" in Jewish writings], *an area which comprised . . . administrative buildings, stores, stables, and bazaars.* The area outside the temple on the Mount was accessible to everybody, including the impure and unwashed: there was no restriction of movement in it, or any limitation, restriction, or supervision of trading. It is true that, for their business, all the traders speculated on the needs of temple visitors: moneychangers converted the coins brought by the pilgrims from their districts into the shekel (or half-shekel), the only currency circulating as the prescribed temple gift (Exod. 21:13-16), *and three weeks before the festivals, when the great pilgrimages to the temple started, the moneychangers had already to be at their counters. There is an ancient report that on the mount there stood two large cypresses: under one were four booths for the sale of pure sacrificial animals, under the other so many dovecotes that, from the birds bred in them, not only all temple requirements but the markets all over Israel could be supplied.*[60]

As a matter of fact, the Mount referred to as harboring the four Temple booths and two ancient cypresses is not at all the Temple Mount but is the "Mountain of the House", the southern hill of the Mount of Olives. It was often termed the "Mountain of the House" in the earliest Midrash and Talmud. The later rabbis called it "the *Mount of the House*", and it was here the markets (*Chanuyoth beney Chanan*) were located (*b. Hag.* 78a). The *Chel* (or Porch) portion of the Eastern Cloisters, where Jesus had driven out moneychangers, was actually a rampart, or bridge built "arches upon arches", over which

---

59. "Bethphage", J.E., p. 124.
60. Cohn, *Trial and Death*, pp. 55–56; *y. Ta'an.* IV 5.

the Red Heifer was led to be sacrificed on the Mount of Olives "outside the gate". Adin Steinsaltz, translator of one edition of the Talmud, not only speaks of this "bridge", he states that the Mount of Olives is part of the ecclesiastical district of the Temple.

> In the days of the Temple, the carcass of the heifer was burned on the Mount of Olives opposite the Temple, *and this is one of the reasons why this spot is considered sacred; a special bridge* [the "street", porch, Colonnade called the "Descent of the Mount of Olives" and also called the Chel] *was constructed between the temple mount and the Mount of Olives* lest there be any suspicion of pollution en route.[61]

The Mishnah, that body of laws codified during the second century, describes it as well.

> And they *would make a causeway from [south of] the Temple mount to the Mount of Olives*, arches upon arches, an arch directly above each pair, because of the grave in the depths [Valley of Kidron], on which the priest who burns the cow, and the cow, and all those that assist it go forth to the Mount of Olives.[62]

We are specifically told in the *mishnayot* that there was also a house for immersion there.

> And the elders would precede [them] on foot to the Mount of Olives. *And a house for immersion [bet hamikvaot] was there.*[63]

This immersion tank is likely at the location of the large deep cistern located under the ancient Eleona Church. The Plaza of Gulgoleth (or "ridge") was really a complex of arched and colonnaded "stalls", each chamber called by the name of the function it served. These buildings or "houses" were used for any number of administrative purposes.

Situated in or near that location; for example, a school house (more properly, "house of interpretation" called *Beth HaMidrash*); a lunar signal station (*Beth Zedek*); the house of the pit of ashes for purification ceremonies and the Miphkad altar (*Beth HaDeshen/Beth HaMiphkad*); a merchant trading station in which accounts were settled (*Beth HaKana*); the courthouse (*Beth Din*); and a house of census or numbering (*Beth HaSephar*) among others. It was divided into three portions, two holy and one profane. It might be that this area was the real Court of the Gentiles. Most of the "buildings" of the Temple were located across the Kidron Valley on the Mount of Olives opposite the hill of Ophel and situated in such a manner that the high priest, during the Red Heifer ritual, might gaze over the low eastern wall to view the Sanctuary. Some of these buildings, however, were located in the priestly village of Bethphage, all a part of *Beth Pagi*, which was surrounded by its *own* wall.

> It would appear that Bethphage (Tos. Pes. viii.) was near, yet outside, Jerusalem (בית פגי Sotah 45a). Yet it is referred to as surrounded by a wall (Pes. 63b, 91a; Men. 78b).[64]

---

61. Steinsaltz and Galai, *Essential Talmud*, p. 196.
62. *m. Par.* 3:6a–c.
63. *m. Par.* 3:7 f–g.
64. "Bethphage", J.E., p. 124.

> The first spatial distinction is between the camp and outside the camp, which serve as one set of locations for the pure and the impure. The next spatial distinction is between the camp and the sanctuary, or the Tent of Assembly, in its center, which serves as another and more differentiated set of locations for the pure and impure respectively. At the center is the Tent of the seat of the cult.[65]

There were "houses of immersion" situated at both the "Stone House" and near the Plaza of Gulgoleth, in which the priest was immersed prior to the rites of holy events. The "house of immersion" situated near the *Beth HaDeshen* [Place of Fat Ashes] was beside the Miphkad Altar. As such it was called the "place (plaza) of appointment" [*Beth HaMiphkad*].

> And the elders of Israel would precede [them] on foot to the *Mount of Olives. And a house for immersion was there*. And they would render the priest who burns the cow unclean, because of the Sadducees, so that they should not say, "It is done by one on whom the sun has set." They placed their hands on him, and they say to him, "My lord, High Priest, immerse one time".[66]

The modern Hebrew term for "district" is, in fact, *galeel* (*galal*) from which *gulgoleth* (the *top* of the head, or ridge of the cranium) is derived. In ancient times, it was also termed *medinah* (jurisdiction), a word derived from *din* meaning "to judge" and from which the area's name finds its root. So it was at Beth Pagi (or the "district house") that the judicial Beth Din met for "first" adjudication. The illusive Miphkad Gate was the Eastern Gate Shushan, the entrance of which led to the altar of the Red Heifer and probably situated on the Mount of Olives. This gate led to the Plaza (or gathering place of pilgrims) on the Mount of Olives near the Miphkad Altar, "outside the camp". "Outside the camp" was always known to have been toward the east.

The reason for placement of the "unclean" in the east was that the wind originated in the west and blew eastward. Since "leprosy" was believed to have been contagious, unclean persons had to reside "outside the camp" on the eastern side. It will be remembered that Miriam, the sister of Moses, when struck with leprosy, was forced to stay outside the camp until she had been pronounced "clean". Ezekiel, in describing the Millennial Temple, refers to this Plaza near the southern summit of Olivet as the "appointed place of the house (*Beth haMiphkad*), *outside* the sanctuary (*naos, kodesh*)" (Ezek. 43:21]) i.e., near the Plaza of the Temple where the Red Heifer and Atonement Goat were to be slain. The "appointed place", in fact, is translated as the *Beth Miphkad* and refers to the Miphkad Altar, which during the first century was situated at the Plaza of Gulgoleth, and was also where these special sinbearer sacrifices were "wholly burnt". Ezekiel's vision was certainly influenced by his remembrances of Solomon's Temple as it stood prior to its destruction by Nebuchadnezzar; i.e., before the Babylonian Captivity. The altar Miphkad referred to as a "sin altar" is patterned after the "sin that lieth at the door" that God had provided for Cain to purify himself from the sin of death (Gen. 4:7).

Another point must be made concerning the "house" of the high priest: the *nasi* (Caiaphas, the High Priest) resided in the Parwah ("Stone House"), while his substitute,

---

65. Wieseltier, "Congregation", *Commentary on Leviticus*, p. 35.
66. *m. Par.* 3.7 f–h; 3.8a.

the *ab bet din* (Annas) resided at the *village* of Bethphage near the *hedra* (the third *beth din*), the "room (or cave) formed by an open or columned recess often semicircular in shape and furnished with seats for 'conversation'". Both "houses" were lunar-shaped. Since the Hanan family owned property and the bazaars where items for purification were sold on the Mount of Olives, it is likely this location is where the Beth Din met.

> The [judicial] Sanhedrin was [arranged] *in the shape of a half of a round threshingfloor* [semicircular], so that the judges should see one another.[67]

Sylvester Saller excavated one such cave in Bethphage that fits the description. The interior is semicircular in nature and appears to have been used in some administrative function. In it were found numerous first century coins and other administrative artifacts.[68]

THE BELOVED DISCIPLE

Since the Beloved Disciple becomes an active participant in the trial of Jesus, it once again, becomes necessary to digress from our narrative. It will be pointed out that the Gospel of John was written from the perspective of an eyewitness, one who apparently was "kin" to the high priest Caiaphas. A plethora of recent evidence has been uncovered concluding that John might have been the first canonical gospel written and not the fourth. If this is so, then we have a better perspective of the Jewish trial of Jesus. Certainly, kinship to Caiaphas would indicate the Beloved Disciple was one of the priestly caste himself. Whether he might have any influence on the judges is another matter, and though he might have been able to enter the judgment hall he might not have been influential enough to speak on behalf of Jesus or persuade others in their opinions of him. He might also have been kin to Jesus, but as a kinsman or because of his association with him, he would have been excluded from the process.

> There are some scholars now who would place the composition of Mark's Gospel as early as 55 CE, and there are those who believe *that the Fourth Gospel might have been composed in 30-50 CE*, passing through a second revision by 65 CE. The New Testament could well be closer in time to Jesus than was once supposed.[69]

Evan Powell, for example, has explored this in his book *The Unfinished Gospel*. The conclusion of Mr. Powell's research concerning the gospel, itself, appears to be quite sound. His premise is that the Gospel of John was written during the early 50s CE. His claim, that it is supported by the structure and similarity of the early writings of the apostle Paul (i.e., Gal., 1 Cor. and 1 Thess., 50s CE) has much to commend it. Mr. Powell identifies a number of structural arguments concerning these similarities: 1) that both apostles focus on the spiritual rather than historical aspect of Jesus; 2) that neither are aware of any institutionalized "church" structure substantiated in other latter first century documents; 3) that the gospel is totally devoid of technical "church" vocabulary

---

67. *m. Sanh.* 4.3 a–c.
68. Saller and Testa, *Archaeological Setting*, pp. 10–14.
69. Wilson, *Jesus, A Life*, p. 91.

which was only introduced in the 90s CE; 4) that Mark, Luke, and Matthew appear to have expanded the historical details rendered in John; and 5) that the author of the Gospel of John is the only one who claims to have been an eyewitness to the actual events.[70]

We must add to these points the Jewish nature of the gospel and that the use of the Light/Dark motif supports an early composition since it is similar to the structure of the Essenes' writings found at Qumran which are dated a hundred years BCE. One argument put forth for an early dating is that many of the geographical sites mentioned in the gospel and previously believed to have been fictitious, have been discovered. One site often mentioned by the author of the gospel is the Sea of Tiberius. It would have been within contemporary usage to refer to the Sea of Galilee by that name only during the 30s CE since Herod had just completed building the new city of Tiberius. John, the apostle, could not have been the Beloved Disciple because there is evidence that he had shown his pettiness by vying for the first place in the Kingdom, and this was, instead, inherited by the Beloved Disciple as we shall soon learn. The gospels make note that *all* the disciples fled and hid themselves, but the Beloved Disciple (not one of the twelve) stood at the foot of the tree, unafraid of the authorities. The author also appears to have been a priest, having knowledge of priestly duties and legalities, as well as a deep understanding of the Jewish concept of spiritual unity with YHWH. As confirmation of this point, it will be remembered that this disciple was "known to the high-priest" and allowed within the chamber, while Peter was to remain *outside* in the courtyard. The plain fact is no layman was allowed to enter into the Beth Din, especially during feast days when there was a danger of defilement, while any *priest* could come and go as he so chose. There is, however, a minor exception to this rule, and this exception will be discussed a little later. The Greek word translated as "known", in fact, means "intimate with", and as we shall attempt to establish, the author might well have been "intimate" with the high priest and his family.

There is ample supporting data to conclude that the author of John was, in fact, Lazarus (Eleazar), whom Jesus had raised from the dead. Lazarus is the Latin rendering of the name Eleazar, and it is that name we shall use for the rest of our narrative. Eleazar is a name found *only* in priestly lineages. That he was also the "rich young ruler" is evident in that we note the fact that Jesus "loved him".

> And when he was gone forth into the way, there came one running, and kneeled to him, and asked him, Good Master, what shall I do that I may inherit eternal life . . . Master, all these have I observed from my youth. Then *Jesus beholding him loved him*. One thing thou lackest: go thy way, sell whatsoever thou hast, and give to the poor, and thou shalt have treasure in heaven . . . and follow me. And he was sad at that saying, and went away grieved: for he had great possessions (Mark 10:17–22).

Only here and in the Gospel of John is there any statement made to the effect that Jesus "loved" any particular individual. In John, however, we note the evidence that Jesus loved him in that "Jesus wept". We are told specifically over and again that Jesus "loved" Eleazar.

---

70. Powell, *The Unfinished Gospel*, pp. 157–198.

The Night of Watching

> Therefore his sisters sent unto him, saying, Lord [Master], behold, *he whom thou lovest is sick* (John 11:3).
>
> Now *Jesus loved* Martha and her sister and *Lazarus* [Eleazar] (John 11:5).
>
> *Lazarus* [Eleazar], *our dear friend* sleepeth (John 11:11).
>
> *Jesus wept.* Then said the Jews, *Behold how he loved him!* (John 11:35).
>
> There they made him a supper; and Martha served, but *Lazarus* [Eleazar] *was one of them that sat at the table with him* (John 12:2).

Eleazar was also the "naked young man" of Mark's narration. He had been wearing a white linen garment [a *kittel*, the *priestly* garment] that was torn from his body as he sought to flee. We have it from Clement (Paul's friend and a disciple of Peter) in a letter to one Theodore, that there had been more testimony attached to Mark than was presently available. Within this so-called secret gospel was a discussion of the young man Eleazar. After Jesus raised him from the tomb, Eleazar went to the Garden of Gethsemane clothed in a fine white linen garment (the priestly *kittel*) over his naked body for rites of "initiation", an initiation not unsimilar to priestly ordination in the Temple. The earliest Nazaraeans actually performed the ritual of immersion ("baptism") naked. Clement's testimony also states that Eleazar was a *"wealthy" young man.* A special point might be raised here as to the expense (about $10,000 at today's cost) of the "pure nard" that Mary used in anointing Jesus. It might be expected that the ordinary Jewish family could not have afforded such expensive anointing oil. That would not pose a problem for an individual belonging to an aristocratic priestly family involved in the incense trade. Note what Clement has to say in the epistle to Theodore concerning the ending of Mark:

> But when Peter died a martyr, Mark came over to Alexandria, bringing both his own notes and those of Peter, from which he transferred to his former book the things suitable to whatever makes progress toward knowledge. *Thus he composed a more spiritual gospel for the use of those who were being perfected . . .* nor did he write down the hierophantic teaching of the Lord, but to the stories already written he added yet others . . . To you, therefore, I shall not hesitate to answer the questions you have asked, refuting the falsifications by the very words of the Gospel. For example after "And they were in the road going up to Jerusalem," and what follows, until "After three days he shall arise," *The secret gospel brings the following material word for word*: "And they came into Bethany. And *a certain woman whose brother had died was there.* And, coming, she prostrated herself before Jesus and says to him, 'Son of David, have mercy on me.' But the disciples rebuked her. And *Jesus, being angered, went off with her into the garden where the tomb was, and straightway a great cry was heard from the tomb.* And going near Jesus rolled away the stone from the door of the tomb. And straightway, *going in where the youth was, he stretched forth his hand and raised him, seizing his hand. But the youth, looking upon him, loved him and began to beseech him that he might be with him.* And going out of the tomb they came into the house of *the youth, for he was rich . . .* Jesus told him what to do and in the evening *the youth comes to him, wearing a linen cloth [i.e., a kittle] over his naked body . . .* And after the words, "And he comes into Jericho," the secret Gospel adds only, "And the

sister of *the youth whom Jesus loved* and his mother and Salome were there, and Jesus did not receive them".[71]

Since Eleazar and the "rich young ruler" appear to be the same man, we must recommend that he, as a member of the aristocratic ruling class, was also a member of the Sanhedrin. The same designation ("ruler") is used to describe Nicodemus and others who held that official capacity. The use of the term "Jews" in the Gospel of John has sometimes been said to refer to the ruling class, i.e., the members of the Sanhedrin. The inference is that the "Jews" in attendance with Mary and Martha were the associates of Eleazar within the exclusive tribunal body of the Sanhedrin. It would logically follow that Jesus might have been angered by them (as he usually was).

> When Jesus, therefore, saw her weeping, and the Jews also weeping with her, he groaned in the spirit, and was troubled, And said, Where have ye laid him? (John 11:33; see also John 11:37–38).

It is in the writings of Josephus that we find these same men described as the "leading men of the nation". Since a number of these were known to have informed the high priests and Pharisees in Jerusalem of Jesus' whereabouts, it might logically be assumed they were members of that same aristocratic body. To see anything anti-Semitic within the gospel's use of "Jews" is not truly feasible. Josephus, a Jew himself, used the same term to describe them.

> Then many *of the Jews [rulers] who came to Mary* and had seen the things which Jesus did, believed on him; *but some of them went their ways to the Pharisees*, and told them what things Jesus had done. Then gathered the chief priests and the Pharisees a council . . . (John 11:45–47).

A number of points then are to be made in behalf of "Lazarus" as the author of John:

1. His Hebrew name was Eleazar, and that name designates him as a member of the priesthood;
2. he is the only person in all New Covenant writings that is specifically mentioned as being "loved" by Jesus;
3. he is mentioned by name only in the Gospel of John;
4. as a "ruler", he might enter into the *beth din*, while Peter, a layman, was required to remain "outside";
5. he is known to the high priest;
6. as a priest fearing Levitical defilement he races ahead of Peter to the tomb of Jesus but *does not enter*, while Peter has no sensibilities about purification;
7. he would have had an especial closeness to Jesus after his own resurrection from the dead;
8. the rumor in John 21 "that this disciple would not die" is logical if one has already been once raised from the grave.

---

71. Barnstone, *Other Bible*, p. 341–342.

The Night of Watching

Since Eleazar would not die again there would also be curiosity about "this one". It might also be noticed that the Beloved Disciple, in the last chapter (21) *had already named the "sons of Zebedee"* as being present on the shores of Galilee, with Peter and "two other disciples." In keeping with the structure of his writing, it becomes illogical that "John", who had consistently called himself the "Disciple Whom Jesus Loved" throughout the gospel, would now change that designation of himself to one of the "two sons of Zebedee". Likewise, this Eleazar lived in "Beth Hini", an area believed to have been the residential district for the Tannaim.

Furthermore, we are told that all the "twelve" deserted Jesus at the time of the arrest and were scattered (Matt. 26:56). This one, then, who stood *without fear* at the foot of the tree (John 19:26–27) could not have been one of "the twelve" but someone close, someone to whom Jesus would entrust his mother's welfare and become the beneficiary of his earthly estate and responsibilities. Only a kinsman would have been allowed to stand near the condemned as "family" for last words. Mary's family is said to have included Elizabeth, the mother of John the Immerser, who was "a daughter of Aaron" (Luke 1:5), that is, the priestly tribe. Joseph, too, was also of a priestly lineage, referred to as a "scribe". For this reason, it seems reasonable to suggest that this Eleazar and Jesus were of some kinship. This would make Eleazar a near cousin to Jesus and would explain why he often stayed in Bethany at Eleazar's home. This, too, is logical since the name Bethany might have been derived from *Beth Tanna*, where members of the priestly caste (Tannaim) lived. There is evidence that Eleazar, in fact, took Mary into his own home in Bethany near Jerusalem since she is also found in company with the apostles on the day of ascension (Acts 1:14). It might be worthwhile at this point to digress just a moment to the events of Pentecost some ten days after the ascension. When Pentecost had "fully" come (meaning midnight), they were gathered in one place.

> It is customary *to delay the evening service until dark to make sure that the Kiddush will be chanted after the stars have emerged.* Thus we fulfill the biblical command that *"seven complete weeks"* (Lev. 23:15) elapse from the sixteenth of Nisan [Firstfruits]. The practice of staying awake through the first night of Shavuot was first mentioned in the Zohar (Lev. 98; published in the 13th cent.). The Zohar attributed this custom to *chasidei kadmai* ("early zealots").[72]

The words in the KJV "they were all with one accord *in one place*" are redundant. When translated properly, it should read "they were all with one accord *in the Spirit!*" The "house" in which they gathered was not the upper room (a third story room where they had chosen the replacement for Judas, which occurs at a different time and has been run together by Christian tradition). It was one that was open to the public where other festive pilgrims from the Diaspora had also gathered for Pentecost. This "house" was, in fact, the open Plaza of Gulgoleth where *all* Jewish pilgrims awaited the opening of the Temple doors at midnight. These pilgrims had heard their own languages spoken by these Galileans gathered *in the plaza* on the Mount of Olives! It was here Peter stood up (probably in the very spot where Jesus was executed and from where he also ascended) and made his oration concerning final judgment and the execution of Jesus (Acts 2). The

---

72. Bloch, *Biblical*, pp. 248–249.

A Book of Evidence

Holy Spirit had descended upon them in the Plaza where Jesus had been executed as a *witness*. Because of this, some 3000 individuals believed and repented. This spot is exactly a Sabbath's Day's journey from Jerusalem. One point that deserves special mention is that the apostle John lived in Galilee and was the son of Salome and Zebedee. He was a simple fisherman, with little or no education in the law, and from all indication, John returned to that region after the resurrection of Jesus. We have this from Justin Martyr writing in about 150 CE.

> For from Jerusalem there went out into the world, men, twelve in number, and these *illiterate, of no ability in speaking*.[73]

It is also confirmed in the book of Acts.

> Now when they saw the boldness of Peter and John, and perceived *that they were unlearned and ignorant men*, they marvelled; and they took knowledge of them, that they had been with (Acts 4:13).

On the other hand, the author of John has a clear, intelligent grasp of the Hebrew spiritual relationship with YHWH that only one of the Jewish priesthood might have had. The writing does not fit the character of John, whose intellect and selfishness we might determine by his desire to be "first" in the Kingdom. It might be further noted that it is the author of John who *mentions* the family of Eleazar (Mary and Martha) almost exclusively. Mary of Bethany is mentioned only twice in the Gospel of Luke and in no other. A special point is made in John that Eleazar *reclined* with Jesus, and that the Disciple Whom Jesus Loved later reclined with Jesus and laid in his bosom at Passover. The tradition of "lying in the bosom" is an idiom for a testamentary procedure by which an heir is appointed. Evan Powell quotes W. H. Brownlee in giving an example, Jacob, while reclining on his deathbed, confers his final blessing on his grandson. In other words, this traditional Hebrew procedure of designating an heir and known as "lying in the bosom" is prerequisite for conferring on one the blessings and substance of the testator. It would also include the responsibilities and duties that the decedent would leave behind; i.e., accepting the duty of the firstborn in caring for a widowed mother. The author might well be identified as Yohanan Eleazar (Lazarus), the younger John (or "youth") spoken of by Polycrates [189-199 CE] and quoted by Eusebius.

> Moreover, *John, that rested on the bosom of our Lord, who was a priest that bore the sacerdotal plate [πεταλον petalon] [i.e., he was a priest!], both a martyr and teacher.*[74]

This younger Yohanan (John, the "presbyter") is identified as the disciple who rested on the bosom of Jesus during the Passover! The fact that he wore both the linen garment (*kittel*) and the plate of the mitre certainly identifies him as a member of the priesthood. It is likely that Yohanan Eleazar, who lived at Bethany was a member of the Boethus family, a son of Simon Cantheras Boethus (probably the "Leper"). Simon Cantheras was a son of Simon Boethus and his alleged wife Mary Caiaphas, a sister

---

73. Bush, *Classic Readings*, p. 23.
74. Eusebius, *Eccl. Hist.*, xxiv, p. 208.

to none other than Joseph Caiaphas, the judge at the trial of Jesus. For this reason he would certainly have been "intimate" with the high priest. Furthermore, the Talmudic notation that Jesus was close to the "government" or "royalty" might also be reflected in this relationship. If Eleazar was, in fact, a priest, this would have enabled him to use the highly technical priestly symbolism in the book of Revelation, which only a priest having served in the Temple might have used. Furthermore, the John of Revelation never *claimed* to be one of the twelve disciples. This one stood beneath the tree while they all scattered, but in Revelation calls himself instead a "prophet" ("Blessed is he that readeth, and they that hear the words of this *prophecy*") and his writing bears remarkable similarity to the announcements of the Old Covenant prophets (i.e., "Thus saith YHWH"). Eusebius records fragments of *An Exegesis of the Dominical Logia*, compiled by Papias in five volumes in which Papias states:

> But if I met with any one who had been a follower of the elders any where, I made it a point to inquire what were the declarations of the elders. What was said by Andrew, Peter or Philip. What by Thomas, James, *John [the disciple]*, Matthew, or any other of the disciples of our Lord. What was said by Aristion, and *the presbyter John [the priest]*, disciples of the Lord.[75]

The "presbyter" John was the younger of the two. Both lived in Ephesus, and both died and were buried there. There is some indication that Mary, the mother of Jesus, lived in that area with John. This might well be the Beloved Disciple, Yohanan Eleazar, the priest, Lazarus, who had become the beneficiary of Jesus' earthly estate, and whose responsibility it was to care for the mother of the Messiah. It was this John who said that Mark was the "interpreter" of Peter. He went on to note: "he wrote with great accuracy but not however, in the order in which it was spoken or done by our Lord, for he neither heard nor followed our Lord."[76] John probably made mention of this because he himself had just written a more accurate historical account, clarifying and expanding some points in his own gospel that Mark had overlooked, adding other events that Mark had not mentioned. The entire gospel, in fact, seems to clarify Mark's narrative. His own gospel is an accurate depiction of the entire three and one-half-year ministry of Jesus. Tertullian, in *De praescriptione haereticorum*, 36, states that John was *in insulam relegatus*, that is, he was sent to Patmos "for the word of YHWH and the testimony of Jesus" (Rev. 1:9). This would make him a member of the *honestiores*, the reputable upper class of Jewish society.[77]

> J.N. Sanders, who inferred from Tertullian's reference that John of Patmos belonged to the upper classes of Jewish society, argued further that if John's relgatio was imposed for his Christian activity—"for the word of God and the testimony of Jesus", as he says himself (Rev. 1:9)—it must have been before such activity became a capital offence, that is, before A.D. 64/65; and that *he may have been the "other disciple" of John 18:15f who was "known", and possibly related, to the high priest*; "John of Ephesus, the seer and exile of Patmos, *was a Sadducean*

---

75. Eusebius, xxxix, p. 125.
76. Eusebius, xxxix, p. 127.
77. Sanders, "St. John on Patmos", NTS 9, pp. 75–85.

aristocrat, a Jerusalem disciple of Jesus, and last survivor of the eye-witness of the incarnate logos, but not the son of Zebedee."[78]

In the Gospel of John, the ministry of Jesus appears to have continued for three and one-half years. Jesus began his ministry at the beginning of the Sabbatical year on the Day of Atonement, the last day of the Feast of Trumpets (the Jewish year 4000 from Ha Adam). He stood up to read Isaiah 61 at this time, which is the portion allotted for the Jubilee. At this point the shammash, a kind of sacristan of the synagogue, took from the wooden ark (*'aron*) the parchment scrolls of the [Torah] and the prophets, waiting for some member of the congregation to volunteer to read from them in Hebrew, in which they were written, and comment on them in Aramaic. In our times, the sacred texts are divided into fifty-two portions (parashot), one for each Saturday, so that the reading of the whole requires a year, but it appears that in the time of Jesus *there were one hundred seventy-five parashot, the completion of which required almost three and a half years.*[79]

His partial reading of Isaiah 61:1–3, which relates to the release of captives (the year of "the Lord's release") is among those typically read near the 1st of Tishri at the time of the new civil year, Rosh Hashanah, the Day of Atonement, and the Feast of Tabernacles. On that day, the "law" was to be read before all Israel in their hearing (Deut. 31:10-11). Jesus commented on the text by proclaiming that the Scripture was that day fulfilled in their hearing. He was referring to the fulfillment of the beginning of the Jubilee (50-year sabbatical) and Sabbatical year (the 7th year when the land was to lie fallow) more specifically than to his own messianic claim. It might also be that his reading was to prepare Israel for the messianic redemption in which they had placed their hopes. There were certainly reports that the Messiah, by calculations made within the Hebraic calendar, was, indeed, to appear in the land of Israel during the very years of Jesus' ministry (*b. RH* 11a). He had been immersed by John in August (the month of Elul) of that year. The *haftara* reading of the *Nitzavim* (the last of the seven *Haftarot* of Consolation, all taken from the book of *Isaiah*), occurs on the seventh Sabbath after Tisha B'Av. It coincides with the Sabbath that precedes Rosh Hashanah (or in the event that the Sabbath occurs on Rosh Hashanah, the last would be read that day). It is the reading of Isaiah 61:10 – 63:9. The Torah reading is from Deuteronomy 29:9 – 30:20. The reading is meant to be a reaffirmation of the Covenant with YHWH. Here, we find the themes of loyalty to YHWH, a reminder of refreshing and renewing the Covenant, repentance, blessings and cursings. All these would become important to Jesus in his attempt to "freshen" and "renew" the Covenant, which the later third century Christians so inaptly named the *"New" (kainos)* Covenant. The reading of the foregoing *haftarot* is designed to set the stage for the Days of Awe that follow, and the Day of Atonement, which Jesus was to provide by his substitutionary death. The Beloved Disciple gives us the chronology necessary to understand the symbolism and figurative language used by Jesus. It was this Beloved Disciple, Yohanan Eleazar, who was allowed into the priestly quarters. At some point, he returns to Peter *outside* and brings him into the chamber. For what purpose we shall shortly learn.

78. Bruce, *Peter*, pp. 148–149, n. 78.
79. Wilson, *Jesus, A Life*, p. 88.

THE PROCEEDINGS

When Jesus was brought to the first "house" of the high priest (Annas at Bethphage), an initial investigation was made by Annas as the *ab bet din*. Had the true charge been "blasphemy" in the strictest sense, utterance of the divine name, one might suspect that Annas would have questioned Jesus concerning *that* crime; rather, Annas questioned him regarding "his disciples" and "his teaching" (John 18:19). His interrogation would indicate the charge agreed with the crime of the enticer, or *mesith*, the crime of leading astray the nation by errant teachings that would turn the population away from the Temple Cult. After forming the accusation at the judicial *beth din* at Bethphage, Jesus would have been taken to the roof of the Parwah Chamber (the "Stone House") to the other high priest, Caiaphas. Here, many "false witnesses" were brought forward to testify as to these things. The witnesses were the "suborned men" who had been sent to espy the activities of Jesus during his three and a half-year ministry. While there is subtle mention in the New Covenant writings of their success, no witnesses could be found to agree in all circumstances. There were, however, two witnesses who were willing to testify in behalf of Jesus during this introductory investigative procedure: Peter and Eleazar, the Beloved Disciple. Eleazar, as a "ruler" and priest and having been "known by the high-priest", perhaps even a kinsman, had entered into the "house" with Jesus. When the point in the procedure came that required the necessity of witnesses, Eleazar went out to the "courtyard" to bring forth Peter.

> And Simon Peter followed Jesus, and so did another disciple: *that disciple was known unto* [intimate with] *the high priest, and went in with Jesus into the palace* ["house"] *of the high priest. But Peter stood at the door without.* Then went out that other disciple, which was known unto the high priest, and spake unto her that kept the door, and brought in Peter. (John 18:15–16).

Only as a witness could a layman have entered into the court of the high priest, especially during the week of purification prior to Passover, lest the priest become "defiled" by his presence. There were certain requirements that witnesses had to meet in order to attain entrance into the court area. It must have been first determined whether or not he might be *qualified* to give testimony. An entire section of the Mishnah is devoted to the qualifications of witnesses. Very specific questions were asked of these individuals including "In what septannate? In what year? In what month? On what day of the month? On what day of the week? At what time? In what place" . . . Do you know him? Did you warn him of the consequences of his deed".[80] Whether the testimony was for or against the accused, a rigorous examination was made for the agreement of witnesses. If Annas was as sly and crafty as history makes him out to be, he could have easily flustered the bumbling Peter. Some have suggested that as a kinsman Peter might have sought to testify for Jesus, but this could not have happened. More likely, he would not have been considered qualified to render testimony because he was a "friend", or one who might be considered a "groomsman" (a servant, disciple).

---

80. *m. Sanh.* 5:1a–c.

Furthermore, however much Eleazar might have wished to testify, he, too, would have been denied the opportunity.

> These are reckoned as kinsfolk: a brother, paternal or maternal uncle, brother-in-law, father's and mother's brother-in-law, step-son, father-in-law, wife's sister's husband—these together with their sons, their sons-in-law, and a man's step-son (but not the latter's children). R. Jose said: Such is the Mishnah of R. Akiba; but the first Mishnah included uncle, first-cousin, and *all eligible to be heirs*, and those who at the time were relatives; but relatives who had since become estranged were eligible (as judges or witnesses). R. Jehuda holds that if a man's daughter die and leave children, her husband is still reckoned as a relative. A friend or an enemy (is disqualified). Who is counted as a friend? *One's groomsman*.[81]

The charge leveled against Jesus regarding the "false prophecy" of the destruction of the Temple was, apparently, brought forward by the "suborned men" who had heard him say it. Jesus, who knew it was an offense to speak or act against the sanctity of the Temple and its precincts, had been prepared for their testimony. He knew the Sanhedrin was allowed to pronounce and execute the sentence of death for such offenses, and he did not intend to be tried for that crime. It was for this reason that Peter and the Beloved Disciple had entered into the high priest's court, not to act as witnesses but to refute the testimony of the "suborned men". Jesus, knowing he could not be made to admit nor deny the charge [as previously mentioned], made reference to the presence of the only other witnesses to what he had actually said.

> Why askest thou me? *Ask them which heard me, what I have said unto them* ... [as the law required](John 18:21).

Jesus was referring, of course, to two eyewitnesses who had been with him when he made the statement regarding the "Temple" and who would have been able to describe and explain the events of that day in detail. Peter and Yohanan Eleazar would have been two witnesses who could have given the most reliable testimony of all. Unfortunately, their testimony would not be heard. The testimony of Eleazar, as a ruler and priest of the Sanhedrin himself might have been given ultimate consideration (or at least it might have appeared so on the surface), but he would have been immediately disqualified, because he was Jesus' heir.

> If one say, "I have something to plead on behalf of the defendant," they listen to him; but if it be against the interests of the defendant, they silence him with a rebuke. A witness cannot plead either for or against the defendant; but R. Jose, the son of R. Jehuda, says that *he may plead for, but not against, the defendant*.[82]

Peter, however, was a Galilean whose testimony the high priest was certain to have found most "unreliable" and highly suspect. There were a number of reasons. First of all, it was in Galilee where the Zealots thrived, and there is some reason to suspect Peter, who was a native of Galilee, might have been involved with that sect.

---

81. Danby, *Tractate Sanhedrin*; M. Sanh. III.4–5; *Tosef. Sanh.* V.3.
82. Danby, *Sanhedrin*; *Tosef. Sanh.* IX.4.

The Zealots were also called 'Galileans'. Judas, the organizer of the freedom movement, bears, both in the book of Acts (5.37) and in Josephus, the sobriequet 'the Galilean'. The stubborn resistance in Galilee against Herod, and the insurrection after his death, show that *this province was early on a centre of revolutionary opposition to the foreign power and its clients*. It was quite natural, then, for rebels throughout the land to be called 'Galileans'.[83]

Secondly, since Caiaphas would have viewed Peter as an illiterate fisherman, he might have been considered an unreliable witness, although it must be stated here that in that priest's view anyone who did not know the "law" was thought to be "illiterate". He would have been labeled as a member of the *ammei ha aretz*, the uneducated people of the land. His testimony was sure to have been scorned by the highly educated Annas, who would have made it quite difficult and confusing for Peter to testify if, indeed, he were allowed to do so at all. There is evidence within the Mishnah that witnesses were often purposely confused in order to gain knowledge of the true events. Peter's intellect, as we know from New Covenant writings, was not "quick".

Furthermore, Peter would have been in great fear of the authorities. He had been frightened and slow to learn, and for this temptation Jesus was known to have upbraided him with the words "Get thee behind me, Satan". It was Peter, too, who at the Passover meal had motioned to the Beloved Disciple and asked who it was that would betray Jesus. Although Judas was the intended, Jesus was fully aware that Peter, through a lack of confidence, might also deny him. Whether Peter unintentionally denied him during the questioning or whether it was through his fear, or confusion, if, indeed, he was allowed to testify at all, his testimony apparently did not help Jesus. It was, therefore, nullified. Finally, Peter was a follower of Jesus, a "friend", "disciple", or "groomsman". His testimony would have been considered biased.

The charge of prophesying the destruction of the Temple, even though Jesus meant it metaphorically, was one that Annas had been legally allowed to consider. Erich H. Kiehl, a lawyer and author of *The Passion* has this to say:

> To speak against a temple was a very serious offense in the time of Jesus. To desecrate a temple in any way was regarded as sacrilege, a crime carrying the death sentence . . . [S]igns warning Gentiles not to enter the sacred area explicitly stated that doing so would subject the transgressor to execution. Jeremiah's experience clearly demonstrates that speaking against the temple was also considered a crime worthy of death.[84]

This was only a part of the accusation, but Annas was determined, however he could, to have Jesus tried and executed for despoiling the Temple precincts and interrupting and interfering with his personal financial welfare. Since no favorable *or* unfavorable testimony was forthcoming, Jesus was indicted for the trumped-up charge of "leading the nation astray". Such a charge would include the other crimes of which he was accused as well, and it would accomplish the purpose of Annas. Jesus had been bound and sent to Caiaphas who was residing in his own chamber of the Parwah. Annas

---

83. Zeitlin, *Jesus and the Judaism*, pp. 30–31.
84. Kiehl, *The Passion*, p. 87.

would have joined the party. Gathered with him would have been the priestly entourage necessary for fulfillment of the priestly Passover preparations, many members of the House of Hanan. There would be a quorum present to act as a judicial Sanhedrin that morning. At the Parwah Jesus would be tried and convicted for bringing down upon the heads of the entire nation of Israel the wrath of YHWH.

3

The Jewish Trial

THERE IS AN ONGOING debate as to whether or not Jesus' appearance before the judicial body of the Sanhedrin was a trial or an investigatory hearing; whether it was legal or illegal; and whether or not it was before the full Sanhedrin. In this chapter, I will endeavor to show that the appearance of Jesus before this governmental tribunal was, in fact, a trial, entirely legal in every principle of the law, and that it was held before the twenty-three-member judicial Sanhedrin; that at morning light he was taken to Beth Pagi to be flogged with thirty-nine stripes save one; that Jesus was brought before a Jewish criminal court headed by Caiaphas in order to answer a Jewish criminal accusation, and that the charge was fully defined as blasphemy by Jewish law.

THE SANHEDRIN

There were, during the time of Jesus, three Sanhedrins: 1) a three-judge panel; 2) a twenty-three-member judicial Sanhedrin; and 3) a full seventy-one-member religious Sanhedrin. Only the twenty-three-member Sanhedrin was qualified to try criminal cases. Individuals accused of capital crimes were brought before this court over which the *nasi* and *ab bet din* presided. At the time of Jesus the Sadducees held the powerful offices of the criminal court.

> Cases involving the death penalty are judged before twenty-three [judges].[1]

The Great Sanhedrin [sometimes called the *Great Beth Din*] was a tribunal body consisting of three chambers: the Chamber of the Chief Priests; the Chamber of the Scribes; and the Chamber of the Elders (sometimes called counselors). These three chambers were divided into twenty-three members each, which when combined constituted a body of sixty-nine members. Added to this were the two high priests: the *nasi* and the *ab bet din*, making a total of seventy-one members in all. This legislative unit was responsible only for

---

1. *m. Sanh.* 1:4a

the administration of the Temple. The only capital cases brought before it were those involving women who had committed adultery and cases against the priesthood, or the high priest himself. This court was authorized only to administer the "bitter water" to those women caught in adultery, and to sentence members of the priesthood.

> It [the Great Sanhedrin] sat in judgment on women suspected of adultery, and sentenced them to drink the bitter water (Sotah i. 4).[2]

The exception to this rule was in the case where the accused adulteress was an *arusah* (a priest's daughter), who was "singled out by the Divine Law [and punished] by stoning [instead of burning or strangulation]".[3]

The Chamber of Priests included the leading priests and their Levitical attendants. Their duties consisted of the administration of various *sacrificial* functions of the Temple. The majority of these priests were Sadducean. They were often in opposition to the Pharisees in that the Sadduceans were more political and held a stricter interpretation of the written Mosaic law. During the time of Jesus, the Sadducees, who had formed an alliance with the Romans, had become materialistic, greedy, and political. They did not believe in the resurrection of the dead nor an afterlife, but did, however, follow the strictest tenets of Mosaic criminal law. It was this aggregate of priests who found Jesus a threat to the *economic and political stability of the priestly oligarchy and their Temple Cult.*

The Chamber of the Scribes was a group of scholars (called sages), primarily composed of Pharisees. They received their titles (*soferim*) because, originally, it was their duty to count the words of Torah in order to determine if texts were corrupt.

> Why is a scribe called a *sofer*? The Hebrew word *sofer* (plural, *soferim*) means "one who counts." The Talmud informs us that some of the early scribes were called *soferim* because they used to count all the letters, words, and verses of the Torah. They did so in order to make certain that letters or words were neither added nor omitted and that a Torah scroll represented as correct was indeed so. This practice of counting words, verses, and lines was well known in the literary world of the Greeks and Romans and appears to have been introduced by the librarians of the great library in Alexandria, Egypt, in the second or third centuries B.C.E. Authors and copyists would indicate at the end of their works all or some of these vital statistics for two reasons: to help teachers and students refer to passages and to enable buyers of manuscripts to check whether the exact number of words and lines were copied—without addition or deletion.[4]

In New Covenant writings they are called "lawyers" in that they interpreted the Mosaic law by oral tradition and set down precedents for future legislation. While the Sadducees had objected to Jesus on political grounds, it was this group who found offense in Jesus' *teachings*.

> No teacher could base his teaching merely on his own authority; and the fact that Jesus did this, was no doubt one of the grievances against him on the part of the Jews . . . the statement (Matt. vii. 28, 29) that Jesus *taught them as one*

---

2. "Sanhedrin", J.E., p. 44.
3. *b. Sanh.* 50a
4. Kolatch, *Torah*, p. 88.

> *having authority and not as their scribes*, was certainly cause sufficient that the people should be *astonished at his teaching*, and that the scribes should be incensed and alarmed.[5]

Scribes, like lawyers today, were known to have cited at least one authority (and preferably more) when trying to establish law. Without such citations, scribes could be held accountable for "leading the nation astray" through the teaching of "false and misleading" doctrines. The scribes and Pharisees of the New Covenant are one and the same; the title scribe denotes their occupation, the word Pharisee denotes their affiliation.

> The Pharisees were neither a 'party' nor a 'sect', but rather a socio-religious movement. And we should note that within the boundaries of the Pharisaic movement one can discern at least two different religious approaches to a given situation. The different approaches became especially evident when Palestine was ruled by a pagan power or by a Jewish government friendly to it . . . One wing of the Pharisaic movement, then, exercised some influence on the revolutionary trend which gained ground among the Jews in the first century. It is therefore quite evident that prior to AD 70 'Pharisaism', so-called, far from being a monolith, was a rather complex and heterogeneous religious movement.[6]

While there were several splinter groups from the Pharisaic movement, at least four factions of Pharisees can be identified within the first century: Essenes (the seclusive radicals), Zealots (the militant radicals), those simply called "Pharisees" in the gospels (Hellenistic radicals), and the more conservative group within which Jesus was accepted as *hasidim*. The most extreme of the Hellenistic Pharisees were those who were connected to the Sanhedrin as members of the Chamber of the Scribes.

> The early Scribes were, as Bickerman suggests, similar to the "Roman *juris periti* of the same period, who were the legal advisers of the pontifices." Some think that these Scribes were the predecessors of the Sages and eventually, the Rabbis—Masters or teachers of Torah.[7]

It was also this brotherhood of scribes which later was to become the dominant sect. They later became responsible for instituting and recording the Mishnaic Code from what they believed was the traditional "oral" law handed down from Moses. Hillel and others thought this contemporary view of the law was a more feasible corpus of law for the nation of Israel within the Hellenic culture of the first century than was the written Mosaic legislation adhered to by the Sadduceans.

> The naive and artless interpretations of the Torah, offered by the Midrash, would no longer suffice in an age of intellectual vigor. The rabbis began to *add Greek reasoning to biblical revelation*. The result was the Mishna, the work of a new set of Jewish scholars known as the Tannas . . . like the Midrash, it kept on diluting the Word of God with liberal quantities of fallible human opinion.[8]

---

5. Herford, *Christianity*, p. 9.
6. Zeitlin, *Jesus and Judaism*, pp. 14–15.
7. Hammer, *Classic Midrash*, p. 18.
8. Phillips, *Exploring*, pp. 56–57.

A Book of Evidence

The Chamber of the Elders, also called "senators" or "councilors", were men of aristocratic lineage who maintained the view that the nation should remain faithful to the written law of Moses. While many were Pharisees, themselves, they were generally adverse to the policies of the extreme Pharisaic Chamber of Scribes. It is clear there were a number of different factions within the "brotherhood" of the Pharisees. As mentioned earlier, it is believed some of the more radical among them were the Zealots and Essenes. The conservative Pharisees with whom Jesus was congenial generally associated themselves with the Chamber of Elders. This is the reason that Jesus sometimes is found dining with, conversing with, and visiting with some Pharisees. It was to this conservative group that Nicodemus and Joseph of Arimaethea belonged. Unfortunately, this chamber was the least influential of the three chambers and had nothing to do with criminal law. In order to apply for membership in this elite political and religious governing assemblage one must (eliminating both kinship and wealth) meet the following criteria and possess the following qualifications:

"1. He must have been a Hebrew and a lineal descendant of Hebrews.

'2. He must have been learned in the law, both written and unwritten.

'3. He must have had judicial experience; have begun with one of the local courts and passed through two magistracies in Jerusalem (Jose b. Halafta, I.c). He must have been especially well grounded in astronomy, medicine, chemistry, and familiar with the arts of the necromancer.

'4. He must have been an accomplished linguist, familiar with all the languages of the surrounding nations. The reason for this is found that interpreters were not allowed in Hebrew courts. After 70 A.D., the Sanhedrin discouraged learning the Greek language.

'5. He must have been modest, popular, of good appearance and without haughty demeanor.

'6. He must have been pious, strong and courageous."[9]

7. He must have been qualified for a regular trade, occupation, or profession. Unless he could meet this qualification, he would not at all be qualified for membership.[10]

8. In addition to these requirements, he must have been genealogically qualified to intermarry with women belonging to the priestly families.

From the seventy-one members of this great tribunal (Great Sanhedrin) were taken the twenty-three-member criminal court. Members consisted of the Chamber of Priests and the Chamber of Scribes. The Chamber of Elders had nothing to do with criminal jurisdiction. Its duty was to judge the priesthood. It was this twenty-three-member judicial Sanhedrin before which Jesus was tried. The criminal bet din actually consisted of twenty-one members (extracted from the sixty-nine of the *Great Beth Din*), along with the *nasi* (President/High Priest; Caiaphas) and the *ab bet din* (Vice President/High Priest; Annas). While the official presiding officer of the body was the *nasi*, it was the *ab bet din* who held the real power over these individuals. The group required to hear criminal cases also constituted a quorum of the larger body. It is for this reason that neither Nicodemus nor Joseph (conservative Pharisees and Elders) were present for Jesus' trial.

9. Aiyar, *Legality*, pp. 49-50.
10. Aiyar, p. 50.

The Jewish Trial

The majority of these individuals, then, could be hand-picked by Annas in order to assure the verdict he desired. Since at least a quorum was in opposition to Jesus on both economic-political (Sadducees), and religious grounds (Pharisees/Scribes), it would not have been difficult to pick a group willing to put him to death. The members of this court, therefore, could have been hand-picked by Annas himself, who chose members from his own family and his financial partners who would be willing to put Jesus to death. Ordinarily, this group of individuals would have been above reproach.

> The laws that not all [persons] are eligible, and that twenty three judges are necessary, are but one—There is yet another [difference]: for it has been taught: 'We do not appoint as members of the Sanhedrin, an aged man, a eunuch or one who is childless . . . People of illegitimate birth are ineligible as judges in capital cases because a court of twenty-three holds the status of a minor Sanhedrin, with whom pure descent is essential; hence they are counted as one.[11]

But look what happens when the case of a *mesith* (one who leads the nation astray) is to be tried: the requirement is *purposely reversed*!

> It is the reverse in the case of a Mesith, for the Divine Law states, *Neither shalt thou spare, neither shalt thou conceal him* . . . Because such are more or less devoid of paternal tenderness (Cf. Tosef. Sanh. vii and x).[12]

Furthermore, the trial for such an accused might be legally held in one day (or night) [a decision for the hour, or *horaat sha'ah*], and he *can* be convicted by a unanimous verdict of guilty.

> His case may be begun by day and finished by night; they may begin and end it on the same day, whether he be guilty or not; they may arrive at a verdict by a majority of one whether it be for conviction or acquittal; *All may plead for acquittal or all for conviction*; one who pleads for acquittal may retract and plead for conviction. *The eunuch and the childless can act as judges, and, according to R. Jehuda, even those who are biased in the direction of severity.*[13]

As we know, this is exactly what occurred during Jesus' trial. Many attempts have been made to exonerate the Jewish Sanhedrin by claiming that the trial was highly irregular and illegal, but upon closer examination of the law, we shall learn that this is simply not the case. These judges were unanimously determined to put Jesus to death for his interference in their affairs. An investigation might be made into those members of the Sanhedrin who might have been most likely chosen by Annas and present during the trial of Jesus. Authorities have long recognized that these individuals were primarily Sadducees connected with the House of Annas and the infamous oligarchy in control of the Temple Cult, those having an interest in the Temple traffic.

---

11 *b. Sanh.* 36b and 36b, n.4.
12. Danby, *Tractate Sanhedrin*, p. 105; *Tosef. Sanh.* VII and X; *b. Sanh.* 36b and 36b n.6.
13. Danby, p. 105; *Tosef. Sanh.* X, 11.

A Book of Evidence

> He [Jesus] was held in custody in the house of the high priest. Temple scribes and priests had been called to the house. These were Sadducee members of the committee responsible for the functioning of the Temple.[14]

THE JUDGES

The following individuals then might be the most likely candidates to serve as judges (or *elohim*) in the trial proceedings:

1. Caiaphas [Houses of Kithros/Hanan]: Caiaphas held the office of high priest during the entire term of Pilate's procuratorship (25-36 CE). He was appointed by Valerius Gratus in 25 CE.[15] Little is known about him, except that his "father-in-law" (*or ab bet din*) was Annas. As stated earlier, I believe, perhaps, it was to his title that the author of John referred, rather than to any notion of kinship by marriage. That is not to say Caiaphas was not a member of the House of Hanan. He was, however, a mere puppet who held no real political power. In the case of Jesus, he presided as *nasi* over the Sanhedrin and pronounced the final verdict of blasphemy. He was deposed from his office in the same year that Pilate was recalled to Rome. This fact would seem to indicate that the two were, perhaps, intimately connected.

2. Annas (Ananus) [House of Hanan]: Annas was the former high priest, holding office five years under Coponius, Ambivus, and Rufus (7-11 CE).[16] He was called by Josephus the "ancientest of the high-priests"[17]. He also states that it was Annas' death that "was the beginning of the destruction of the city".[18] Annas was slain in the midst of Jerusalem. At the time of Jesus' trial and execution, he served as *ab bet din*, the "father of the court". It was his duty to bring forth the formal accusation. As stated above, while Caiaphas was the high priest, Annas held the actual power. History is quite clear about this. His wealthy family, in fact, held the office of the high priesthood for fifty years without interruption. In the words of one scholar they were "haughty, audacious, and cruel".[19]

3. Eleazar ben Hanan [House of Hanan]: Eleazar was the eldest son of Annas. He was high priest under Valerius Gratus, holding that office between 23-24 CE. He had replaced Ismael ben Phabi I, who had already served one term as high priest. When Eleazar had served for one year, Gratus gave the office to Simon ben Camithus (who also served about a year).[20]

4. Jonathan ben Hanan [House of Hanan]: Jonathan, another son of Annas replaced Caiaphas as high priest for one year[21] and was deposed by Vitellius and Herod the tetrarch (Antipas) in 37 CE, who installed in his stead Jonathan's brother Theophilus

---

14. Potok, *Wanderings*, p. 374.
15. Josephus, *Ant.*, 18.2.2.
16. Josephus, *Ant.*, 20.9.1.
17. Josephus, *Ant.*, 4.3.7.
18. Josephus, *Ant.*, 4.5.2.
19. Foreman, *Crucify Him*, p. 110.
20. Josephus, *Ant.*, 18.2.2.
21. Josephus, *Ant.*, 18.4.3

at the death of Tiberius.[22] Jonathan was again appointed High-priest by King Agrippa, who deposed Simon [II] [Boethus] Cantheras, but Jonathan, who had held the office before refused the honor and offered it to his brother, Matthias.[23] During the siege of Jerusalem, he was the first man murdered by the sect of the Sicarii [Zealots]. These sicarii were called by that name because of the concealed daggers they carried in their cloaks.[24] The Sicarii terrorized the priesthood because it was sympathetic to Rome. Jonathan was mentioned in the book of Acts (4:6), along with Annas, Caiaphas, and Alexander (his kinsmen) as present at the examination of Peter and John. This places the disciples' arrest prior to 37 CE since that was the year Jonathan replaced Caiaphas as high priest.

5. Theophilus ben Hanan [House of Hanan]: Theophilus, another son of Annas was high priest after his brother Jonathan.[25] He held the office for five years until 42 CE and was replaced by another brother Matthias (but this was not until after Simon, the son of Simon Boethus had served in that capacity). Not much is known about the activities of this man. Josephus here contradicts himself and tells us he was replaced by Simon [II], the son of [Simon] Boethus, appointed by King Agrippa, "whose name was also Cantheras, *whose daughter* [the daughter of Simon I] *King Herod had married*".[26] Josephus tells us the high priesthood now returned to the family of Boethus for a time, but as we have stated before Matthias officiated for two years during this time. Unless this Matthias, brother of Jonathan, and son of Ananus (Annas) was also related to the Boethus family, this is not possible. We note that this first Simon's name was also "Cantheras", indicating that intermarriage within the four families of the high priesthood (and also with the Herodians) was a fairly common practice.

> In the Second Temple period, the leading priestly families made a practice of endogamous marriage; but under suitable circumstances they were not unwilling to establish matrimonial ties with influential families not included among the priesthood.[27]

6. Matthias ben Hanan [House of Hanan]: This son of Annas became high priest for two years (42-44 CE), succeeding his brother, Jonathan.[28]

7. Ananus ben Hanan [House of Hanan]: Ananus, son of Annas. This was the high priest who was said to be a Sadducee of "extravagant zeal". This Ananus II was the priest who illegally condemned James and other Nazaraeans to be stoned and was deposed by Albanus (who replaced the prefect Portius Festus), the representative of the Roman government in 62 CE.[29] The more conservative Pharisees contacted King Agrippa, who deposed Ananus and replaced him with Jesus, the son of Damneus. Ananus II was said to be ineffective and cruel.

22. Josephus, *Ant.*, 18.5.3.
23. Josephus, *Ant.*, 19.6.4.
24. Josephus, *War* 2.8.3.
25. Josephus, *Ant.* 18.5.3.
26. Josephus, *Ant.*, 19.6.3
27. Ben-Sasson, *A History*, p. 195.
28. Josephus, *Ant.*, 19.6.4.
29. Josephus, *Ant.*, 20.8.1.

8. Joazar ben Boethus [House of Boethus]: Joazar, the son of Simon Boethus (I) served for six years (4 BCE – 2 CE). He was brother-in-law of the high priest Matthias ben Hanan, and replaced Matthias in that office. It was during his tenure that Cyrenius, the Roman senator, became the governor of Syria and, along with Coponius, imposed a census in Judea, "being sent by Caesar to be a judge of that nation, and to take an account of their substance".[30] This is the census to which Luke refers (Luke 2:1–3). It was Joazar ben Boethus who persuaded the Jews to accept the taxation imposed on them.[31] This census was concluded in the "thirty-seventh year of Caesar's victory over Antony at Actium"[32] (which occurred in 31 BCE). It occurred during the year Joazar was installed in the priesthood (4 BCE).

We might here mention that it was also during this time frame that Jesus was born. Both Luke and Josephus seem confused in their narratives. Herod the Great had just died. Here, we find a discrepancy in the writings of Luke, since Herod was *supposed* to have slain all infants in Bethlehem "two years old and under". The phrase would suggest that Jesus had been born in 6 BCE, his family immediately fleeing to Egypt. They would not return until Archelaus was king (4 BCE) (at the time of the taxation), because it was at this time that the kingdom of Judea was to revert to Archelaus. It was at this time that Antipas was appointed tetrarch of Galilee and Berea.[33]

Archelaus deposed Joazar and replaced him with his brother Eleazar ben Boethus.[34] After three months, the priesthood was then transferred to Jesus ben Sie.[35] Josephus again contradicts himself, stating that "he [Archelaus] deprived Joazar of the high-priesthood, which dignity had been conferred on him by the multitude, and he appointed Ananus [Annas], the son of Seth, to be high priest".[36] Apparently, Eleazar held the office for three months, then Jesus ben Sie, who held the office for five or six years until 7 CE when he was replaced by Annas, who resided as *ab bet din* at Jesus' trial.

9. Eleazar ben Boethus [House of Boethus]: Eleazar, the son of Simon Boethus I served only three months as high priest in 2 CE. He replaced his brother, Joazar.[37] Joazar replaced the high priest Joseph ben Elim who had substituted for Matthias ben Theophilus on the Day of Atonement.

10. Simon Cantharus ben Boethus [House of Boethus]: This is the Simon (II) mentioned above, the third son of Simon Boethus. He served only a few months as high priest in 42 CE.[38] At this time "Herod of Chalcis petitioned Claudius Caesar for the authority over the temple, and the money of the sacred treasure, and the choice of the high-priests, and obtained all he petitioned for".[39] Afterward, this Herod installed

30. Josephus, *Ant.*, 18.1.1.
31. Josephus, *Ant.*, 18.1.1.
32. Josephus, *Ant.*, 18.2.1.
33. Josephus, *Ant.*, 17.8.1.
34. Josephus, *Ant.*, 17.13.1.
35. Josephus, *Ant.*, 17.13.1.
36. Josephus, *Ant.*, 18.2.1.
37. Josephus, *Ant.*, 17.8.1.
38. Josephus, *Ant.*, 19.6.2,4.
39. Josephus, *Ant.*, 20.1.3.

The Jewish Trial

Joseph, the son of "Camus" or "Camydus" [Gamus] as high priest,[40] who after serving a short period of time in office was succeeded by Ananias, the son of Nebedeus [Hananiah ben Nedebai], before whose tribunal Paul appeared (Acts 23:2–5).

11. Ishmael ben Phiabi (Fabus, Phabi) [House of Phiabi]: Ishmael ben Phiabi was high priest for nine years under Valerius Gratus, the predecessor of Pontius Pilate. He is said to have been "the handsomest man of his time, whose effeminate love of luxury was the scandal of the age".[41] His grandson is believed to have been Rabbi Ishmael of the sages, who was said to have been tortured at the hands of the Roman soldiers for having studied Torah.[42]

12. Jesus ben Sie: Jesus ben Sie held the high priesthood for five or six years (1-6 CE) just prior to the introduction of our infamous Annas into the high-priesthood.[43] This Jesus had replaced Eleazar ben Boethus, who held the office only three months.

13. Simon ben Camithus [Camithi]: Simon ben Camithus served as high priest for one year (24-25 CE). He is often ridiculed in the Talmud (*b. Yoma* 47, for example). Joseph Caiaphas was his successor.[44]

14. Joshua ben Phiabi [House of Phiabi]: This man served as high priest under Herod the Great. He was an Alexandrian Jew and his descendants served in the office of high priest at various times during the following years.

> The greatness of the third priestly family, the house of Phiabi, which also seems to have come from Egypt, is reflected in the fact that it supplied three High Priests: the first, Joshua ben Phiabi, held office under Herod himself; the second, Ishmael ben Phiabi I functioned as High Priest under the early Roman governors; the third, Ishmael ben Phiabi II, was appointed by Agrippa II.[45]

15. Alexander ben Hanan [House of Hanan]: Josephus says that he afterward (after his term of office) became an Alabarch—first magistrate of the Jews in Alexandria.[46] It is said he was very rich and at one time loaned King Herod Agrippa two hundred pieces of silver.[47] One source claims he was "a priestly partner of the sons of Annas in the Temple traffic".[48] He is the Alexander mentioned in Acts 4:6. It was this Alexander (a *Jewish* high priest) who commanded that Simon and James, the two sons of Judas, the Galilean Zealot, be crucified![49]

16. Hananiah ben Nedebai (Ananias ben Nebedeus): Ananias was a high priest under Ventideus, Cumanus and Felix. He served for twelve years (47–59 CE).[50] Ananias (the high

---

40. Josephus, *Ant.*, 20.5.2.
41. Aiyar, *Legality*, p. 53.
42. Wiesel, *Sages and Dreamers*, pp. 212–213.
43. Josephus, *Ant.* 17.13.1.
44. Josephus, *Ant.*, 18.2.2.
45. Ben-Sasson, *A History*, p. 256.
46. Josephus, *Ant.* 20.5.2.
47. Josephus, *Ant.*, 18.6.3.
48. Richards, *Illegality*, p. 16.
49. Josephus, *Ant.* 20.5.2.
50. Josephus, *Ant.* 20.5.2; 20.6.2; 20.9.2–4.

priest) and Ananus II (the "commander of the Temple" i.e., the Captain of the Temple at that time) were sent in bonds to Rome to appear before Claudius Caesar for their report on a recent Samaritan revolt. The two must have been received favorably because Ananus II is found again in Jerusalem as high priest in 62 CE when James was executed. He was infamous for his excessive gluttony, and was exceptionally wealthy. A tradition has been preserved in the Talmud (*b. Gittin* 56a) that there were three other rich men of Jerusalem who could supply Jerusalem with all that was needed to withstand a siege for a number of years (twenty-seven years): Nicodemus ben Gorion (who might have been the Nicodemus of the New Covenant); Ben-Kalba Savua and Ben-Zitzit Hakkesset.[51]

> Three men of great wealth, Nakdimon ben Gorion, Ben Kalba Savua, and Ben Tzitzit ha-Keset, lived in Jerusalem. Nakdimon ben Gorion was so called because the sun continued shining (*nakedah*) for his sake. Ben Kalba Savua was so called because one would go into his house hungry as a dog (*kelev*) and come out full (*savea*). Ben Tzitzit ha-Keset was so called because his fringes (*tzitzit*) used to trail on cushions (*keset*). One of the three said, "I will keep the people of Jerusalem in wheat and barley." A second said, "I will keep them in wine, oil, and salt." The third said, "I will keep them in firewood." (The sages considered the offer of wood the most generous. They pointed out that R. Hisda [used to hand all his keys to his servant, except the one to the woodbin, for, he] would say, "To bake one load of wheat requires sixty loads of wood.").[52]

Ananias, after the Zealots had set fire to his house on the 14th of Av, was slain in 66 C.E. by the Sicarii,[53] along with his brother Hezekiah (Ezekias), while hiding in an aqueduct. It was about this time that the Bazaars of Annas were destroyed. It is noted by Josephus that after the burning of Ananias' house, the Zealots "carried the fire to the *place where the archives were reposited*, and made haste to burn the contracts belonging to their creditors, and thereby dissolve their obligations for paying their debts; and this was done, in order to gain the multitude of those who had been debtors, and that they might persuade the poorer sort to join in their insurrection with safety against the more wealthy; so the keepers of the records fled away, and the rest set fire to them".[54] At that time, this "vaulted" structure (called the Arch of Accounts or *Bet HaKana*) was located upon the Mount of Olives.

17. Helcias ben Phiabi [House of Phiabi]: Helcias (or Chelcias) was the keeper of the sacred Treasury. He is called "Helcias the Great" by Josephus, who states that he and the other "principal men of that family" went to Petronius (a Roman publican) to persuade him to reason with Caius (Caligula) Caesar concerning the bringing of his own statue to Jerusalem to be placed in the Temple".[55] Helcias is believed to have been the Chief Treasurer of the Temple during the trial of Jesus and would have been responsible for giving the thirty pieces of silver to Judas Iscariot (not out of character for these families, who were often known to have made "bribes") to betray his Master.

51. Ben-Sasson, *A History*, p. 270.
52. Bialik and Ravnitzky, *Legends*, 189–190:2.
53. Josephus, *War* 2.17.9.
54. Josephus, *War* 2.7.6.
55. Josephus, *Ant.*, 20.8.4

18. Joseph ben Cabi: The son of Simon Cantheras son of Boethus.

19. Jonathan ben Uziel (Yonathan ben Ouziel): He was a scribe and translator of the prophets (except for the book of Daniel). He is said to have been the best scholar of the School of Hillel.[56]

20. Rabbi Nachun Halbalar: He was another scribe who acted as a judge in Jesus' case. He was known to have been a member of the Sanhedrin in the year 28 CE.[57]

21. Narada ben Zitzit Hakkesset (Hacksab): Narada, a Pharisaic Elder who it has been said "proclaimed to the full body, the question of guilt of Jesus".[58] His father, as mentioned earlier, was one of the three richest men in Jerusalem.

22. Doras: A treacherous man, Doras was known to have been persuaded by the procurator Felix to bring "robbers" (Sicarii) against his most faithful friend Jonathan ben Hanan (the high-priest and son of Annas) in order to murder him.[59] It was at Jonathan's request that Felix was brought to Judea as prefect.

23. Matthias ben Boethus [House of Boethus]: He served as one of the high priests and was betrayed by Simon, a former high priest, to the Romans during the Jewish War. His three sons were put to death before his eyes prior to his own execution.[60] They were left in the streets to rot.

The foregoing list of participants seems the most likely to have been among the judges during the trial of Jesus. All belonged to the exclusive Temple Cult, all were among the four families controlling the priesthood, and all were partners in the Bazaars of Annas and the Temple bank. These corrupt priestly families, intermarried among themselves and with the Herodian royal house (whose sons were raised in the Roman Emperor's own household), and were those before whom Jesus stood because he had dared to confront them with their avarice, politics, and irreligion. The Pharisaic rabbis and sages of the latter first century and onward, for the most part, held these individuals in utter disdain.

> What a plague is the *family of Simon Boethus*; cursed be their lances! What a plague is the *family of Ananos*; cursed be their hissing of vipers! What a plague is the family *of Cantharus*; cursed be their pens! What a plague is the *family of Ismael ben Phabi*; cursed be their fists! They are high priests themselves, their sons are treasurers, their sons-in-law are commanders [captains], and their servants strike people with staves [thus verifying the words of Josephus about the servants of Annas].[61]

Of the foregoing assemblage of Priests, Scribes, and Elders we find at least eight members of the House of Hanan, four members of the House of Boethus, and three members of the House of Phiabi. The rest are their kinsmen. Their influence in the government of Israel and on Rome, itself, was extremely powerful. The populace hated them because of their close political ties to both the Herodian royal house and the Roman

---

56. Wiesel, *Sages and Dreamers*, p. 162.
57. Aiyar, *Legality*, p. 56.
58. Aiyar, p. 58.
59. Josephus, *Ant.*, 20.7.5.
60. Josephus, *War* 5.8.1.
61. *b. Pes.* 57.

government. It is difficult to imagine that these four families might be amenable to the teachings of Jesus. In their opinions, this man's teachings were in opposition to their governmental persuasions. He stirred up the dissatisfied people, already ripe for revolt. When Jesus was brought before Annas, that *ab bet din* found in him little to commend in light of the political and economic policies of the Temple Cult of which he was the chief. After Annas completed the formal accusation at Beth Pagi, Jesus had been bound and sent to Caiaphas, who was temporarily residing in the "house" of the Temple ("Stone House"). It is also here that we find the council chamber in which were gathered the infamous judges. The gospel narrators tell us that witnesses were procured. These would necessarily have been the same witnesses who had testified during the initial accusation phase of the trial. Peter was, apparently, released from further duty as an "unreliable" witness, for we learn that he awaits the outcome of the trial in the "porch" or "place of blowing" [*Beth Chatser*] alongside the guard and temple servants. Yohanan Eleazar (Lazarus), on the other hand, as a member of the Sanhedrin (but not of the criminal court) was allowed to remain as a spectator to the travesty. It is the testimony of that disciple to whom we owe our debt of gratitude for the report of the trial proceedings.

> This is the disciple which testifieth of these things, and wrote these things: and we know that his testimony is true (John 21:24).

Yet the report is not entirely rendered in the Gospel of John. It is to the other gospels (who received that oral testimony) that we must now turn. Mark, as a disciple of Peter, would likely have had this tradition from both the author of John and from Peter, yet not even all the tradition was reported at that time. Luke and Matthew are known to have taken parts of their own gospels from Mark, and each gives details from a different viewpoint that help us to understand the trial. Academicians have insisted that the Jewish trial was highly illegal and an unexcused breach of the existing law. At first glance, this seems feasible. An investigation into the finer points of the law will prove otherwise. The arguments made by the proponents of an illegal trial are listed below. Some of the evidence used below has already been covered in the chapter entitled "The Crime: Apostasy From the Law", but for the sake of clarity a few citations bear repeating.

1. Capital cases are said to begin with the defense of the accused rather than the prosecution.

> . . . in capital cases they begin only with the case for acquittal, and not with the case for conviction.[62]

There appears to have been no attempt to first pursue acquittal at Jesus' trial. To the contrary, "the High-priest and all the High-council were seeking against Jesus testimony, *with the intent to put him to death*" (Mark 14:55).

2. Mark informs us that "the High-priest rising up into the midst *questioned Jesus*" (Mark 14:60). Talmudic law states this is highly illegal in that the accused is never required to testify against himself. Adin Steinsaltz explains:

> The basic assumption in *halakhah* is that a man does not belong only to himself; just as he has no right to cause physical harm to others, so he has no right to

---

62. *m. Sanh.* 4.1e.

inflict injury on himself. *This is why it was determined that the confession of the defendant had no legal consideration.* This rule, which has its own formal substantiation, served courts for centuries as a powerful weapon *against attempts to extract confessions by force or persuasion.* Not only can no man be forced to incriminate himself through his own testimony, but *self-incrimination has no significance and is unacceptable as evidence in court.*[63]

That Caiaphas sought such a confession from Jesus, even to the point of placing him under oath, is ordinarily seen as nullifying the proceedings.

> It goes even farther, *for it makes no use whatever of admissions or of confessions of guilt, either in or out of court; (Deut. xix. 15) is understood as excluding the mouth of the accused; and the principle is laid down,* "No one can make himself out guilty" (or "wicked"), and it appears often throughout the Talmud.[64]

3. Caiaphas, upon hearing Jesus' statement claiming he was "Son of Man" (i.e., a frail human), that he would sit on the right hand of "Power" and come in the clouds, declared no further need for witnesses. Mishnaic law, if on no other single point, is quite clear about the necessity of qualified eyewitnesses, two or three, agreeing as to what they had seen.

> Capital punishment in rabbinic law, or indeed any other punishment, must not be inflicted, except by the verdict of a regularly constituted court (Lesser Sanh.) of three and twenty qualified members (Sanh. 1:1; Sifre, Num. 160), and except on the most trustworthy and convincing testimony of at least two qualified eyewitnesses to the crime (Deut. xvii.6, xix.15; Sotah vi. 3; Sifre Num. 161; *ib.* Deut. 150, 188; Sanh. 30a) who must depose that the culprit had been forewarned as to the criminality and the consequences of his project (Sanh. v. 1, 140b *et seq.*).[65]

Caiaphas' statement concerning no further need for such witnesses would seem to invalidate the trial.

4. Trials for capital punishment were not to take place on either the eve of the Sabbath or on a festival day. Furthermore, the trial and the verdict could not be confined to a single day.

> In capital cases they come to a final decision for acquittal on the same day, but on the following day for conviction. (Therefore they do not judge capital cases either on the eve of the Sabbath or on the eve of a festival).[66]

Yet we know that Jesus *was* brought to trial, a verdict was rendered, sentence passed, and execution carried out in a single day (beginning about 3:00 a.m. and ending at 3:00 p.m. on 14 Nisan) and that day was both the eve of the Sabbath and the Eve of Passover.

5. The Sanhedrin was not allowed to render a unanimous verdict of guilty.

> ... in capital cases they decide by a majority of one for acquittal, but only with a majority of two [judges] for conviction.[67]

---

63. Steinsaltz and Galai, *Essential Talmud*, pp. 167–168.
64. "Accusatory", J.E., p. 163.
65. "Capital Punishment", J.E., p. 556.
66. *m. Sanh.* 4:1k–l.
67. *m. Sanh.* 4:1f.

A Book of Evidence

We are told in the gospel of Mark that "they *all* condemned him to be worthy of death" (Mark 14:64). At first glance, these irregularities seem to completely invalidate the trial's proceedings and thus close the case. The fact is, however, these proceedings, which would have been highly illegal in any other capital trial, were not illegal in the case at bar. We only need to look to the nature of the crime and what the Sanhedrin tractate of the Tosefta and Talmud says about the requirements concerning trial proceedings in order to establish legality. As mentioned before, when an individual is brought to trial, charged as a *mesith*, the entire order as narrated above is then *reversed*!

The reversal process is one of the finer points of Jewish law during the first century, and we have only to recite the two all-inclusive Jewish statutes concerning the *mesith* to prove our case.

> His case may be begun by day and finished by night; *they may begin and end it on the same day, whether he be guilty or not*; they may arrive at a verdict by a majority of one whether it be for conviction or acquittal; *all may plead for acquittal or all for conviction*; one who pleads for acquittal may retract and plead for conviction. *The eunuch and the childless can act as judges, and, according to R. Jehuda, even those who are biased in the direction of severity*... [furthermore he is] *brought to Jerusalem* and kept in prison till a feast *and killed at a feast*, for it is written: *and all the people shall hear and fear, and do no more presumptuously*... therefore *they kill him at once*...[68]

Since anyone could perform the duties of "judge" in cases such as this, Annas was able to choose any number of corrupt judges to do his bidding.

> In capital cases they begin not with the case for prosecution, but with the case for the defence, *except only in the case of a beguiler to idolatry* (Mesith), and, according to R. Jehoshua, the son of Karha, *the case of one who leads a town astray*.[69]

In just such a case, the defendant might even be allowed to testify and accuse himself. As mentioned in a previous chapter, Caiaphas had every legal right to place Jesus on oath and could use his testimony to condemn him. Did Jesus confess his "crime"? We shall learn later that, in fact, he did, but he had not elaborated in his "confession", and it was the failure to elaborate which would have condemned him.

They had wanted to cross-examine him further, but as they related to Pilate, it was "not lawful" to put a man to death. That statement has absolutely nothing to do with any notion that capital jurisdiction and the death penalty had been taken away from them at the time. The word "lawful" is the Greek *exetazo* or *etazo* meaning "to examine" or "to test thoroughly (by questions)", "to ascertain or interrogate". Thayer's defines it as "to search out", "to examine strictly", "to inquire ... by direct question". What they were saying to Pilate was, in effect, "We cannot by our law interrogate Jesus in the way we would like because our law does not permit it, but you, as a Roman prefect, might legally ask the questions we cannot." The rulers' hypocrisy is quite blatant, and Pilate would have recognized it. For this reason, when he was questioning Jesus *for them*, his scorn for their hypocrisy would be reflected in such statements as "Am *I* a Jew?", and

---

68. Danby, *Sanhedrin Tractate*, p. 105, 111; *Tosef. Sanh.* X.11; XI.7.
69. Danby, p. 69; *Tosef. Sanh.* VII. 2a.

"What is truth?" It is clear the Sanhedrin did not want to accept full responsibility for Jesus' execution. They used a point of Jewish law to force Pilate's hand in the matter. By claiming they were not allowed to question Jesus directly (since capital law forbids it), the court was attempting to "pass the buck", so to speak, to the Roman administration who was hated even more than the Sanhedrin itself. Furthermore, they were required to seek Roman authorization to carry out their sentence. Their attempt to coerce Jesus into a *mesith's* confession by placing him on oath had resulted, not in the confession of a clear capital crime as they had desired, but in what they considered the foolish "vain oath", a lesser crime for which Jesus might be flogged with thirty-nine stripes. We must not be deceived, however, for that legislative body had found him guilty of blasphemy by enticement, and this is clearly evidenced by the *niddui*, or excommunicative process. The author of *John* merely mentioned that the death penalty had been abolished at the time to point out the hypocritical nature of the criminal court. While the court did, indeed, have to seek approval for its judgments from the Roman governor, it continued to carry out its own executions. There is a Talmudic reference regarding the abolition of the death penalty. It is assumed that forty years before the destruction of the Temple that capital cases could no longer be tried. This assumption is due to the fact that "the Sanhedrin were exiled and took up residence in Hanuth,"[70] and since they were no longer situated in the Hall of Hewn Stone could not try capital cases. However, the Sanhedrin continued to try capital cases in Beth Pagi at the site of the Bazaars of Annas:

> That these, *like capital charges* could be tried only in the chief seat of the Sanhedrin—the Hall of Hewn Stones! *These cases could, in fact, be tried anywhere in Palestine.*[71]

Here is the statement as recorded in the Talmud:

> More than forty years before the Temple was destroyed, capital cases were removed [from the authority of the Beth Din].[72]

The fact of the matter is that capital cases were tried and the death penalty exacted throughout the next two centuries. The book of Acts records at least two more instances against the followers of Jesus, as well as the attempted trial and execution of Peter and John. The first was only a few years after Jesus' execution when the Sanhedrin put Stephen on trial, finding him guilty and further enforcing the penalty of stoning (Acts 6:12). The second example of this type of conduct by the Sanhedrin is in the case of Paul (Acts 22:23 – 23). It might be noted that the Roman captain who first arrested him, believing the proper jurisdiction lay within the authority of the Jewish political sphere, *delivered Paul to the High Council*. We have, on authority of the Talmud, numerous instances of the same practice. The most historical of the sources, some would believe, is Josephus, who tells us Ananus II in 62 CE "assembled the Sanhedrin of judges, and brought before them the brother of Jesus, who was called [Messiah], whose name was James, and some others [Nazaraeans or Ebionites]; *and when he had formed an accusation against them as*

---

70. b. Sanh. 43a.
71. b. Sanh. 43a n.6.
72. y. Sanh. 18a

breakers of the law, he delivered them to be stoned".[73] If the statement in the Talmud is to be taken seriously, then the Sanhedrin often broke their own law. What was theory and what was reality were two different things. One historian explains:

> Nevertheless, we sometimes get the impression that the Jews were accustomed to trying capital cases. A comparative study of the sources leads to the following conclusions: (1) in principal, criminal jurisdiction was indeed transferred from the Jewish institutions to the Roman administration; (2) *in the case of offenses directly involving desecration of the Temple, the Sanhedrin was entitled to pass death sentences*, though even here there was a measure of supervision by representatives of the Roman administration; (3) the degree of supervision was liable to change according to the circumstances . . . and *when the circumstances were favorable the Jews could give a broader interpretation to their residual powers of capital jurisdiction and include religious offenses connected only indirectly with the Temple*; (4) even in matters that were not in any way related to the Temple or its cult, the Roman authorities sometimes voluntarily authorized the Sanhedrin and the high priest to try capital cases.[74]

The leading authorities simply did not want to recognize a claim of a legitimate heir to of the House of David.

> Judah and Hezekiah, the sons of R. Hiyya, once sat at table with Rabbi and uttered not a word. Whereupon he said: Give the young men plenty of strong wine, so that they may say something. When the wine took effect, they began by saying: The *son of David cannot appear ere the two ruling houses in Israel shall have come to an end*, viz., the Exilarchate in Babylon and the Patriarchate in Palestine, for it is written, *And he shall be for a Sanctuary, for a stone of stumbling and for a rock of offence to both houses of Israel*. Thereupon he [Rabbi] exclaimed: *You throw thorns in my eyes, my children!* At this, R. Hiyya [his disciple] remarked: Master, be not angered, for the numerical value of the letters of *yayin* is seventy, and likewise the letters of *sod*: When *yayin* [wine] goes in, *sod* [secrets] comes out.[75]

The statement above reflects the fear of the rulers and those in power that the nation of Israel would come to an end. Had they recognized Jesus as Messiah, they knew the Romans would destroy the nation and take away their powerful positions. They chose to be ruled by the Romans because it was advantageous to them, both politically and financially.

The fact is these rulers *knew* Jesus claimed to be the promised Messiah. His parable in the Gospel of Matthew makes that clear.

> There was a certain householder [YHWH], which planted a vineyard [Israel; Isa. 5:7, Surely the vineyard of Yahweh of hosts is the house of Israel], and hedged it round about, and digged a winepress in it, and built a tower, and let it out to husbandmen [rulers], and went into a far country. And when the time of the fruit drew near he sent his servants [the prophets] to the husbandmen, that they might receive the fruits of it. And the husbandmen [rulers] took his servants [the

---

73. Josephus, *Ant.* 20.9.1.
74. Ben-Sasson, *A History*, p. 250.
75. *b. Sanh.* 38a

prophets], and beat one, and killed another, and stoned another. Again, he sent other servants [prophets] more than the first: and they did unto them likewise. But last of all, he sent unto them *his son*, saying, They will reverence my son. But when the husbandmen [rulers] *saw the son, they said among themselves, This is the heir; come let us kill him, and let us seize on his inheritance. And they caught him, and cast him out of the vineyard* ["outside the camp"] *and slew* [executed] *him* (Matt. 21:33–39).

This is the reply of the rulers to Jesus' parable:

And when the chief priests and Pharisees had heard his parables *perceived that he spake of them* (Matt. 21:45).

Herod Antipas, too, would have perceived Jesus as a threat to his position. While his title was tetrarch, Antipas viewed himself as a "king", a member of the royal household of Israel and Roman official. He had, in fact, already contested his father's Will unsuccessfully. Herod the Great had several wills and codicils. In his last will he had made Herod Antipas his heir; however, by codicils to the last will, he had named his son Archelaus as king after him. Antipas, went to Rome and challenged his kingship, based on the fact that the will should have prevailed over the codicil. The Emperor Augustus, however, decided it would be politically wise to name Archalaus ethnarch and give the title of tetrarch of Galilee to Antipas. Antipas had recently put John the Baptist to death, proving that he, too, had the power to enact the death penalty when he so desired without Roman intervention. The statement that Jesus was "connected with royalty" (*b. Sanh.* 43a) would have been of great significance to him. He, like his father Herod the Great, would have been greatly suspicious of and disturbed at the prospect of any rumor circulating that a "usurpation" of the kingdom by a *legitimate* heir of the House of David was at hand.

Whether correctly understood or not, his prophecy of the kingdom was interpreted by the *Roman tetrarch Herod Antipas (son of Herod the Great) in a political manner*.[76]

Since Antipas and his wife Herodias (great granddaughter of Mariamne I, the Hasmonian) were of some kin to the priesthood (as well as allied with them), he would have agreed wholeheartedly with their wishes in this matter. Josephus gives us the history of the Sanhedrin during the days of the Temple.

Accordingly the number of the high-priests, from the days of Herod [The Great] until the day when Titus took the temple and the city, and burnt them, were in all twenty-eight; the time also that belonged to them was a hundred and seven years. *Some of these were the political governors of the people under the reign of Herod, and under the regin of Archelaus his son, although, after their death, the government became an aristocracy, and the high-priests were intrusted with a dominion over the nation.*[77]

Herod Antipas was a member of that aristocracy because of his kinship with the priestly families. Both Josephus and the gospels inform us of his lavish lifestyle. He was

---

76. Idinopulos, *Jerusalem*, p. 131.
77. Josephus, *Ant.* 20.10.1.

often called "king" and was certainly viewed by the populace as the reigning monarch. There is every indication that Pilate sent Jesus to Herod, *the Roman-appointed tetrarch of Galilee*, to investigate the possibly of any treasonous act against Rome, but Herod had found no legal *Roman* crime. This is not to say that he found no *Jewish* crime in Jesus' activities. There is certainly evidence in New Covenant writings that Herod envied Jesus as much or even more than he had envied John the Immerser. In fact, we are told that he had sought "to slay him" (Luke 13:31). The Hellenistic and self-seeking Herod, as acting "king" of Judea, would have envied the "miracles" of Jesus. Like Vespasion afterward, his Hellenic background would have required him (as "king") to verify his rule by "miracles". He sought to learn the "magician's tricks" through the help of Jesus to attain such an affirmation of "divinity". He had heard rumors that there were those among the population (probably Zealots) who desired to make Jesus king. There is also no reason to assume that because Herod had found no legal Roman crime against Jesus that the proceedings of the Sanhedrin were nullified. While Herod was a Roman puppet, he was also powerful in his own right as a Jewish ruler, and while entitled tetrarch, there can be no question that his lifestyle and power was that of a king. His primary interest was in the survival of the Jewish-Roman economic-political structure that he had inherited from his father, Herod the Great, over which he maintained complete control. If we are to give any credence to the apocryphal Gospel of Peter, it was, indeed, Herod who gave final approval to the Sanhedrin for the execution of Jesus, and whoever the anonymous author of the gospel was, he certainly believed Herod was king.

> And then *Herod the king* commandeth that the Lord [Master] be taken saying to them, *what things soever I commanded you to do unto him, do*.[78]

As mentioned above, The Talmud (*b. Sanh.* 43a) mentions the fact that Jesus is connected with *malkhut*, and it has been compromised by Jewish scholars to mean the "Roman government". Nothing could be further from the truth. While the word "malkhut" *can* mean government, it means most specifically *royalty* and in Jewish writings, it particularly designates that royalty as being the government of Israel! Since we are tackling the task of determining what it means to be the Hebrew messiah, we must look at how the *Jews* of the first century (and even later) define the word *malkhut*. It is defined in the *Zohar* as "community" or "kingdom" and refers only to the *government of Israel*!

> The Zohar's expression "Community of Israel" (*Knesset Yisrael*) refers *not* to the actual people Israel, but symbolically to the tenth and final *Sefirah, Malkhut* or *Shekhinah* [that is, as Rabbi Eleazar defines it, the *Kingdom of Israel*].[79]

Yet the *Malkhut* or *Shekinah* is also connected with the royalty of the Son of David, the object of YHWH's love, since it is said to reside in him. Midrashic interpretation of Jeremiah 2.2 states: "This verse refers to the *Community [or kingdom] of Israel* (*malkhut*) when She was walking in the wilderness along with Israel".[80] Jewish interpretation of the word *malkhut* is, then, expressed as the royal kingdom of the House of David and

---

78. Gosp. Pet., *Lost Books*, p. 283.
79. Holtz, *Sources*, p. 331.
80. Holtz, p. 331; Jer. 2.2.

thus relates to the Messiah and the messianic government. Since the Sanhedrin and the Herodians were allied, the fact that Jesus is sent to Herod for examination would tend to indicate that the tetrarch's involvement was more than cursory. Mention has already been made in a previous chapter of Herod's complicity, but there would appear to be some verification in a custom dating to 38 CE, just five years after the execution of Jesus which was invented to ridicule the Herodian family.

> In particular it has been observed that the buffoonery in which . . . [the] soldiery engage for their diversion has a *parallel* in a sequence of theatrical street-performances *enacted by the Alexandrian mob that ridiculed [Herod] Agrippa I [the brother of Herodias; brother-in-law of Antipas] when he visited their town in 38*. Philo's *In Flaccum* preserves a fairly detailed account of the manner in which the mob of *Alexandria took pleasure in making fun of the king of the Jews—Agrippa*. On the occasion of his visit, the rabble collected and proceeded to enact a sort of mime: they dressed a well-known street-lout named Καραβς [Karabas, whose name means the "Lamb of the Father"], *decked him out in royal style, putting a papyrus shrub on his head as if it were a diadem, hanging a doormat around his shoulders in place of the Χλάμυς [chlamus, robe], and putting in his hand a papyrus stick for a sceptre*. Thus adorned like a carnival-king, Karabas was led by the mob through the streets of the city receiving mock-homages from the merry-making crowds. *The Alexandrians' intention was to hold Agrippa up as an object of ridicule*.[81]

The custom (38 CE) might well have originated with the events occurring during the interview between Jesus and Herod, or else it was a custom in situ for messianic pretenders. We might note that after the execution of Jesus many Nazaraeans migrated to Alexandria (for instance, Mark, Barnabus, and Aristobulus III are said to have lived there early on) where the Nazaraean community was quite large. We also find large Jewish communities there as well. It is not unreasonable to surmise that the Nazaraeans had great scorn for the family of Antipas, and their ridicule of the Herodian king would have been meant to ridicule the artificial king and the Herodian family for their involvement in the case of Jesus. Further, it cannot be conclusively proven that it was Roman soldiers who mocked and scorned Jesus. It cannot be coincidental that the first notation concerning his treatment during the Herodian interview is that *"Herod with his soldiery*, having set him at nought, and *mocked him, threw about him a gorgeous robe*, and sent him back to Pilate" (Matt. 27:27–31). The passage in Matthew would indicate that it was Herod who was "governor" of Israel and it was *his* band who put the scarlet robe on Jesus.

> Then the soldiers of the governor [Herod] took Jesus into the common hall [the judgment hall], and gathered unto him *the whole band* [perhaps a combination of the Temple guard, Herodian soldiery, and Romans] ("of soldiers" not in the original manuscript). And they stripped him, and *put on him a scarlet robe* (Matt. 27:27–28).

Three groups of soldiers are said to have mocked Jesus in the same way, and three different descriptions of the robe were given: scarlet, purple, and "gorgeous" [or radiant,

---

81. Winter, *On the Trial*, p. 103.

magnificent]. It is within this context that we might determine just who the majority of those soldiers might have been. Herod's robe would have been the one called "gorgeous". The indication is that it was Herod's robe (a *royal* robe) that was draped around Jesus' shoulders. Neither the Roman military guards nor the Temple guard would have been in possession of such a fine seamless garment, nor would Pilate, since his dress would have been of the military type. Josephus tells us just what sort of royal robe it was in his description of the type of robe King Herod Agrippa The Great was wearing when he was arrested by the emperor Tiberius. It was the robe of state.

> Upon which [Herod] *Agrippa* betook himself to make supplication for himself, putting him [Tiberius] in mind of his son, *with whom he [Agrippa] was brought up*, and of Tiberius [his grandson] whom he had educated, but all to no purpose, for they led him [Agrippa] about *bound even in his purple garments*.[82]

During the Jewish War Simon bar-Giora (the "leader" of Jerusalem) wore the same habit during his attempt to escape the Romans.

> Dressed in a white tunic *over which floated an ample purple robe*, he emerged suddenly, like a phantom, from beneath the earth, amid the ruins of the Temple area.[83]

The royal robe's color hue might easily have been described as scarlet or purple (as only royalty might wear) and was definitely "gorgeous" [magnificent]. It is a fact that this color is often described *subjectively*; individual viewpoints might differ as to the varying hues of the fabric which might range from blue, bluish-purple, red, and purple. William Wilson defines the Hebrew word for this "color".

> תכלת [*Tekeleth*: blue] *f.* a shell-fish . . . This colour distinguished the dress of princes, &c., imported from remote countries, and is supposed to have been procured from the juice of a purple shell-fish in the Mediterranean sea, conchylium of the ancients, *helix ianthina*, Linn.; or from indigo. This word is almost constantly joined with ארימן ['*argaman*: purple] reddish purple; Exodus xxv. 4, &c.[84]

In the book of Exodus (25:4) the color is described as a *mixture* of the three colors: "blue, and purple, and scarlet". Because of the difficulty in identifying a single color, it was sometimes called scarlet, sometimes purple, and sometimes blue, depending upon the observation of the individual. The Greek word *chiton* here is equivalent to the Hebrew *kuttoneth* and means "robe", not tunic as it is so often mistranslated. It is derived from the Hebrew *katheph* meaning "to clothe the shoulder proper, the spot where the garments hang." There is little doubt that it was Herod's robe of state that the attendants at the execution did not want to rend. Shem-Tob ben-Isaac ben-Shaprut, author of the fourteenth-century treatise, *Even Bohan*, included an entire Gospel of Matthew in Hebrew therein primarily for the purpose of providing rebuttal students and proselytes to Christians of his day, even though Jews were forbidden to read these gospels. He makes it clear that it was the Jewish government who carried out the execution of Jesus.

---

82. Josephus, *Ant.*, 18.5.4.
83. Mazar, *Mountain*, p. 93.
84. Wilson, *Word Studies*, p. 43.

The Jewish Trial

> Pilate when he saw that he had no power of resistance and was unable to make any peace with them, before a great dispute among the people might arise because of this, took water and washed his hands before the people and said: I am innocent (of the blood). *Be careful what you do* (Matt. 27:24–25).[85]

When the people answered that his blood be upon them and their seed . . .

> Then he released Barabbas (to them), and delivered to them Jesus for beating and affliction that they might hang him. Then the horsemen of the court took Jesus under guard and came together before a great company of many people. They clothed Jesus with silk garments and covered him with a greenish silk robe.

> They made a crown of thorns and placed it on his head and set a reed in his right hand and were bowing down mocking him [saying]: Peace be upon you, king of the Jews. They spit in his face and took the reed and struck his head. When they had mocked him (much), they stripped the robe from him, dressed him in his own clothes, and gave orders to hang him (Matt. 27:26–31).[86]

Any discussion of the Jewish trial would be incomplete without the Sanhedrin's perspective of the political nature of Jesus' activities. He was known to have consorted with the worst elements of society; in particular, tax collectors and "robbers" (lestai), who were often connected with the faction of Zealots. Some scholars believe that many of Jesus' own disciples were Galilean Zealots, and there appears to be some evidence that this might be so. Galileans were viewed as "suspicious", primarily because of the messianic contender, Judas. The most obvious among them is Simon Zelotes (the Zealot), but there are others who might well have been involved with that movement as well (i.e., Judas Iscariot). For instance, it is thought by some scholars that Peter's appellation "Bar Jonah" should instead be read Peter, the *barjona*, or terrorist and not as indication of his name.

> The baryonim or biryonim (An Akkadian loanword) were outlaws or terrorists; according to TB Gittin 56a they gained control of the temple area during the first Jewish revolt against Rome, under the leadership of one Abba Siqera [from which the word sicarii is believed to have derived][87]

Peter did, indeed, keep a short sword beneath his cloak (John 18:10). When Peter rebuked Jesus for speaking of his death, some have seen an attempt by Peter to tempt Jesus into becoming militant (Mark 8:31–33). Matthew is believed to have been the "tax collector" Levi, who would have been regarded by them as a Roman "robber", and even Judas Iscariot is thought to have been the disgruntled Zealot who had become disenchanted with Jesus' peaceful program. The Sanhedrin distrusted Galileans, in general, since it was that region that fomented the zealous patriots who threatened their status. We must also remember that Jesus was executed with two supposed robbers, or *lestai*, who Josephus, in using the same word, calls the rebellious *sicarii* (Zealots). The fact that Jesus was well acquainted with such people led the Sanhedrin to try Jesus as a *mesith*, killing two birds with one stone, because that crime is both of a political and a religious

---

85. Howard, *Hebrew Gospel of Matthew*, p. 145.
86. Howard, p. 145.
87. Eisler, *Messiah*, pp. 252 ff, as quoted in Bruce, *Peter*, p. 16n.

nature. He could thus be described as a revolutionary, and as such could be taken "outside the camp" to the Mount of Olives as one *smitten* by God (i.e., with leprosy; Isa. 53). The Messiah has been called the "Leper Scholar" in Jewish writings. The precedent for punishment of a rebellious person is based upon Moses' reaction to his sister's leprosy (Num. 12:14). For this reason, the face is covered and the individual is spat upon.

> But the Lord said to Moses, "if her father spat in her face would she not bear her shame for seven days?" (Num 12:14). R. Ahai b. R. Joshia says, "It is as if she were doubly chastised".[88]

One of the purposes for excommunication was to insult and debase the accused. As evidenced by the list enumerated below, Jesus was excommunicated for a number of reasons.

> Later authorities enumerate the twenty-four [reasons for excommunication] as follows: (1) *insulting a learned man*, even after his death . . . (5) *dealing lightly with any of the rabbinic or Mosaic precepts* . . . (13) *taking the name of God in vain;* (14) *causing others to profane the name of God* ("hillul hashem") . . . (17) *putting a stumbling-block in the way of the blind*, that is to say, tempting one to sin.[89]

All these "crimes" were blasphemous and said to have profaned the name of God. The "vain oath" had resulted in the thirty-nine stripes, "the beating of a lawless man". This is described by the Greek word *dero* [for smote] in Luke 22:64, meaning "to flay", or "to scourge". More definitively, the word "smote" in Matthew 26:68 is the Greek *paio*, "to sting as a scorpion". Both terms indicate that a whip was used for this purpose. He was also beaten with the palms of their hands. The events of the trial narrative within the gospels are sketchy at best, but I believe it is possible to determine the proceedings of the Jewish trial of Jesus. Following the Talmudic passage pertaining to the execution of Jesus (*b. Sanh.* 43a) is a cryptic passage concerning "five disciples" of Jesus. The passage has baffled scholars for centuries, and most have passed it off as impossible to decipher. The passage is quoted below in its entirety. I have placed the Scriptures to which the dialogue is referred at the end of each phrase in brackets.

> Our Rabbis taught: Yeshu [Jesus] had five disciples, Matthai, Nakai, Nezer, Buni and Todah. When Matthai was brought [before the court] he said to them [the judges], Shall Matthai be executed? Is it not written, Matthai [when] shall I come and appear before God [Ps. 42:3, an "Instructive" Psalm]? Thereupon they retorted: Yes, Matthai shall be executed, since it is written, When Matthai [when] shall [he] die and his name perish [Ps. 41:5]. When Nakai was brought in he said to them: Shall Nakai be executed? It is not written, Naki [the innocent] and the righteous slay thou not [Exod. 23:7]? Yes, was the answer, Nakai shall be executed, since it is written, In secret places does Naki [the innocent] slay [Ps. 10:8]. When Nezer was brought in, he said: Shall Nezer be executed? Is it not written, And Nezer [a twig] shall grow forth out of his roots [Isa. 11:1]. Yes, they said, Nezer shall be executed, since it is written, But thou art cast forth away from the grave like Nezer [an abhorred offshoot] [Isa. 14:19]. When Buni was

---

88. Hammer, *Classic Midrash*, p. 263.
89. "Excommunication", J.E., p. 286.

The Jewish Trial

brought in, he said: Shall Buni be executed? Is it not written, Beni [my son], my first born [Exod. 4:22]? Yes, they said, Buni shall be executed, since it is written, Behold I will slay Bine-ka [thy son] thy first born [Exod. 4:23]. And when Todah was brought in, he said to them: Shall Todah be executed? Is it not written, A psalm for Todah [thanksgiving] [Ps. 100:1]? Yes, they answered, Todah shall be executed, since it is written, Whoso offereth the sacrifice of Todah [thanksgiving] honoureth me [Ps. 50:23].[90]

R. Travers Herford, who studied in-depth the Talmud and Midrash for traces of Christianity, like other scholars who have tried to tie the disciples to those of the gospels, states:

Little or nothing can be learnt from the names of the five disciples; only the first, Matthai, has any close resemblance to a name in the list of the twelve (Matt. x. 2-4). The last, Thodah, is not unlike Thaddaeus; but in Hebrew that name would be Thaddai, not Thodah. The others, Naqi, Netzer, and Buni, have no parallels in the list of the Twelve; indeed, it is doubtful whether they, and Thodah, were ever names of persons at all. At most they may have been nick-names, and they certainly *raise the suspicion that they have been chosen for the sake of the texts*. I suggest that the case stands thus:—five disciples of Jesus, i.e., five Christians, were on some occasion condemned to death, that their real names, if known, were not mentioned, that one of them was designated Matthai with reference to the name attached to the first Gospel, that the play upon his name suggested a similar device in the case of the others, and that for them other names were invented, *each of which had some reference to Jesus, as regarded of course by Christians.*[91]

Mr. Herford recognizes two major themes appearing in the passage: 1) that the names were "chosen for the sake of the texts," and 2) that each name was a "reference to Jesus." But there is more to the text than the recalling of the trials of five unknown disciples. I suggest that within the Scriptural references we are to find hidden messages that give us the very transcript of the Jewish proceedings during the trial of Jesus. That the rabbis chose to hide the traditions of the trial through such "fencing" is not at all unusual, and in this way they might prevent the "church", whose anti-Semitism had caused the censorship of their precious Talmud, from understanding their discussion. The stories and legends of the Midrash and Talmud are, many times, presented as parables or fables in order to discuss events in a "hidden way" through Scriptural commentary. Certain linguistic devices are merely used as symbols for those who studied the Hebrew language with such exactness. The sages believed that one needed to "work" and "suffer" to obtain a true meaning of the writings. It is for this reason that much of the Talmud and Midrash seems "silly" to most westerners. The plain fact is that many of the "legends" (which are based on placing a "fence" around Torah) are tied to Scripture. The real meanings of those legends can be derived from Scripture.

Another interpretation: *May my discourse come down as the rain* Deut. 32:2). The Sages say, "Moses said to Israel, 'Perhaps you do not know how much I suffered

---

90. *b. Sanh.* 43a.
91. Herford, *Christianity*, pp. 92–93.

A Book of Evidence

for the Torah, how much effort I put into it, how much I toiled for it'—teach it by suffering—*make it difficult or expense to acquire.*[92]

It is, therefore, thought to be the mark of a great sage to be able to discover the secret messages hidden with the Talmud. Such parables as "growing cucumbers", connoting magic, using biblical names such as Balaam to refer to Jesus, and the four sages' excursion into "Pardes" (Paradise; a mnemonic: *Pesat* = literal interpretation; *Remez* = allegorical interpretation; *Deras* = homiletic interpretation; *Sod* = mystical interpretation); are based on Scripture and are ways of discussing the "secrets of God" or other subjects too sensitive to discuss openly. The passage above is another such example. Prior to further investigation into the tradition, I shall attempt to reconstruct the examination of Jesus before the Sanhedrin in transcript form. These appear to be the main points in the trial. Both the questions and the responses are based on Scripture. I do not here state that these are the actual words of the participants; however, it is clear that the wording of the cryptic passage suggests some similar rendering. It would go something like this:

Sanhedrin (Caiaphas): "I put thee on oath by the Living God, that to us thou say—whether thou art the [Messiah], the Son of God?" [Matt. 26:63]. What is your name? What "god" do you worship? [Implying that Jesus was a *mesith*]. *Jesus*: Jesus remains silent. He does not recognize this *beth din* as the authority of God [Matt. 26:63]. He refuses to answer their question, instead fencing with the Masters (as is characteristic of their debates). *When* [Matthai] am I to appear before *righteous* judges (*elohim*) and appear before YHWH's true representatives? [This is a rhetorical question].

Sanhedrin: When [*Matthai*] will you be executed and your name perish? *What* is your name? [The High-priests consider his reply an insult to the integrity of the court and reply in like manner, pressing for his name].

Jesus: I am innocent [*N'ki*]. Will you slay me? "If I should tell you in nowise would ye believe, And if I should put questions in nowise would ye answer" [Luke 22: 67–68].

Sanhedrin: You are leading the innocent [*Naki*] astray by teaching them your false doctrine in *secret*. (Again a reference to a charge of "mysticism", "sorcery", or slanderous conduct toward the scribes.) What is your name?

Jesus: "I openly have spoken unto the world,—I ever taught in synagogue, and in the temple, where all the Jews gather together; and *in secret* spake nothing" [John 18:19]. I am a Nazaraean, the branch [*Nezer*] from the stock of Jesse. I am the Messiah.

Sanhedrin: We believe you are a detested and abhorred offshoot [*Nezer*], an impostor. What is your name?

Jesus: I am the Son [*Beni*] of God, his firstborn son.

Sanhedrin: We are going to execute you if you persist in these appellations. Don't you know we shall execute you if you continue saying you are the firstborn [*Bine-ku*]? What is your name?

---

92. Hammer, *Classic Midrash*, p. 345 and n.

Jesus: God desires thanksgiving, praise [*Todah*] and mercy, *not sacrifice* of animals by which you gain your wealth and power. "Hereafter ye will see the Son of Man sitting on the right hand of power, and coming upon the clouds of heaven [Matt. 26:64].

Sanhedrin: This is a confession to the crime. He tells us in our presence that he is against the priesthood of the nation, against the Temple, and he has desecrated the Name of God and the authority of the *Beth Din* while under oath. We shall honor God by offering [*Todah*] Temple sacrifice and by offering [*yadah*, the root of *todah*, stoning and hanging and used as referring to "making confession" or atonement by death] this *mesith* as a "lawless man". "What further need have we for witnesses. Heard ye the profanity? What to you doth it appear?"

Sanhedrin (Judges): Guilty on all counts [Mark 14:64].

Since Jesus was pronounced guilty, ordinarily, he would have been sent to Beth Pagi "outside the camp" for sentencing. It was only here that a criminal sentence might be pronounced; however, the high priest could not leave the "Stone House" due to ritual impurity, and the verdict was pronounced there. Once the judges had gathered (at daybreak), the following verdict would have been added to the trial transcript.

Verdict: The verdict is unanimous. The accused is to be flogged with thirty-nine stripes for the indiscretion of the "vain oath". After consulting with the Roman authorities (both Pilate and Herod), he is to be taken to the *Beth haSeqilah* ("Place of Stoning") at Gulgoleth, on the Mount of Olives, where he shall be hanged alive and stoned for the crime of blasphemy. The high priest goes to a ewer and washes his hands.

Within the *Toldoth Yeshua* is an interpolated text of the same proceedings, and for confirmation that this cryptic Talmudic passage relates to the trial proceedings of Jesus, that portion (4:11–19) is quoted here.

> (11) Immediately the wise men perceived this, they rose up against him, and seized him. (12) [[They say unto him, What is thy name? He saith unto them, Mathai. They say unto him, How establishest thou this? He saith unto them, When (*mathai*) shall I come and appear before God? They say unto him, When (*mathai*) shall he die, and his name perish? (13) Again they say unto him, What is thy name? He saith, Naki. They say unto him, How establishest thou this? He saith, Innocent (*n'ki*) of hands, and pure of heart. They say unto him, The innocent (*nakeh*) he will not clear. (14) Again they say unto him, What is thy name? He saith, Buni. They say, How establishest thou this? He saith, My son (*b'ni*) my firstborn, even Israel. They say, Concerning thee it was said, Behold, I will slay thy son (*binchah*), even thy firstborn. (15) And they say again, What is thy name? He saith, Netser. They say, How establishest thou this? He saith, A branch (*netser*) shall spring forth from his roots. They say unto him, Thou art cast out of thy grave like an abominable branch (*netser*). And in like manner, much more, *as he stated in his behalf many other names.* (16) Forthwith *they held him*, and his three hundred and ten disciples were unable to deliver him. (17) Now the same hour that he saw himself brought to death, he began and said, Did not David prophesy concerning me and say, For thy sake we are killed. But of you said Isaiah, Your hands are full of blood. And of you said the prophet before the Holy One, blessed be he, And thy prophets they slew with the sword. (18) then began the insurgents

> [disciples] to lament, but they were not able to deliver him. (19) *And in that same hour [they brought him down to the place of stoning] . . . and was he put to death.*[93]

Although the tradition in Verse 22 describes the later Pharisaic method of stoning an individual prior to hanging him on the tree, the Sadducean practice was the biblical method, to be stoned by the Whole Congregation of Israel and hanged on a tree. Did this occur? We shall examine this in our chapter on "The Execution". This part of the text describes part of the punishment:

> [F]or while he was *yet alive* he knew the custom of Israel that they would *hang him*, and knew his death, and the manner of his being put to death, *that at the last he would be hanged on a tree.*[94]

Five times Jesus was asked who he was. The first time he would have asked to be fairly treated. Each time the judges determined that the verdict should be guilty. What Jesus basically said was this: "When can I be brought before righteous judges? I am innocent of the charges. My residence is in Nazareth (I am a Nazaraean), and I am the "branch" of Jesse, of the royal House of David. I am the expected legitimate Messiah. I am the Son of God. God desire's mercy and thanksgiving, not the sacrifice that you render to him in the Temple." The judges would have immediately seized upon this last Scripture as being in opposition to their Temple graft and banking hierarchy, a confession to his "crime". They would have declared him guilty of the crime of political and religious insurgency; he would have been labeled a *mesith*, one who was leading the nation of Israel astray by his teachings, and one who found the scribal interpretations of the rulers objectionable.

As Caiaphas said, "What further need have we for witnesses. Heard ye the profanity? What to you doth it appear?" (Mark 14:63–64). At this point, "they *all* condemned him to be worthy of death" (64). This cryptic passage that has eluded us for so long becomes clear when taken in conjunction with the gospel narratives. The original Hebrew Gospel (Gospel of the Hebrews) conforms to the Gospel of John in that it clearly states the Jewish *rulers* were responsible for the execution of Jesus.

> It is written in the Gospel of the Hebrews that . . . The Jews [rulers] grew envious of him and came to hate him. *They changed the custom of their law* and they rose up against him and laid a trap and caught him. They turned him over to the governor [Herod? Pilate?], *who gave him back to them to crucify [hang]. And after they had raised him on the cross [tree]*, the Father took him up into heaven to himself.[95]

In light of the evidence presented in this chapter, it simply cannot be said that the trial of Jesus was illegal in any way. Perhaps the Sanhedrin was corrupt and self-serving, but that same Sanhedrin governed Israel as its supreme authority. As the supreme Jewish authority, it had every *legal* right to try Jesus (even on trumped-up charges) and to put him to death. The Sanhedrin simply sought to exercise that option. In hindsight, we see the Sanhedrin's actions as a moral crime. This indictment is not a

---

93. Schonfield, *According*, pp. 49–50, and n.2.
94. Schonfield, p. 50.
95. Miller and Funk, *Complete Gospels*, ASV, p. 430, Gosp. Heb.

The Jewish Trial

condemnation of the Jewish people as a whole but *only* that corrupt government as it existed in the first century. While centuries of study have enabled us to recognize and more fully understand the spiritual character and nature of Jesus, as well as his doctrine, the chaotic state of political affairs in Judea during the first century and the rigid legal rules of the scribes, would have made it impossible for the ruling class to view Jesus in a favorable light (just as God had willed it). They found him a threat to their system of graft, to their Hellenized society, and a threat to what they deemed national security. In their own understanding and under the legislation current at that time, Jesus could be tried as a *mesith* and a blasphemer; he was deemed a threat to their political existence. The rulers did not, however, want to be held responsible by either the Roman government for fear their positions might be placed in jeopardy (which would lead to complete Roman authoritarian rule over Israel), nor by the population of Israel for fear the Zealots would revolt and kill them (which they eventually did anyway). They had tried to maintain a delicate balance between the two, but their plan, while at first succeeding, backfired on them. They would not only lose their powerful positions, they would lose their nation and their lives. But it was with that plan in mind that they bound Jesus and took him to Pilate.

4

The Roman Pseudo-Trial

WITHOUT SOME GLIMPSE INTO the history and conditions existing at the inception of Roman assimilation in Judea and a portrayal of Pontius Pilate, the Roman prefect, as well as the reputation of the Herodian Dynasty, there can be no real comprehension of the Roman proceedings pertaining to Jesus. The circumstances occurring shortly before and running concurrently with the advent of Jesus provide insight into just what really did occur that day when Jesus was sent to Pilate.

ROMAN ADMINISTRATION OVER JUDEA

Roman administration over Judea, the area later called Palestine, can be said to have effectively begun in 6 CE with the appointment of Coponius, the first prefect. It was also during this year that the Zealot movement was born in Galilee in opposition to Roman rule. Until the year 44 CE these "governors" held only the title of "prefect". It was only after Agrippa's death that they received the official designation of "procurator". Prefects, in general, were not very powerful. They were generally ineffective diplomats; some were military men who had risen in rank; others senators from Rome. They were appointed directly by the Emperor of Rome, usually through some favor to individuals having acted in a friendly capacity toward the government. As such, their rule in Judea against the patriotic, extremely religious, if not fanatical, Jews was never quite what was intended. The Jewish nation at the time of the death of Herod the Great was not easily ruled. Its citizens' patriotic and religious fervor eventually led to the destruction of the Temple and the City of Jerusalem in 70 CE. Josephus places the blame on the population of Zealots, whom he called sicarii (or robbers, *lestai*).[1] For the most part, Rome had allowed Judea its separatism. The prefects were generally not very interested in Judea's alien religion and laws. The Roman Empire found it most desirable to allow its territories to act independently in religious matters. The ineffectiveness of the prefects might be

---

1. Josephus, *War* 4.3.11-14.

said to stem from the fact that Rome had not completely assimilated Judea into the Roman Empire. Thus Rome had found the best military and political management for ruling Judea was to allow the local authorities to maintain direct rule over affairs that did not concern Roman interests.

> Disinterested in the religious concerns of the subject and associate populations, the Romans fastidiously refrained from interfering in the domain of jurisdiction on matters of Jewish religious law. It was, in fact, an undertaking on the part of Rome that *the ancestral Jewish law should continue to be applied and should be protected by the imperial representative* .²

During the earliest period of Roman assimilation, the Roman Senate had, in fact, confirmed the royal leadership of King Herod the Great. For the period in which he reigned, Herod possessed exclusive rights in trying political legal cases, while the Sanhedrin's authority was denigrated to those concerning only religious issues. At Herod's death, the Sanhedrin, having sent a deputation to Rome, requested that Rome allow them complete autonomy under the rule of one of Herod's sons. They believed their liberty would be better served if joint rulers, one a Roman prefect and the other a son of Herod, were appointed to rule in Judea. Rome was not at all opposed to this solution of indirect rule and, in fact, found it beneficial. A race whose nationalistic and religious tendencies ran so parallel was thought by Rome to better serve the pax Romanus. Rome was disinterested in the internal affairs of the Jewish nation. The first prefect was thus sent to Judea at the request of the Jewish rulers solely to safeguard the Syrian-Egyptian highway. The prefect himself was expected to respect Jewish religious law and customs without interference.

> Cases between Jew and Jew were left to the adjudication of their own tribunals, from the village judges up to the high court in Jerusalem. It was the general policy of Rome to leave local matters . . . to be settled in the native courts by native law . . . Religious issues would certainly be . . . referred to the Sanhedrin . . . The Romans . . . allowed native courts considerable latitude, *including civil and criminal competence as well as merely religious [affairs]* . . . In Palestine Greeks as well as Jews had jurisdiction in non-political matters over their respective citizens, and the Romans were as a rule careful not to encroach upon these prerogatives.³

The administrative capital of the province was not located in Jerusalem but in northern Caesarea Philippi where the military was garrisoned and the seat of the prefect was situated. The governor of Syria, however, frequently intervened in the affairs of Judea, his power overshadowing that of the prefect assigned to that province. The Judean prefect thus answered to the more powerful Syrian governor.

Rome's desire for cooperative rule, however, was not through any particular notion of kindness. Should Judea's cities be destroyed, she could yield no taxation monies to the government. Neither could its prefects and their agents skim their share from Rome's profits.⁴ Thus three corrupt groups arose in wealth and status during those earliest decades of the first century: 1) the Babylonian-Alexandrian-Herodian oligarchy of priests,

---

2. Winter, *On the Trial*, p. 11.
3. Winter, p. 14.
4. Blaiklock, *Compact Handbook*, pp. 63-69.

including the families of Hanan, Boethus (to a lesser extent), Kimchit, and Phiabi; 2) the Herodian rulers and royal administrators known to have ties with the powerful families of the priesthood; and 3) the Roman prefect and his agents, the tax collectors who themselves were many times bought with bribes. Yet there existed an ironic ring of hatred and fear among these three groups. The system of graft they shared kept these groups tightly bound into an improbable brotherhood of sorts, working together cooperatively only to maintain their self-indulgent lifestyles. Pontius Pilate proved to be no more or less susceptible to the system than those prefects preceding or succeeding him.

PONTIUS PILATE

Pontius Pilate, quite the weakest of the prefects to rule over Judea was (as testified by Josephus) specifically sent to Judea in order to do away with self-rule among the Jews. Josephus tells us he brought in images of the Emperor that infuriated the Jewish people.

> But now Pilate, the procurator of Judea, removed the army from Caesarea to Jerusalem, to take their winter-quarters there, *in order to abolish the Jewish laws. So he introduced Caesar's effigies*, which were upon the ensigns and brought them into the city; whereas our law forbids us the very making of images . . . Pilate was the first who brought those images to Jerusalem, and set them up there.[5]

This particular incident initiated a series of clashes between Pilate and the government of Israel. It seems he was ever embroiled in some political intrigue.

> Under the first Roman governors, with the exception of Pilate, relations between the Jewish nation and the Roman Empire were not markedly hostile . . . From the time of Pilate onwards, reports of unrest and riots become more frequent, and a gradual disillusionment from the hopes that had been attached to Roman rule is evident . . . *The first serious deterioration between the Jews and the Roman administration did not occur until the days of Pontius Pilate (26-36), who is remembered as a harsh, stubborn governor, not easily appeased* . . . One of the most dangerous incidents during his term of office was his decision to bring the banners of a Roman army unit, bearing the image of the emperor, into Jerusalem . . . *Yet another dispute broke out when Pilate wanted to bring shields dedicated to the Emperor Tiberius into Jerusalem*. The Jews put up an organized, determined resistance, led by four of Herod's sons. Following intervention by the emperor himself, the shields were removed from Jerusalem to Caesarea.[6]

Pilate was caught between the proverbial rock and hard place. His life and career would be burdened by the constant strain of attempting to maintain his *personal* status quo while, at the same time, trying to appease his patron Sejanus and the opposing directives of his emperor, Tiberius. The insurrectionist, Sejanus, once a minister in Tiberius' counsel and second only to the emperor himself, had been instrumental in having Pilate appointed to the post in Judea. It was Sejanus who had instructed Pilate to "abolish the Jewish laws", not Tiberius. It might well have been Sejanus himself who advised Pilate to bring the

---

5. Josephus, *Ant.* 18.3.1.
6. Ben-Sasson, *A History*, pp. 251–252.

images into Jerusalem. There is evidence that it was Tiberius' wish that the Jewish people be left to their own religion. There is further ancient evidence by Eusebius that Pilate did not attempt this at the request of the emperor himself, but at the urging of his patron.

> First, then, he relates, that in the reign of Tiberius, at Rome, *Sejanus*, who was then in great favour with Tiberius, *had made every effort to destroy the whole nation of the Jews from the foundation*, and that in Judea Pontius Pilate, *under whom* [not *by* whom] the crimes were committed against our Saviour, having attempted something contrary to what was lawful among the Jews respecting the temple at Jerusalem, which was then yet standing, excited them to the greatest tumults.[7]

There is every indication that Sejanus was not only Pilate's patron but that it was through the powerful Sejanus that Pilate had been appointed prefect in Judea. Although many stories have been told of Pilate's ruthless character, he often wavered between rage and submission on account of the Jewish peoples, his patron, and his emperor.

> We have it on the authority of Philo, as reported by Eusebius, that *Sejanus*, the all-powerful minister at the emperor's court, had taken "energetic steps to exterminate the whole Jewish race": it is assumed that, with this purpose in mind, *he had prevailed upon Tiberius, or his predecessor, to send Pilate as governor to Judaea*—he was strong-minded, ruthless, and dependable enough to be entrusted with a mission of that nature . . . But there are those who think—and there is no evidence to the contrary—that he acquired his evil ways *only after he came to Judaea*. He was certainly not an ideal governor, Eduard Meyer writes, "but if even their own rulers could never cope with the Jews, and each measure they took provoked immediate criticism and fanatical resistance—a normal Roman officer must have been driven by them to utter despair . . ." Add thereto the never ending acts of violence of the bandits, always covered up by religio-political motives. That the governors then occasionally grew wild and attacked blindly, ought only too well to be understood.[8]

Tiberius had no desire to offend the Jews nor did he want to confront any unnecessary problems in a foreign land while warring in other regions. On having been made aware of Pilate's insensitivity, Philo informs us that Tiberius dispatched to him a command to withdraw the shields. After the execution of Jesus, Pilate was accused by Vitellius, governor of Syria, of the massive slaughter of Samaritans in the village of Tirathaba. That incident resulted in Pilate's being recalled to Rome to face Tiberius.[9]

> It seems that Pilate's conduct in Judea was inspired by Tiberius' minister Sejanus, the real power behind the throne in those days. *After Sejanus' fall in 31*, Pilate's influence gradually dwindled, and when he treated the Samaritans too severely, he was recalled (in 36).[10]

Sejanus, however, had plotted to overthrow the Roman Emperor Tiberius. This single event, superimposed over the delicate situation Pilate found himself in, must have

---

7. Eusebius, *Eccl. Hist.* 2.5.7; p. 55.
8. Cohn, *Trial and Death*, pp. 14–16.
9. Josephus, *Ant.* 18.4.2,3.
10. Ben-Sasson, *A History*, p. 253.

thrown Pilate into an even more precarious political situation. He had become guilty by association. His political position had become unstable with the Roman government, and he found himself wavering between the pressure of the Jews on one hand, the ever-watchful eye of Antipas in between, and Tiberius on the other. It is no wonder that some scholars have suggested Pilate's erratic behavior might have been attributable to paranoid schizophrenia.

> Pilate was originally appointed prefect in A.D. 26 at the request of *Aelius Seianus* [Sejanus], a high ranking Roman of great influence with Emperor Tiberius. Pilate's job was to keep the rebellious peoples of the far eastern edge of the Roman Empire at peace. Despite his blunders he remained a favorite of the Emperor's. But *in A.D. 31*, Aelius Seianus himself was caught plotting to overthrow Tiberius. *Pilate, a thousand miles away in Jerusalem, had no part in the scheme, but a cloud of suspicion descended on him. Since Pilate had no powerful protector in Rome to speak well of him to the emperor, he was in grave danger.*[11]

Josephus describes for us the history of Sejanus' fall:

> She [Antonia] had also been the greatest benefactress to Tiberius, when there was a very *dangerous plot laid against him by Sejanus*, a man who had been her husband's friend, and *who had the greatest authority, because he was general of the army, and when many members of the senate, and many of the freedmen, joined with him, and the soldiery was corrupted, and the plot was come to a great height.* Now Sejanus had certainly gained his point, had not Antonia's boldness been more wisely conducted than Sejanus's malice; for when she had discovered his designs against Tiberius, she wrote him an exact account of the whole, and gave the letter to Pallas, the most faithful of her servants, and sent him to Capreae to *Tiberius, who, when he understood it, slew Sejanus and his confederates.*[12]

There had not been one but two incidents in which Pilate had tried to introduce the images of the Emperor into Jerusalem. In the second Pilate ordered his men to disguise themselves and mix with the Jewish crowd.

> Now when he was apprised aforehand of this disturbance, he mixed his own soldiers in their armor with the multitude, and ordered them to conceal themselves under the habits of private men, and not indeed to use their swords, but with their staves to beat those that made the clamor. He then gave the signal from his tribunal (to do as he had bidden them).[13]

Sometimes, Pilate cowered before the Jews; sometimes, he was ruthless. His constantly changing behavior has been mystifying in the study of the man's psyche. Certainly, the stress of his position in attempting to pacify the Jewish nation and Herod Antipas, while at the same time trying to please his emperor were, in the end, enough to cause Pilate to take his own life at his recall in 36–37 CE.

Philo's testimony concerning the introduction of the shields into Jerusalem attests to the fact that Pilate feared the Jewish leaders might send a deputation to Tiberius in

---

11. Foreman, *Crucify Him*, p. 130.
12. Josephus, *Ant.*, 18.6.6.
13. Josephus, *War* 2.9.4.

The Roman Pseudo-Trial

Rome with complaint of his conduct. The Jewish influence in Rome was quite substantial during the Julio-Claudian period. It has been said that there had already been made against Pilate some several complaints, and the emperor was growing weary of hearing of his failures. Coupled with the sedition of his patron Sejanus, Pilate had ample reason to fear the emperor's wrath.

> He [Philo] states that *Pilate feared lest Jewish notables should send a deputation to Tiberius and explose his arbitrary government in Judaea*, denouncing his insolence, his rapacity, his high-handed treatment of his subjects, and his disposition to cruelty which led him in numerous cases to order the execution of people without previous trial.[14]

That Pilate was growing quite anxious for his position and, indeed, for his very life is universally known. He wanted no problems from the Jews, nor indeed from Antipas, who was in even greater favor with Tiberius than himself. After all, Antipas and his brothers had been raised and educated alongside the Emperor's own son and in his own household. It is certain Antipas held this affinity with Caesar's household over the lowly prefect's head. The rulers of the Sanhedrin, themselves, had found the powerful instrument by which they could gain their own will in both political and religious matters.

> On three several occasions he had brought himself into hostile relationship with the Jews by his sycophantic desire to make a display of his loyalty to Tiberius. He had come to regard the Jews with scornful contempt, and *yet also with a certain feeling of fear lest they should by some complaint of his administration lodged at Rome, awaken the suspicion of Tiberius, with the result of his removal from place and power*. That these apprehensions on the part of Pilate were well grounded we learn from Josephus, who relates that Pilate in fact lost his position as Procurator through just such a complaint; and that within a year or so after the crucifixion of Jesus.[15]

Pilate's political maneuvering had finally placed him in ultimate danger of losing, not only his position, but his life as well. Apparently, he feared the outcome of the emperor's decision so much that he decided not to wait for it. Had he done so, his fears might have come to naught since Tiberius died before Pilate could reach Rome.

> It is proper also, to observe, how it is asserted that this same Pilate, who was governor at our Saviour's crucifixion, in the reign of Caius, whose times we are recording, fell into such calamities that he was forced to become his own murderer, and the avenger of his own wickedness.[16]

Josephus records the account that removed Pilate from his jurisdiction in Judea. It appears that Pilate had attempted to keep the Samaritans from worshipping on Mount Gerazim. Since a great number of these individuals gathered there to see the "sacred vessels which were laid under that place",[17] Pilate believed they were insurrectionists. He gathered together his troops, killing a great many of them and taking others captive.

14. Winter, *On the Trial*, pp. 53–54.
15. Richards, *Illegality*, p. 22.
16. Eusebius, *Eccl. Hist.* 2.7; p. 57.
17. Josephus, *Ant.*, 18.4.1.

> But when this tumult was appeased, the Samaritan senate sent an embassy to Vitellius, a man that had been consul, and who was now president of Syria, and accused Pilate of the murder of those that were killed . . . So Vitellius sent Marcellus, a friend of his, to take care of the affairs of Judea, and ordered Pilate to go to Rome, to answer before the emperor to *the accusation of the Jews*. So Pilate, when he had tarried ten years in Judea, made haste to Rome, and this in obedience to the orders of Vitellius, which he durst not contradict; but before he could get to Rome, Tiberius was dead.[18]

At the same time Pilate was told to return to Rome, Vitellius deprived Caiaphas of his high-priestly office, appointing instead Jonathan, a son of Annas, to serve in that capacity. Jonathan was, perhaps, the most ineffective member of the House of Hanan, and for that reason refused the second offer of the high-priestly office. Annas held the greatest of power in the political arena. It is obvious the relationship between Caiaphas and Pilate would be detrimental to the political affairs of Israel. It might be that this was a political maneuver by Annas, himself.

TIBERIUS

Once timid and introverted, the emperor Tiberius was known to have become a suspicious and unrelenting tyrant. When he had taken the imperial office, the Senate had just begun to review matters of dynastic inheritance in the election of the emperor. He had not been the first choice to fill the office, and he was disliked and misunderstood. It was only through his marriage to Julia, the former wife of Marcus Agrippa, that Tiberius had managed to secure the office. In order to do this, however, he had had to divorce his own wife who he loved dearly. The marriage to Julia had been a political move, and Tiberius soon found himself both regretting the marriage and disliking Julia and her three sons. It was for this reason that Tiberius, in 6 BCE, retired to the island of Rhodes, where he focused on his own private education. Because of his constant paranoic fear of rebellion and conspiracy, Tiberius instituted the law of *maiestas* (or treason). He did not, at first, employ the law because if the accuser was successful, he might receive a share of the convicted man's estate, and Tiberius saw this as a misuse of privilege. However, after the fall of Sejanus in 31 CE, his mental instability caused him to embark upon a reign of terror. Tiberius had secluded himself from his ministers and the Roman senate on the island of Capri in 27 CE, the year Jesus began his ministry in Israel, and he remained there until his death in 37 CE. It was during this period of time that Sejanus had sought to usurp his position, that Pilate feared Caesar's suspicion resulting in a charge of treason, that the Sanhedrin moved to the Bazaars (*khanoot*) of Annas located on the Mount of Olives at Beth Pagi (*b.Shabb.* 15a, *b. A.Z.* 8b, *b. Sanh.* 12a, 41a, *b. R.H.* 31a), and Jesus was executed.

> Tiberius Caesar was the most morbid, jealous and capricious tyrant which had, thus far, donned the imperial purple as Emperor of the Roman world. The slightest suggestion of treason in any part of his empire aroused his suspicious

---

18. Josephus, *Ant.*, 18.4.2.

temperament to intense activity. Tacitus records 52 cases of prosecutions for treason during his reign, many of these for the most flimsy and trivial causes.[19]

It is small wonder that Pilate might have feared Jewish complaints to the Emperor concerning his behavior, especially since his patron Sejanus had just been executed. The sons of Herod the Great, having had close associations with Rome from their youth and favored by the Emperor probably kept him fearful. Pilate, in effect, was walking a tightrope in Judea; one wrong step and his life and career would topple. His personality is often seen as paradoxical: at one time he was cruel and arrogant; at another he was a weakling, giving in to Jewish demands. It is under these precarious conditions that Jesus was brought before the prefect by the Sanhedrin. It will be shown in the discussion that follows that Pilate had much less to do with the execution of Jesus than has been commonly believed. It will also be shown that prefect was blackmailed by the political Sanhedrin and that it was Herod Antipas who sanctioned the execution. Pilate was in dire need of Herod's support and influence with the Roman emperor at the time of Jesus' trial. His decision to send Jesus to Herod was less an attempt to "pass the buck" or neglect his duty than to gain the emperor's favor. If Pilate could reconcile with the tetrarch, perhaps Herod might use his influence with Tiberius to restore Pilate's reputation. The Gospel of Luke makes note that from that day forward they became "friends" (Luke 23:12). In other words, they formed a closer political alliance; Herod Antipas (who Jesus calls a "fox" in the gospels) now had Pilate exactly where he wanted him. This same Herod was known to have been subversive toward other individuals and served somewhat as a spy for Tiberius in order to remain in his favor. Antipas, always the politician, would do whatever he deemed necessary to insure and promote his own rule over Israel. Josephus records one such example of his malignant political behavior.

> [B]ut Herod [the tetrarch], being desirous to give Caesar *the first information* that they had obtained hostages, sent posts with letters, wherein he had accurately described all the particulars, *and had left nothing for the consular Vitellius to inform him of*. But when Vitellius's letters were sent, and Caesar had let him know that he was acquainted with the affairs already, because Herod had given him an account of them before, *Vitellius was very much troubled* at it; and supposing that he had been thereby a greater sufferer than he really was, *he kept up a secret anger upon this occasion, till he could be revenged on him*; which he was after Caius had taken the government [Antipas was exiled].[20]

This political "brown-nosing" provides evidence of his character and motives. Like his father before him, Antipas was "useful" to Rome.

THE HERODIAN DYNASTY

The Herodian Dynasty which had ruled over Judea was founded by Herod the Great, an Idumean, *said* to be of Jewish blood but in reality only a proselyte to Judaism. Politically, his allegiance was to Antony and Cleopatra and, later, to Augustus who conferred upon

---

19. Richards, *Illegality*, p. 21.
20. Josephus, *Ant.* 18.4.5

him the title of king. It was through Roman military aid that Herod had solidified his position in Judea by defeating the Jewish Hasmonean kings. Herod was a strong and crafty military commander and a shrewd ruler. His character and reputation earned for him the felicitude of Rome. He was known to maintain continuous contact with his Roman friends, while entertaining and employing his principle ministers and administrators from among the Greeks. He knew little of Jewish culture nor religion. It might be noted that in the Gospel of Matthew (2:7) he was unaware of any messianic prophecies. He had found it necessary to call in his puppet priests to respond to the inquiries of the magi (astronomers). Herod's own sons were tutored by foreigners and sent to Rome at early ages in order to be instructed in Hellenic culture and court manners. It was in that household that they became fast friends with the family of Tiberius. Because of the continuous political intrigue that characterized the family of Herod, he executed three of his own sons on charges of conspiracy because he suspected them of collaboration with the Romans. It was Herod who instituted the Hellenic Babylonian-Alexandrian priesthood in Judea. These priests were especially composed of the families of Boethus (to a lesser extent) and Phiabi, who became his political allies. He appointed as the first high priest one Hanamel, a Babylonian. To add to his political security, he married Mariamne I, a royal granddaughter of Hyrcanus the priest, and having put her to death, married another, Mariamne II, the daughter of Simon Boethus, a man he later appointed as high priest. It was their granddaughter, Herodias, who had married Herod Antipas, her living husband's half-brother. The Jewish population was outraged by such an affront to their religious sensibilities. These complaints of the people were vocalized by John the Immerser. The Hellenistic and Babylonian influence upon the Jewish priesthood would forever change Judaism. These individuals were known to have demonstrated the views, political, religious, and economic, of their crafty monarch. Together, the Herodians and the priesthood, became the aristocratic ruling class in Judea, reflecting Roman politics and Greek culture and learning so prominent in the pagan societies surrounding Judea. Herod's building projects reflected the architecture of these cultures as well.

Having been brought up and educated in Rome, Herod's surviving sons continued his policies after his death. Herod Antipas, tetrarch of Galilee and Peraea, continued his father's luxuriant lifestyle. He practiced his father's politics, still appointing foreign administrators to royal offices. He also alienated the Jews by his marriage to a Samaritan woman, Malthus. The breach became intolerable when he divorced her (resulting in a war) and married Herodias, his cousin and his own (half) brother's wife. A great deal of intermarriage within this family and the newly installed priesthood was to shape the historical events that caused John and Jesus to begin their ministries against the Temple Cult. Herod Antipas also succeeded his father in his building projects. It was Antipas who founded the city of Tiberius (17–22) in Galilee (in honor of Caesar) as the administrative capitol. Because the city was newly built at the time the author of John wrote his gospel, he frequently referred to the Sea of Galilee as the "Sea of Tiberius". Since the author was from Jerusalem and not a Galilean himself, he would have called the city *only* by that name.

Although his tetrarchy did not include Jerusalem, Herod's influence was felt there. He was closely allied with the Babylonian-Alexandrian priesthood (who held estates in Galilee) instituted by his corrupt father and the pseudo-Sadducean "Herodians" who had governor that Pilate would be removed from his office a few years hence. Thus we find Pilate's resentment and scorn toward this group of rulers reflected in his remarks. He knew the Sanhedrin was politically shaken by the fact that Jesus (as they well knew) was the legitimate royal heir. Had Jesus been proclaimed king, and Herod Antipas deposed, their own world would come tumbling down. Pilate could not resist one final dig at their sensibilities: he stated to them derisively: "Behold your King" (John 19:15). He brought him out to them, having scourged Jesus to prove a point, proclaiming to them that Jesus was not the emperor-god nor nationalistic messiah they had claimed, that he was only a man, albeit the legitimate royal heir to the throne of Israel, yet one who held no real political power and, therefore, not perceived by him as a threat. The Jewish rulers had claimed that Jesus, like the emperor-gods, had wrought "miracles". Pilate determined that Jesus was no more than a man, no threat at all to the Roman government, and this after sending him for examination by Herod.

> Pilate therefore went forth again [outside], and saith unto them, Behold, I bring him forth to you [outside], that ye may know that I find no fault in him. Then Jesus came forth [outside], wearing the crown of thorns and the purple robe. And Pilate saith unto them, *Behold, the man!* (John 19:4--5).

To be sure, this was after *Herod's* soldiery had set him "at nought" and "mocked him". Now, it becomes important to note one very important historical fact. The Romans did not practice scourging as a prerequisite to crucifixion until 64–66 CE during the time of Florus Gessius.

> They also caught many of the quiet people, and brought them before Florus, *whom he first chastised with stripes, and then crucified.* Accordingly, the whole number of those that were destroyed that day, with their wives and children (for they did not spare even the infants themselves), was about three thousand and six hundred; and what made this calamity the heavier, was *this new method of Roman barbarity; for Florus ventured then to do what no one had done before,* that is, to have men of the equestrian order *whipped and nailed to the cross before his tribunal.*[25]

Another practice that is said to have occurred at Roman hands is the parting of Jesus' clothes, casting lots for his seamless garment, yet this, too, is expressly forbidden by Roman law.

> Clothing of which a man can be stripped are those things which he brought with him when he was placed in prison, and with which he is attired when he is conducted to punishment, as the name itself indicates. *Hence, neither the executioners nor their assistants can claim these things as spoils at the moment when the culprit is executed.*[26]

It is, in fact, the *custom* of the Jewish priesthood to divide the clothes of the accused at his death by casting lots for them.

> Our Rabbis taught: The property of those executed by the State [note 3: The reference is to the *Jewish* State; e.g. those executed for treason against the King

---

25. Josephus, *War* 2.14.9.
26. Ulpianus, *Digest.* xlviii. 20, 6; http://www.constitution.org/sps/sps11.htm.

> (YHWH)] belongs to the King (YHWH, or his representatives); the property of those executed by the Beth din belongs to their heirs ... hence it is said, Naboth did curse God and the King [note 1: pointing to his culpability for treason to the king [government] in addition to blasphemy, which is punished by the Beth din; *hence his estate would fall to the crown [government)].*[27]

As we shall learn in a later chapter, the execution is carried out in a Jewish fashion down to the most minute details.

While Pilate saw little significance in the Jewish charge, Herod, on the other hand, stood much to lose if the populace took it upon themselves to crown Jesus as king. Much like his father, Herod the Great, Antipas felt threatened by the legitimate heir to the throne. There is evidence from Irenaeus, one of the early church fathers, that Herod had, in fact, been the instigator of the death of Jesus.

> Irenaeus relates that Herod [Antipas] and Pontius Pilate came together and condemned Jesus to be crucified. *"For Herod was frightened lest he be ousted by him (= Jesus) from the kingship* ... while *Pilate was constrained [forced or blackmailed] by Herod and by the Jews [rulers] around him to deliver [Jesus] unwillingly to death on the grounds that not to do so would be to go against Caesar* by liberating a man who was given the title of king".[28]

It is evident here that Pilate had not wanted to put Jesus to death, but was *constrained* to do so. The word "constrain", as defined by Webster: "to force by imposed stricture, restriction, or limitation." In other words, Pilate was blackmailed! Melito of Sardis states: *"Though Jesus must needs be crucified, Israel should have let him suffer at the hand of the Gentiles*, by the oppressor's hand, *not by Israel's action".*[29]

Melito's statement, and those of other historians and church leaders in those first few centuries, implies that it was not by Pilate's decree that Jesus was executed but by the decree of the judicial Sanhedrin and by Herod Antipas, those who would stand to lose the greatest political power and influence in the land. It is well known that the Jewish rulers sometimes gave bribes to their Roman overlords in order to attain their desires.

Even the Jewish people, who certainly have no reason to admit to the execution, often reference this incident within the writings of the Talmud and Tosefta. The references of a Jewish execution are, in fact, so numerous that it is to be wondered why they are not taken seriously. After all, nothing anti-Semitic can be found in them, since the aristocratic members of the Sanhedrin themselves were afraid of a revolt of the Jewish people.

The so-called *trial* before Pilate cannot really be called a trial at all but a simple investigation into the facts of the case. A probe into the mode of examining capital cases of non-Romans before Roman jurisdiction will prove that no such trial took place. There are three elements to a Roman trial: 1) the *inscripto*, 2) the *nominus receptio*; and 3) the *citatio*. The *inscripto* is the indictment document initiated by a prosecutor and signed by witnesses. At the time these written charges are presented a trial date is set for some *future* date, allowing ample opportunity for *both sides* to gather evidence. The *citatio*

---

27. *b. Sanh.* 48b; 48b n. 1,3.
28. Winter, *On the Trial*, p. 58.
29. Winter, p. 58.

The Roman Pseudo-Trial

was the part of the process in which the accused appeared for the *first* time in court. In the case of Jesus it cannot be said that the trial followed these guidelines. No written indictment was formed and presented, certainly no future trial date set, and no corpus of evidence was gathered by the *Roman authorities*. Instead, the *citatio* begins immediately. The trial should have been public while the governor sat on the *bema*; however, the examination of Jesus was held in closed chambers. This is reflected in John 18:28 wherein the members of the Sanhedrin did not enter into the judgment hall at all, nor were other witnesses present inside. While Pilate and Jesus remained alone *inside* for the interrogation, only the prefect, at times, came *outside* to speak to the members of the Sanhedrin.

> Then led they Jesus from Caiaphas unto the hall of judgment [Solomon's Hall of Justice]: and it was early; *and they themselves went not into the judgment hall*, lest they should be defiled; but that they might eat the passover [the Saducees ate the Passover on the 15th of Nisan]. *Pilate then went out unto them* (John 18:28-29).

The two Jewish accusers (Annas and Caiaphas), who would have also served as prosecutors, would have been *required by Roman law* to stand face-to-face with the accused to present the charges. At no time did the high priests stand face-to-face with Jesus during the Roman proceedings. Jesus was *inside*; they were *outside*.

> Then Pilate *entered into the judgment hall again*, and called Jesus (John 18:33).

The accused had a right to defend himself. If he refused to do so, he was given three opportunities to change his mind. This, however, was *also* done in interrogating witnesses to determine whether the case might have merit. Pilate gave Jesus that opportunity. In this case, Jesus did not choose to defend himself. That Pilate and Jesus both knew Jesus had committed no crime is evident by Pilate's questions. Jesus asks Pilate if *he* is making any accusation against him; Pilate responds indignantly that he is not a Jew, and that it was the Sanhedrin who had brought forth the charges, *not himself* (John 18:34-35). Jesus goes on to make the statement that "everyone who is of the truth hearkeneth unto my voice", to which Pilate, twice, responds with a rhetorical question: "What is truth?" He asked this almost as if he were addressing his own dilemma. Had this statement been made in any other profane document, Pilate's ironic sarcasm and cynicism would have been easily detected. He *knew* the truth, that Jesus might be the legitimate heir to the throne of David but that he had no real political power, and that Pilate, himself, had been placed in a difficult political position; yet he had been made powerless by the influence of Antipas, who had the emperor's ear, and the Sanhedrin, that was allied with him, to do other than he did. This is evidenced in Mark 15:10 and in Matthew 27:18.

> For he knew that the chief priests had delivered him *for envy* (Mark 15:10).

Pilate's favor with Tiberius had gradually waned. He sought now to redeem himself in Caesar's eyes. Because of numerous administrative blunders, and the most recent, the spilling of Galilean blood (Luke 13:1), Pilate found himself between the proverbial rock and hard place. He could do nothing but pacify the Sanhedrin and hope for better relations with Herod Antipas who, as we earlier demonstrated was known to have often undermined the Roman governors by his self-serving patronage to Tiberius. He had acted like a petulant child, seeking to get undeserved attention and favor from Caesar. The Herods were notorious for their political intrigue and their self-centered and self-indulgent whims.

Even though Jesus stood silently before the charge, merely questioning Pilate as to what crime he had committed, *Pilate found no fault in him* and did no more than scourge him, thinking to satisfy the Sanhedrin. After the third interrogation, Pilate had returned him to the Sanhedrin, having found him innocent of the charges they had made.

> See! *I lead him unto you outside*, that ye may take knowledge that no single fault do I find in him (John 19:4).

Pilate, however, was not so easily duped by the Sanhedrin's ploy to trick him into sanctioning the execution of Jesus, thus relieving *them* of the responsibility. His response to Jesus betrays his understanding and his increasing scorn of what the Sanhedrin was attempting to do.

> Jesus answered—Of thyself art thou this thing saying; or did others tell thee concerning me? Pilate answered—*Am I a Jew? Thine own nation and the high-priests delivered thee up unto me!* (John 18:34–35).

That the Sanhedrin was attempting to blackmail Pilate is not easily denied.

> According to the Gospels, the political charges against Jesus were spoken, not presented in writing. *This may have been because the Sanhedrin was merely seeking a confirmation of its own death sentence and not expecting formal trial from the Romans.* Whatever their motives, Pilate, as a Roman magistrate, was unwilling to rubber-stamp their decision.[30]

As the Roman representative of the Emperor, Pilate had the right to seek the advice of an investigatory committee. This simply did not occur. In fact, the only advice by a Roman citizen recorded in the gospels is the advice of his wife.

> When he was sat down on the judgment seat, his wife sent unto him, saying, Have nothing to do with that just man: for I have suffered many things this day in a dream because of him (Matt. 27:19).

During the first century, superstition was commonplace among the surrounding nations; it was found in the most civilized societies, whether Rome, Greece, or even Israel. The Romans, especially, feared the gods and their reprisals. It was not that Pilate had any particular twinge of conscience concerning the sentencing of Jesus but that he had feared some "divine" personal catastrophe might befall him should it happen that Jesus be joined to the pantheon of Roman gods. It might well have been this very fear that spurred him into reporting as he did to Tiberius the affair of Jesus. Eusebius makes mention that Tiberius encouraged the Roman senate to deify him (though that is unlikely).

> The fame of our Lord's remarkable resurrection and ascension being now spread abroad, according to an ancient custom prevalent among the rulers of the nations, to communicate novel occurrences to the emperor, that nothing might escape him, Pontius Pilate transmits to Tiberius an account of the circumstances

---

30. Foreman, *Crucify Him*, p. 134.

concerning the resurrection of our Lord from the dead, the report of which had already been spread throughout all Palestine. In this account, he also intimated that he ascertained other miracles respecting him, and that having now risen from the dead, he was believed to be a God by the great mass of the people. *Tiberius referred the matter to the senate, but it is said they rejected the proposition, in appearance, because they had not examined into this subject first, according to an ancient law among the Romans, that no one should be ranked among the gods unless by a vote and decree of the senate.*[31]

While it is not probable that this occurred, it does reflect the manner in which the Romans established their gods. The early dispatch referred to here must not be confused with the infamous Gospel of Nicodemus.

Sentence must have been, by Roman law, pronounced while sitting on the *bema inside* the praetorium. This was not done. Pilate, in accommodation to the sensibilities of the ruling Jews, placed the bema outside on what is called the Gabbatha, or tessellated (polished mosaic stone) and raised pavement, the Pavement of the Moqed.

> Pilate, therefore, *when he heard these words led Jesus outside, and sat down upon a rasied seat* [bema] *in a place called pavement*, but in Hebrew *Gabbatha* [this word means "a stumbling stone"] (John 19:13).

The fact that Pilate sat upon the *bema* represents his final word in the matter. The passage introducing the formal sentencing by Pilate is indeed, illuminating: "Then, therefore, *he* [Pilate] delivered *him* [Jesus] *unto them* [the Sanhedrin] that *he* [Jesus] might be crucified [*staroo*, hanged on a living tree] (John 19:16).

> And Pilate *consented that their request should be granted*; and released him who for revolt and murder had been cast into prison, whom they [the Sanhedrin] claimed—whereas *Jesus delivered he up unto their will* (Luke 23:24).

As Shem-Tob translated in his Hebrew Gospel of Matthew "Then he released Barabbas (to them) *and delivered to them Jesus for beating and affliction that they might hang him.*"[32]

It is a fact that Pilate found *no fault* with Jesus, *even after sending him to Antipas* who was ultimately responsible for sanctioning the execution. Herod, himself, had to admit that Jesus had committed *no crime against the Roman government*. It was then that Pilate had offered to chastise Jesus by scourging him. But the Sanhedrin, even *after* the Roman scourging [a regular punishment, not the scourging before a crucifixion], was determined to put Jesus to death. The rulers merely wanted Pilate to "do the dirty work".

> But he *the third time* said unto them—Why! what base thing hath this man done? Nothing worthy of death found I in him. Chastising [i.e., *having already chastised*] him then *I will release him!* (Luke 23:22).

At this point, Jesus had already received the punishment to which Pilate had sentenced him. After having made several attempts to reason with the Sanhedrin, Pilate at

---

31. Eusebius, *Eccl. Hist.* 2.2; p. 51.
32. Howard, *Hebrew Gospel of Matthew*, p. 145.

last consented to their wishes. To be fair, he did not, however, take the responsibility (even though he has been burdened with it throughout the centuries).

> And Pilate seeing *that nothing it availed but rather a tumult was arising, taking water, washed his hands of it before the multitude* [against the Sanhedrin], *saying— innocent am I of the blood of this man—ye shall see to it for yourselves* . . . Then released he unto them Barabbas, but scourging Jesus, *delivered him up, that he might be crucified* [*staroo*, hanged on a tree] (Matt. 27:24–26).

He used a purification custom that the Hebrews claim as their own, washing the hands to allay himself of guilt. Much has been made of this incident by scholars, who claim the practice was solely of Hebrew origin. There are those who claim this portion of our gospel has been tampered with by the church to cast favorable light on Pilate. Pilate, as a Roman, would have had little personal knowledge of the elaborate purity rituals of the Hebrews. Pilate used the ritual in conformity with Jewish law to make it clear to the judges of the Sanhedrin, that he, too, claimed to be innocent of the blood of the defendant. This custom is also the method used by the Jewish high priest in *silently* pronouncing a verdict of guilty. When the temple guards see the high priest wash his hands, it is a signal to them to take charge of the accused and lead him to his execution. The procedure was simply a device by which the verdict of guilty might be made without verbal sentencing.

> After the testimony was taken the . . . men cast lots or voted, and their decision was shown to the high priest. As he was too holy to act of himself, but only as the mouth-piece of God, *he went up to a basin or ewer, as it is called by them, and washed his hands in token of the innocency of the court, thus testifying that the criminal's own action had brought condemnation on himself.* As soon as the soldiers saw this, they took the man to the *place of execution [bet haSeqilah], and there stoned him till he was dead. Not one of them was allowed to speak, not even to whisper, while the execution was going on.* Nothing was heard but the pelting of stones and the shrieks of the criminal.[33]

Pilate had been coerced into affirming the Sanhedrin's own sentence of death. He fought them in the only manner he knew: he tried to release Jesus, as a "Passover reward". The Sanhedrin, however, was determined that the blame fall on Pilate's shoulders instead of their own. Should it appear to the populace that the Jewish Sanhedrin was responsible for the death of Jesus, the nation might revolt against them, not only endangering their delicate political positions but also their financial security and their lives. The Sanhedrin was not publicly popular; they knew they were on shaky ground. Had the Jewish people revolted against their own government, the rulers knew their positions would have been in danger. Under no circumstances, however, might they allow Pilate to release Jesus. Had he done so, their chances to *legally* execute him were forever nil.

> If the guilt of the accused is not established by the witnesses and proofs (evidence being also adduced in defense) *to the satisfaction of the judges or jurors, an acquittal follows and the accused goes free.*[34]

---

33. Mahan, *Archaeological*, p. 5.
34. "Accusatory", J.E., p. 163.

The Roman Pseudo-Trial

They had sought the sanction of Pilate, as the highest Roman representative in the land of Judea. If their ploy had failed, they could not again try Jesus. He was considered more dangerous to the political welfare of the nation than was even the Zealot criminal they eventually released from prison. Jesus had been acquitted by Pilate! The "crowd" that gathered with the rulers were not the commoners, as often misrepresented; they were the Herodians and the Sadducean partners of priestly mercantilism. The clause that Jesus "was crucified under Pontius Pilate" was incorporated for the first time at the Council of Nicea (325 CE) in the Nicene Creed. This creed was formed from an earlier document, the so-called "Apostle's Creed", which says nothing explicitly about the divinity of Jesus, nor of the Holy Spirit, nor of the crucifixion. These documents were created in order to bring all faiths and nationalities into one fold, into the universal Roman church, thus separating forever the earliest Jewish histories espoused by the apostles, themselves, from their original contexts.

We find extant an account of the execution of Jesus in an ancient translation of Josephus (and said to have been issued around 71–73 CE under the title *Peri Haloseos*). It is generally suppressed by both the church and Israel, because it is not favorable to the Sanhedrin. I quote from Haim Cohn's translation. The document is said to be authentic by Hugh Schonfield (see *According to the Hebrews*) and Berendts and Grass (*Flavius Josephus vom juedischen Kriege nach der slavischen Uebersetzung, passim*) as well as other scholars. It is also in harmony with the gospel narratives to some degree, conforms to the charges leveled against Jesus by the Sanhedrin, displays the fear of the Sanhedrin that the Romans might take away their "place" (position) and nation, and that the Scribes were "envenomed" by his teachings. The fact that this particular word is used in the document shows that it corresponds to the writing of Josephus in his histories in that he is known to have called Annas and his family "whisperers" or "vipers".

> At that time also a man came forward—if it is fitting to call him a man. His nature as well as his form were a man's, but his showing forth was more than that of a man. His works were godly and he wrought wonder deeds, amazing and full of power. Therefore it is not possible for me to call him a man, but in view of the nature he shared with all, I would also not call him an angel. And all that he wrought through some kind *of invisible power, he wrought by word or command.* Some said of him: Our first lawgiver [Moses] has risen from the dead and shows forth many cures and arts. But others supposed that *he was sent by God.* He opposed himself in much to the law, and did not observe the Sabbath *according to ancestral custom. Yet he did nothing reprehensible nor any crime, but by word solely he effected everything.* And many from the folk [ammei ha-aretz] followed him and received his teachings; and many souls [Zealots] began to waver, supposing that through him the Jewish tribe would be freed from Roman hands. *It was his custom often to walk outside the city, preferably on the Mount of Olives [i.e., at the Outer Court near Gulgoeth]*; it was there that he dispensed his cures to the people. And there gathered around him a hundred and fifty servants [i.e., disciples], and from among the people a great number. When they saw his power, *and that he accomplished everything he wanted by word of mouth,* they urged him that he should enter the city, massacre the Roman soldiers and Pilate, and rule over them [they tried to "make him king"]. But he scorned it. Later, the *leaders of the Jews* [Sanhedrin; called by Josephus the "leading men"] obtained

knowledge thereof and *they convened [after the resurrection of Lazarus] with the high priest and said: We are powerless and too weak to withstand the Romans, like a bow that is bent. Let us tell Pilate what we have heard, and we shall have no trouble; if he should hear it from others, our goods may be confiscated, we may ourselves be beheaded, and our children may be exiled* [the Romans might take away their "place" and "nation"]. So they went and informed Pilate. He sent his men, who killed many of the people, and they brought this miracle-worker before him. *He interrogated him, and he found that he did good and no evil, that he was no revolutionary, and that he did not aspire to royal power; and he discharged him.* For he had healed his wife who had been dying. He went to his accustomed place [the Mount of Olives, in the Temple Precincts at Beth Pagi] and wrought the accustomed works. And as an ever increasing number of people gathered around him, he won great reputation among them all. *The teachers of the law were envenomed with envy, and they gave thirty talents [thirty pieces of silver] to Pilate that he should kill him. Pilate took the money and gave them permission to carry their purpose into effect themselves. They seized him and crucified him, not withstanding the laws of the ancestors.*[35]

Hugh Schonfield states:

The canonical records inform us that Pilate wanted to release him. In the Slavonic Josephus that release is actually effected. Unless there was some persistent and reliable authority for such an assertion, one cannot believe that any Christian would have invented a story so at variance with his New Testament. And it is to be noted that both here and in the *Toldoth* the conclusion is the same, Jesus goes away and renews his miracles.[36]

Alan Watson and G. A. Williamson agree:

"It is to be observed also that the forging of these passages for propaganda purposes could not have rendered the least service to a Christian apologist; they could never influence anyone not already convinced by the Gospels; they are in many points irreconcilable with Christian tradition; and they clearly reveal their author not as a believer but as a doubting, if curious, onlooker".[37]

Whatever approach one takes to the passage from the *Jewish Ant.*, the argument for authenticity of the Slavonic *Jewish War* remains: it is inconceivable that a passage inserted at some stage into Josephus's *Jewish War*, whether in Slavonic or in Greek that was subsequently translated into Slavonic, should have some correspondence with a passage in the *Jewish Ant.*, which itself was tampered with. That would involve an impossible editorial link between the two passages from two different works.[38]

It is relatively certain that the "Jesus" passage in the *Greek* translation of Josephus was inserted, or at the very least, that certain words were added to an existing paragraph in order to favor Christianity. It is a historical fact that Origen (185–255 CE) is known to have twice stated Josephus was not a Christian! Although, it is unlikely that Josephus

---

35. Cohen, *Trial and Death*, pp. 312-313.
36. Schonfield, *According*, pp. 166–167.
37. Williamson as quoted in Watson, *The Trial of Jesus*, p. 130.
38. Watson, *The Trial of Jesus*, p. 132.

wrote it, there is much to commend in this Slavonic Josephus (although doubtfully written by Josephus). Specific references to the use of the hands with a spiritual "word" in Jesus' healings would have been understood by a Jewish audience; to Gentiles, these phrases would have meant nothing. The passage from the Slavonic Josephus manuscript agrees with Scripture.

> When Jesus therefore *perceived that they would come and take him by force, to make him a king*, he departed again into a mountain himself alone (John 6:15).

Other ancient documents also clear Pilate of ultimate responsibility. One such example, as we have noted in our last chapter, is the incomplete Aramaic *Toldoth Jeshu* in which the "five disciples" are tried before the Sanhedrin. This source states that the priests who hated Jesus not only hung him on a tree *but stoned him as well*! This was done to ensure that a resurrection was impossible in that the body would be in a state of absolute destruction when buried. The acknowledgment lists the dates of the execution, a display of the body, a curse on the followers of Jesus, and the names of Roman and Jewish authorities who witnessed the events. Adler's incomplete translation seems to correspond to the account given by the Talmudic sages (*b. Sanh.* 43a). The two documents appear to carry forth some validity. Herford agrees: "We can only regard this fencing with texts as a *jeu d'espirit, occasioned no doubt by some actual event*.[39]

As we have seen in the preceding chapter, the "actual event" was the trial and execution of Jesus. Christianity itself has preserved ancient writings on the death of Jesus that might give further insight into the nature of the proceedings. The earliest "Christian" writer, Justin, a Samaritan, Semitic himself by birth, wrote his *Apology* (between 148 and 154 CE), declaring that it was the Sanhedrin that was responsible for the death of Jesus.

> And indeed David, the king and prophet, who uttered these things, suffered none of them; but Jesus Christ stretched forth his hands, *being crucified by the Jews speaking against him, and denying that he was the Christ*[40] . . . And this the Jews who possessed the books of the prophets did not understand, and therefore did not recognize Christ even when [h]e came, but even hate us who say that [h]e has come, and who prove that, *as was predicted, he was crucified by them*.[41]

It was not in the hands of the populace that the ancient books of the prophets were kept but in the hands of the interpreters of the Torah. These interpreters were the Scribes of the Sanhedrin. Just as the "dark ages" were the result of the Bible being kept in the hands of a few church leaders, so the Scriptures were held by the Sanhedrin. There can be no doubt that the populace, nor even the apostles, might have had possession of the books of the prophets. What they had learned about the prophets had been learned in synagogues controlled by the Sanhedrin. It is in this anomaly that we know Jesus had received the education required to become a member of the Sanhedrin, a Master, and a Scribe, perhaps even a priest since he was also Aaronic. Justin apparently derived his

---

39. Herford, *Christianity*, p. 92.
40. Bush, *Classical Readings*, p. 21; The First Apology of Justin.
41. Bush, p. 22.

information from some early oral and written traditions as reflected in his comments that it was "Jews" who executed Jesus.

> And again, when he says, "They spake with their lips, they wagged the head, saying Let him deliver himself" [Ps. 22:7]. *And that all these things happened to Christ at the hands of the Jews, you can ascertain.* For when He was crucified, they did shoot out the lip, and wagged their heads, saying, "Let him who raised the dead save himself".[42]

Justin goes on to give the *reason* for the execution by the Sanhedrin:

> But lest anyone should meet us with the question, What should prevent that He whom we call Christ, being a man born of men, *performed what we call his mighty works by magical art, and by this appeared to be the son of God?* we will now offer proof, *not trusting mere assertions*, but being of necessity persuaded by those who prophesied [of Him] before these things came to pass, for with our own eyes we behold things that have happened and are happening just as they were predicted; and this will, we think, appear even to you the strongest and truest evidence.[43]

There must have been some common rumor that Jesus had been tried and executed for the crime of "sorcery" or "leading the nation astray" (as a *mesith*) in circulation at the time. Otherwise, there should have been no need for Justin to deny it, and that crime, as most are now aware, was not a Roman crime but a Jewish one. The "mere assertions" are mirrored in the Jewish documents we have been examining. There is no reason to see in Justin's apology any anti-Semitic tendencies. He is clearly Semitic, himself, and would have nothing to gain from it. He is describing, like the author of John, the "rulers" of Israel, the Sanhedrin, *not the race*.

We have further testimony from Tertullian (160–230 CE) that the execution of Jesus was effected, not by Pilate, but by the Sanhedrin. Here, he is claiming that Pilate was *blackmailed*!

> But the Jews were so exasperated by his teaching, by which their *rulers and chiefs* were convicted of the truth, chiefly because so many turned aside to Him, that at last they brought Him before *Pontius Pilate*, at that time Roman governor of Syria [sic]; and, by the violence of their outcries against Him, *extorted a sentence giving him up to them to be crucified.*[44]

The author of the Gospel of John was a witness to this accusation, for he makes a point of placing the blame where it is deserved, squarely on the shoulders of the corrupt *government* of Israel.

> Pilate saith unto them—your king shall I crucify? The High-priests answered— we have no king but Caesar! Then, therefore, he [Pilate] delivered him [Jesus] *up unto them* [the Sanhedrin], that he [Jesus] might be crucified [*staroo*, hanged on a tree]. *They [the Sanhedrin] took possession, therefore, of Jesus* (John 19:16).

After Jesus' resurrection, Luke makes this statement about the execution:

---

42. Bush, p. 23.
43. Bush, p. 17.
44. Bush, pp. 93-94.

> In what way also *our high-priests and rulers delivered him up unto a sentence of death and crucified [hanged] him [on a living tree]* (Luke 24:20).

Likewise, Peter confronts the high priests at his own trial (about 36 CE), claiming in his defense that he had healed in the name of resurrected Jesus: "the God [YHWH] of our fathers raised up Jesus, whom ye slew and hanged on a tree" (Acts 5:30). He, again, in speaking to Cornelius claims to be witness to the fact that the "Jews" [meaning the leaders of the Sanhedrin] "slew and hanged on a tree" (Acts 10:39). Even Paul refers to the Jewish [not Roman] law when he states in Galatians 3:3 that "cursed is everyone that hangeth on a tree", claiming that Messiah was, indeed, made a curse, and in 1st Peter 2:24, the author speaks of Jesus "[w]ho, his own self bare our sins in his own body on the tree". It is clear that the earliest followers of Jesus believed it was the government of Israel who had executed him. Furthermore, all the earliest documents clearly indicate that it was the Sanhedrin who "crucified" Jesus. If Pilate, himself, had intended to have Jesus crucified in the Roman fashion, there would have been no reason for him to deliver Jesus up *to the Sanhedrin*. The plain fact is the rulers stood to lose both their positions of power and their personal wealth. They wanted Jesus out of the picture so that they might continue the graft of the Temple Cult; Pilate did not. In his own mind, it would have made little difference whether the king of Israel was Herod Antipas or Jesus. The disputes over a royal lineage within the weakened Judea would have been irrelevant to him, a moot point. If anything, he might have preferred Jesus as king over Antipas. By the time Pilate had become prefect, the Jewish nation had already begun to revolt against its oppressors.[45] The rulers had, after all, forced Pilate to remove the golden shields bearing the image of Tiberius from the palace of Herod, and were quite skilled in maneuvering the Roman puppet into serving their own purposes, whether by blackmail or by bribe. They had concluded, wrongly it seems, that Pilate would have taken the claim of Jesus' royalty as an affront to the emperor-god and would have had him executed for treason against Rome. However, many gods were worshipped by the Romans. One more would have made little difference. New "gods" were often added to the Roman pantheon by a majority of senatorial vote. After the resurrection event, Pilate had begun to think of Jesus as a "god", as testified by Eusebius. His superstitious nature had prevented him from carrying out the execution, himself; however, he *did* fear retaliation of that "god" for the consent that he had given. It was common to expect such retaliation by wronged deities in his civilization. His political well being heightened only when his life and position were threatened by a "god" more tangible to him than Jesus: Tiberius Caesar. It was for this reason that he sent a small execution detail (as was customary) to oversee the Jewish execution. Pilate, however, could not resist one final taunt to the Jewish rulers: the *titulus* upon which he wrote, ironically, in three languages (Hebrew, Greek, and Latin) that Jesus, the Nazaraean, was King of the Jews; he, ironically, wrote the truth! He had his revenge against them; the Sanhedrin would have to deal with the population after all. The indignant reaction of the Jewish Sanhedrin is recorded in the gospels:

> The High-priests of the Jews, therefore, were saying unto Pilate—Do not be writing *The King of the Jews*; but that *he said* King of the Jews I am. Pilate answered

---

45. Ben-Sasson, *A History*, pp. 251–252.

[well pleased with himself to be sure] *What I have written, I have written!* (John 19:21–22).

Although Pilate had sent a representation of Roman soldiers to be present at the execution, it was *not* those soldiers who hanged him on the tree: it was the temple captains. John 19:16–18 clearly states it was the Jewish authorities who executed Jesus.

> Then therefore he [Pilate] delivered him [Jesus] up unto them [referring to the High-priests and the sanhedrin], that he [Jesus] might be crucified [hanged on a tree]. They [the Jewish authorities] *took possession*, therefore of Jesus. And bearing for himself the cross [gibbet, that is the yoke that was to be attached to the tree] he [Jesus] went forth unto the so-called Skull-place [*sic*, "ridge", ha-Rosh on the Mount of Olives, the *bet haSeqilah* or "Place of Stoning"], which is named in Hebrew Golgotha [this is the Greek transliteration of the Hebrew Gulgoleth, place of the mountain ridge]; where him [Jesus] *they [the Jewish authorities] crucified [hanged] him [on a living tree]* (John 19:16–18).

It is well documented that the Roman prefects often allowed the Jewish government to administer their own punishments. At first glance, the indication is that the Sanhedrin took no actual part in the execution. This is quite misleading, as we shall learn in the chapter entitled "The Execution".

5

Beth Pagi: The Place of the Crux

During the first century there was an ecclesiastical district on the Mount of Olives called Beth Pagi, where Jesus was put to death. It is the same site where Stephen and James the Just were later stoned. This important ecclesiastical district has been designated by many names in Scripture and in Jewish writings. The area included portions of the two central mountains in the Olivet chain. It has been called, as is customary in Hebrew practice, by a variety of appellations: Beth Pagi, Beth Hini, Beth Hanuyoth, the "Fountain", the Plaza, the Outer Court, the Spine, the Ridge, the Corner, the Wall, and most importantly, Golgotha. Sometimes, it is referred to in Jewish writings by the governmental departments located there; for example, *Beth HaKana* (the "Market") or *Beth HaSephar*. It was also called the Footstool of *HaShem*. In the Talmud it is most often referred to as Beth Pagi, and in the Copper Scroll it is symbolically called Secacah and Beth Kerem (House of the Spine). This important site was, in fact, the most important ecclesiastical district for the City of Jerusalem. It is at this site that the armies of Israel had been mustered, where lepers had gathered, where merchants sold their wares, where the New Moon was determined, and where the judicial Sanhedrin met for *criminal* adjudication. It was important during the first century because it was the seat of the Temple Cult and the headquarters for the government of Israel. When Jesus and his disciples sat "opposite the temple" (*hieron* - temple precincts), it was the buildings at this *governmental site* to which he referred (Matt. 24). This "branch" of the Temple extended from the Hill of Ophel on the west to the eastern extremity of the village of Bethphage. That village derived its name from the district of Beth Pagi (Place of Meeting) in which it sat. The region is sometimes referred to as the Beth Galeel (House of the Circle) or the Beth Din (House of Judgment). It was also the place of public execution. Note the wording of the New Covenant reference.

> And Jesus went out, and departed from the *temple* [*hieron*]: and his disciples came to him to shew him the *buildings* [*oikodome*] *of the temple* [*hieron*] (Matt. 24:1).

A Book of Evidence

Herod's Temple was a *singular* structure located upon the southern end of the present Temple platform. It was not the Herodian Temple sanctuary [*naos*] to which the disciples were referring but to the "*buildings (oikos) of the temple*" situated on the Mount of Olives. Mark 13:3 states that "he [Jesus] sat upon the Mount of Olives over against [opposite] the temple", but the word for temple here is *hieron*. Strong's Concordance indicates that it was "a sacred place; i.e., *the entire precincts* of the Temple" [whereas 3485 (*naos*) denotes the central sanctuary itself]. The word *naos* derives from the root *naio* and literally means "to dwell", so it was not the usual "dwelling-place" of the *Shekinah*, that is, the Temple sanctuary, to which Jesus referred but the place where the Shekinah rested when it left the Temple (Eze. 11:23). It has already been established that the activities performed on the Mount of Olives were of a sacred nature, and that the Mount of Olives, itself, was considered a holy site (*b. Ber.* 9:5; *b. Yom.* 68b) primarily because the "glory" of YHWH had last rested there. These buildings, as we shall see, were located in the Plaza of Gulgoleth, perhaps extending as far as the village of Bethphage. The Bordeaux Pilgrim locates the village at one thousand paces (i.e., one thousand yards) southeast of the northern summit of Olivet. Jesus had said that "one stone would not be left upon another," yet there are many stones and structures left on and near the Temple Mount. This has been adduced by modern archaeological experts. He was, however, not speaking of the Herodian Temple Mount at all. Jesus was referring to these other *buildings* (plural) attached to the Hill of Ophel in the form of a lateral appendage, or a *wing* that extended from the Women's Court (at the Miphkad Gate) east of the Temple at Ophel, over a bridge that covered the Kidron Valley, and over the hill toward the Village of Bethphage) [this "wing" should not be confused with the "pinnacle" of the temple; to be sure there is also an ecclesiastical "wing" at the site of the pinnacle as well]. Part of the region of Beth Pagi was sometimes called the *topos* (as in the gospels), the "plaza". In the Old Covenant it had been referred to as the "Wall. Since there are various archaeological ruins attached to the site of the Temple Mount, these could not have been the "buildings" to which Jesus referred. An investigation into the extent of the Temple precincts (the *hieron*) will show that there is not a single whole stone to suggest that the "wing" or "outer court" (the ecclesiastical district) ever existed at all. It has been leveled to the ground. The Kidron Valley, which was at one time deep enough to accommodate a structure some six hundred feet in height, is now filled with centuries of debris. As a matter of fact, Beth Pagi is today a cemetery! Even the once important priestly village of Bethphage has been destroyed. Yet historical, Scriptural, and archaeological sources prove that the village and the Plaza at Beth Pagi *did* exist during the first century, and that these sites were the meeting places for the government and the seat of the *criminal* courts [*beth din*] [there is a great difference between the criminal court and the court of the priests]. The Outer Court, traditionally depicted as being situated on the Herodian Temple Mount was actually on the Mount of Olives. It is here we find the meeting place for the rulers of the government of Israel. They were referred to as "heads" of State.

> Another interpretation: Do not read it as *and I will appoint them (wa-'asimem) as your heads* but *Their guilt (wa-'ashmom) is on your heads.*" This teaches that the guilt of Israel rests upon the heads of their judges. Thus it says now, O mortal, I have appointed you a watchman for the house of Israel; and whenever you hear a message from my mouth, you must transmit my warning to them . . . *your heads*

will be preserved—Appointing the judges as your heads means that your heads, i.e., your very lives, are dependent on your obedience to them; upon the heads of their judges—Judges are responsible for the actions of the people. The term judges is here used in the sense of leaders or elders.[1]

Naturally enough, one of the reasons the area became known as Gulgoleth (Golgotha) is because it was the site of meeting for the "Head" of the government yet there are other reasons as well. These "heads" of State were additionally known as the *elohim* or judges of the land.

> The Hebrew word is *elohim*, which usually means God but is sometimes taken to refer to human judges.[2]

In *b. Sanh.* 2b *elohim* occurs three times for "judges". In the New Covenant, too, Jesus (in John 10:33–38) declares himself a judge (*elohim*) of Israel. The Sanhedrin resented his implication intensely, for by so-doing he usurped their authority. As the "*elohim*" of Israel, these men claimed exclusive rights of adjudication. Moses Maimonides explains:

> The term *elohim* signifies "judges"; comp. "The cause of both parties shall come before the "judges" (*ha-elohim*; Exod. xxii.8). It has been figuratively applied to angels, and to the Creator as being Judge over the angels.[3]

The Plaza of Gulgoleth was one of the two "polling" stations or customs houses, places where the "head" (poll) tax was collected and the collection chest was maintained. Individuals who entered the Plaza by the Jericho Road (north/south) would pay their taxes at the Plaza station, while those entering through Bethphage (east) would utilize the "district house" located there. Various types of coins dating to the 30s CE have been found at the site of the exedra in Bethphage. It was used throughout the Hellenistic and Roman periods. Numerous Israelite armies had been mustered in Beth Pagi, and it was from this location that the Tenth Legion of Rome's army besieged Jerusalem in 70 CE.

> He [Titus] set up his headquarters on Mount Scopus, a region to the north and east of the city, with three of the legions at hand *and the tenth legion camped on the Mount of Olives.*[4]

Byzantine tradition (on which one can hardly rely) tells us Jesus was executed on a hill, but there is absolutely no indication for that belief *anywhere* in the pages of the New Covenant. This inference derives only from third and fourth century Christian *tradition*. There is, on the other hand, every indication that he was executed in the public square. This public square was located near the intersection of the Jericho Road with the path from Bethphage. The following examination clearly shows Jesus was executed, not on the stony western hill known as "Calvary", but east of Ophel, on the western ridge of Olivet at the very site on which the physical "Ark of the Covenant" had once stood. It will also show that he had been formally sentenced and flogged at the "House of Meeting"

---

1. Hammer, *Classic Midrash*, p. 296 and 296n.
2. Hammer, p. 505.
3. Maimonides, *Guide*, p. 317.
4. Mare, *Archaeology*, p. 191.

in the village of Bethphage. By following the patterns found in Genesis and the writings of the Talmud, we find that the locale of the Plaza is entirely historical and Scriptural. David himself had worshipped God in this same region on one of the two hills of the Mount of Olives (2 Sam. 15:30). When he had crossed over the brook Kidron, he crossed over due east from Ophel, the site of Solomon's Temple.

Beth Pagi was quite important during the first century. At one time, it included the priestly city of Nob, where David had eaten the Bread of the Presence. There has been great debate as to the precise location of Beth Pagi. Some scholars have placed it on the western slopes of Olivet, others at the Village of Bethphage, itself. Each location has its merits. Little thought, however, has been given to the premise that it comprised *both* areas. It was on Olivet that the Tabernacle had once stood (1 Sam. 21). The word *Pagi* is a corruption of the Hebrew *pogesh* which means "to meet" (from *pegeeshah*, a "rendezvous" or "meeting"). Because this area has been little understood, few recognize it as the symbolic "Har Megiddo" (mountain of *rendezvous*) of the book of Revelation. "Armageddon" is, in fact, Har Megiddo, the "mountain of meeting" and the "mountain of mustering" armies (as is quite logical). The Hebrew word Megiddo (meaning "rendezvous" or "gathering") is, in fact, derived from the root *gadad*, to "assemble troops". This assembling of troops is the major event of the Great Day and signals a return of the Messiah.

Origen confirms that the village of Bethphage was inhabited by priests (*b. Sot.* 45a, Note 12). Beth Pagi, the region in which it sat, was comprised of both the eastern *and* western slopes of Olivet and included a threshing floor, one that David bought for fifty pieces of silver from Araunah the Jebusite. His purpose was to set up an altar in order to stave off a plague (2 Sam. 24:15–25). This particular altar was especially provided to prevent a *plague*. The plague might well have been *leprosy*! The only site where one might be "cleansed" by purification from leprosy is, in fact, on the *eastern side* of the Temple near the Miphkad Altar. The threshing floor David bought for *silver* must be distinguished from another on Mount Ophel. David had purchased this *second* threshing floor from Ornan (the names are similar and have been connected in error) for six hundred pieces of *gold*! (1 Chr. 21:17–25; 2 Chr. 3:1). Thus, one was bought with silver and the other with gold; the amount of purchase was different; and the two owners were Jebusites with similar sounding names. It is apparent that these were two different threshing floors! The second threshing floor was on the Mount of Ophel. It formed the site of Solomon's Temple. The evidence for this east-west orientation will be presented in the pages that follow. The rabbis spoke of the *eastern* threshing floor in their Talmuds.

> If he [the owner] anticipated [the tithing] whilst it was yet in ear. But [even] on R. Judah's view, does it not require the wall [of Jerusalem]? [Note 5: I.e., since he tithed the crops in ear, nothing thereof is to be consumed—not even by beasts—outside the walls of Jerusalem. How then may the animal thresh it unmuzzled?] *He threshed it within the walls of Beth Pagi* [thus there was a "threshingfloor" in Beth Pagi, which was also surrounded by a wall]. [Note 6: The outer wall of Jerusalem, added to the original limits of the town; v. Sanh. (Sonc. ed.) p. 67, n. 9].[5]

---

5. *b. b.m.* 90a; 90a n. 5.

Beth Pagi: The Place of the Crux

This district on the Mount of Olives was always considered "holy". Over time, the Israelites had forgotten the reason. It is sometimes referred to as the "Rib" because of its half-moon shape. The word *sheleph* is used to describe this "rib" of Jerusalem. It derives its meaning from Adam and Eve. The Woman was created from the *rib* of Adam; she was "pulled out" of the flesh of man. The Woman, of course, is the *havah*, the symbolic dwelling-place of God's children. Furthermore, this region begins to form a curve near this spot, like a "rib". The Latin word for "ridge" is *crux*. Webster's gives the following definition for "ridge": "L. *cruc-*, crux, cross, *curvus*, curved - *crown* [from which the words crucify and cross are derived], an elevated body part (as along the backbone), a range of hills or mountains". Now, this "Place of the Skull" was merely a designation for the "Place of the *Cross*" but *having nothing to do with a "Roman" cross* and really meaning the place of the *crown* (or "*rosh*" - head), which is, in fact, a little hill on the Mount of Olives. The Shekinah of God, thus, would rest in this spot.

The only time the topography of the Mount of Olives has been described in any detail is in 2 Sam. 16:13 where David is said to have traveled along the "hill's side" (*har tsela*). The Hebrew word *tsela/tsalah*, when translated properly, actually means "a rib (as *curved*), a quarter," the "corner" or "side chamber". At that time, David was travelling along the area of what later came to be known as Beth Pagi on the Mount of Olives, on to Bethphage and along the southeastern path to Bethany and Jericho. The same passage also refers to the site of Nob (Bethphage), which at the time would have been east of the future temple sites, near the third hill in the Olivet chain. Smith states plainly that there are actually *four hills*, rather than three in the Olivet chain.

> Next to it [the principal portion of the mount] on the southern side, separated from it by a slight depression up which the path mentioned above as the third takes its course, is *a hill, which appears neither to possess, nor to have possessed, any independent name.* It is remarkable only for the fact that it contains the "singular catacomb" known as the "Tombs of the Prophets].[6]

This unnamed third hill will figure quite prominently in our discussion. From all available evidence, it appears that this "hill" with no name is the historical Gareb ("scab" or "whiteness" of leprosy, a clean condition), the twin of Ophel ("boil" of leprosy, an unclean condition). It was only in this eastern region that one might be washed "white as snow" by means of purification. It is here the mountain chain begins a southern curve (like a rib or "cross"), and forms the shape of a crescent moon.

Another description in the Ethiopic Book of Enoch gives us more information about the mountain "in the east".

> And I saw *toward the east* another mountain [Mount of Olives] *higher than the first* [thus the "Lower City" is on Ophel]; *and in the midst of them* [Olivet and Ophel] *a valley deep and narrow* [the Kidron Valley], *and through it* [the Kidron], *a stream ran alongside this higher* [eastern] *mountain* [Olivet] [the Kidron is a winter torrent-bed]. And to the west thereof was another mountain [the mountain designated as the traditional site of the Zion], lower than it [Olivet] and of no great height, and a valley at its foot between them [Hinnom Valley], deep and dry, and all the valleys deep and dry at the farthest parts of the three mountains

---

6. Smith, *Dictionary*, p. 469.

> [i.e., the Kidron/Hinnom valleys]. And all the valleys were deep and narrow, of flint-rock, and no tree was planted in them. And I marveled at the rocky ground and I marveled at the [depth of the] valley; indeed, I marveled exceedingly.[7]

This book which was written during the inter-testamentary period, describes Jerusalem as consisting of both the eastern mountain of Olivet, the mountain of Ophel, and a third western mountain [that which is *now* called the City of David]. The late Israeli archaeologist, Benjamin Mazar, has proven that the traditional Zion of the "Upper City" did *not* exist in that location.

> The Mount Zion tradition concerning the Tomb of David apparently was derived from *an erroneous statement made by Josephus, that the City of David was situated on the western hill. In other words, although this tradition is of ancient origin, it is without historical basis, and has no archeological support, even thou it has been boosted on traditional or folkloristic grounds (like so many other sites in the Holy Land throughout the centuries) into a focus of pilgrimage. Vestiges of ancient structures are visible on this sensitive site on Mount Zion, though their age is uncertain* ...[8]

This region on the eastern mountain (Olivet), which was, during the first century referred to as Beth Pagi has been *called* both Bethany *and* Bethphage interchangeably.

Throughout the centuries, these villages were known to have been associated with both the House of Hanan (Annas) and the Hanan family dove aviary.

> Three of the five references to "Bethania" in Talmud Bqavliy show this place named spelled ... (*Beyt Hiyniy'* ... *Pesakhim* 53a [twice] and *Bava M'tziya* 88a). The other two references spell this place name ... (*Beyt Y'vaniy'*; Hellenic House, *Eyruviyn* 28b [twice]). This refers to the *bazaars of "stores" set up on the Mount of Olives for the supply of [doves] and other commodities required for sacrifices, and owned by the powerful priestly family [Khanan* ... *], to whom they proved a source of wealth."* ... The name in Talmud Y'rushalmiy is ... (*Beyt-Khanan*; House of Khanan). [Hanan; i.e., Annas] was the family name of a priestly family (above) mentioned in Yirmiyahu 35:4. This seems the most likely original name of the village that was also known for the Khanan family dove aviary ...[9]

Yirmiyahu Ben-David also investigated the possibility of the association of Bethany with *Beyt Tanna*, the House of Tanna. The name would indicate that many members of the Sanhedrin (sages called Tannaim) resided in that village. These Tannaim were the Pharisaic teachers of the Mishnaic period (from 1 CE to 220 CE) with whom Jesus debated. It is entirely likely, however, that the two villages, Bethphage and Bethany, received their New Covenant names from the region in which they were situated and the functions performed there. It is certain both were considered a legal part of the City of Jerusalem, and both were, apparently, "outside the city", yet within the limits of Beth Pagi which itself was walled separately. These villages were also connected with the priesthood and the Bazaars of Annas. The wing of the Temple on the Mount of Olives was the outermost court of the Temple (which at one time had been constructed on Ophel). In describing the walls of Jerusalem,

---

7. First Book of Enoch.
8. Mazar, *Mountain*, p. 185.
9. Ben-David, NRM, Vol. II: Miydrash, II:21, 17.1.

Beth Pagi: The Place of the Crux

it is clear Josephus places a "bridge" at Ophel and over the Kidron Valley (this is verified by the Talmud). In another place he describes these Eastern Cloisters for us. Note that he specifically states that these cloisters were built over the Kidron Valley.

> But the next day the Romans burnt down the northern cloister entirely, *as far as the east cloister, whose common angle* [the wing] *joined to the valley that was called Cedron* [Kidron], *and was built over it*; on which account the depth was frightful.[10]

Situated outside the gate of the bridge on the Mount of Olives was the "plaza" and marketplace. This Plaza was located near the intersection of the Jericho Road and the eastern path from Bethphage. All this area was "outside the camp". Since this entire wing of the Temple was called Beth Pagi, there has been much confusion in locating it. It was in this walled area that the Red Heifer and the Atonement Goat were burned on an altar called Miphkad, and from which the (Eastern) Miphkad Gate derived its name. Near the Miphkad altar was also a pit, the *Beth HaDeshen* [Place of Fat Ashes]. That these areas were once in existence and served as a pattern for the New Temple of the Messianic kingdom we have evidence from the Dead Sea library.

> And we are of the opinion that the sanctuary [is the 'tent of meeting' (temple)] and that Jerusalem is the 'camp', and that 'outside the camp' [is outside Jerusalem], that is, *the encampment of their settlements* [i.e., Beth Pagi]. It is outside the c[amp [at Beth Pagi] where one should . . . the purification offering and] take out the ashes of [the] altar and bu[rn the purification offering. For Jerusalem] is the place which [He has chosen] from among all the tribes [of Israel . . .].[11]

The Temple Scroll, also discovered at Qumran near the Dead Sea, states that outside the third encampment of Israel *on the east* was *another* area divided into three sections or "encampments": 1) an area to be designated for the unclean—which we know *must* reside "outside the camp" of Israel, 2) the execution site, *Beth HaSeqilah*, and 3) the clean place, in which is situated the *Beth HaMiphkad* and a "pit".

> You shall make *three areas to the east of the city, divided from one another*, where [shall come] the lepers, those suffering from a flux and men who have had a (nocturnal) emission XLVII . . .[12]

In order to understand the significance of this area, it is important to investigate each of these three portions of Beth Pagi. The site was destroyed during the invasion by Nebuchadnezzar, but it had been rebuilt after the exiles returned from Babylon. It is this structure that Mazar believes was completed in 30 CE when the Sanhedrin removed from the Hall of Hewn Stone to Beth Hanuyoth. It is within the Plaza that we find the "Arch of Accounts" of which it is said, "Outside of Jerusalem there was an arcade called the Arch of Accounts, and when people had accounts to settle, they used to go and settle them under the arch".[13] The purpose for this was so that grief might not be allowed to occur in the city that is called "the joy of the whole earth". One was only to experi-

---

10. Josephus, *War* 6.3.2.
11. Qimron and Strugnell, MMT, *BAR*, Vol. 20, No. 6, pp. 58–59.
12. Vermes, *Dead Sea Scrolls*, p. 144.
13. Bialik and Ravnitzky, *Legends*, 372:118.

A Book of Evidence

ence grief "outside the camp" in the Plaza at Beth Pagi. Beyond the Eastern Gate is the "religious" Outer Court (the Plaza) that forms the "Wall" of Jerusalem, the boundary of which on the eastward side is where Gentiles and the unclean might gather. Beth Pagi was included within the enclosure wall built by Titus around Jerusalem. This area had already been separated from the City of Jerusalem by its own surrounding wall.

> To hasten the surrender Titus built an enclosure wall around the whole city of Jerusalem. We cannot locate all the sites that the wall encompassed, as listed by Josephus (*War* 5.499). We know that the wall took in the Mount of Olives on the east, Siloam on the south, and the area north of the temple called New Town.[14]

Because the region of Beth Pagi was surrounded by its own wall, it is referred to, in Scripture, interchangeably as "The Wall" and "The Street" of the City. The Hebrew words used to describe the bridge and administrative plaza [public square] outside the camp are, in fact, *rechob* and *charuts*, respectively. Like Beth Pagi itself, they are quite confused in Scripture as if the two areas were considered a unit, yet distinct from each other. The reason for this is because the two structures were considered a single unit (a "branch" of Zion) "outside the camp" which belonged to the "outer court". It might be interesting to investigate the reason these areas were defined as they were. The translations of the two Hebrew words are so similar as to be indistinguishable. The Greek words, on the other hand (*plateia* in particular) are quite specific in their meanings. We have been told many times in the New Covenant exactly where Jesus was executed. We have just been too blinded by the generality of the Greek language to see it. The reason for this blindness is because of the general translation of the word "place" (or *topos*). The Greek New Covenant uses only one of several translations for the word. Just as the word "house" (*oikos*) is translated in a general sense to describe numerous kinds of "houses" (for example, palace, temple residence, household, family, assembly, place, and so forth), the word *topos*, generally translated as "place" can also mean "status", "position", "spot", "quarter", "room", and "plaza". Thayer's defines it as "any portion of space marked off, as it were, from surrounding space", or "a parcel of ground". It is the equivalent of the Hebrew word *meqomah*, which is used for describing the clean place "without the camp" in Leviticus 1:16 and 4:12, the site of the Miphkad Altar which was situated eastward of the Tabernacle in the Wilderness.

> It seems that this gate was not in the wall of Jerusalem, but that the part of the wall facing it was to the east, between the Horse Gate and the Sheep Gate. Indeed, it is not mentioned among the gates of Jerusalem in Neh. xii. 31 et seq. The word מפקד [miphkad] designates in Ezek. xliii. 21 the place near the Temple where the sin-offering was burned, and it seems to mean "an appointed place," to which this gate may refer ... Jerome translates it by "porta judicialis," [the Gate of Judgment] which induces Lightfoot ("Horae Hebraicae," ii 27) to suggest that it may refer either to the hall of judgment in the Praetorium or to the east gate of the Temple."[15]

The Latin term "judicialis" means "belonging to the law courts." It is derived from "judicium", judgment. This Gate of Judgment led to the seat of the criminal Sanhedrin and the execution site, as well as the altar of the Red Heifer (Miphkad Altar) in Beth

---

14. Mare, *Archaeology*, p. 191.
15. "Miphkad", J.E.; http://www.jewishencyclopedia.com/articles/10867-miphkad.

Beth Pagi: The Place of the Crux

Pagi. This "spot" also served as a pattern in the future Temples for placing the Miphkad Altar and the Pit of Ashes (as well as the execution site) outside the camp toward the east on the Mount of Olives. Below is a comparison of the two Greek words for "place" and the Hebrew words for the same, and how the various translations of the Scriptures translate (and thus define) the "Place of the Skull" [crux] and the "Wall" of the City.

Greek New Covenant	*plateia*
Bible Version	Definition: Plat, plaza
ERB	Broadway
YLT	Broad-place
KJV	Street
Interlinear	Street
CBN	Street

Greek used with Golgotha	*topos* Place, plaza
Translation of "Place of the Skull"	
EBR	Skull-place
YLT	Place (a proper name)
KJV	place
Interlinear	"that called the place"
Companion	"of a skull" (there is no translation at all for the word "place")
ROSN	"the so-called Skull-place"
ISR	"so-called Place of a Skull"

Hebrew Old Covenant	*rechob*	*charuts*
Definitions	Chel of Decision	Decision Place
JPS	Moat [trench]	Square [wing, open place; i.e., plaza]
EBR	Broadway	Wall
YLT	Rampart	Broad-place
KJV	Street	Wall
Interlinear	Ditch	Plaza
CBN	Street	Wall

159

A Book of Evidence

Please note that the word *charuts* indicates an "open space" where decisions might be made. The Companion Bible translator give this footnote about the "wall".

> [C]haruz. *Whatever it may mean, it cannot be "wall"*, for that is *homah* (that which surrounds). Haruz = something cut in or dug out; and may well be used of what is *narrow, and then that which is narrowed down to a deciding point, a decision or determination*, as in 9.26; 11. 36 Cp. Isa. 10.22. Job 14.5,&c . . . the street = *the broadway or open space by the gates or elsewhere.*[16]

The Wall (*charuts*) of the city is this "open place". The word *charuts*, or "wall" occurs in the book of Daniel. It is prophesied that it will be rebuilt in times of trouble. The word *charuts* is derived from the root *charats* meaning "to wound" and "to decide". It, again, signifies both a place of determination and a place of execution. This, of course, corresponds with the dual nature and purpose of the ecclesiastical district "outside the camp". A portion of this Plaza was designated as clean; the other two portions as profane or "unclean". The word moat [trench] or *rechob*, ordinarily defined as a long, narrow and usually steep-sided depression or channel for water between hills is often translated as "avenue" or "broadway". It is the same "broad" way (*plateia* or "street") of the city on which the bodies of the two witnesses of Revelation 11:7–8 lie slain (*"where also our Master was slain"*). This should not to be confused with another "street" [plaza] within the Temple, which is at the Nicanor Gate. The word translated most often as "street" in Revelation 11:8 is, in fact, the Greek *plateia* meaning "a wide plat" or "open square"; i.e., a plaza. The description of it as a "street" is not at all similar to what we today would refer to as a "street". The word *plateia* is derived from *platus*, which means to spread out "flat" as broadened and is a plaza formed by flagstones (*plasso*). The author of the book of Revelation emphatically states that our Master was executed in that Plaza!

> And their dead bodies lie upon the *broadway [street or plateia (Plaza); the fountain plaza or "open place"]* (of the Great City the which is called spiritually Sodom and Egypt), *where their Lord also was crucified [hanged]* (Rev. 11:8).

Unfortunately, the reader's attention has been drawn to "the great city" (Jerusalem, likened to Sodom and Egypt) rather than to the "street" (Plaza) where Jesus was executed. The Greek word *plateia*, from which the various translations derive, also means "open square" or plat. Webster's defines a plat as "a quadrate". The definition of a quadrate is quite simply "to make square; being square or approximately square". In fact, a quadrate is often signified by a "heraldic cross". An illustration of a quadrate shows that it is simply a square with a four-way *intersection*, and this, again, forms our Plaza of Gulgoleth where the path from Bethphage intersects with the Jericho Road.

---

16. CBN, p. 1199.

Beth Pagi: The Place of the Crux

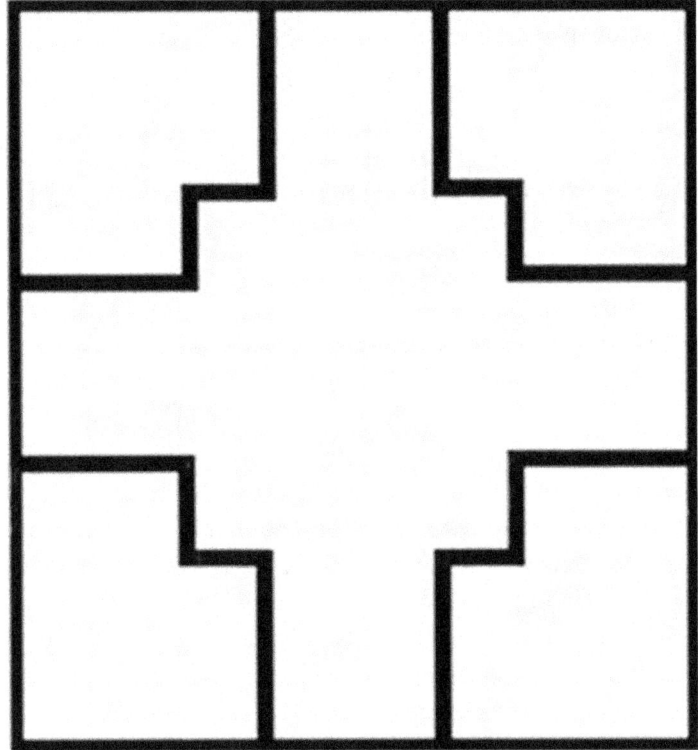

The earliest followers of Jesus used a "plus" sign to indicate the site of his execution. It had nothing to do with the "cross" invented later by the universal church. Jesus was, in fact, not executed on a Roman cross but on a *living tree*!

In Lamentations, Jeremiah has made a point of describing this area of Jerusalem after the first destruction. He has designated the "trench" and "street" as a rampart (*chel*).

> Yahweh hath devised to lay in ruins the *wall* of the daughter of Zion ["branch" of Zion], He hath stretched out a line, He hath not turned back his hand from *swallowing up—thus hath he caused to mourn the rampart* [*chel*, trench, wall, referring to the area of the bridge *and* the "plaza"] *and wall* [*chomah*, the joining or Azal wall; see Zech. 14:5]. Together have they languished! (Lam. 2:8).

He is referring to both the Temple area and the regular public meeting place at the Plaza of Gulgoleth within the parameters of Beth Pagi, where the Sanhedrin was known to meet for criminal adjudication. The word for "trench" can also mean "decision" and describes symbolically the first-century bridge that led to the house of judgment (*beth din*) outside the gate. The word *chel* is also defined as "an intrenchment", a "rampart", or a "trench". It suggests the mustering place of an army. Its root is *chayil* meaning "army", "host," or "power," which again is derived from *chiyl* meaning "to writhe in pain" or to "be wounded" and suggests that this *chel* also led to a place of execution.

The word "square", as in our preceding chart, is rendered "plaza" or *topos* in Greek. A plaza is an "open area often featuring a *walkway and shops*, usually located near urban buildings" [i.e., a public square, forum, or agora]. Anciently, all cities had these public

A Book of Evidence

squares. Since it was the public square that attracted visitors and marketers to the city, it was designated as the "place" of the city. The Greeks called them *agoras*.

> AGORA (PLACE) [Gk. Agora]. A gathering place in the city of town that was used for business, social, and political purposes. The word derives from *ageirein*, meaning "to bring together" . . . In the Gospels, the word is [often] rendered "market place," and the contexts show that it referred to a place where more than buying and selling went on.[17]

Strong's Concordance defines an *agora* as "*the town-square*" or "*street*". The town square is often called a "quarter", an "ell" or a "wing", and a wing is a part or feature which is a lateral appendage from a main or central object [in this instance, an extension of the Temple] (Webster's). It is sometimes called a "quarter" of the Temple because Sabbath measurements were to be made from the Holy of Holies in the Temple Sanctuary and formed a circumference around it that was divided into four quarters.

It is the boundary of the circumference that forms the Sabbath Limit. Another Hebrew term might also describe the site of the Sabbath Limit. *Chagag*, meaning "the path from Bethphage intersects with" is where the *chag* (sacrifice) was slain. The word indicates traveling in a circle, or going around. The illustration below will provide a glimpse of Beth Pagi and its own three encampments as it relates to the Holy of Holies with its private encompassing wall. It also shows the three encampments of Israel, along with its four quarters, including the temple walls, city walls, and the Miphkad Gate leading to the Eastern Cloister over the Kidron Valley with its accompanying bridge.

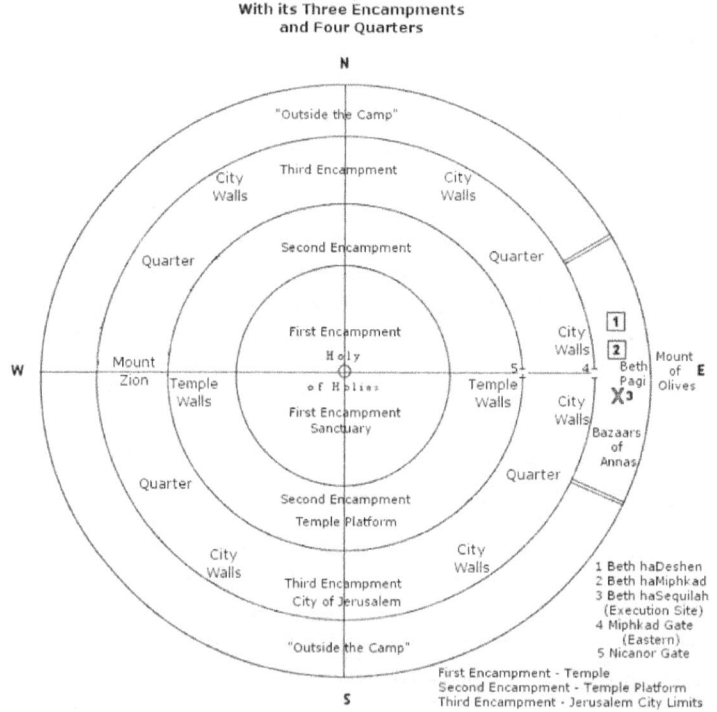

17. ABD Vol. I, p. 92.

Beth Pagi: The Place of the Crux

The reader will recall that when Ezra accused the people, they were gathered in the "street of the House of God" (Ezra 10:9), and it was here also that Hezekiah gathered his people (2 Chr. 29:4; 32:6]. Nehemiah, too, had gathered the people in the Plaza for the consecration of the walls of Jerusalem (Neh. 8:16-17). To be sure, we are quite clearly told in the Talmud that the Sanhedrin sat in the "naval" of the earth. In another section of the Talmud it is specifically mentioned that the Sanhedrin sat at Beth Pagi for judgment, *thus the navel* (*shor* - umbilical cord to Upper Jerusalem) is Beth Pagi, a place of nourishment and resurrection! This is why the Jews wanted to be buried on the Mount of Olives.

> R. Aha b: Haninah said: Scripture states, *Thy navel is like a round goblet* [aggan ha-Sahar] *wherein no mingled wine is wanting*. 'Thy navel'—that is the Sanhedrin. Why was it called 'navel'?—Because it sat at the navel-point of the world. [Why] 'aggan?—Because it protects [meggin] the whole world. [Why] ha-Sahar?—Because it was moon-shaped. [Why] in which no mingled wine is wanting—I.e., if one of them had to leave, it had to be ascertained if *twenty-three, corresponding to the minor Sanhedrin [the judicial Sanhedrin], were left*, in which case he might go out; if not, he might not depart.[18]

The "navel-point" is moon-shaped, meaning it formed a "ridge" or crux (curve) like a crescent moon, the description of this area on the Mount of Olives. It was to this "Daughter of Zion" that the Messiah was to come riding on the colt, the foal of an ass.

> Exult greatly, *O Daughter* [bath = branch] *of Zion*, Shout in triumph, *O Daughter of Jerusalem*, Lo! thy king cometh unto thee Vindicated and victorious is he— Lowly and riding upon an ass. Yea upon a colt, a young ass (Zech. 9:9).

Jesus partially fulfilled this prophecy when he made his "triumphal" entry into Jerusalem during the first century. It was not to *Zion* (the Ophel region) that he was appearing but to the *Daughter* of Zion (on the Mount of Olives at the crossroads).

> And when they drew near unto Jerusalem and came unto the (Village of) *Bethphage* [in the region of Beth Pagi] unto the *Mount of Olives* then Jesus sent forth two disciples; saying unto them—Be going into the *village* that is over against you, and straightway ye shall find an ass bound, and a colt with her—loose them and lead them unto me . . . But this hath come to pass, that it might be fulfilled which was spoken through the prophet, saying: Tell ye the *Daughter of Zion*, Lo! thy King is coming unto thee, Meek and mounted upon an ass, And upon a colt the foal of a toiling ass (Matt. 21:1-5).

Having descended the path from Bethphage and having entered into the Outer Court from the East, Jesus was making a statement that the rulers of Israel simply could not miss. Jesus had come to this Plaza where the hub of social, political, and business activity flourished, where the *Beth Din* sat, and where purification occurred. There is evidence within the New Covenant that clearly distinguishes this site as the one in which the Miphkad Altar was situated (on the Mount of Olives).

> And when the chief priests and scribes saw the wonderful things that he did, and the *children* [pais, a boy (as often beaten with impunity), a slave or servant

---

18. *b. Sanh.* 37a

(especially ministering to God); i.e., these were young boys who served as attendants to God] crying in the temple [*hieron*; precincts], and saying, Hosanna to the son of David; they were sore displeased, And said unto him, Hearest thou what these say? And Jesus saith unto them, Yea; have ye never read, Out of the mouth of babes and sucklings thou hast perfected praise? (Matt. 21:16).

These boy servants (attendants to God) were those who were consecrated by the priesthood from birth to aid the priests in the rites of the Red Heifer. They remained in caves carved beneath the Temple Mount until they reached adulthood so that they might not become Levitically defiled and thus be disqualified from administering the "water of separation". This "water of separation" was administered both on the Mount of Olives and at the Nicanor Gate. The "boys" administered it on the Mount of Olives, while the priesthood administered it at the Nicanor Gate.

> There were courtyards in Jerusalem, *built on rock*, and *under them was a hollow*, [which served as a protection] against the graves in the Kidron Valley below]. And they bring *pregnant women, who give birth there, and who raise their sons there [in these hollow caves, so that the children might remain pure]*. And they bring oxen, and on them are doors [boards], *and the youngsters sit on top of them, with cups of stone in their hands [so that they might not be defiled by the ground]*. [When] they reached the Siloam [referring here to the Gihon Spring], they descended and filled them, and mounted and sat on top of them [i.e., they took the boards and placed them on the ground to keep their bare feet from touching the defiled ground], and mounted and sat on top of them. They came to the Temple mount and dismounted. The Temple mount [on Ophel] *and the courtyards—under them is a hollow against the grave in the depth. And at the door of the courtyard* [i.e., the Eastern Gate] *was set up a flask of [ashes of] purification.*[19]

Alfred Edersheim describes these "children" in more complete detail.

> The next care was to find one to whom no suspicion of possible defilement could attach, who might administer purification to such as needed it. For this purpose a priest was not required; but any one—even a child—was fit for the service. *In point of fact, according to Jewish tradition, children were exclusively employed in this ministry*. If we are to believe the *Mishnah*, there were at Jerusalem certain dwellings built upon rocks, that were *hollowed beneath*, so as to render impossible pollution from unknown graves beneath. Here the children destined for this ministry were to be born, and here they were reared and kept till fit for their service. Peculiar precautions were adopted in leading them out to their work. The child was to ride on a bullock, and to mount and descend it by boards. He was first to proceed to the Pool of *Siloam* [or Gihon], and to fill a stone cup with its water, and thence to ride to the Temple Mount, which, with all its courts, was also supposed to be free from possible pollutions by being hollowed beneath. Dismounting, he would approach the [Eastern] . . . Gate, where the vessel with the ashes of the red heifer was kept.[20]

It was these boys who administered the water of purification on the Mount of Olives in the Plaza and who recognized Jesus as Messiah. Since their duties were directly

---

19. *m. Par.* 3:2 a–d; 3:3a.
20. Edersheim, *The Temple*, p. 354.

connected with the Red Heifer ritual, and we know the Red Heifer was slain "outside the camp" on the Mount of Olives, that the ashes were kept in one of three places (one being on the Mount of Olives), and that the administration of the "waters of separation" required one to be purified *before* entering into the Temple, this could only have taken place at the Plaza in Beth Pagi.

Since we have already discussed the Arch of Accounts as being located "outside the city" of Jerusalem, it might be well to state that an "arch" is simply a column or pillar. There is some confusion about the "arched" Red Heifer bridge that extended from Ophel to the Wing of the Temple. It was not actually "arched" but pillared. Webster's defines an arch as an arcade, "a long arched building or gallery; 2) an arched covered passageway or avenue (as between shops); 3) a series of arches with their columns or piers; or 4) an amusement center". This exactly describes the Red Heifer bridge and the area of the broad Plaza. The criminal court of the Sanhedrin met "outside the camp" for sentencing and execution, but they also had to meet inside the Temple prior to execution.

> And was *the place of stoning [beth haSequilah] only just outside the [inner] court and no further?* Has it not been taught: The place of stoning was outside the three encampments?—True, it is even as you say, yet he teaches it thus, *so that one may infer from it that the Beth din (lesser Sanhedrin) went forth and stationed itself outside the three encampments.*[21]

The *first* three encampments of Israel were "inside" the city walls of Jerusalem, yet judgment and execution were to occur only "outside the camp" at the "Wall". The "Wall" was so-called because the region of Beth Pagi was originally "outside the camp". Eventually, this area was itself surrounded by its own wall and used as an "extension" of the city limits of Jerusalem. A portion of this region was used for ecclesiastical and purity purposes, while two parts were reserved for profane use. It was considered the "Sabbath Limit" for the City of Jerusalem. The eastern gate in the "Wall" of Beth Pagi is sometimes confused with the Eastern Gate of the temple itself. Since the surrounding wall of Beth Pagi essentially cut off the Temple platform from the Kidron Valley and Mount of Olives, the Miphkad Gate (and two others) stood on its western side, facing the gate of the Temple Mount. At least three bridges were created to cross the Kidron Valley and enter through these western gates onto the Mount of Olives. This ensured that no profane or impure person might enter in onto the Temple Mount.

> In Jerusalem they were situated as follows: The first was confined to the space of the Temple court [the Inner Court]; the second to the Temple Mount and the third occupied *the rest of the city.*[22]

Where the walls of the City were situated has been a cause of much misunderstanding in the scholarly community. Once the sacred portion of the Wing of the Temple is included within the general boundaries of the City, Nehemiah's description makes more sense. We are told that a man named Hur was the ruler of this "half-part" of Jerusalem. The words "half-part" simply mean the divided or separated part of Jerusalem. This tells

---

21. *b. Sanh.* 42b.
22. *b. Sanh.* 42b; n. a-8.

us that the two parts of Jerusalem might well have been divided by the Kidron Valley. Since Bethphage (part of Beth Pagi) was sometimes considered a part of the City of Jerusalem, the placing of the "city walls" has been difficult. The explanation, however, appears to be quite simple. Just outside the three encampments of Israel, which were walled, there is also the joining wall (*chomah*) forming a separation between the Outer Court (Beth Pagi, the *rechob* and *charuts*) and the Inner Court. This joining wall was probably the mysterious *soreg*, forming the boundary for both the City of Jerusalem and the sacred Inner Court. Beyond this point no Gentile might pass. They might gather at the Plaza on the Mount of Olives but were unable to pass beyond the Eastern Gate (at which the ashes of the Red Heifer were placed). This gate led out onto the bridge westward. This outer portion of the "temple" precincts was thus called in the New Covenant the "Court of the Gentiles", which was not mentioned in Old Covenant Scripture as a part of the Temple proper. While the Village of Bethphage was considered a separate village at times, the "city" limits were finally extended to include the entire area of Beth Pagi, which was also enclosed by its own walls.

> But [even] on R. Judah's view, *does it not require the [chomah or joining] wall [of Jerusalem]?*—He threshed it *within the walls of Beth Pagi* . . . I.e., since he tithed the crops in ear, nothing thereof is to be consumed—not even by beasts—*outside the walls of Jerusalem . . . the outer wall of Jerusalem, added to the original limits of the town*; v. Sanh. (Sonc. ed.) p. 67, no. 9.[23]

The reference to the three encampments having been located inside the city walls, then, expressly indicates that the *Beth Din* stationed itself "outside" the *city* walls and outside the *soreg*, yet within the surrounding wall of Beth Pagi (which itself was called the "Wall" of the City). There is further evidence within the same tractate serving to illustrate this point. In a rather long and involved discussion relating to the number of members belonging to the Great Sanhedrin who must go *out* the Eastern Gate to sit for judgment at *Beth Pagi,* (the area of the Plaza and eastward), we are told that this *is* the place of judgment, where decisions are to be made. Please note there were two eastern gates, the Nicanor Gate inside the Temple sanctuary and the Miphkad Gate (sometimes called the Muster or Inspection Gate) in the wall of the City of Jerusalem. The temple's eastern boundary was also the boundary of the City of Jerusalem.

> R. Joseph said, Come and hear: If they found a rebellious elder in *Beth Pagi*, and he rebelled against them, it is possible to think that his act of rebellion is punishable; therefore there is a text to state, *Then shalt thou arise and get thee up unto the place [the Plaza of Gulgoleth, called the topos in the New Covenant Greek].* This teaches *that the 'place' [the "town square"; Plaza] determines [whether the act of rebellion is punishable].* Now how many of them had gone forth [from the Great Sanhedrin to Beth Pagi]? . . . *if they met in Beth Pagi, and [an elder] rebelled against them . . .* [This verse is applied to the Sanhedrin, called *'navel'*, because *it sat in a place [plaza] which was considered to be the centre of the world [the naval; daughter of Zion, the branch of Zion; part of Beth Pagi].* 'Mingled wine' is defined (Shab. 77a) as diluted with two-thirds of water. Hence *one third of the Sanhedrin must at least be present* at a session] . . . e.g., they went forth to carry

---

23. b. b.m. 90a; n. 5, 6.

out a measurement in connection with the heifer, or to add to the boundaries of the city [of Jerusalem] or the Temple-courts, it is possible to think that his act of rebellion is punishable; therefore there is a text to state, *Then shalt thou arise and get thee up [etc.].* This teaches that the *'place'* [plaza at Beth Pagi] *determines [whether the act of rebellion is punishable].*[24]

This citation gives us the site for the seat of the criminal court; i.e., "one third" of the Great Sanhedrin, and referred to as the Lesser Beth Din. It was near the Plaza of Gulgoleth ("cranium", "ridge", "crux"; i.e., the area where the mountain began to curve) in the area of Beth Pagi that the *Beth Din* met, just *outside* the Eastern Gate [i.e., the Miphkad Gate], in the area translated in Scripture as "the Wall" (*charuts,* plaza). The reason it is so called is because it was the jurisdictional limit of Jerusalem. Scripture calls it meeting "in the gate". The "wall" separating the Outer Court from the Inner Court is, no doubt, the *soreg*. Since the village of Bethphage was also considered a part of this wing, it, too, was enclosed in its own separate wall. Bethphage and Bethany, the path from from them, and the Plaza were known by the single appellation, Beth Pagi, but sometimes referred to as Gulgoleth, the "Fountain" (or the top of the skull where the cranium joins; i.e., the mountain "ridge") or the *"infant"*, the Daughter (or "Branch") of Zion. The Plaza was "outside the city" proper and also outside the lower eastern wall of the later Temple Mount. It was also the execution site, Golgotha, which the gospels tell us was "outside the gate" and "outside the city".

> Whence is this inferred?—From what our Rabbis taught: *Bring forth him that hath cursed without the camp: i.e., without the three camps:* but may it not mean simply outside one camp?—It is here stated, *Without the camp;* and *in reference to the bulls that were [wholly] burned [near the Miphkad Altar], it is also said without the camp: Just as there,* [it means] *without the* three *camps* [the Inner Court, the Temple Platform, and the City of Jerusalem], *so here too*. And whence is that derived there?—From what our Rabbis taught: *The whole bullock shall he carry away without the camp—i.e., without the three camps.*[25]

In the above passage criminals who are accused of "blasphemy" are compared to "sinbearers" (or "sinners") that are burned "outside the camp" on the Mount of Olives. The place of public execution is, likewise, in the same general area that "sinbearers" are wholly burned. These criminals are more specifically compared with the sin-offering of the High-priest's bullock on the Day of Atonement, which is burned near the Miphkad Altar. This area "outside the three camps" is located on the *ridge* [cranium or crux] of the two central mountains of Olivet, which were anciently known as *Gulgoleth,* the Place of the Crux (Cross) or Skull (as the New Covenant verifies). But the word *gulgoleth* implies the *top of the head,* and more particularly, the *place* or fontanel ("fountain") on the top of an infant's skull, along the "ridge" of the cranium. Most ancient plazas were recognized because in their center they had a "fountain" or "eye", which is the reason the word *ayin* (eye) in Hebrew has a meaning of "fountain" as the "eye" of the landscape. It is thus also connected with the word *luz* (eye). In Jewish literature there is a portion of the body (in

---

24. *b. Sot.* 45a (1987 ed.).
25. *b. Sanh.* 42b; n. 2.

the spine) also called "luz" or the "nut" of resurrection (*os resurrectionis*): "According to the *midrash*, there is a bone at the bottom of the spine, likewise called the 'luz' or 'the nut of the spinal column', from which human beings will blossom forth at the Resurrection." [*Eccl. Rabbah* 12:5;].[26] The Mount of Olives is associated with resurrection from the dead and this area might well have been the ancient city of Luz, sometimes associated with Nob. Since *luz* also means "almond" (as in the *shape* of an eye), it is connected with the blossoming of the almond branch (an allusion to resurrection).

Christians have long envisioned the place of execution as the "face" of a skull, or have assumed that skulls were lying around near the site. The latter idea is absolutely preposterous. It is a well-known fact that after execution, criminals were taken down and buried (before nightfall). Certainly, no skulls would have remained at the site. The infant's skull represented the state in which YHWH had found Israel as an "infant" (Ezek. 16). It also represents the state of the future "virgin bride", the Daughter of Zion, when she is (re-) born from above. This site (also known as the "navel" or umbilical cord) is the place of Israel's "force" or "strength", implying that it was at this site that armies were mustered, and the "princes" (rulers, judges, and priests) of Israel sat to make decisions, a place where the infant is nourished. It was, for that reason, designated as the "chief" or "head" place of activity for the government of Israel and the place of criminal adjudication. The Hebrew term *Gulgoleth* also means "head" or "poll", and it refers to numerous functions of governmental management. The word means more specifically "round like the top of the head" but by implication a head or poll, a place of muster. It is derived from the root *galal* (circle) which means a "body as rolled together", i.e., a united group of individuals serving as the chief administrative power of the nation. The word was intended to portray *unity with God*. This area might have been the "private property" mentioned by the sages of the Mishnah.

> The paths of *Bet Gilgul*, and the like of them—[they are] private in regard to the Sabbath and *public domain with regard to uncleanness [i.e., where the gathering of lepers might occur]*. Said R. Eleazar, "The paths of Bet Gilgul were mentioned only because they are regarded as private property for both purposes.[27]

This "private property" was the suburbs of the priests. *Gulgoleth*, in fact, might also be identified as a "cross" place. At this "cross" place we find the narrow western ridge (called the neck or scarp) of the Olivet mountain chain where the Jericho Road intersects with the path from Bethany. Furthermore, it was represented by the Greek letter "chi" which is formed like a capital "X", the same symbol used as a cross by the early Gentile church. The chi also appears as graffiti #6 on the tomb of Jesus.

For Hebrews this "chi" *always* represented the four corners of the earth, the creation of God. The Roman religion adapted the practice of "crossing" from the Jewish priestly consecration of the meal offering and perverted the earthly directional blessing (referring to God's creation of the whole world) to represent both the Roman "cross" of Jesus and the "communion" rites.

---

26. Frankel and Teutsch, *Encyclopedia*, p. 6.
27. *m. Toh.* 6.6 f-h.

> All meal offerings which are prepared in a utensil [a baking pan, or a frying pan] require three applications of oil: (1) pouring [oil into the utensil], (2) stirring [the meal into the oil], and [then again], (3) putting oil into the utensil prior to their preparation. "And as to the loaves [baked in an oven], one stirs them [with oil]", the words of Rabbi. And sages say, "The fine flour [alone is used for preparing them but no oil]." The loaves require stirring. *The wafers are anointed. How does one anoint them? In the form of a chi [that is, in the form of a cross; i.e., in the four directions of earthly creation].*[28]

The earliest followers of Jesus understood that "cross" as a meeting of two ways, a balance. It was recognized that the world had been "out of joint" since the fall of the first man. It was believed that the Messiah would come to again put things in order, once again forming a balance in God's world. This will be discussed more fully in "The Lamp of the World". "Cross" [*crux*] actually means "ridge" [*crux*, or curve], and sometimes refers to the "summit of a mountain" which lies between two other peaks (the cranium or "bowl" that holds the brain; *gullah*). The two peaks referred to are the two central mountains (northern and southern) of the Olivet chain. This chain consists of, not three, but *four* elevations which form a ridge: 1) Mount Scopus; 2) the highest or northern summit known as Ha-Rosh; 3) the "unnamed" southern summit, which is itself sometimes referred to as Ha-Rosh; and 4) the Mount of Offense. William Smith, in his description of the Olivet chain, states:

> *It is not so much a "mount" as a ridge*, of rather more than a mile in length, running in general direction north and south, covering the whole eastern side of the city. At its northern end the ridge bends round to the west, so as to form an enclosure to the city on that side also . . . *The word "ridge" has been used above as the only one available for an eminence of some length and even height.*[29]

The third unnamed hill is due west of Ophel (the latter means a leprous boil, but it also means a rounded swelling or a rounded elevation). Ophel is often translated "emerod" or "gloom" in the King James Version. The reason for this will become clearer as our discussion continues. A "ridge", however, can imply not only the bones of the cranium but can also mean the *ridge of the top of the head or skull* (again as rounded). The description seems to refer to the area east of the narrow ridge or "crossroads" (the *place* of the "cross"), within the confines of Beth Pagi.

The Strait Gate mentioned by Jesus is none other than the gate called Miphkad. It is the eastern gate of the City of Jerusalem that led out onto the Plaza "outside the camp". It was near the "water gate" which was "eastward" because that gate led to the Gihon Spring and this (not Siloam) is where the young boys would go for the water of "separation" used in the rites of the Red Heifer (which, again, is connected with the Miphkad or Strait Gate). The word "Strait" is, in fact, derived from the Greek roots *stao* and *histemi* from which the word "cross" is formed, the gate of burden. It is the gate of the Outer Court. It literally means "narrow" and refers to execution. This "Strait" Gate, through which Jesus stated we should enter, can also be called the "Cross" Gate

---

28. *m. Men.* 6:3 a–h.
29. Smith, *Dictionary*, p. 469.

or "Crucifixion" Gate (Gate of Hanging, Gate of the "Ridge") because it led to the "crucifixion" or hanging site (*Beth HaSeqilah*) in the Plaza of Gulgoleth. It was from this ridge that the Temple was most clearly viewed. When the priest sprinkled the blood of the Red Heifer *he looked due west toward the door of the Holy of Holies* on Ophel, which also tells us exactly where the Holy of Holies was located.

> They bound it [the Red Heifer] with a rope of bast and placed it on the pile of wood, with its head southward and its *face westward [due west]*. The priest standing at the *east [side], with his face turned [due] west*, slaughtered [it] with his right hand and received the blood with his left hand . . . *He dipped and sprinkled seven times toward the house of the Holy of Holies.*[30]

The *traditional* site for the Miphkad Altar would require the priest to look both westward and to the *north* toward the Holy of Holies of the Herodian Temple Mount. The cow's face must also be turned to the west, and to position it in a northwesterly direction would have been extremely awkward. This indicates to us that this Mishnaic tradition comes from an ancient time, a time when Solomon's Temple was situated on the Mount of Ophel.

To recapitulate, the word *gulgoleth* might mean many things: 1) that the area is smooth and round (like the top of a head or cranium); 2) that it is the area where the chief or head of the government met for deliberations; 3) that it is the place of execution; 4) that it is the place of the "poll" (head-count) tax, and a place of census where male pilgrims report for the three yearly festivals and, therefore, a place of muster where armies might be gathered; 5) that it is a place where accounts might be settled; 6) that it is the place designated to intercalate the "head" of the month (New Moon) and year (New Year); 7) that it was the place of "mutual appointment" where purification occurred so that one might be able to commune with YHWH; 8) that it was the place where laws were enacted; 9) that it was a place of study (literally "house of interpretation") and meditation; 10) that it was a public marketplace, square, and "promenade"; 11) that it was the place of the crux ("cross", "ridge"); and 12) that it was the place where the criminal Sanhedrin met for final adjudication. "Sitting in the gate" is a phrase employed for the sitting of the Sanhedrin (rulers) in the office of jurisprudence. Outside the gate, we find the administrative "houses", or "places", a number of chambers (or stalls, really) wherein various temple functions were performed. The entire Sanhedrin (including the religious Sanhedrin, called the Great Sanhedrin), who had originally sat in the "Hall of Hewn Stones" to the south of the Temple Mount, removed to the Plaza in the district of Beth Pagi about 30 CE. (*b. Shab.* 15a, *b. A.Z.* 8b, *Sanh.* 12a, 41a; *R.H.* 31a).

> "Correspondingly the Sanhedrin wandered to ten places of banishment, as we know from tradition', namely, *from the Chamber of Hewn Stone to Hanuth [Lit., 'shop', 'bazaar'"]* . . . Derenbourg, Essai p. 467 identifies it with the *Chamber of the Sons of Hanan [Annas] (a powerful priestly family*, (cf. Jer. XXXV, 4) mentioned in *J. Pe'ah* I, 5].[31]

---

30. *m. Par.* 3:9 a–d, f.
31. *b. R.H.* 31a, 31a Notes 3, 4.

In other words, the Sanhedrin, like the Shekinah (of which the above is an analogy) removed from its original location to various other sites, ending at the Hanuth (on the Mount of Olives), and logically, the last place the Shekinah was seen.

> And the glory (Shekinah) of the LORD went up from the midst of the City and *stood upon the mountain which is on the east* [i.e., the Mount of Olives] (Ezek. 11:23).

Benjamin Mazar, the late Israeli archaeologist, tells us the move from the Hall of Hewn Stone to the Bazaars of Annas was connected with Solomon's Colonnade.

> John's statement (2:20) is supported by Talmudic references (Sanhedrin 41:2; Aboda-Zara 8:2) which state that the seat of the Sanhedrin was transferred from the Lishkat Hagazit, "Chamber of Hewn Stone"... to the place called the Hanuyot in the Temple precincts... forty years before the destruction of the Lishkat Hagazit, i.e., about A.D. 30. *This is very probably the time when the monumental Hanuyot colonade was completed.*[32]

Please note the date (30 CE) that it was destroyed. Originally, the religious Sanhedrin had sat in the Hall of Hewn Stone, but the criminal Sanhedrin had always sat in the Plaza. For some reason, the Great Sanhedrin was removed from that location to sit with the criminal court near the Bazaars of Annas on the Mount of Olives. It is important to understand that the judges of the Lesser Sanhedrin (known specifically to try criminal cases) had already been situated "in the gate", even prior to the religious Sanhedrin's removal to Beth Hanuyoth [near the Plaza]. There are numerous Old Covenant Scriptures that refer to the process of judgment occurring "in the gate" of the city, *near the marketplace*, and the marketplace, as we have already determined was the "place" of the city. Actually, judgment occurred *just outside the gate*. Some of the more obvious examples are given below.

SITTING IN THE GATE

1. 2 Sam. 15:2–6:

> And Absalom rose up early, *and stood beside the way of the gate*: and it was so, that when any man that had a controversy came to the king *for judgment*, then Absalom called unto him, and said, Of what city art thou? And he said, Thy servant is of one of the tribes of Israel. And Absalom said unto him, See, thy matters [cause of legal action] are good and right, but there is no man deputed of the king to hear [a legal lawsuit] thee. Absalom said moreover, *Oh that I were made judge in the land, that every man which hath any suit or cause [a legal complaint] might come unto me, and I would do him justice!*

Absalom makes known his desire to be a *judge* of the peoples of Israel. This, however, does not refer to the "gate" of *any temple* platform since the Temple was yet to be built. Absalom wanted to sit in the "gate" of the City of David.

2. 2 Ki. 7:1–4:

---

32. Mazar, *Mountain*, p. 112.

A Book of Evidence

> Then Elisha said, Hear ye the word of the LORD [YHWH], Thus saith the LORD [YHWH], To-morrow about this time shall a measure of fine flour be sold for a shekel, and two measures of barley for a shekel, *in the gate* of Samaria. Then a lord [*officer*] on whose hand the king leaned [*in the marketplace or plaza of the city*] answered the man of God, and said, Behold, if the LORD [YHWH] would make windows in heaven might this thing be? And he said, Behold, thou shall see it with thine eyes, but shalt thou not eat thereof. And there were *four leprous men at the entering in of the gate.*

This reference is to a marketplace where hungry lepers are gathered at the gate in Samaria during a famine. Elisha's prophecy indicates that the "judges" influenced by YHWH's word will lower the cost of fine meal and barley so that the people of Samaria would not starve. The important point to emphasize here is that the marketplaces (plazas) of the cities were where the unclean and the "lepers" are gathered; i.e., at the "gate". In our present case, even the hill above Bethany and "outside the gate" of the Plaza was probably the true Hill of Gareb ("hill of the scab" of leprosy, the healed state of leprosy) (Jer. 31:39). It is mentioned in connection with the rebuilding of the City of Jerusalem from the Tower of Hananeel "as far as the gate of the 'corner' (the wing of the Temple); then shall go forth again the measuring-line straight forward, over the hill Gareb (opposite the western hill of Ophel, the boil of leprosy), and it shall go round to Goah" [the Sheep Market and Gate], which is purported to have been east of the two pools referred to in Scripture *Beth Esda* (and in the Copper Scroll, *Beth Esdatayin; Esdat (plural) ayin*, two fountains or flowings). King Uzziah, known to have had leprosy, was originally buried in the Tombs of the Kings, but his bones were later removed to the Beth Pagi, where lepers were buried. A stone inscription concerning his burial was found in the region of Beth Pagi and was taken to the site of the Russian Church on the Mount of Olives, just above the Village of Bethphage.

> It may be inferred that the tomb of King Uzziah was originally located there [in the Tombs of the Kings]. In the Bible it is reported that the king was laid to rest "in the burial field which belonged to the kings" (II Chronicles 26:23). However, *according to a much later Aramaic inscription found on a stone slab which had been in the collection of antiquities in the Russian church on the [summit] of the Mount of Olives and is now in the Israel Museum, his remains were transferred for reasons unknown during the days of the second temple.* The Aramaic inscription reads: "Hither were brought the bones of Uzziah, king of Judah, do not open." Apparently it *had been discovered and brought to the Russian church* at the end of the nineteenth century A.D. Some scholars relate this find to the above-mentioned passage in Chronicles which relates *that King Uzziah was a leper*, and was therefore not buried in the tombs of the House of David, but somewhere else . . .[33]

The presumptuous and pseudo-pious leaders *during the days of the second temple* had removed his bones from the Tombs of the Kings and had re-interred them in a place where lepers were buried. He was presumed to have been buried at Siloam, nearby. The Tombs of the Prophets is situated on this third mountain near the Jewish Cemetery, and there must have been a cemetery for lepers in the region as well. The second temple

---

33. Mazar, p. 187.

priesthood was, in fact, in the process of *removing* cemeteries during the days of Jesus. Jesus had upbraided the leaders of Israel for having built the "Tombs of the Prophets" in the region of the unnamed third mountain, the sacred mountain termed the "Mount of the Prophets" by Smith.[34]

> Woe unto you, scribes and Pharisees, hypocrites! because ye build *the tombs of the prophets*, and garnish the sepulchres of the righteous, And say, If we had been in the days of our fathers, we would not have been partakers with them in the blood of the prophets (Matt. 23:29–30).

The Tombs of the Prophets is the only site to distinguish this mountain.

> The only important hypogeum which is wholly Jewish in its arrangements, and may consequently belong to an earlier or to any epoch, is that known as *the tombs of the prophets in the western flank of the Mount of Olives*. It has every appearance of having originally been a natural cavern *improved by art*, and with an external gallery some 140 feet in extent, into which twenty-seven deep Jewish loculi open.[35]

Jesus recognized the seat of the Sanhedrin as being in the Plaza (which was also a marketplace). He was referring to the judges at Beth Pagi in Matthew 11:16, where he likened them to "children [*padeia*, a play on *paideno*: educated, trained, or instructed; i.e., in Torah] sitting in the market-places" piping a song that Israel will not dance to. The Greek word for "piping" is *auleo*. He was referring to the words that came from their throats. The sages compared the "windpipe" to the shofar since it was through that "instrument" that they might praise God. Jesus used the same analogy to indicate the disapproval of Israel's common people for the harsh judgments and scribal law rendered by the *beth din* at the Plaza and at Bethphage. It was they who, by their exorbitant traffic, oppressed the poor of Israel.

3. Job 29:7–17:

> When I went out to the gate through the city, when I prepared my seat [of judgment] in the street ["street", rachob; a plaza]! The young men saw me and hid themselves: and the aged [Elders] arose, and stood up [in respect]. Princes [rulers] refrained talking, and laid their hand on their mouth. The Nobles held their peace, and their tongue cleaved to the roof of their mouth. When the ear heard me, then it blessed me, and when the eye saw me, it gave witness to me: Because I delivered the poor that cried, and the fatherless, and him that had none to help him. The blessing of him that was ready to perish came upon me [upon his own head]: and I caused the widow's heart to sing for joy. I put on righteousness, and it clothed me [like a judge's robe]: my judgment was as a robe and a diadem [mitre]. I was eyes to the blind, and feet was I to the lame. I was a father to the poor, and the [legal] cause which I knew not I searched out [in Torah]. And I brake the jaws of the wicked, and plucked the spoil out of his teeth [both civil and criminal adjudication].

Job was a "ruler" and a priest who judged the people. At the end of his trials God appointed him High Priest. The Hebrew word used here for street is again *rechob* (the

---

34. Smith, *Dictionary*, p. 469.
35. Smith, p. 705.

"broadway" or public square). The word "seat" is the Hebrew *moshab*, "a seat", a "site", "a place of abode, by implication the population (a census place), assembly, sitting, or situation". The word *moshab* is derived from the root *yatsab* meaning "to sit down specifically as a judge", or "place" (plaza, or *topos* in the Greek). In Jerusalem, during the days of the Herodian Temple, this "place" is "outside the camp" in the region of Beth Pagi and is called the Plaza of Gulgoleth or the Plaza of the Ridge.

4. Deut. 17:5–8; 25:7:

> Then shalt thou bring forth that man or that woman, which have committed that wicked thing, unto thy gates, even that man or that woman, and shalt stone them with stones till they die . . . If there arise a matter too hard for thee in judgment, between blood and blood, between plea and plea, and between stroke and stroke, matters of controversy *within thy gates then shalt thou* [the Plaintiffs] *arise and go up unto the place* [*maqom*, a designated spot or locality; i.e., the town square] *which the LORD thy God* [YHWH] *shall choose; and thou shalt come unto the priests the Levites, and unto the* judge [i.e., the criminal Sanhedrin sat "outside" in a plaza by the gates of the city], *that shall be in those days, and enquire; and they shall shew thee the sentence of judgment.*

In this Scripture is the command by which criminals are explicitly said to be judged and executed "outside the gate", and "outside the camp" of Israel. We have previously learned that the "Place" is the town square. The Talmud (as previously quoted) indicates that the "place" is in Beth Pagi.

5. 2 Chr. 23:4–6 ("foundation" gate); 19–20 (the Gate of Lepers):

> This is the thing that ye shall do; A third part of you entering on the sabbath, both of the priests and of the Levites, shall be porters of the doors; And a third part shall be at the king's house, and a third part at the gate of the foundation [Foundation Gate; i.e., the criminal court or beth din]: and all people shall be in the courts of the house of the LORD [YHWH]. But let none come into the house of the LORD [YHWH], save the priests, and they that minister of the Levites; they shall go in for they are holy [consecrated]: but all the people [leaders of the *ma'amadot* or stations throughout the land] shall keep the watch of the LORD [YHWH].

The Eastern Plaza was lower than Solomon's Temple, and it is for this reason that the priest who burned the goat "outside the camp" on the Day of Atonement was unable to see the high priest at the Nicanor Gate (beyond the Women's Court) when he was reading Torah to the people.

> The high priest came to read [in the Women's Court] . . . He who can see the high priest when he is reading cannot see the bullock and goat which are burned. And he who can see the bullock and goat when they are burned cannot see the high priest when he is reading. But this is not because he is not permitted to do so, but because it was quite a distance. And the rites concerning both of them were done simultaneously.[36]

---

36. *m. Yom.*, 7:1a; 7:2 a–d.

Beth Pagi: The Place of the Crux

Again, this is an indication that the site of the Miphkad Altar had been moved from its original place. During the days of the Herodian Temple it is clearly stated that the high priest who burned the cow could see into the doors of the Sanctuary.

The Miphkad Gate could also be referred to as the "appointment" gate (or festival gate, again "to meet for appointment"), where one-third of the Sanhedrin (the twenty-three-member judicial Sanhedrin) was to meet. It was, as well, the "gates of the unclean". Again, this refers to the "place of meeting" outside the Eastern Gate in Beth Pagi. The gate receives its various names because of the sacred functions performed nearby by the heads of state. The "appointment gate" (Miphkad Gate) refers to the "appointments" of God, the festivals. *Miphkad* in Hebrew means "an appointment", "appointed place", or "a census spot" and derives from *paqad* "to muster", "to do judgment", or "to oversee". It is from this root that the name of the gate is sometimes called the Muster Gate. It also means "to punish" and "to count", which would indicate it also led to the site of execution and the place where scribes "counted" the letters of Torah. It is at this *maqom* (place or "plaza") that the chest (or collection box) was kept (2 Chr. 24:8–11). In other words, this was the locality of the Treasury House of the Temple, or what is referred to in the Copper Scroll the "*Old* House of Tribute". Both money and tithe-offerings were kept here. This Scripture is rendered more clearly in the Jewish Tanach.

> And at the king's commandment they made a *chest* and *set it without at the gate of the House of the LORD* [YHWH]. And they made a proclamation through Judah and Jerusalem to *bring into the LORD* [YHWH; i.e., the tax imposed on Israel] that Moses, the servant of God laid upon Israel in the wilderness. *And all the princes* [officers] *and the people rejoiced, and brought in, and cast into the chest until they had made an end* [i.e., until it was full]. Now it came to pass, that at what time the chest was brought unto the king's office by the hand of the Levites, *and when they saw that there was much money, the king's scribe and the high priest's officer came and emptied the chest* [into the Temple Mount "bank"], and took it, *and carried it to his place again* [outside the gate in the Plaza at Beth Pagi]. (2 Chr. 24:8–11).

The money put into the chest (the Treasury of the Temple) was collected at the Plaza of Gulgoleth (and also at Bethphage). After it was collected, it was then taken to the Temple Mount where the main vaults were located, emptied, and "carried back to its place", the "plaza" of the census, the customs house. For a period of time prior to 30 CE the Treasury of the Temple was probably situated at the Hall of Hewn Stone. Above this customs house and "treasury" was the royal *summer house* (or *parwar, a* Persian term), the Hall of Justice, the temporary house of the high priest during the week before the Day of Atonement. It was connected (underground) by the vaults to the Temple to what later became known as the "praetorium". Since Pilate had commandeered this hall for his own private use, he was able to access the Treasury of the Temple, and it was this that provided him funds with which to build the aqueducts designed to bring water into Jerusalem (probably from Siloam).

> But Pilate undertook to bring a current of water to Jerusalem, and *did it with the sacred money*, and derived the origin of the stream from the distance of two hundred furlongs.[37]

It was probably on this riotous occasion that the Tower of Siloam fell, causing the death of several Galilean zealots. After 30 CE, however, the customs house was removed to its former site. This pattern is found in 2 Chr. 24:8–11 as the site for the collection of taxes and became permanent. We can also find this same "customs house" (the original meaning of Bethphage and connected with it) operating to collect the poll tax of Rome during the days of Jesus.

> In Jesus' day the Temple was not only the central religious shrine, *it was also the major industrial and banking facility of the nation*. It received the annual Temple tax paid by Jews throughout the world. Great sums of money were deposited at the Temple by wealthy families and by the hundreds of elderly Jews who had come to retire in the Holy City. The daily sale of sacrificial animals was routinely conducted in the Temple area. At the Passover, with the city's population bloated by pilgrims . . . one can imagine the congestion of pilgrims, priests, beasts, blood, and money. Conduits carried blood drained from the sacrificed animals down the southern side [the JPS Tanach reads "southeastern" side] of the Temple into the Kidron Valley, where it was used as fertilizer for vegetable gardens. The Temple itself gleamed from the sheer amount of gold, marble, and bronze used in its construction. And *outside the walls of the Temple were artisan shops of gold and silver, and other shops of incense and shewbread catering directly to temple needs*. One need not have had so lofty a view of religion as Jesus to have found himself nauseated by such sights in a city whose ritual purity was promptly restored at sunrise each morning by an army of street cleaners. It was Jesus' preaching of the coming kingdom at the Temple that drew the adverse reaction of Temple officials . . .[38]

The phrase "sitting in the gate" was not employed without reason. It was used to denote the symbol of power (for instance, see Gen. 22:17; Ruth 4:1–12; Isa. 24:12; Amos 5:10; Matt. 16:18). It was also flanked by towers (2 Sam. 18:24, 33), the Tower of Meah for the Captains of Hundreds, the Tower of Hananeel, and the "Citadel" itself, the three "towers" that Aristeas tells us were shaped in a semi-circle like a "theatre".

Beth Pagi was destroyed the first time by Nebuchadnezzar in his siege on Jerusalem.

> The LORD [YHWH] hath purposed *to destroy the wall* [*chomah*, Joining] *of the daughter of Zion*: he hath stretched out a line, he hath not withdrawn his hand from destroying: therefore he made *the rampart* [*chel*, trench, wall; i.e., Solomon's Colonade and plaza] *and the wall* [*chomah*, the joining wall that connected the wing to the temple] to lament; *they languished together.* (Lam.2:8).

This Scripture refers to both the adjoining wall *and* the colonnade of the Temple, the "branch" at Beth Pagi. Josephus makes mention of this locality in both his *Wars of the Jews* and in the *Antiquities*. The Roman army swept through the Temple area from north to south, burning the Eastern Cloister (which was attached to the Wing and extended over the Kidron Valley) at the south.

---

37. Josephus, *Ant.* 18.3.2.
38. Idinopulos, *Jerusalem*, p. 134.

> But the next day the Romans burnt down the northern cloister entirely, *as far as the east cloister* [Solomon's Porch at Ophel, which was considered part of the outer court], *whose common angle* [the corner or wing] *joined the valley that was called Cedron* [Kidron] *and was built over it*; on which account the depth was frightful.[39]

> *These cloisters belonged to the outer* court [i.e., the administrative buildings in the Plaza of Gulgoleth at Beth Pagi], *and were situated in a deep valley* [Kidron] *and had walls* that reached four hundred cubits.[40]

The original colonnade had been built down into the valley itself, beginning at the scarp of northern Ophel and was known as the original "Stairs of David". Undoubtedly, over time, this became the Red Heifer bridge. Because the cloisters were first built down into the Kidron, they formed a "trench", thus it was also called Solomon's "Trench".

In the Masoretic Text of 1 Sam. 20:19 the word (*hrygb/heribah*) which Allegro translates "watchtower" in the Copper Scroll (which means "ruins" referring to David's Fallen Sukkah, which might well have been the original site of the Tabernacle of David) is translated as "*Ezel eben*" (Joining Stone, or Assembly Stone). The Ezel *eben* was the boundary line of the "secret" place in the field near Nob (the Village of Bethphage), where David met with Jonathan. Once again, the Plaza and David's "watchtower" with David's Fallen Sukkah, *Beth Ezel*, the "House of Assembly" is connected with the earthquake fissure and Azal (the root of *Ezel*) which Zechariah tells us will reach "very near" in the day of the final earthquake when refugees will flee from Jerusalem (on the west) to the Mount of Olives (on the east). The word "Azal" is sometimes translated "to disappear" or "depart", but this translation seems to refer to the "boundary" stone or Sabbath Limit, the Wall of Jerusalem. This boundary was simply the *eben* (stone) Ezel mentioned above where David and Jonathan had agreed to meet after the feast of the New Moon.

It was a place designated as the "fountain" beneath the throne of Ein Sof (Eternal Fountain) above, and connected by an umbilical cord (from which the infant Israel below is nourished with life), the *tree of life* which is represented by an olive tree, a tree of light-giving oil! If this is the *mishneh* (or "second"), we have another coincidence: another meaning for *shanah* is "to transmute' or *resurrect*. The word indicates that the Garden of Eden (the original foundation) will again be resurrected when Messiah appears. Again, this would be represented by the plaza protected by its own wall, a place spiritually defined as being surrounded by a "wall of fire" or "hedged about with thorns". In Revelation 21:17 the "wall" (*teichos/tikto*) of the future city is the "fixed limit" (boundary) or place of "deliverance", a place of "being born" and the "seed from the mother" (Zion above). It is symbolic of the "unity" that Israel is to have with God, and represents the "arm" (or Army) of God. It is also symbolic of the 144,000 "witnesses", the "living stones" (or "jewels") of the New Kingdom. We are also told that in that day a "little one shall become a thousand" (Isa. 60:22), and the word for "thousand" in Hebrew is Aleph (the numerical value of which is "one", it being the first letter of the Hebrew alphabet). Isaiah used it much like Jesus did (i.e., the First will be Last, and the Last will be First; Matt. 19:30; Mark 10:31; and Luke 13:20). The word Aleph simply symbolizes the "unity"

---

39. Josephus, *War* 6.3.2.
40. Josephus, *Ant.*, 20.9.7.

of God with His Family (of like mind, one purpose, one spirit). The cubit symbolizes the "mother" kingdom as being bound together ('em). The Hebrew word indicates that the mother is the "bond of the family". The Heavenly Kingdom is described in various sacred writings as "the Pearl", and the pearl is constituted of "mother of pearl", which is translucent, iridescent, transparent, and precious. It is found as concentric layers of nacre, enclosed in a protective covering (a shell), again symbolic of "unity" with God in his Sukkah (hedged about with thorns). The "Trench" (Colonnade) was later built "arches upon arches" (meaning pillar upon pillar and also designated in the Mishnah as "causeway" or "rampart") over the Kidron Valley because of the "graves in the depths", which had multiplied over the centuries and might have defiled the high priest who was to offer the Red Heifer.

> And they would make a causeway [compare 1 Chr. 26:16, David's "causeway, or *mesillah*; staircase that goeth up"] from the Temple mount [this refers to the original platform on Ophel] to the Mount of Olives, arches upon arches, an arch directly above each pair, because of the grave in the depths [which would make them "unclean"], on which the priest who burns the cow [the Red Heifer], and the cow, and all those that assist it go forth to the Mount of Olives.[41]

While there were probably three bridges eastward over the Kidron Valley during the days of the Herodian Temple, the Mishnah describes this particular bridge as the one used for leading the Red Heifer over to the Mount of Olives on which the Miphkad Altar (where the cow was slain) and the Beth HaDeshen (the pit in which it was burned) were situated. It was also the bridge over which criminals were led.[42] At opposite ends of the bridge (on the west at Ophel and on the east at the Mount of Olives plaza) were placed the urns (kalal) that contained the ashes of the Red Heifer.

> [When] it was burned up [the heifer], they beat it with rods and sift it in sieves. R. Ishmael says, "With stone hammers and with stone sieves was it done." A black [cinder] on which is ash they crush. And that on which is none do they leave. The bone, one way or the other, is crushed. And they divide it into three parts. *One is placed on the rampart [the bridge], and one is placed on the Mount of Olives [at the plaza in Beth Pagi], and one was divided among all the [priestly] watches.*[43]

It was at this site in the east, *outside* the Eastern Gate Miphkad, at the "Wing" of the Temple, that the lepers congregated (2 Ki. 7:1–4) and the unclean gathered to be purified or consecrated by the priests.

> And the head of the priestly watch then had the *unclean* people stand at the eastern gate.[44]

The Talmud is clear in placing all unclean (and lepers) on the eastern side of the Temple "outside the camp" (*b. Kel.* 1.7). The citizens of Jerusalem refused to walk to the east of these individuals in fear of contagion.

41. *m. Par.* 3:6 a–c

42. Due to the fact that they were compared with "sinners", or sin offerings that were burned outside the camp.

43. *m. Par.* 3:11 b–i.

44. *m. Tam.* 5:6 c(3).

> Moreover those that had the gonorrhoea and the leprosy were *excluded out of the city entirely*; women also, when their courses were upon them *were shut out of the Temple*; nor when they were free from that impurity, were they allowed to go beyond the limit before-mentioned; men also, that were not thoroughly pure, were prohibited to come into the inner court of the temple; nay, the priests themselves that were not pure, were prohibited to come into it also.[45]

Since the prevailing winds in the east blew from the west, lepers and others who were "unclean" were kept to the east of the city so that the "clean" might not become infected. The words "Ophel" (boil) and "Gareb" (scab) describe the condition of the lepers. It was in the area to the east that the unclean and leprous congregated for purification and healing. They presented themselves at the Eastern Gate singly where they might be pronounced "clean" by an "inspector" after having been subjected to the rites of purity (*b. Neg.* 3.1).

That gate has been named by some archaeologists the "Inspection" Gate. After being pronounced clean by an authorized medical examiner (a priest trained to recognize leprosy) they were then allowed to advance into the Eastern Cloisters of the Temple and enter only through the northern Tadi Gate into the Temple. The Mishnah informs us it was north of the Temple. The Tadi Gate has been excavated by Benjamin Mazar. The word Tadi, which must have been originally called the Tavi, might have been derived from the Hebrew letter Tav or Tau ת, meaning "marked".

> The entrance on the north was through the "Tadi" gate, i.e., the gate of obscurity or privacy, it being used only by those who were ceremonially unclean and by mourners and those under the ban.[46]

> That is why that Hebrew who was asked by Origen regarding the paternal tradition regarding the letter *Taw* in *Ez.* 9, 4, replied: The letter *Taw* (one of the 24 letters used by the Hebrews) is *the last* in the order in which they are arranged. For this reason this *last* has been chosen to indicate the perfection of those, who on account of their own virtue lament and grieve over the sins of the people and have compassion with sinners. Another said that the letter *Taw* is a symbol of those who observe the law, and precisely on this account it is called *T(orah)* by the Hebrews because *Taw* is the letter with which the name begins and represents those who observe it. Also R. NAHMAN was wont to say that the *Taw* "refers to the man who has observed the law from '*Alef* to *Taw*". For Jewish circles T meant perfection, the end, either of God or of the one who observes the law or of human life; it was, therefore, an eschatological letter. This is the reason why it was associated with final judgment, of life for the good and of condemnation and eternal death for the wicked. The rabbis said: It was a word of condemnation; RABBAH said: From the moment that he used it in every affair it could stand for: Be confounded! or: May you live! Rabbi HANINA ben Isaac said: It indicates: the merits of their forefathers are finished. In the *Babylonian Talmud* it is written: "The Holy One said to Gabriel: Go and put on the forehead of the just a *Taw*

---

45. Josephus, *War* 5.5.6.
46. "Plan of Second Temple", J.E., http://www.jewishencyclopedia.com/articles/14307-temple-plan-of-second.

> in ink . . . and on the forehead of the wicked a *Taw* in blood . . . And why a *Taw*? The *Taw* means: you shall live (*tihyeh*) and you shall die (*tamuth*)".[47]

Whether the reason the lepers and mourners had to enter through this particular gate was because they had followed the "letter of the law" through purification, or whether it marked them as "dead" is difficult to ascertain. It *is* interesting to note that the sick were not healed until all their sins were forgiven. Since it was the priesthood who controlled the inspection of the unclean, they were the authority to which the *ammei ha-aretz* looked for forgiveness of sin. It was this type of activity that Jesus condemned. It might be well to note that Jesus consorted with the lepers at Bethany, which might well have been a "colony" for the unclean.

The "house in the gate" during the early first century is to be identified with the structure housing the *beth din* at the Plaza of Gulgoleth. It must not be confused with that "place of exercise" called the *Xystus*, which was situated on the *west* of the Temple after the Sanhedrin removed from the Bazaars of Annas.

> Whereupon they built *a place of exercise* at Jerusalem according to the customs of the heathen.[48]
>
> A building in Jerusalem, erected, as is shown by the name, in the Hellenistic period, probably under the Herodians. The term properly denotes *a covered colonnade in the gymnasia*, although the Romans employed the word "xystus" to designate open terraces before the colonnades of their country homes.[49]

The word *Xystus* derives it name from the Latin term *xustos*, "polished" flagstones,[50] and was apparently the site of the western plaza, the Gabbatha. The place of exercise was not built by the Herodians but by Jason during the Maccabean period. It might well be that such an existing structure replaced the Hall of Hewn Stone and the Plaza during the mid-first century as the seat of the *Beth Din*. The Jewish records indicate that the Sanhedrin removed first from the Hall of Hewn Stone to the Plaza at Beth Pagi, then again removed to Jerusalem. Josephus in *War* 6.6.2 states it (the *Xystus*) *"joined the temple plateau by a bridge"*. It is entirely possible that another portion of the path of the Red Heifer bridge had a *corresponding* western bridge which connected Ophel to the present "Upper City".

In any event, the *Xystus* must not be connected with the seat of the Sanhedrin at the Plaza in the "outer court". The "Outer Court" was on the eastern side of the Temple, the *Xystus* on the west. Given the evidence presented by Mazar, and given the logic of Scripture, it is not unreasonable to suggest the western Hill of Ophel (the southern end of the present temple platform) as the site of Solomon's Temple and the eastern hill, the Mount of Olives, as the site for the "branch" of Zion. There is clear differentiation in the book of Nehemiah for the two "half-part" sections of Jerusalem (Neh. 3:9; 3:12). We are also told by Josephus (who contradicts himself in an earlier statement) that Titus pitched his own tent north and east of the "city" about two furlongs (about 1212 feet) distant from the *wall, at that part of it where was the corner* (i.e., the "corner" or "wing"

---

47. Saller and Testa, *Archaeological Setting*, pp. 109–110.
48. *The Apocrypha*, p. 140; 1 Macc. 1:14.
49. "Xystus", J.E., p. 575
50. Allegro, *Treasure*, p. 87.

of the Temple at Beth Pagi on the Mount of Olives) . . . but the other part of the army fortified themselves at the tower called Hippicus, and was distant, in like manner, but two furlongs (1212 feet) from the city".[51]

It was this northeastern portion of the city that the Romans had a problem conquering. It must be remembered that the Roman Tenth Legion had conquered and destroyed the Qumran community prior to marching "westward" through the Judean wilderness to the "corner" at Beth Pagi where they besieged Jerusalem.

> Since it would appear from this passage [Josephus, *War* II, 152-3] that the Romans were persecuting not individuals, but a group, it is tempting, bearing in mind *the arcaeologists' claim that the Qumran settlement was destroyed by the Romans*, to associate it with the story of Essenes captured by the Dead Sea. If such a surmise is correct, the sect's disappearance from history may well have been brought about in the lethal blow suffered by its *central establishment during the fateful summer of A.D. 68*.[52]

By the time the Romans had besieged Jerusalem, they had cut down all the trees on the Mount of Olives, including the tree on which Jesus was executed and the two ancient cypress trees belonging to the Bazaars of Annas.

> Now, when Caesar perceived that the upper city was so steep, that it could not possibly be taken without raising banks against it, he distributed the several parts of that work among his army, and this on the twentieth day of the month Lous [Ab]. Now, the carriage of the materials was a difficult task, since all *the trees*, as I have already told you, *that were about the city, within the distance of a hundred* furlongs [7,272 feet; about a mile and a half in a circumference around the city], *had their branches cut off* already, in order to make the former banks. The works that belonged to the four legions were erected on the *west side* of the city over-against the royal palace, but the whole body of the auxiliary troops, with the rest of the multitude that were with them, [erected their banks] at the Xystus, whence they reached the bridge, and that tower of Simon [on the Temple Mount], which he had built as a citadel for himself against John, when they were at war one with another.[53]

Titus had pitched his own camp "within the city" at a place called "the Camp of the Assyrians".[54] Tradition places this site to the west of the Temple Mount; however, Josephus, who again seems to contradict himself, has already told us that Titus pitched his tent near the "corner" on the northeastern side.

Scripture gives us its more exact location. It is the site where the army of the "Assyrian" aggressor (Sennacherib) was turned back. Only from an area on the northern summit of the Mount of Olives, above Bethphage (Nob), a "priestly city", might he have "brandished his hand" toward the Mount of the Daughter of "Zion" (the Plaza area on the Mount of Olives).

---

51. Josephus, *War* 5.3.5.
52. Vermes, *Dead Sea Scrolls in English*, p. 35; see also Shanks, *Understanding*, p. 187.
53. Josephus, *War* 6.8.1.
54. Josephus, *War* 5.7.2.

> O my people that dwellest in Zion, be not afraid of the *Assyrian* . . . As yet shall he remain at *Nob* [Bethphage] that day: he shall shake his hand against *the mount of the daughter of Zion, the hill of Jerusalem* [the southern peak of the Mount of Olives] (Isa. 10:24, 32).

Sennacherib would have been interested in conquering Solomon's administrative complex, the seat of Israel's government, and that complex was located on the Mount of Olives near the Plaza. The Maccabees repaired the "wall" of Beth Pagi and the Plaza.

> And making the walls of Jerusalem higher, and raising a great mount between the tower and the city, for to separate it from the city, that so it might be alone that men might neither sell nor buy in it. Upon this they came together to build up the city, forasmuch *as part of the wall [plaza, "wall"] toward the brook on the east side was fallen down, and they repaired that which was called Caphenatha.*[55]

The *Caphenatha*, with which scholars have had linguistic problems, might simply mean "bend of appearing" or "curve of appearing". It is to be identified with the curve (crux) of the Mount of Olives. The reason it was called the "bend of appearing" was, perhaps, fourfold: 1) the sun rose from the east over the Mount of Olives; 2) it formed the "curve" or ridge enclosing Beth Pagi; 3) it was the site where the Shekinah rested after Ezekiel's vision; and 4) it was the site of the final resurrection, the revelation of the Messiah, and the return of YHWH to His people. It is also the site of the Messiah's parousia [appearance] (Zech. 14:4–5) in the Shekinah of YHWH, who is prophesied to appear on the Mount of Olives in the east. This is exactly where Jesus is said to "return" in that day:

> And when he had spoken these things, while they beheld, he was taken up; and a cloud received him out of their sight. And while they looked stedfastly toward heaven as he went up, behold, two men stood by them in white apparel; Which also said, Ye men of Galilee, why stand ye gazing up into heaven? This same Jesus, which is taken up from you into heaven, shall so come in like manner as ye have seen him go into heaven. *Then returned they unto Jerusalem from the mount called Olivet, which is from Jerusalem a sabbath day's journey* (Acts 1:9–12).

The area in which he ascended was on the Mount of Olives and was at Beth Hini (Bethany):

> *And he led them out as far as Bethany* [Beth Hini], *and he lifted up his hands, and blessed them. And it came to pass, while he blessed them, he was parted from them, and carried up into heaven* (Luke 24:50–51).

The Sabbath limit during that time was at Beth Pagi (or Beth Hini). We are told by Zechariah that the Messiah in his Father's Shekinah will appear on the Mount of Olives *on the east*! Thus the Miphkad Gate is to remain closed (or hidden) until Messiah comes to Israel. As Jeremiah tells us this gate is "sunk in the ground". It is not to be confused with the *traditional* Eastern Gate on the present Temple Platform. The Byzantines erroneously refer to that gate as the "Golden Gate".

> Walls have their gates, and Jerusalem's old city gates are wide, handsome mouths opening into a tiny universe of priests, pilgrims, peddlers, plotters, dreamers,

---

55. *The Apocrypha*, p. 165; 1 Macc. 12:36–37.

rabbis, and Muslim holy men. But one gate is never open: the Golden Gate, through which Jesus entered the Temple Mount on Palm Sunday. *The Turks sealed the Golden Gate, fearing the legend that when Christ appears through the gate the world empires will fall.* Sealed with stones, the Golden Gate's double-door outline seems more like an etched decoration in the eastern wall than an actual gate. But the people who live in this city know the gate is there, and they will tell you stories which speak volumes about their yearnings and fears. Legend has it that when Titus burned the Temple the Divine Presence—the Shekinah, as it is called in Hebrew—fled the conflagration, exiting from the earth through the Golden Gate. To this day the most pious of Jerusalem's Jews believe that on the Day of Judgment the Shekinah will return to earth and reenter the Temple Mount through the same gate. On that day the righteous souls will ascend to heaven through the southern (Mercy) portal and the wicked will be cast down into hell through the northern (Repentance) portal. The judgment will take place in the Valley of Jehosophat, below the Mount of Olives. Then a bridge will appear across the valley, a bridge "as thin as hair and as sharp as a sword." Muslims believe that the righteous Muslims will cross the bridge safely but that the wicked will fall to their ruin below. The Jewish version of the same legend contains a different fate. The bridges are two, one of iron, the other of paper. The Muslims and Christians will cross the iron bridge which will collapse under them, while Jews will pass safely over the paper bridge.[56]

All this sounds well and good; however, there is just one tiny problem. *That* gate has *already been opened* by human Christian hands near the year 1049 CE and onward. It could not be the one to which Ezekiel refers!

> *At dawn a multitude would gather in the village of Bethany*, a few miles east of the Mount of Olives, to retrace the footsteps of Jesus' fatal journey. Standing behind the True Cross [so it is called], or what was left of it, the patriarch led the bishops of all the churches, followed by knights, monks, town merchants, village priests, peasants, and hordes of pilgrims from every nation—the whole of the city in one grand procession, minus the few Muslims and Jews who hid out during this week. Their path was cleared by white-robed boys incensing the ground to drive away demonic spirits. Slowly the procession walked to the Mount of Olives to pray at the stone which bore the footprints of Christ when he ascended to heaven [he really ascended from Beth Hini]. From there the column made its way downhill to the Garden of Gethsemane to witness to the Lord's sorrow. *Then it marched up the [present] Temple Mount through the Golden Gate as Jesus had done; the gate was opened once annually for this occasion.* The devout prayed first in the Templum Solomonis and then walked across to the Templum Domini for more prayers at the altar constructed over the Moriah stone. As they exited they knelt before the great picture of the Madonna which was affixed to the door of the former Muslim shrine of the Dome of the Rock. From the Temple Mount they went immediately to the Praetoriaum to follow Jesus' footsteps on the Via Dolorosa. They stopped at ten stations of the cross, which took them into the Church of the Holy Sepulchre and to the final four stations covering the Crucifixion and burial. Finally they would

---

56. Idinopulos, *Jerusalem*, pp. 14–15.

gather at the tomb to sing hymns of praise through the day, feeling the excitement that would fill them this entire week.[57]

From time to time there was, apparently, some need to repair the walkway and bridge since a heavy amount of traffic would traverse there. During King Herod Agrippa's reign, he was enticed to again repair them.

> [S]o they persuaded him [King Agrippa II] to rebuild the eastern cloisters. These cloisters belonged to the outer court [Beth Pagi], and were situated in a deep valley [the Kidron], and had walls that reached four hundred cubits [in length] [600 feet], and were built of square and very white stones, the length of each of which stones was twenty cubits, and their height six cubits. This was the work of king Solomon, who first of all built the entire temple.[58]

Clearly, Solomon's "Trench" was destroyed, and with it all traces of the "buildings" of the temple [hieron] at Beth Pagi. Since Jerusalem proper had no "town square", the priests had incorporated an area on the Mount of Olives into the "city limits". Here, they might have their "plaza" or public square "outside the camp" so as not to profane Jerusalem. It consisted of a "walkway" between pillars. Solomon's Colonnade had once led to the administrative complex on the Mount of Olives, at the conclusion of which was the public square.

This building logic would have been entirely acceptable because the area east of the Eastern Gate was considered "profane" (i.e., secular) by the seventh century BCE. Since the ceremony of the "beheaded heifer" (Deut. 21:1–8) might not be performed to atone an unknown murder in Jerusalem, (and this must be adjudicated in the town square), the "open space" (Plaza of Gulgoleth) in the region of Beth Pagi satisfied the requirement.

The area of the Plaza became known as the "Wing of Abomination". It was here the Bazaars of Annas, with all the corruption and graft associated with them, stood. Knowing what we now know of the Hellenistic priesthood of the first century, the idea of the "abomination" is not so farfetched. It was the area of Beth Pagi near the unnamed hill that Daniel (9:27) called the "wing of abomination" or as in the Jewish Tanach, simply an "appalling abomination" at the "corner [wing] of the [Miphkad] altar". It is referred to in the KJV as the "overspreading of abominations" (i.e., the "wing" of abominations). The genealogically pure priestly families were scandalized by the merchandising of the Plaza. The area must have been a constant controversy for the pious. Even Nehemiah, at the time of the rebuilding of Solomon's Temple, was offended by the merchants who gathered there.

> In those days saw I in Judah some treading winepresses on the sabbath, and brining in sheaves, and lading asses; as also wine, grapes, and figs, and all manner of burdens, which they brought into Jerusalem on the sabbath day: and *I testified against them in the day wherein they sold victuals. There dwelt men of Tyre also therein, which brought fish, and all manner of ware, and sold on the sabbath unto the children of Judah, and in Jerusalem . . . So the merchants and sellers of all kind of ware lodged without Jerusalem* ["outside the camp"] *once or twice. Then I testified against them, and said unto them, Why lodge ye about the wall?* if ye

---

57. Idinopulos, pp. 177–179.
58. Josephus, *Ant.* 20.9.7.

do so again, I will lay hands on you. From that time forth came they no more on the sabbath. And I commanded the Levites that they should be *cleansed* [purify] *themselves* [which could only occur at the site of the Miphkad Altar] and keep the gates, to sanctify the sabbath day (Neh. 13:15–16; 20–22).

Jesus, several centuries later (as well as other pious individuals mentioned in the Talmud), was offended by these same practices still occurring there. The Family of Hanan, however, were notorious for their mercantile and financial pursuits. Pure lineal descent for the priesthood had come to an end during the previous two centuries, replaced by the Maccabees and by the Herodian and Roman-appointed Hellenists in political favor with Rome. *Both* groups, however, were allied with the Roman government. When Jesus spoke about the "abomination of desolation", however, he was more specifically referring to the Tenth Legion "standing in a holy place" during the siege of Jerusalem.

> Thou must know and understand: From the issuance of the word to restore and rebuild Jerusalem until the time of the Anointed Leader is seven weeks; and for sixty-two weeks it will be rebuilt, *square* [*charuts*] *and moat* [*rechob*], *but in a time of distress* . . . *during one week he will make a firm covenant with many. For half a week he will put a stop to the sacrifice and the meal offering. At the corner of the altar* [otherwise translated "wing of the temple" or "overspreading of abominations"] *will be an appalling abomination until the decreed destruction will be poured down upon the appalling thing* (Dan. 9:24–27, JPS)

The building of the Temple precincts continued throughout the years after the execution of Jesus until Jerusalem was destroyed, certainly a "time of distress". The entire wing was destroyed during the siege of Jerusalem in 70 CE, thus fulfilling the prophecy made by Jesus that "one stone will not be left upon another". It was here that the Roman Tenth Legion trod underfoot the sacred Miphkad Altar. The words used by Jesus indicate the "abomination of desolation" will stand in the secular plaza where the (*hagio*) "victim is slain"; i.e., at the "corner" or "wing" of the Miphkad Altar. As quoted earlier, the Romans had encamped only 1212 feet from the "corner" or "wing" of the Temple. The "corner of the altar" [that is, the "quarter" or wing by which the Miphkad Altar of the first century stood] was in this vicinity.

The practices of the corrupt priesthood had made the Mount of Olives a place of "abomination", literally a "den of thieves". Since it later became the foreign merchant exchange and the seat of the apathetic government of Israel, it might have been viewed as a place of "filthy" lucre and "detestable" practices, a veritable "wing of abomination". We must remember that Jesus cleansed this area of the temple precincts twice, because the practice of merchandising and traffic (i.e., graft) was abominable to YHWH. In speaking of Hiram, the Prince of Tyre (who we know was a "type" of Lucifer) Scripture states:

> With thy wisdom and with thy understanding thou hast gotten thee riches, and has gotten gold and silver into thy treasures: By thy great *wisdom and by thy traffic* hast thou increased thy riches, and thine heart is *lifted up* [and] Thou hast *defiled thy sanctuaries by the multitude of thine iniquities, by the iniquity of thy traffic* (Ezek. 28:4-5; Ezek. 28:18).

Remember, it was this prince who encouraged David to build a "house of cedars" and who aided Solomon in the building of the Temple on Ophel. Ezekiel might have been describing the leadership of Israel during the days of Jesus. As depicted by Jesus we might be inclined to expect that the "pavillion" "or palace-home" [*'appeden*] of the "god of forces", which the heathen enemy pitches and places "between the seas [Dead Sea/Mediterranean Sea] towards the *beautiful holy mountain* [i.e., the Mount of Ophel] (Dan. 11:45) might well be the "abomination of desolation" standing in a holy place [*topos; makon (foundation); miqdash* (Dan. 8:11)]. The plaza at which Israel's leaders ruled might well have been the place where David's own "pavillion" (sukkah) had been placed. That canopy or marquee (tent) covered the Ark of the Covenant as it sat upon the Shetiyyah Stone (*eben* Ezel), a "fountain" or eye of the landscape. As already stated, Jesus was referring to the Roman destruction of Jerusalem. Remember Jesus had told his disciples that they were to flee to the wilderness of Judea (the "mountains"), and this was just east of Beth Pagi in the Olivet mountain chain. But the passage also indicates another more future time, and that time is when the armies of the False Messiah encompass "Jerusalem" (just as the Romans did). Any investigation into the patterns of Genesis will firmly establish this "wing of appointment" [corner of the altar] and the Foundation Plaza of Gulgoleth in Beth Pagi as the site of the execution of Jesus. He was executed in the midst of that "street", at the Footstool of God.

6

The Execution

NOW THAT THE PLACE of execution has been firmly established in our minds, our next step is to determine the events that occurred *that* day, the day the Messiah of Israel was executed. Jesus had spent a wakeful and anxious morning. He had been brought before the two high priests, the Roman prefect of Judea, the Roman prefect of Galilee and Perea (and Jewish "king"), had his hair pulled, his beard plucked out; he had been spit upon, cursed, beaten, scourged, and humiliated. Finally, he was condemned. It was just before the "third hour", or 9:00 a.m. that the Sanhedrin led Jesus (and the two Zealots) to the *Beth HaSeqilah* at the public square for execution. Some scholars have argued that the Sanhedrin was not allowed to execute more than one individual at a time. Because there were two others executed that same day, a few academicians have rejected the notion that the two "thieves" (or robbers) were actually executed with Jesus. They claim the motif must have been a literary device used within the text in order to provide the reader with a spiritual sense of what it was to accept or deny Jesus. While the motif does enhance the benefits of accepting Jesus as Israel's Messiah, it was *not* a literary device. Clearly, what the scholars suggest is impossible because it contradicts Jewish law (i.e., that only one execution can occur in a single day). Two, three, or more individuals might be executed on a single day if they had been convicted of charges carrying the same death penalty. It was the *mode* of execution that determined whether multiple individuals might be sentenced and executed on the same day.

> Why? Shall we say, because two [men] may not be tried [and sentenced] on the same day? But R. Hisda said: This was taught only with reference to [charges involving] *two different modes of execution*; whereas [cases that involve only] *one mode of execution may be tried?*—But it was so, that the fierce anger of the Lord may turn away from Israel.[1]

Clearly, the two "robbers" were Zealots who had been sentenced to death for their radical religious and political beliefs. They, too, would have been classified as *mesith*.

---

1. *b. Sanh.* 35a.

A Book of Evidence

They would certainly have been inciting the populace against the leadership of the Temple Cult, as history confirms. Four years before the destruction of Jerusalem by the Romans in 70 CE the Zealots had finally attained their goal, having put a legitimate high priest in office, after having assassinated, one by one, the members of the powerful priestly oligarchy.

The two criminals might well have gone through much the same process as Jesus himself did. What is certain is that each was excommunicated from the community of Israel. As the shofar sounded the blasts announcing excommunication from the congregation of Israel on the Pinnacle of the Temple, a flagman (lactee), stood near the southeastern cloisters of the Women's Court near the Miphkad Gate with a red flag. Each man would have been led separately over the Red Heifer bridge to the execution site on the "ridge" (or "cranium", "spine", or "crux") of the Mount of Olives (Gulgoleth). A second lactee riding a white horse and carrying a wooden plaque upon which the charge was written, led the execution party to that public square, the gathering place for the festal pilgrims situated near the Bazaars of Annas. Pilate had written on that plaque that Jesus was the "King of Israel"! No other charge was represented on the plaque.

> A man was stationed at the door of the court with a signalling flag in his hand, and a horseman was stationed at a distance yet within sight of him, and then if one says, 'I have something [further] to state in his favour', he [the signaller] waves the flag, and the horse-man runs and stops them. *And even if he himself [the condemned] says, 'I have something to plead in my own favour', he is brought back, even four or five times, providing, however, that there is substance in his assertion.*[2]

Jesus, however, "opened not his mouth" in his own behalf but allowed the execution squad to lead him to the tree situated in the Plaza. He had accepted his duty and his "cup", and it was for this reason, and not the Christian tradition of remaining silent during his trials (which he clearly did *not* do), that fulfilled the prophecy of Isaiah.

> Hard pressed—yet he humbled himself, *Nor opened his mouth—As a lamb to the slaughter is led, And as a sheep before her shearers is dumb—Nor opened his mouth. By constraint and by sentence was he taken away,* And of his age who considered that he was cut off out of the land of the living, For my people's transgression did the stroke fall on him (Isa. 53:7–8).

The sentence after describing his silence clearly states it was in connection with his execution that he remained silent. Jesus had had every opportunity to defend himself, even up to the very point of execution.

> [A]rguments in favor of acquittal may be raised *even after sentence, up to the very moment of execution.* Only when all doubt is at an end the condemned criminal is exhorted to confess, in order that he may find forgiveness in another world.[3]

As the Mishnah and Tosefta inform us, even the convicted himself might bring forth evidence.

---

2. *b. Sanh.* 42b.
3. "Accusatory", J.E., p. 163.

The Execution

> Even if the convicted one say, "I have something to plead in my own defence," he is to be brought back, it may be four or five times, provided his plea is reasonable; then if he be acquitted he is set free, and if not, he is again taken out to be stoned.[4]

Jesus, however, knew what they could not know, that it was YHWH's will to bruise him.

As the horseman proceeded to the execution site, he announced a message similar to this:

> [Yehoshua], son of [Yoseph], is going forth to be [executed], in that he has committed the offense of blasphemy by leading the nation of Israel astray from the teachings of the scribes and from worship in the Temple. He has shown disrespect for his elders and for the Beth Din. Anyone who knows anything in his defense, let him come and witness.[5]

His apostles, many of whom were probably Zealots themselves feared for their own lives and scattered. Just as no one could be found to witness that he was *not* Messiah, no one stepped forward to say *he was*!

When Jesus was led from the Miphkad Gate toward the public "Street" or Plaza at Beth Pagi, professional mourners lamented and mourned. Since it was believed he, as one having been convicted as a *mesith*, had called down the wrath of God on the nation, they mourned his condemnation, not out of any peculiar compassion but simply out of duty. Women were traditionally the first to mourn, and would not only lead a funeral procession but also an execution procession. Jewish commentary states that woman, who brought death into our world, ought to lead the way in such processions. It was here Jesus had spoken to them.

> And there was following him a great throng of people *and of women who were smiting themselves and lamenting him*. But turning towards them Jesus said—Daughters of Jerusalem! Do not weep for me; But for yourselves be weeping, and for your children (Luke 23:27).

Their mourning for him prompted his sorrowful warning. The reader will recall that he had wept over Jerusalem when he had first entered the city.

By this time, however, Simon the Cyrenian who had come in from the "field" (probably from the area around Beth Hini) and had been, himself, entering the public "street" in order to join the crowd gathering in the Plaza, had already been impressed to carry the yoke. Perhaps this was because of the wounds Jesus had received at the hands of the Temple captains. It must here be noted that the "yoke" was not what Christian tradition claims. It was not the Roman "cross" or even the crossbeam of the cross. It was, instead, a sturdy piece of wood fitted over the neck like the yoke of an ox, one that might easily be attached with ropes to another living tree and could be removed after execution.

> As to the gibbet [yoke, *patibulum*], it must not be a natural [as part of a living tree] or *permanent* one, like a tree, but an artificial arrangement, easily removable

---

4. Danby, *Tractate Sanhedrin*, p. 87; M. Sanh. VI. I.
5. Danby, p. 87; Adapted from *Tosef. M. Sanh.* 6.1.

[from the tree]; and when once used, must be buried out of sight (Sanh. vi. 4, 46b; Sifre, Deut. 221).[6]

The reason the artificial yoke had to be buried was because "it was regarded as part of the body and must be carried with it when moved" (Cf. *Nazir* 64b, *b. Sanh.* 45b).

> But has it not been taught: 'The stone with which he [the condemned] was stoned, the gallows on which he was hanged, the sword with which he was beheaded, or the cloth with which he was strangled, are all buried with him?[7]

This is why the Gospel of Peter (verse 10) describes the "cross" as following Jesus from the tomb at the time of his resurrection. The "yoke" had been buried with him after he had been brought down from the tree. The practice, and consequently, the law, was instituted during the days of Joshua when the sinner Achan had been hanged on a tree (Josh. 19–25).

Once the procession had passed over the Red Heifer bridge and through the Miphkad Gate into the region known as Beth Pagi, the *Beth HaSeqilah*, the place of execution, was directly in view.

When the execution squad approached within ten cubits (about 17-1/2 feet) of the execution site, Jesus was asked to confess (not necessarily his crime but his sins).

> When ten cubits from the stoning-place they say to him, "Confess: for it is the custom of all about to be put to death to make confession; and every one who confesses has a share in the world to come; for so we find it in the case of Achan. Joshua said to him: My son, ascribe glory to the LORD, the God of Israel, and *make confession unto him*; and tell me now what thou hast done; hide it not from me. And Achan answered Joshua, and said, of a truth I have sinned against the LORD, the God of Israel, and thus and thus have I done. Whence do we know that his confession expiated his crime? It is written: "And Joshua said, Why has thou troubled us? The LORD shall trouble thee this day—this day thou art to be troubled, but thou art not to be troubled in the time to come." If he does not know how to make confession, he is told to say, *"May my death be an expiation of all my sins."* According to R. Jehuda, if he know himself to be condemned wrongfully, he says, "Let my death be an expiation of all my sins save this." But it was replied, "If so, every one would say so to clear himself" . . .[8]
>
> . . . Those who are put to death by the court have a share in the world to come, because they confess all their sins. *Ten cubits from the stoning-place they say to the condemned man, "Confess!"* It happened to one who went out to be stoned, that when they told him to confess he said, "May my death be an expiation of all my sins; and if I have done this, let it not be forgiven me, and let the court of Israel be innocent." When this was reported to the judges their eyes trickled with tears, but they said, "It is not possible to reprieve him, for then there would be no end to the matter; but his blood is hung on the neck of his witnesses".[9]

---

6. "Capital Punishment", J.E., p. 557
7. *b. Sanh.* 45b
8. Danby, *Tractate Sanhedrin*, p. 88; *M. Sanh.* 6.2.
9. Danby, p. 89; *Tosef. Sanh.* IX. 5.

The Execution

Jesus did not "confess". He, instead, later prayed from the tree that YHWH might *forgive them* for their ignorance in putting him to death.

"Father! *forgive them*; For they know not what they do" (Luke 23:34).

Afterward, Jesus would have been led to another locale just four cubits (about 7 feet) from the execution site, itself. Here Jesus would have been divested of his clothing. The reason for this was to humiliate the accused and cause him shame.

> Four cubits from the stoning-place the criminal is stripped.[10]

Only a man was stripped naked prior to execution. A woman would have been allowed a covering over her bosom, not for her own modesty's sake, but in order to prevent the priests from lusting after her naked body. We have already discussed the parting of his garments by the Temple captains in another chapter. After Jesus had been stripped, he was offered the compassionate drink of wine and olibanum (myrrh and laudanum, a narcotic mixed with watered wine) by the wealthy women of Jerusalem.

> And coming to a place called Golgotha, that is to say Skull Place [the entire area on the Mount of Olives is called Golgotha, but Jesus was actually executed in the Plaza or "Place" southeast of the summit or Ha-Rosh], they gave him to *drink wine with gall mingled* (Matt. 27:34).

This drink was designed to blunt the sensibilities of the condemned man, so that he might become stupefied and not realize his painful end. It was considered an act of mercy.

> When one is led out to execution, he is given a goblet of wine containing a grain of frankincense, in order to benumb his senses, for it is written, *Give strong drink unto him that is ready to perish, and wine unto the bitter in soul*. And it has also been taught: The noble women in Jerusalem used to donate and bring it. If these did not donate it, who provided it?—As for that, it is certainly logical that it should be provided out of the public [funds]: since it is written, '*Give*' [the implication is] of what is theirs.[11]

Jesus, however, did not accept the drink (Matt. 27:34; Mark 15:23; Luke 23:36), and it must have made his pain even more acute. Perhaps it was because he did not accept the narcotic that he died within such a short period of time. One should not confuse the "vinegar" which he later accepted as the narcotic offered at first. The vinegar was simply watered wine. After Jesus refused the narcotic, his wrists would have been nailed to the yoke. No nails would have been placed in his feet. The Gospel of Peter (verse 6) makes mention of the fact that when Jesus was taken from the tree, they pulled the nails from his hands, but the feet were not mentioned. When Jesus verified his identity to the disciples, he offered to show them his hands and his side, mentioning nothing about his feet (John 20:20–27). As a matter of fact, the inclusion of "and feet" in the Lucan narrative (Luke 24:40) is omitted in all the earliest Greek manuscripts. It had been interpolated later by some Christian scribe to conform to execution on a Roman cross. Once the nails had been driven through his wrists, he would have been hoisted up the tree by

---

10. Danby, *Tractate Sanhedrin*, p. 88; *M. Sanh. 6.3*.
11. *b. Sanh.* 43a

ropes. The yoke would have been attached either by ropes or by nails to a living tree, and the accusation plaque attached to the tree above his head. While the Jewish "hanging" was generally a procedure that occurred only after death, the Babylonian-Alexandrian priesthood had adopted the methods of their predecessor Alexander Jannaeus, who had *hanged alive* eight hundred Pharisees. The Qumran documents make it clear that the practice was clearly Alexandrian.

> [And chokes prey for its lionesses; and it fills] its caves [with prey] and its dens with victims (ii, 12a-b). Interpreted, this concerns the furious young lion [who executes revenge] [Alexander Jannaeus] on those who seek smooth things [Pharisees] and *hangs men alive* . . . *formerly in Israel. Because of a man hanged alive on [the] tree,* He proclaims, 'Behold I am against [you, says the Lord of Hosts']. [12]

The missing words before "formerly in Israel" are translated by scholars in contradictory ways: 1) "as was never done" and 2) "as was done". The controversy makes little difference to our present case. Whether Israel had always hanged their criminals alive or whether it had just begun to do so makes little difference. The fact is Alexander Jannaeus, the Hellenized leader of Israel during the first century BCE, *did* hang men alive on the tree. Josephus gives us the gruesome details.

> Now as Alexander fled to the mountains, six thousand of the Jews hereupon came together [from Demetrius] to him out of pity at the change of his fortune; upon which Demetrius was afraid, and retired out of the country; after which the Jews fought against Alexander, and being beaten were slain in great numbers in the several battles which they had, and when he had shut up the most powerful of them in the city Bethome, he besieged them therein; and when he had taken the city, and gotten the men into his power, *he brought them to Jerusalem, and did one of the most barbarous actions in the world to them; for as he was feasting with his concubines, in the sight of all the city, he ordered about eight hundred of them to be crucified [hanged]; and while they were living, he ordered the throats of their children and wives to be cut before their eyes.*[13]

From the time of Alexander's death in 78 BCE, with a brief respite until 69 CE, the nation of Israel was primarily ruled by the Babylonian-Alexandrian priesthood, having been imported by Herod the Great from both Babylon and Egypt. As stated numerous times already, this priesthood (the Temple Cult) was both illegitimate and corrupt. They had Hellenistic origins and were associated with the Romans and the self-seeking Herodian dynasty (which itself also had close ties to the Roman emperors).

> After Mark Antony's suppression of the revolutionary activity by Aristobulus' two sons Alexander and Antigonus in the next generation, who like John the Baptist after them were *beheaded; the priests officiating at the Temple all owed their positions to Roman and Herodian power.*[14]

The temple itself had evolved into a corrupt financial institution, and the priesthood served as its bankers. It was not until the destruction of Jerusalem in 70 CE that

---

12. Vermes, *Dead Sea Scrolls*, p. 280.
13. Josephus, *Ant.* 13.14.2.
14. Eisenman and Wise, *Scrolls Uncovered*, p. 121.

The Execution

the Pharisees again gained control of Israel's religious affairs, the primary reason that the Jewish writings reflect the Pharisaic death penalties. The Saducean mode of execution was, however, different. John the Baptist calls them a "brood of vipers", reflecting the Hebrew equivalent *ma'ase 'eph'eh* "creatures of the Snake".[15] The execution of Jesus was primarily instigated by a single corrupt family: the family of Hanan (Annas). It is obvious that the Jewish people during the first century, who had absolutely nothing to do with the death of Jesus, recognized this Saducean priesthood as overlords. Both Josephus and the rabbis of the Talmud referred to them as "hissers" or "whisperers" and connected them with the evil serpent. Jesus, himself, referred to them as "vipers" and compared them to their "father"; i.e., the ancient serpent of Genesis. Members from the Babylonian-Alexandrian priesthood, ruling during the first century, had first been appointed by the Edomite King, Herod. These Herodian-appointed Babylonian priests were primarily Saducees, and it was this group to which Alexander Janneus allied himself. It was Alexander Janneus, too, who had hanged men *alive* on trees! The Pharisees of the first century BCE had found the practice to be utterly abhorrent, and this is reflected in the writings of the Essenes. Within the *order* of the language, another Qumran manuscript seems to imply that hanging convicted criminals on a tree while still alive was a fairly common practice, at least during the years prior to the rabbinic period after the destruction of Jerusalem.

> If a man is guilty of a capital crime and flees (abroad) to the nations, and curses his people, the children of Israel, *you shall hang him also on the [living] tree and he shall die*. But his body shall not stay overnight on the tree. Indeed you shall bury him on the same day. *For he who is hanged on the tree is accursed of God and men*.[16]

Please note that this document states the criminal is to be *first* hanged upon a tree, and then *secondly*, that he shall die. The statement would seem to imply that this was the ordinary practice during the years the Babylonian-Alexandrian priesthood (who were Saducean) ruled in Israel. Taken in conjunction with the *Nahum Pesher* quoted earlier, there seems to be enough evidence to at least suspect this to be a true statement.

> The passage ordains that *the death penalty shall be carried out by "suspending" the convict alive for the charge of treason* on the basis of Deuteronomy 21:22-23. What we have *here is a pre-Christian halakhic interpretation of Deuteronomy 21:22-23 (crucifixion in the form of a hanging on a tree)*.[17]

The *Nahum Pesher* continues with the same wording as the Temple Scroll.

> If a man slanders his people and delivers his people to a foreign nation and does evil to his people, *you shall hang him on a tree and he shall die*. On the testimony of two witnesses and on the testimony of three witnesses, he shall be put to death [a reversal in wording here] and they shall hang him on the tree. If a man is guilty of a capital crime and flees (abroad) to the nations [i.e.,

---

15. Shanks, *Understanding*, p. 212.
16. Vermes, *Dead Sea Scrolls*, p. 156.
17. Fujita, *Crack*, p. 133.

> a *mesith*], and curses his people, and the children of Israel, *you shall hang him also on the tree, and he shall die.*[18]

The Sadducean priesthood took full responsibility for the execution of Jesus. The "crowd" of priests and Herodians shouting from the third story of the Temple offices demanded Pilate condemn him. These, along with the witnesses (the accusers, who would have been the priests themselves) made a statement that reflects exactly upon whose shoulders the blame should rest.

> And all the people, answering said, *"his blood be upon us and upon our children!"* (Matt. 27:25).

This Jewish euphemism referred to as *demehem bam* was used *only by the judges in a capital case*. It was designed to make them think about the responsibility they take upon themselves in rendering a verdict. It was well known that if the judges of Israel found one guilty of a capital crime, the verdict necessarily made them responsible for not only the blood of the accused but of the physical descendants that might have followed him had he been acquitted. What is indicated more particularly by the expression, however, is the *type* of death the accused was to suffer.

> With reference to all other capital offenses [blasphemy included], the law ordains that the perpetrator shall die a violent death, occasionally adding the expression, *"His (their) blood shall be upon him (them)."* This expression, as we shall see presently, post-Biblical legislation *applies to death by stoning* . . . the law says (Lev. xx. 27), *"They shall stone them with stones; their blood shall be upon them (*דמיהם בם*).* Here the expression "Demehem bam" is plainly used in connection with death by stoning: hence it is argued that, *wherever the same expression occurs in the Pentateuch in connection with the death penalty, it means death by stoning*, and consequently the punishment of the crimes mentioned in Lev. xx. 9, 11, 12, 13, 16, is the same: *death by* stoning [Mek., Mishpatim, 17; Sifra, Kedoshim, 9; Sanh. 53b, 66a].[19]

In the case of Jesus, it was meant to infer that the judges themselves would take responsibility for his death. Anyone who was sentenced to death by stoning was also hanged. While we presently view stoning as a barbaric and inhumane practice and cannot imagine that our Messiah might have been stoned, this mode of execution was entirely legal and accepted during the first century. The Pharisaic and Sadducean methods of stoning an individual were, however, entirely different. Whereas the Pharisees used only one large stone and threw the individual down from a great height, the Sadducees demanded the whole congregation of Israel have a part in putting the accused to death. Each person passing by the execution site would have been required by law to pick up a stone and cast it at the accused, thus "casting out" that individual from the nation of Israel. It was a process similar to the placing of hands on the Sinbearer Goat to be "cast out" into the "wilderness" as a "curse" of God. Since the Sadducean priesthood was the powerful sect during the lifetime of Jesus, we must assume it would have been their law that carried the day. We shall examine the evidence in Scripture to

---

18. Vermes, p. 156; *Nah. Pesh.*, Col. 1, Lines 1-11 (4Q169).
19. "Capital Punishment", J.E., pp. 554-555.

The Execution

determine whether or not Jesus might have been stoned. I make no assertion concerning this question. I merely list the facts below. The reader must weigh the evidence for himself. One of the prophecies applied to "prove" the "crucifixion" of Jesus by Christianity is Psalm 22:16–18. Unfortunately, the etymology of that Psalm has never been properly examined.

> For dogs have surrounded me—an assembly of evil doers have encircled me, *they have pierced my hands and feet, I may tell all my bones, they [his bones] look for—they [his bones] behold me!* They part my garments among them, and for my vestment they cast lots (Ps. 22:16–18).

The only manner in which a man's bones might view him is if they were no longer enclosed in flesh. We have no problem with the "assembly of evil doers" nor the parting of the garments, but there is a very important discrepancy in wording here that has failed to receive close scrutiny. The word "pierced" does not mean "to pierce through". The Hebrew word here is *'aryeh* and is derived from the root *'arah*. Those words literally mean "to pluck away skin" as a young lion might maul and tear the flesh of a carcass, exposing the whitened bones. Anyone who has ever been slapped by a cat knows that the skin is not pierced through but literally pulled away. A stone, especially if sharp, would have the same effect as a lion's claw. William Wilson gives the following exact usage of the word: *'arah*, "like a lion". Again, crucifixion could not "pluck" into the flesh and tear it away. Had the prophecy been meant to imply a puncturing of nail marks, the word *daqar* (as used in Zech. 12:10), "to stab or thrust through", would have been used instead. The word for "feet" is *pudenda* and indicates the generative parts of a man's body, but might well refer to the abdominal cavity in general. Certainly, anyone who was stoned would receive wounds all over the body. It is interesting to note that the nailing of the feet is mentioned only once in the New Covenant (Luke 40); however, on closer examination we learn that the words "and feet" have been interpolated from a late Greek manuscript. A few scholars, including Paulus claims that his feet were not "nailed".[20] The feet were usually tied with a rope to the tree. But it is the portion of the Psalm (mentioned earlier) that gives us the best evidence of stoning. Looking down upon his own body from the tree, the individual speaking in the Psalm *sees his bones*, and *they behold him*! The phrase would indicate that there is no flesh on his bones, that the skin had been removed from them. The wording is used to indicate that the bones are bared and stare back at him. The fact is the scourging by either party (either the Sanhedrin or the Romans) would have been injurious *to his back*, not the front, where he might look down and view his own bones. He would not have been able to see his back while hanging on the tree. Crucifixion, in no way, would cause bones to be so exposed as to be viewed by the victim himself. The most important theological argument about the execution of Jesus is the "blood" that he shed, yet crucifixion alone would not account for the amount of blood Christian traditions implies he would have shed.

---

20. Paulus, *Das Leben Jesu*, III, 669, 754.

A Book of Evidence

An iron spike was driven through the middle part of each wrist between the carpal bones. *The loss of blood was moderate since the spike did not penetrate a major artery.*[21]

Another Scripture used to imply a Roman crucifixion of Jesus is Isa. 53:5.

Yet he was *pierced [wounded, KJV; daka]* for transgressions that were ours, was *crushed [bruised, KJV; daka]* for iniquities that were ours—The chastisement of our well-being was upon him, and by his *stripes [chaburah,* a stripe, weal, or wound] there is healing for us.

Two of these three words (wounded, bruised) are exactly the same Hebrew word, *daka*, and simply means "a stripe, weal, bruise; i.e., a weal", or black and blue mark itself—a bruise, that is, "the mark or print of blows in the skin, in which blood and humours [water] appear, spoken of the consequences of sin, and the sense of divine wrath".[22] These words, which are indications of stoning, give clearer meaning to 1 John 5:6.

That is he that came through means of *water and blood* [the bruise], [Jesus Messiah]: Not by the water only, but by the water and the blood—and the Spirit it is that is bearing witness, because the Spirit is the truth (1 John 5:6).

It was necessary that Jesus be "bruised", and it was YHWH's purpose to "bruise" him. Thus the phrase in 1 John is made clearer. The next prophecy that might also give evidence of stoning is found in Isaiah, chapters 52 and 53. While the King James translation is quite vague, the Hebrew words in these passages are more specific. They give us an indication of what the Messiah was to experience.

Yet he was pierced [wounded, bruised, *stoned; daka*] for transgressions that were ours, was crushed [bruised; emasculated; *daka*] for iniquities that were ours—The chastisement for our well-being was upon him, And by his stripes [*chaburah*; i.e., "weal, black-and-blue mark itself"] there is healing for us (Isa. 53:5).

The first word "pierced" is the Hebrew *daka*, which means "stoned", but for certainty we must also identify the other relevant terms in this Scripture. One of these words is "crushed" (bruised in KJV). The Hebrew word here is *daka*, and it is more specific in its rendering. When it is used it always refers to "stoning". William Wilson gives the best translation of the word:

דכה *f.* Daka: *a crushing*: Deut. xxiii, 1, wounded or mutilated by by bruising, by crushing, sc. in the testicle, i.e., *in order to produce emasculation.*[23]

Strong's Concordance states it is "to bruise, crush, smite". The word would imply that the Messiah would be stoned, and that the effect of that penalty would be emasculation, that is a destruction of his abdominal cavity if not his genital organs. This is not to imply that the object of the penalty was to emasculate the genitals in particular, but during the process of stoning the Messiah was to be so physically damaged he would

---

21. Kiehl, *The Passion*, p. 128.
22. Wilson, *Word Studies*, p. 490.
23. Wilson, p. 490.

be unable to produce physical descendants even if he were to live. Isaiah makes it clear (53:8) that the Messiah would have no *physical* descendants.

> ... and who shall declare his generations? (KJV)
> ... and who can speak of his descendants? (NIV)
> ... Who could describe his abode [house or descendants]? (JPS)

Yet in the same manner that all were made spiritual descendants of Abraham, he, too, would have *spiritual* descendants.

> But the LORD chose to crush him by disease, That, if he made himself an offering for guilt, He might see *offspring and have long life*. And that through him the LORD'S purpose might prosper. Out of his anguish he shall see it; He shall enjoy it to the full through his devotion (Isa. 53:10, JPS).

It is important that the word *daka* is used here because it infers that the Messiah is to be cursed by God. The same word, which is seldom used in Scripture, is the one used to describe an individual "cursed of God".

> Surely no man in whom is any blemish shall come near—No man who is blind or lame, or hath a flat nose, or is lanky; nor any man who hath a broken foot, or a broken hand; or is hump-backed or a dwarf, or hath defective vision—or hath scurvy or scab [leprosy], or is *crushed in the stones ['eshek,* testicles] (Lev. 21:18–20).

But there is another word in the Isaiah prophecy to link the execution to stoning. That word is "stripes". The word is *chaburah*, and it means the "black and blue mark", the "weal". That word is used specifically to refer to the type of wounds one might receive from the penalty of stoning.

Perhaps one of the most important Old Covenant prophecies to study in regard to the penalty of stoning is Isaiah 52. In it we have a clue as to why the disciples might not have, at first, recognized Jesus after he had been resurrected.

> The more that Many were amazed at thee *so marred [disfigured] beyond any man's was his appearance—and his form [unrecognizable] beyond the sons of men,* the more *doth he startle many nations [in astonishment],* Before him have kings closed their mouth—for that which had not been related [told] to them have they seen, and that which they had not heard [that the Messiah had been stoned] have they diligently considered (Isa. 52:14-15).

Had Jesus been stoned (as seems to be prophesied) he would have been so marred (or disfigured) and so malformed as to be indistinguishable as a man at all. The result of having been stoned would have obscured his identity, and not even his closest disciples would have, at first, recognized him (John 20:14–15; Mark 16:12; John 20:19–25; John 21:4, 12). It was probably for this reason that Mary the Magdalene did not recognize him until he *spoke* to her (John 20:14–15). He would have been so marred that Thomas, the one apostle who was even willing, at first, to follow Jesus into Judea to his death (John 11:16), only *truly believed* Jesus had been resurrected when he had placed his hands into the nail prints and into his side (John 20:24–29). He hadn't even trusted his own eyes!

There is other evidence in the New Covenant that we must consider. The apostle Paul had been stoned in Antioch, dragged out of the city and left for dead (Acts 14:19; 2 Cor.

A Book of Evidence

11:25). As a result of having been stoned, Paul carried with him the lasting results. His eyes had been damaged. When a man was stoned, it was the head and eyes that were usually targeted (Mark 12:4). But we have Paul's own words to provide the evidence we need.

> Howbeit ye know that *by reason of a weakness of the flesh* I myself announced the glad-message unto you formerly; *and your trial in my flesh ye despised not, neither spat ye in disgust* . . . For I bear you witness—that if possible *your eyes ye would have dug out and given unto me* (Gal. 4:13–15).

Jesus, himself, had given us the parable of the vineyard (Mark 12:4) that tells us the primary places of injury during stoning: the head and the eyes. It was rare that anyone escaped death when stoned, but when he did he was an outcast from Israel. He would have been called a "leper" and spat upon "in disgust" (Deut. 25:9). How do we know Paul was not a leper but was referring to his having been stoned? Here is what he says.

> For I, the *brandmarks [scars] of Jesus* in my body am bearing (Gal. 6:17).

This is not a reference to any spiritual connection between Paul and Jesus. The word "brandmarks" is the Greek *stigma* (from the root *stizo*), meaning "to make incised or punched marks" [i.e., bruises] that have resulted in "scars". These "brandmarks" that Paul carries in his own flesh are the result of having been stoned, and he claims they are the same as those that Jesus received. We know these marks do not refer to the *crucifixion* of Jesus, because *Paul was not crucified! He was stoned!*

We might also remember that Pilate seemed shocked when he was told that Jesus had already died. He knew that crucifixion sometimes took days, yet it had only been six hours since Jesus had been "hanged" on the tree. Pilate "wondered whether already he was dead," and even "calling near the centurion, questioned him—whether he had already died" (Mark 15:43–44). The reason, perhaps, for Pilate's surprise is because he hadn't expected the Sanhedrin to stone Jesus.

We have one more passage in Revelation 5:6 where Jesus is symbolized as the "Lamb as it had been *slain*". The Greek word translated "slain" in this verse is *sphazo*. It means "to butcher, slaughter, maim, mangle, or wound"; i.e., to stone. Webster gives us the definitions we need for the words: 1) maim—"to mutilate, disfigure". Mutilate implies "the cutting off or removal of an essential part of a person . . . thereby impairing its completeness, beauty, or function;" 2) mangle—"a tearing or crushing that leaves deep extensive wounds . . . to batter"; 3) batter—"implies a series of blows that bruise deeply, deform, or mutilate—to commit mayhem, willing and permanent, upon; crippling, mutilation, or disfigurement of any part of the body"; 4) butcher—"to kill in a barbarous manner"; and 5) slaughter—"to kill in a bloody or violent manner; to strike". The word "slain" then meant more than just "kill". The Hebrew concept of the word, again, is more exact. In Hebrew the word would be *harag*. While it literally means "slew", it was taken to mean, more exactly, *stoned*!

> Since with reference to the enticer to idolatry, the Bible (Deut. xiii 10 [A. V. 9] employs the term *Harag* = "*to slay*" ("Thou shalt surely slay him"), and this is immediately explained by the addition (*ib*. 11 [A. V. 10], "Thou shalt stone him with stones, that he die," it follows *that the term "harag"* used in reference to

> the beast *likewise means to slay by stoning. And as for the criminal himself, his sentence is the same as that of the beast in connection with which he is mentioned* (Sifra *l.c.* x.; Sanh. 54b).[24]

It is interesting, too, that in the book of Revelation the word "Lamb" is not the "lambkin" (*amnos*) of the gospels. Here Jesus is the *arnion* (from *aren/arrhen* or *arsen*) a victorious strong ram. This Greek word is derived from *airo* meaning to expiate [i.e., to atone for] sin. The Hebrew equivalent is *nasa*, the Banner or Flag (Messiah) of God. It is a perfect picture of the execution of Jesus. Traditional Christian belief is founded on the fact that Jesus fulfilled the Passover "appointment", that he was the Passover Lamb who took away the sins of the world. If this is so, then the belief cannot be fully founded unless attention is given to *every* aspect of what happens to the Passover sacrifice, and it is the final part of that sacrificial preparation, the *flaying* of the lamb, that might more completely fulfill the requirements and which fit the word "slain".

> The lamb was then hung upon special hooks or sticks and *skinned*.[25]

As gruesome as it sounds, the penalty of stoning might reflect the final requirement. It is not the author's intention to presume to think for the reader; however, each individual needs to be made aware of the various Hebrew and Greek terms that describe the execution of the Messiah in order to form his own rational opinion about this subject, and in order to understand what his true sufferings *might well have been* as well as what the "blood" of Jesus really means. The Jewish community understands these prophecies to refer to the stoning of the Messiah.

Whatever one believes, we must believe Jesus was hanged alive on a *living tree*. The evidence is overwhelming. From the New Covenant, we have several references to it. Never is the word *xulon* translated as the "cross". The word for "cross" would have been *stauros*, and even then the Greek word only reflects the upright nature of the tree! The word *xulon*, however, is the same that Luke uses in 23:31 for "moist wood" and refers to a *living tree*! The Hebrew equivalent would be the *'ets* (derived from *'atsah*), which is also used as a term for "gallows" in the book of Esther where Haman is "hanged" (Esth. 5:14; 8:7). It is the same word used in Genesis 40:19 and Deuteronomy 21:22 to describe the hanging of an individual on a "tree". These "gallows" do *not* refer to a Roman cross. The word is even used to describe the fruit trees of the Garden of Eden, including the Tree of Life and the Tree of the Knowledge of Good and Evil. In the New Covenant, the disciples were quite clear about how Jesus was hanged, and it wasn't upon a Roman cross. The disciples, in fact, confronted the *Jewish judicial Sanhedrin* later that decade with the ultimate accusation that they had hanged Jesus upon a "living" tree. Here are the passages that reflect the type of execution Jesus endured.

> The God of our fathers hath raised up Jesus—whom *ye* got into *your hands, suspending him upon a tree [xulon]* (Acts 5:30).

---

24. "Capital Punishment", J.E., p. 555
25. "Passover Sacrifice", J.E., p. 556.

> We also are witnesses of all things which he did, both in the country of the Jews and Jerusalem; Whom *they* even slew by *suspending upon a tree [xulon]* (Acts 10:39).
>
> And when they had finished all those things which concerning him had been written, *taking him down from the tree [xulon]*, they put him in a tomb (Acts 13:29).
>
> Messiah hath redeemed us out of the curse of the law [instruction], *having become in our behalf a curse*; because it is *written—Cursed is everyone that hangeth upon a tree [xulon]* (Gal. 3:13).
>
> Who our sins himself bare up in his body *unto the tree [xulon]* (1 Pet. 2:24).

To show that the word *xulon* here means a living tree and not a Roman cross, let's look at Revelation 2:7.

> He that hath an ear let him hear what the Spirit is saying unto the assemblies. Unto him that overcometh I will give unto him to eat of *the tree [xulon] of life*, which is in the paradise of [YHWH].

The passage in Galatians 3:13 refers to the fact that anyone hanged upon a tree [a *xulon* or "living" tree] is considered "cursed of God". The Scripture from which this is taken is found in Deuteronomy 21:22. Jewish individuals were taught from an early age that if they see someone hanged upon a tree, they are to revile them, and this is what we have found in our present case.

> And they who were passing by were reviling him, shaking their heads (Matt. 27:39).

Anyone who did not know Jesus, who happened to be passing by on his way to the Temple would have "reviled" him. The word "reviled" is *blasphemeo*; i.e., they would have blasphemed or "cursed" him. The fact is the "cursing" of one who has been hanged on a tree meant excommunication from the nation of Israel. Since he was to be excommunicated, cast out, and cut off from the nation, and as it was the singular duty of each member of the "congregation" of Israel to cast a stone at a *mesith* so hanged, this simply means that the passersby legally picked up a stone to cast at him. It was a form of excommunication. Just as the congregation was to stone Achan (Josh. 7:25), so was it the duty of the congregation here to perform "justice". The entire Jewish concept of capital punishment is, in fact, based on chapter 7 of Joshua and on Deuteronomy 21:21–23. In them we find the elements necessary on which to base the execution of Jesus: 1) the "accursed thing" or individual who caused the "curse" (Josh. 7:13); 2) the confession of the accused (Josh. 7:20); 3) stoning performed by the "whole congregation" (Josh. 7:25); 4) the "sin unto death" (Deut. 21:22); stoning and hanging upon a tree (Deut. 21:21–22); and 5) not to allow the corpse of the accursed to remain on the tree overnight (Deut. 21:23), because an individual that is hanged is "accursed of God". If that individual is allowed to "rot" on the tree, the land would be defiled (Deut. 21:23) (thus no "skulls" would be lying around the execution site and could not be the reason the place of execution was called Gulgoleth). One other Scripture, in particular, is implicit in the criminal process that requires the "congregation of Israel" to stone the accused.

Cain expresses fear that, for the murder which he has committed, "everyone that findeth me shall slay me" (Gen. iv. 14); in other words, it was the duty of society, and even of the beasts of the field, to avenge the blood of Abel.[26]

Anytime a Jew used the term "hanged on a tree", stoning was automatically assumed. When the disciples accused the Sanhedrin of "hanging" Jesus on a "tree", it was simply a Hebrew idiom for the terminology implying the entire execution process, both stoning *and* hanging. For instance, in the Talmud (b. Sanh. 43a) a herald goes forth announcing that Jesus was to be "stoned"; the passage then goes on to state that he was "hanged". The writers meant that he was both stoned and hanged, and this was a Jewish mode of execution, not a Roman one. Not one aspect of the "hanging" indicated a Roman crucifixion. Likewise, when the Jewish writings indicate that an individual has been stoned and that stoning resulted in his death, it was automatically assumed that he had been hanged afterward.

> And if not, stoning him is [the duty] of all Israelites, as it is said, The hand of the witnesses shall be first upon him to put him to death, and afterward the hand of all the people (Dt. 17:7). "All those who are stoned are hanged on a tree," the words of R. Eliezer.[27]

The type of hanging, however, again depended on whether it was the Pharisees or the Sadducees who did the hanging, and in just what period of time the hanging occurred. Obviously, the Essenes, as we have mentioned earlier, were fully aware that the Sadducean penalty included hanging an individual alive on the tree. The Pharisees, on the other hand, found this abhorrent and when they gained power after 70 CE, they hanged people only after an individual had been stoned to death, and their mode of stoning was with a single heavy stone.

Below is an ancient olive tree in the Garden of Gethsemane. The photograph gives us a good perspective of the size of the ancient olive trees found on the Mount of Olives. Compare the size of the Franciscan monk beside the tree.

26. "Crime", J.E., pp. 357-358.
27. *m. Sanh.* 6:4 g–h.

A Book of Evidence

At the time of Jesus' execution we are told that "there [were] many women from afar beholding". The women who had followed him from Galilee and ministered to him were allowed only to witness the execution from the Women's Court Gallery on the Temple Mount. The distance from the Herodian Temple Mount to the execution site on the Mount of Olives was almost a mile. This would have been considered quite a distance for spectators who were beholding the execution from across the Kidron Valley. The only reason they were able to view the execution at all is because of the low eastern wall. It provided them a view which, if his execution had taken place either to the north, south, or west, *they would not have been able to see him at all*!

> All the walls which were there were high, except the eastern [of the Temple Mount]. For the priest who burns the red cow, stands on the top of the Mount of Olives, and takes his direction looking directly at the door of the heikhal, at the time of the tossing of blood.[28]

The Mishnah connects the sacrifice of the Red Heifer, which we know occurred on the Mount of Olives, with the low Eastern Wall. Since this was the only site where the high priest might have a view of the front of the Sanctuary at all, and we know the Women's Court was two-storied on the east, this statement also connects the execution site with the Mount of Olives. But to confirm that this is so, we also have evidence that it was not Mount Scopus, a part of the Olivet chain, to which the rabbis referred, but the Rosh of the Mount of Olives, because this spot is connected with the Eastern Gate.

> Five gates were in the [wall of the] Temple [i.e., the Sanctuary] . . . *the Eastern Gate*, on it was a picture of the Walled City of Shushan—*through which the high-priest who burned the red cow, the cow, and all who assist, in its rite, go forth to the Mount of Olives.*[29]

It was, in fact, only here where the rending of the veil and the breaking of the stone lintel above the veil might have been viewed. Since we are told that even the Roman centurion responsible for overseeing the execution saw "all these things" happen, it again confirms that the execution site was somewhere on the Mount of Olives.

> A tearing of this curtain *in front of the holy building* at the time of the afternoon sacrifices would have been public and very dramatic in effect. *It would have been visible from the Mount of Olives.*[30]

The fact is the individuals witnessing these events (those near the execution site) could not have seen them *from any other vantage point in Jerusalem!*

From noon until 3:00 p.m. it is stated in the gospels that "darkness" engulfed the land (Mark 15:33). This darkness might have been associated with the coming earthquake. As natural phenomena, earthquakes are sometimes preceded by "darkness". This is because they are the result of volcanic or tectonic activity. This darkness, a natural event used by God, might have been the result of diastrophism near the Dead Sea in what is called the Rift Valley of the Judean Wilderness.

> Fault escarpments to the west and east of the Dead Sea clearly outline its shore . . . Hot sulphur springs, such as those of En Boqeq and Callirrhoe, and the natural salt deposits found in the vicinity also contribute to the exceptionally high mineral content of the sea . . . [They] were known for their medicinal properties, and it was to Callirrhoe that Herod the Great retired in an attempt to be cured of his fatal illness (Jos. War 1.23.5 [656-58]) . . . The account of the battle between the five kings and the four kings in the days of Lot and Abraham mentions "tar [= bitumen] pits" in the "Valley of Siddim" (the Dead Sea area; Gen 14:10). Josephus later describes how in the Roman period the Dead Sea cast up "black masses of bitumen" that floated on the surface . . . [e]arthquakes

---

28 *m. Mid.* 2.4 VI a–b.
29 *m. Mid.* 1.3a, e–g.
30 Kiehl, *The Passion*, p. 141.

A Book of Evidence

are common in the region, and on a number of occasions resulting blockages have stopped the flow of the river [Jordan].[31]

Whatever the cause, the darkness was real. A variety of sources claim it was so dark that people believed night had fallen, and they had failed to remove the corpses from the tree before nightfall. Leaving the corpses on the tree until night had fallen would have brought God's curse on the land.

> To Matt. 27:45-51 cf. Gospel of Peter 5.15-20—Now it was noonday, and darkness prevailed over all Judea, and they were afraid and distressed *for fear the sun had set while he was still alive.* For it is written for them that the sun should not set upon one put to death. And one of them said, "Give him gall with vinegar to drink." And they mixed them and gave it to him. And they fulfilled all things and brought their sins to an end upon their own heads. *And many went about with lamps, supposing it was night, and fell* and the Lord [Master] cried out, "My power, my power, thou hast forsaken me." And, saying this, he was taken up. And in the same hour the curtain of the temple of Jerusalem was torn in two.[32]

By 3:00 p.m.. an earthquake had occurred, damaging the Temple. Jerome, who had access to the Gospel of the Nazaraeans, clearly states that the thirty-ton stone lintel that held the veils in place was destroyed at the time of the earthquake.

> To Matt. 27:51 cf Gospel of the Nazaraeans (in Jerome, *Letter to Hedibia* and *Commentary on Matthew* 27:51) In the Gospel that is written in Hebrew letters we read, not that the curtain of the temple was torn, but that *the astonishingly large lintel of the temple collapsed.*[33]

The collapse of the stone lintel that supported the massive Nicanor Gate would have rended the veils that hung from it. The suggestion that the veils still hung "unrended" over the Temple entrance some years later does not, in any way, refute the tearing of those veils hanging there at the time of Jesus' death. The fact is there were two new curtains made each year.

> Simeon ben Gamaliel said in the name of R. Simeon, deputy [high priest]: The curtain was a handbreadth thick and was woven on seventy-two strands, each strand consisting of twenty-four threads. Its length was forty cubits and its breadth twenty cubits, made up in its entirety of eighty myriads [of threads]. *They used to make two curtains every year, and three hundred priests were required to immerse them.*[34]

The rending of the veils then might well have been an inconvenience, but it is not something they might have noted in their writings. What they do mention in their histories is that the Great Sanhedrin (the religious one) was removed from the Hall of Hewn Stone about 30 CE, joining the seat of the judicial Sanhedrin [criminal Sanhedrin], the Bazaars of Annas at the public square (Plaza) in Beth Pagi.

---

31. Rasmussen, *Zondervan NIV Atlas of the Bible*, pp. 44-45; 54.
32. Throckmorton, *Gospel Parallels*, p. 183.
33. Throckmorton, p. 184.
34. Bialik and Ravnitsky, *Legends*, 160-61:6.

The Execution

Not everything Jesus said at the time of his execution was said from the tree. There are, however, at least three instances in which he *did* speak from the tree. During his last moments, Jesus bequeathed his earthly responsibilities to Eleazar (Lazarus), assigning to him the care of his mother, Mary.

> Jesus therefore seeing his mother and the disciple whom he loved saith unto his mother—O woman, see! thy son! [Eleazar]. Afterwards he saith unto the disciple—See! thy mother! [Mary] And *from that hour* the disciple took her unto *his own home* (John 19:26–27).

We have already discussed the testamentary procedure in an earlier chapter. We can well imagine the torment of Jesus, Mary, and Yohannan Eleazar during these last few moments, yet it was fitting that family members were present to say goodbye for what they believed was the last time. Legally, family and friends were not allowed to be present during the execution until near the time of death, when they were called for last-minute words. It was only when Jesus had spoken these final words that he said "I thirst", and after having been given a merciful drink of water mixed with wine, declared "It is finished".

Jesus was dead. His disciples had fled and were in hiding, anxious for their own lives and disappointed in their Messiah. They hadn't made arrangements for his burial. They assumed Jesus would be treated like other criminals and buried in the criminal's graveyard, perhaps in a grave that was unmarked and would soon be forgotten.

> And they did not bury [the felon] in the burial grounds of his ancestors. But there were two graveyards made ready for the use of the court, one for those who were beheaded or strangled, and *one for those who were stoned or burned*.[35]

Once Jesus was taken down from the tree, even his broken body was in danger, but as we shall learn in the next chapter, YHWH, Himself, would provide a solitary tomb for Jesus, one that still exists and is in usable condition.

---

35. *m. Sanh.* 6:5 e–f.

7

The Lamp of the World

WE ARE TOLD IN the gospels that Joseph of Ari-mathea (Hearth of Matthat), a wealthy but honorable "counsellor" (Matt. 27:57; Mark 15:45; Luke 23:50; John 19:38) went to Pilate to obtain permission to collect the body of Jesus for burial. There is little doubt that he did this because he respected and honored Jesus. Since he had been an Elder of the *religious* Sanhedrin, he would have had little to do with the trial and execution process. It was stated that he had not approved of the trial. We are not told whether Joseph believed Jesus was the supernatural Hebrew Messiah, the Son of God. We do know he believed him to be innocent of the charges, and that he was named as a "secret" disciple (even so, he might have viewed him only as the "nationalistic" messiah). For this reason, he wanted to prevent Jesus' body from ruin and destruction in an unmarked grave. Criminals were *ordinarily* buried in separate graveyards.

> And they did not bury [the felon] in the burial grounds of his ancestors. But there were two graveyards made ready for the use of the court, one for those who were beheaded or strangled, and one for those who were stoned or burned.[1]

Joseph, a rich man, wanted to bury Jesus in his own "new" tomb (referred to as "Joseph's Garden"), and this would fulfill Isaiah's prophecy (Isa. 53:9).

> And why such severity?—*Because a wicked man may not be buried beside a righteous one*. For R. Aha b. Hanina said: Whence is it inferred that a wicked man may not be buried beside a righteous one?—From the verse, *And it came to pass as they were burying a man that behold they spied a band and they cast the man into the sepulchre of Elishah, and as soon as the man touched the bones of Elishah, he revived and stood up on his feet* (2 Ki. 13:21).[2]

We are told Joseph "boldly" went to Pilate for permission to bury Jesus. The Greek word *tolmao* (derived from *telos*) simply means he was determined to retrieve the body

---

1. *m. Sanh.* 6:5 e–f.
2. *b. Sanh.* 47a.

of Jesus. He probably had little to fear from Pilate (although Christian tradition portrays him as fearful). There is some evidence that he had actually been a "friend" (ally) of Pilate, although as a Roman Decurio he outranked Pilate's status as a lowly "prefect". Had the Romans executed Jesus, especially for treason, Pilate would never have given that permission.

> Moreover, *according to Roman law the body of someone executed on a charge of high treason could not be given to relatives or friends for burial*; the idea was to prevent the burial site from becoming a shrine and focal point for any followers.[3]
>
> At present, the bodies of those who have been punished are only buried when this has been requested and permission granted; and sometimes it is not permitted, *especially where persons have been convicted of high treason*.[4]

But Pilate *did* give his permission; therefore, we again find confirmation that Jesus was not executed by Roman law. Pilate was not at all concerned that the tomb of Jesus might become a shrine! He handed over the body to Joseph without further question and showed no interest in upholding the Roman law. The gospels tell us that Joseph had gone to Pilate on the Jewish Preparation Day.

> "Ereb Shabbat" accordingly denotes the day on the evening of which Sabbath begins, or the day on which food is prepared for both the current and the following days, which latter is Sabbath . . . the day is called "Yoma da'Arubta" (Day of Preparation) . . . The same terms are also applied to the days preceding and following any of the festivals; as "Ereb Pesah".[5]

The fact that it was "dawning toward the Sabbath", Yoma da'Arubta made little difference. Joseph hurriedly prepared the body. Even had the preparations extended into the Sabbath it would not have been illegal for him to have completed the requirements of tending to the basic needs of the deceased. It was entirely legal for one to attend to funeral arrangements even on the Sabbath or during a festival, and even outside the Sabbath limit (*b., Ber.* 3.1). He would not have remained long at the tomb, however, for two very specific reasons: 1) mourning for executed criminals was not allowed; and 2) while preparing a body for burial was not illegal, mourning was absolutely prohibited on feast days and other joyous occasions. This is the reason that the women did not mourn at the tomb that day.

> No execution is attended with posthumous indignities, except that the *usual mourning ceremonies are not observed* (Sifra, Shemini, Introduction, 28; Sem. ii. 7; Sanh. vi. 6).[6]

This is reflected in the Gospel of Peter (12:50–13.57):

> And they feared lest the Jews see them and said, 'Even if we were not able to weep and lament him on the day on which he was crucified, yet let us now do so at his tomb' . . . But if we cannot, then let us lay beside the door the things which we have brought in remembrance of him and we will weep and lament until we get home.

---

3. Kiehl, *The Passion*, p. 149.
4. Ulpian, *On the Duties of Proconsul* IX; http://www.constitution.org/sps/sps11.htm.
5. "Calendar", J.E., p. 502.
6. "Capital Punishment", J.E., p. 557.

A Book of Evidence

Most likely, after they identified the tomb in which he was laid, they left to return to their homes in order to prepare the spices and ointments they would use in preparing his body in the proper manner once the Sabbath had passed. Furthermore, they would be able to mourn his death in their own homes, away from the prying eyes of the priests. It would take time to attain and get them ready for use. It was for these reasons that Mary Magdalene, too, only sought to "behold" (*theoreo*), or pay attention to where Jesus was laid, so that she might return after the Sabbath to properly attend to the necessary burial rites.

> [T]heoreo = to be a spectator of, to gaze at, or on, as a spectacle. Our Eng. word "theatre" is from the same root. Hence, it is used of bodily sight, and assumes the actual presence of the object on which the gaze is fixed, and that it is a continued and prolonged gaze.[7]

But there was an even more pressing reason to "gaze attentively" at the tomb; it was to determine *exactly* where Jesus was laid. There were *five* tombs in the garden where Jesus was laid, the other four situated quite near his own. Had there been just *one*, Mary would have had no problem in relocating the specific tomb after the Sabbath had ended. She might have simply glanced around at her surroundings, taking note only of the landmarks nearby. Since there were five tombs in the garden, she had to *positively identify* the one in which Jesus was laid. She was able to do this by noting the rolling stone at the entrance and, perhaps, counting the tombs. The garden tomb in which Jesus was laid was, in fact, only a short distance from the execution site itself.

> Now there was, *in the place* [i.e., Beth Pagi, the region] *where he was crucified [hanged]* a garden; and *in the garden an unused tomb* wherein as yet no one had been laid. So there, by reason of the preparation of the Jews, because *near was the tomb* laid they Jesus (John 19:41–42).

The tomb is situated a short distance, about four hundred feet, southeast of the Shrine of Bethphage. The shrine is attested to by Thecla in the Text of Theodosias (Palestinian Text Society), and is where that martyr believed that Jesus was flogged. The shrine is referred to in that text as "Ancona" (Greek *agchone*) or the place of flogging and execution.[8] It also means "to kill or destroy by preventing access of air or oxygen and to impair the respiration of; asphyxiate." Hanging would create a condition where one might not be able to breathe properly and would result in suffocation.

The series of tomb sites in which it is located has been archaeologically investigated by Sylvester Saller, and one, in particular, that has been used as an example of the type of tomb in which Jesus was buried. Had the archaeologist suspected that Jesus had been executed near a plaza on the Mount of Olives, the tomb might have been more closely examined as a natural consideration for the actual burial site. Nevertheless, this tomb has been studied with utmost care. The rolling stone is still in place, considered a "peculiarity", and the tomb is still in usable condition. It exists in its present condition just as it was during the first century.

---

7. CBN, Appendix 133:I, 11, p. 164.
8. Stedman's Medical Dictionary, p. 66.

The Lamp of the World

This tomb with a round stone for closing its entrance was found on the back (eastern) slopes of the Mount of Olives. The tomb is still in operating condition.[9]

But this is just one reason the tomb might be the one in which Jesus was placed. It is labeled Number 21 by Sylvester Saller, and is just east of tomb sites 19 (an unfinished tomb) and 20. It is also located in a garden. Here is what Mr. Saller says about the tomb.

> Several details are *peculiar to this tomb*. First, the number of graves in each niche differs from tombs 3 and 19 . . . A second peculiarity of this tomb is the rolling stone which is *still in situ in front of the entrance* . . . In lists of such stones which the writer has seen *he does not recall that this one has ever been mentioned* . . . Another reason for indicating its existence is the fact that it is easily accessible and may well serve to illustrate the type of stone used to close the tomb of Our Lord . . . A third peculiarity of our tomb are its graffiti. *Their existence has been known for a long time but for some unaccountable reason they were ignored*, as many other things at Bethphage.[10]

**FINEGAN, Jack; THE ARCHAEOLOGY OF THE NEW TESTAMENT. ©
1969 Princeton University Press, 1997 Renewed PUP
Reprinted by Permission of Princeton University Press**

9. Gundry, *A Survey*, p. 194.
10. Saller and Testa, *Archaeological Setting*, pp. 70–73.

A Book of Evidence

Unlike the traditional sites for the tomb of Jesus, this one has messianic connotations associated with it. A second peculiarity of the tomb is the graffiti etched into the stone. The graffiti peculiar to this tomb was researched and discussed by Emmanuele Testa in the *Excursus* of the report. It is the graffiti (see illustration) that tells us this was probably the tomb where Jesus was laid. Let us consider the significance of that Hebrew and Greek graffiti. The archaic Hebrew and Greek letters are similar to those found in the Copper Scroll. This would seem to indicate that the earliest followers of Jesus might have been associated with the Essene sect situated at the Qumran cave complex near the Dead Sea. Certainly, the symbols represent the types of motifs found in their literature; for instance, we find here as we did at Qumran the Light/Dark motif, with the dualistic notions used by the earliest Jewish and Nazaraean "gnostics". These individuals should not be associated with the many later "heretical" gnostics of the "church age". Clement, writing in the 90s CE, speaks of this original "gnosis", indicating that there was, in fact, a pure Nazaraean gnosis from which the heretical streams flowed. The literature at Qumran also reflects many of the same messianic ideas represented by the symbols. These signs and symbols scratched into the rock surfaces, beginning at the entrance and ending at the head of grave couch "A" tell the story of the Messiah and the purpose of his mission. The overall theme of the symbolic narrative is the coming Kingdom of God. The symbols narrate the coming of the Redeemer Messiah, the cause of redemption, his own resurrection, the resurrection of the dead, the millennial kingdom, and the eternal kingdom. Each of these symbols has a numerical value (called gematria) that tells a hidden story, a method of communication in which the earliest Nazaraeans (and the Essenes) were highly skilled. Josephus tells us the Essenes used gematria in their prophecies and that they were seldom inaccurate. It is my own belief that these symbols were scratched into the rock surface of the tomb as a memorial to its one-time occupant. The marker symbolically names its occupant: Nur (*ner*), the Lamp, the Illuminated One. Jesus, as we know, is the Lamp through which the light shines (the eternal flame). The symbols that tell the story are those used by the earliest Nazaraean followers of Jesus: Hebrew "crosses" (plusses indicating the site of execution), trees, palms, harps, squares and single letters (see illustration).

> It seems that all these signs intend to illustrate a single theme very close to the heart of Jewish-Christian [Nazaraean] circles of the parent church [assembly] of Jerusalem in the first centuries, namely, the idea of a millennium. Jewish-Christians [Nazaraeans] died with the firm conviction and the unshaken hope of a resurrection in order to participate in the glorious earthly rule of a thousand years to be inaugurated by Christ [Messiah] the King [Prince].[11]

---

11. Saller and Testa, p. 84.

The Lamp of the World

S. Saller and E. Testa; *The Archaeological Setting of the Shrine of Bethphage.* ©
1961, Franciscan Press, Reprinted by Permission of Studium Biblicum Franciscan Library

We shall investigate these symbols one by one. As we shall learn, they form an encoded message through the use of gematria, that Hebrew practice of assigning numerical values to letters of the Hebrew and Greek alphabets. Significantly, the name Nur (*ner*) is fitting for the Messiah. The fact is the tomb has been preserved throughout the centuries and exists today much as it did during the first century. Jesus only used the tomb for a short period of time. At the time of his death, the tomb had been newly hewn. The Jewish law states that once an individual was entombed within a sepulchre of this sort, no

211

one except his own children might be placed in it; i.e., it was designed as a family tomb. Joseph, who had intended to use the tomb for his own family, would have had to build another in which to place them. He, himself, could never have reclaimed it.

> Come and hear! 'If one hews a grave for his [dead] father and then goes and buries him elsewhere, *he [himself]* may never be buried therein'?—Here it is on account of his father's honour. That too stands to reason. For the second clause teaches: R. Simeon b. Gamaliel said: Even if one hews stones [for a tomb] for his father, but goes and buries him elsewhere, he [himself] may never employ them for his own grave. Now, if you agree that it is out of respect for his father, it is correct.[12]

These types of tombs were designed for the burial of six to nine persons. Only one niche was ever used, and that for only a short time.

> The caves, or rock-hewn sepulchres, consisted of an ante-chamber in which the bier was deposited, and an inner or rather lower cave in which the bodies were deposited, in a recumbent position, in niches. According to the Talmud these abodes of the dead were usually six feet long, nine feet wide, and ten feet high. Here there were niches for eight bodies: three on each side of the entrance, and two opposite. Larger sepulchres held thirteen bodies. The entrance to the sepulchres was guarded by a large stone or by a door (Matt. xxvii. 66; Mark xv. 46; John xi. 38, 39).[13]

This particular tomb had only six niches (see illustration) but included the rolling stone which is still in place and an ante-chamber in the center.

---

12. *b. Sanh.* 48a
13. Edersheim, *Sketches*, p. 171.

The Lamp of the World

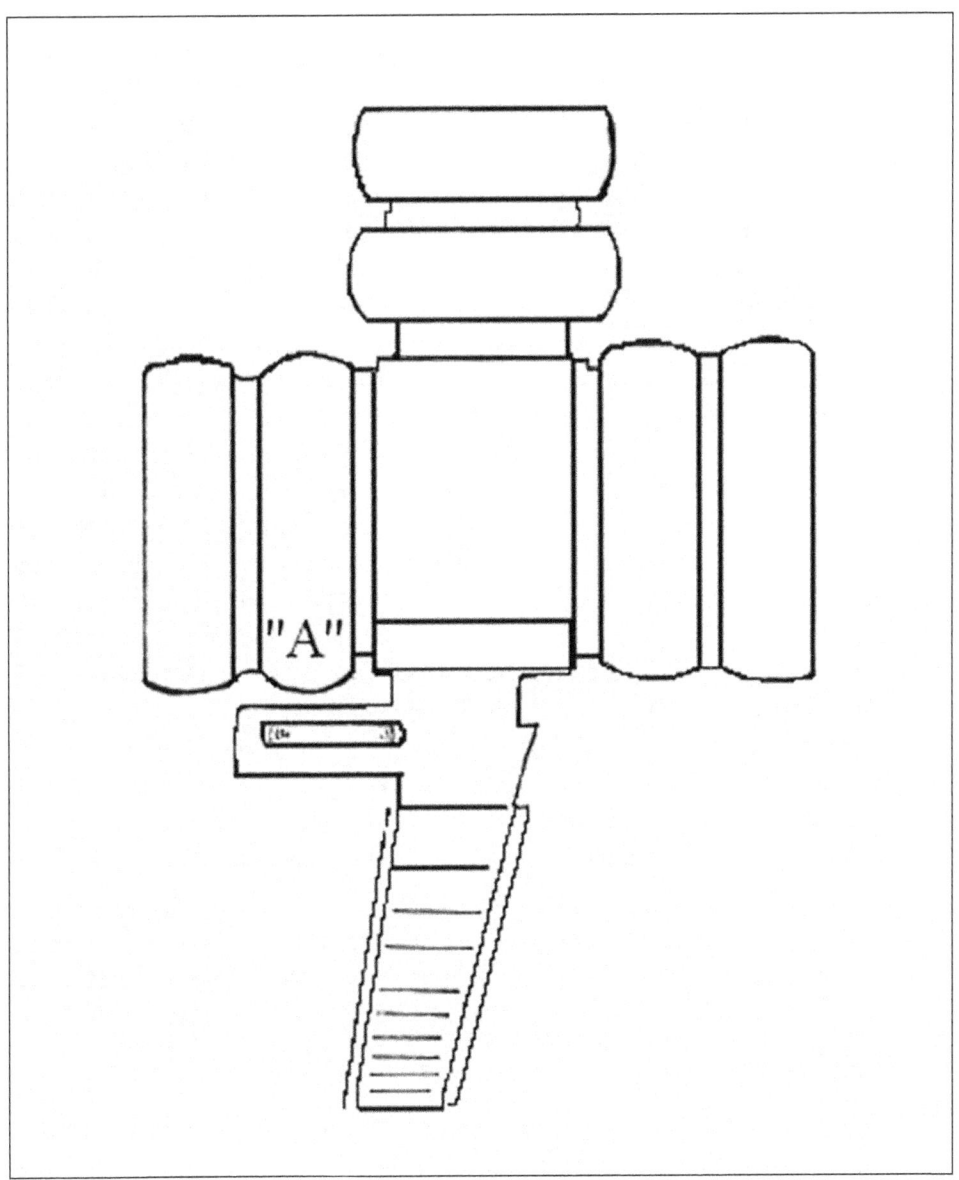

It was this ante-chamber that Peter and the Beloved Disciple entered. The grave couch on which Jesus was placed was grave "A", the one most accessible to the entrance. It would have been in full view. An entire list of the symbols includes: 1) "X" (the sign of priestly blessing and for the Decade or 10); 2) Three inverted Hebrew Vaus forming a "cross"; 3) A cross and a Greek capital Eta (H), forming several other crosses; 4) a net with twelve squares (called a Dodecade, a multiple of twelve); 5) an incomplete palm; 6) the Greek X (Chi); 7) Cross; 8) Greek letter Pi as an abbreviation; 9) A rectangle and cross; 10) Greek "H" intersected by a horizontal Hebrew Vau; 11) Greek "H"; 12) an inscription; 13) a cross with two-pronged horizontal bar; 14) six-pronged cross; 15) three motifs and another inscription; 16) The Greek letter Tau (T) below a Upsilon (Y).

A Book of Evidence

The first symbol is of redemption. It is located on the inner side of the left door jamb. It forms three crosses (or pluses, which in themselves were to represent the four corners of the earth) formed by inverted Hebrew Vaus. These three letters form the sign that alludes to a complete work having been done. *Pleroma* is a Greek word meaning "completion" or "what is filled up". It is used to describe the will of God, the perfection of all things. It is called the Vau-episemon, the numerical value of which is six, and it is connected with the name of Iesous (the Greek rendering of the Hebrew Yehoshua; Jesus), also six. The sign was also connected with the story of the Lost Sheep. Since the fall of Adam, the Knowledge of God (the Word and Wisdom) had become incomplete. The Messiah was sent to place the world back into balance, which is what the "cross" did. The center point of the two ways (the +) balances the opposing points. The world was known to the Nazaraeans as the "Kenoma" (from *kenos*), the "empty" or "vain" place. It is known to be incomplete because the first man, Adam, had sinned and, like the "lost sheep" had "wandered away" from the Truth. Jesus was sent to save that which was lost (Matt. 18:11; Luke 19:10). The "lost sheep" was recovered in the parable (Matt. 10:6; Luke 15:4), and it is this repentance of the sheep that is symbolized by the sign. Continuing on into the vault itself, there is a sign for the "origin of the name of Jesus", "H", having a numerical value of 8 (Greek *Christos*, anointed), which is symbolic for final perfection, and to the "X" (10), Jesus. The sign represents Jesus-Vau-Redeemer, the foundation on which the Kingdom of YHWH will be built. The Hebrew letter Vav (sometimes referred to as a Waw) has as its symbol a nail (tent peg) or a pillar firmly established in the earth, which also was represented during the first century as a "tree" stretching from earth to heaven and providing open communication with YHWH. The "pillar" is also connected with the "key" of the kingdom, the Key of David. It is the righteous path to "salvation".

> MARK the deacon [and the author of the gospel] (who has the same background as the Jewish-Christians [Nazaraeans]) assures us that this cosmic genesis of Jesus consists in the fact that his name was equivalent to the number 888 (I = 10 + η = 8 + σ = 200 + o = 70 + υ = 400 + σ = 200); and resulted as the product of the Ogdoade (= H) and of the Decade (= the Greek I = X [ρειτός] combined in various ways (8 X 10 = 80 X 10 = 800 + 8 = 888).[14]

The sacred Dodecade (twelve, or multiple of twelve) is symbolic of the perfect government. It is also symbolic for the 144,000 Jewish witnesses of the book of Revelation as well as the sacred "pavement" on which the throne of YHWH sits. It is this pavement that represents the Unity of God; i.e., each member is of like mind, of one accord with the will of the Father. Since the latter Gentile church did not fully understand gematria, they condemned these early Nazaraeans as "heretics", but we must remember that these were the earliest followers of Jesus, the ones to whom Jesus imparted the meanings of his parables. Jesus had said that it was given only to the disciples to know the meanings of his parables, not to the general public (Matt. 13:13). This well accords with what we know of the Jewish writings, as well as the ancient doctrines of the "divine chariot" and the "creation", divine secrets of the Jewish Kabbalah that had been handed down from the mouth of prophet to prophet and teacher to student throughout the centuries. It is

---

14. Saller and Testa, p. 90.

in the Zohar (Book of Splendor) that we are introduced to the "Pavement of Sapphires" (*Siferot*), the system of the emanations of God's Unity. Much of the graffiti displayed in this tomb is based on the Jewish traditions of the *Merkavah* and the *Kabbalah* [the "Way" of YHWH]. In the New Covenant we have a description of this pavement of "living stones" (1 Pet. 2:5; Rev. 21:10–21). It is the pavement upon which sits the throne.

The next sign includes two crosses (pluses) and a palm tree. These are used to indicate the *cause* of redemption. The palm tree is used here to symbolize the restoration of the trees of Paradise (Isa. 55:13; 60:13), but it is also assigned as a reward of the elect; it is the Tree of Life. It might also have been a symbol used to describe the execution site, near the "open space" ("street", or "plaza") of the Date Palm Tree; i.e.,; at Beth Hini. Melito (para. 94) said Jesus was executed "in the middle of the Broadway." As discussed in a previous chapter, this "Broadway" was the Fountain Plaza at Gulgoleth on the Mount of Olives.

> But the Scriptures prove that he (Messiah), after having been crucified [hanged] . . . became glorious; for this reason he had, *as a symbol of the cross [tree], the Tree of Life [at the Fountain]*, which, they say, had been planted in paradise.[15]

The reason it is placed between two crosses (or "intersections") is to symbolize it as "the eternal plant between heaven and earth, the support of the universe".[16] This eternal plant is also a symbol of the Kabbalah. It is sometimes called the "umbilical cord", the Tree of Life, or Jacob's Ladder. In the Zohar it is referred to as *Ha Adam Kadmon* (The Ancient Man). But it is also used to symbolize the "mirror image" of the Fountain, which existed not only on earth, but in the Heavenly archetype (Eyeh Asher Eyeh, the Eternal Fountain). The prophets were said to have used mirrors or "glasses" to receive their heavenly visions.

> It is taught: All the prophets looked into a *glass [mirror] that was dim*, as is said, "By the ministry of the prophets I appear dimly (Hos. 12:11). But Moses our teacher *looked through a glass that was translucent*, for him it is said, "The similitude of the Lord doth he behold" (Num. 12:8).[17]

It will also be remembered that Paul claimed we now see only through a "glass darkly". In the *Kabbalah* this earthly structure was said to form a mirror image of the heavenly. Thus it is that the fountain on earth mirrors or reflects the fountain in Aravoth (the unknowable realm of God, meaning "to distil" or "drip", and referring to the Eternal Fountain trickling from "under the throne"). The idea of the "glass" or mirror was that one might reflect God's love and righteousness above on earth; i.e., "thy will be done on earth as it is heaven".

Following the previous symbol are the symbols of Paradise. In particular, the Greek Pi, popular as an abbreviation because so many sacred words began with that letter, is found here. Some of the sacred words were 1) Paraclete (*paracletos*), the Comforter or Intercessor; 2) *pneuma*, breath, Spirit; 3) *Pleroma*, completion, perfection, and 4) Paradise (*paradeisos*). Within this symbol we also have what is called the "*scala*

---

15. Justin, *Dialogue with Trypho*, LXXXVI.
16. Saller and Testa, *Archaeological Setting*, p. 95.
17. Bialik and Ravnitzky, *Legends*, 100:127.

cosmica" (in connection with the palm tree) representing the umbilical cord connecting the "infant" to its "mother" and symbolic of the Ascension. This threefold twisted cord stretches from the heavenly "mother" (New Jerusalem), which nourishes and sustains the earthly "infant" (Zion).

Another inscription gives us the name of the individual who had been purportedly buried there. A well-known Jewish formula (a *shin* used as an abbreviation for *shalom*, Peace) contains the name. It represented the "baptism" by fire which came from Jesus alone.

> The name ["Nur"] is formed form the root נור, fire ["to shine"]. Usually such a name appears in compositions with אב: אבגד, אביגד; or as a theophoric name גדיה and גדיהו; but there are also shortened forms, such as גד, גודא and גודי. This last form could have been preferred by a Jewish-Christian. We know, in fact, that Christians of the early years loved to call themselves the Illuminated Ones or Φωτισθέντες, on account of their baptism by fire (initiation) The wish (לום) ש was one of the most frequent in funerary inscriptions, even when others were also used. Sometimes, as in our case, it appears abbreviated with only ש.[18]

My suggestion is that the name refers to its occupant, the "Illuminator".

Also found here is the symbol for what is called the *psychopompoi*, the sign of the two messengers in John 20:11.

> Howbeit Mary remained standing against the tomb outside, weeping. So then as she wept she stooped aside into the tomb, and *beholdeth two messengers in white garments sitting, one at the head and other at the feet, where had been lying the body of Jesus*. And they say unto her—Woman! why weepest thou? She saith unto them—They have taken away my [Master], and I know not where they have laid him. These things saying she turned round and *seeth Jesus standing, and knew not that it was Jesus* (John 20:11–14).

The two messengers we find in John and in Luke 24:4 were purportedly Michael, the prince of the messengers, and Gabriel, the herald of light. These two were to act as guides in what is called the "good voyage" through the seven dark roads into the seven roads of light (seven levels of Hell and the seven visible levels of Heaven). In many of the inter-testamentary writings (such as the Book of Enoch) and in the known "gnostic" writings, as well as the *Kabbalah*, we are informed that there are in actuality ten levels of each. The upper three levels are the "invisible" heavens, while the lower seven are the "visible", thus the dual term *Shamayim* is used to refer to the combination of the two "heavens". In order to reach the highest visible level of Heaven (the *Shekinah* or *Malkut*) one had to traverse the "staircase" (Jacob's Stairway). It was a common first century Jewish prayer that when one dies he will be guided by these two messengers to the Father. The "Y" symbol represents the two angels who are invoked. The anchor is the symbol of hope and victory through the assistance of these messengers in the "good voyage". The Omega is a symbol for Gabriel, the messenger of light. It was believed that these two messengers, together with the yoke ("cross") entered the tomb with the body (as Jewish law requires, since the execution device was to be buried with the criminal; for instance, the yoke upon which Jesus was executed was thus buried

---

18. Saller and Testa, *Archaeological Setting*, p. 98.

with him). The messengers are to remain in the tomb with the yoke in order to bring about the resurrection of the body. We find these "two youths" in the Gospel of Peter 10, 39–42 (where we also find the "cross" or "yoke" emerging from the tomb behind Jesus and the two messengers) as well as in 2 Enoch 3:15–16; 12:2. It was, of course, in this instance not a physical "cross" (yoke) but a spiritual one. Another inscription (a cross with six prongs) was the sign of Emmanuel (ΙΧΘΥΣ). The sign that accompanies it is that of the *protoctistes*, two gems inscribed with the names of the six messengers Michael, Raphael, Uriel, Sabaoth, Abrasax and Immanuel on one, and on the other Raphael, Renel, Uriel, Iktys, Michael, Gabriel and Azael. This might well have once referred to the twelve tribes of Israel and reflect the names on the stones of Urim and Thummim. These were names of "angels" imagined by the intertestamentary writers. These messengers were believed to have a special role in the *re-creation* of Paradise; i.e., the "new creation" of God, the Infant "Daughter" of Zion. "Through them one gains admission to the church; they are connected with the "scala cosmica", and, according to the Apoc. 21,12, they guard the gates of the heavenly Jerusalem."[19]

There is then another group of symbols that are the signs of the Millennial Kingdom. The first is the symbol of 1000 (Aleph, which also means "One" and signifies unity) and the symbol of the palm tree, representing the *scala cosmica*. The third sign in this group is the Harp of David. The harp is to represent the universal harmony of the Kingdom of God played in the "tent (*sukkah*) of the Father", and again symbolizes unity with God.

> It is in the shadow of the tree of life; it knows the "tongue of angels" and the "voice of the archangels", and is related to the cross with six prongs, to the letter H and to the seven letters (στοιχεγα) [and] the harp of David is the orchestra of the kingdom of heaven, and is connected with *the power of the keys, as Christ [Messiah], who has the Key of David, which opens and no one closes; which closes and no one opens (Apoc. 3,7; see Is. 22,22).*[20]

The group of symbolic letters found next are representative of the Nazaraean doctrine of the two ways and reflects this dualism. This is not in any way similar to the later gnostics to which these earlier Nazaraeans have been compared. The motif of light and dark had been a Jewish concept, derived directly from the pages of the Old Covenant. Qumran scrolls also reflect this doctrine. The letter "Y", for instance, is symbolic for the path leading to the crossroads, the "two ways", which upon arriving at that juncture one must choose the path of darkness or light; i.e., evil or good. The path chosen will determine one's eternal future. The one road leads to a blessed life; the other leads to destruction. It brings to mind the very words of Jesus about the "narrow" way leading to life and the "broad" way leading to destruction (Matt. 7:14). It is also symbolic of our Plaza where Jesus was put to death. We also find the letters O (Omega) and T (Tav). These were considered signs of YHWH, particularly in that He is the First and the "Last—'AHARON". Both Omega (Greek) and Tav (Hebrew) are the last letters of their respective alphabets. They are also the symbol for Torah, because Tav is the beginning

---

19. Saller and Testa, p. 101.
20. Saller and Testa, p. 105.

A Book of Evidence

letter and "represents those who observe it" [E. Testa, p. 110]. It is symbolic of final judgment, the division of the "sheep" and "goats".

> This is the reason why it was associated with the final judgment, of life for the good and of condemnation and eternal death for the wicked. The rabbis said: It was a word of condemnation; RABBAH said: From the moment that he used it in every affair *it could stand for: Be confounded! or: May you live!* Rabbi HANINA ben Isaac said: It indicates: the merits of their forefathers are finished. In the *Babylonian Talmud* it is written: "The Holy One said to Gabriel: Go and put on the forehead of the just a *Taw* in ink... and on the forehead of the wicked a *Taw* in blood... And why a *Taw*? The *Taw* means: you shall live (*tihyeh*) and you shall die (*tamuth*)".[21]

The "sign" of the Son of Man spoken of by Jesus as appearing in the heavens just prior to his parousia (appearance) (Matt. 24:30) was believed by the Gentile church to be the Tav as a symbol of the "cross"; however, the sign of the Son of Man might well be the "rainbow" (i.e., like a prism, a reflection of the "glory" of God), which, like during the days of Noah, appeared *after* the gloom and clouds as a promise. Certainly, the Great Day of YHWH is one of gloom, darkness, and clouds. When Jesus appears, his brilliancy will be like a "rainbow"; i.e., a glittering gemstone. To write an Omega and a Tav together on a tomb was to represent the hope of victory and the second coming of Messiah. There are other sacred letters inscribed alongside these that also represent the appearance of the Messiah.

The letter Sigma is connected with the "seventh millennium"; i.e., the Millennial Kingdom in which Jesus will reign as High Priest and Prince of the World. It refers to that Great Sabbath Rest, the "one day of rest", but it also refers to the *eighth day* of Passover on which he was resurrected. After the Sigma we find the sacred number "H" (the numerical value of which is eight), and this again symbolizes the Eternal Kingdom, or what the rabbis call the World Without End. It is represented by the well-known mathematical infinity symbol [∞]. The *Nun* (Hebrew letter "N") was found there as well, and it represented the *kebar nuna* ("the fish of the tomb"). While we might see in this symbol the very essence of the work of Jesus, the rabbis, without realizing the significance of it, used it as a "charm" to eradicate demons. It was also called the *shepher-nuna* ("the beautiful fish") and the *kedash nuna* ("the sacred fish"). Thus we find the true meaning of the early Nazaraean symbol for the fish.

> *The faithful of the Torah* were the *little fish* which were in the *living water; the Messiah was the Leviathan, that is, the great mythical serpent-fish*, which had two horns and lived in the depth of the sea; its meat would be served at "the banquet of justice", or at the eschatological supper in Jerusalem. He who ate it communicated with the Savior. It was this idea which inspired the use of "the pure supper" (or παρασκευή) which consisted in a plate of fish, which the Jews ate on Friday night in preparation for the Sabbath. This was an eschatological banquet which symbolized immortality and the resurrection, according to the typology of Jonas who was in the fishtomb and came back to life miraculously (see *Mt.* 16,4).[22]

---

21. Saller and Testa, p. 110.
22. Saller and Testa, p. 117.

The Lamp of the World

Jesus had made slight allusion to the eschatological consumption of Leviathan as referring to himself. It was also connected with the "Last Supper".

> Jesus therefore said unto them—Verily, verily, I say unto you—*except ye eat the flesh of the son of man and drink his blood* ye have not life within yourselves. He that feedeth upon my flesh And drinketh my blood *hath life age-abiding*. And I will raise him up at the last day (John 6:53-54).

This fish was also to represent the brazen "serpent" healer in the wilderness (Num. 21:8), a device used even by Jesus in his conversation with Nicodemus when he had come to him by night (John 3:1-9).

The entire series of symbols begins at the door jamb, circles around and ends at the head of the grave, on which is written the very symbolic title of the grave's one-time occupant: *Huios Christos, Son Messiah*! Within the logical cycle of the symbols we have the history and purpose of Jesus. The theme of the tomb is eternal salvation (symbols on the door jamb), which is what Jesus came to provide. The next signs are, in order, redemption by Jesus (the Lamb), the yoke and the Tree of Life (execution and resurrection), the paradise won for us by the Redeemer (through his suffering), the name of the deceased (symbolically Nur, the Lamp through which the Light shines; i.e., the eternal flame, which holds the seven characteristics of YHWH's Spirit), the two messengers who Mary found at his tomb, the story of the Ascension, the Millennial Kingdom, the Eternal Kingdom, and *finally over grave couch "A"*, the two letters "TY", representing the ultimate cause of salvation: *huios christos*, the Son, Messiah.

The importance of this tomb must not be overlooked. The evidence is overwhelming that it is the very tomb in which Jesus was placed after his execution. It is situated approximately four hundred feet from the flogging stone at the Shrine of Bethphage. There are four other tombs that lie alongside and adjacent to it; it is in a garden which is quite near the execution site, and it has a rolling stone which is *still in place*. The symbols of the tomb tell us it is the tomb of "Nur", the (true) Lamp through which YHWH shines, and most importantly, the title Son Messiah is placed over the very head of the grave couch. As stated before, the tomb is in usable condition, even though it was built during the early first century. It seems one must be blind not to detect the uniqueness of this sepulchre. This tomb qualifies more than any other as the true sepulchre of Jesus. It has remained empty since the first century! The earliest Nazaraean followers of Jesus were known to have congregated on the Mount of Olives after the resurrection, and it would be entirely logical that they had placed these symbols in the tomb to mark it as the memorial of the resurrection. We are told by Theodocias that Thecla (an early follower of Paul) that Bethphage claimed Bethphage is Ancona (*angchone*), meaning "to strangle" or "to throttle", but with the final result being "suffocation", which would arise from "hanging". This tomb is the most obvious tomb site to be found anywhere near Jerusalem for the burial site of Jesus. It might well have been preserved by God as a testimony to the death and resurrection of the Messiah who had been executed at the Plaza of Gulgoleth on the Mount of Olives.

The sepulchre had been sealed and guarded by the "captains" of the Temple (not Roman guards as Christian tradition erroneously claims) for just such a reason. Pilate had *refused* to place guards at the tomb!

A Book of Evidence

> Ye [the Sanhedrin] have a guard [the Temple captains]: Go your way, secure it for yourselves, as ye know how. *And they went [the Sanhedrin] and secured for themselves the sepulchre, sealing the stone with a guard [Temple captains]* (Matt. 27:65-66).

The New Covenant Gospel of Matthew clearly states it was the Sanhedrin who took the responsibility of sealing the tomb, yet *tradition* places Roman soldiers around it. We are told that this guard went to the high priests after the resurrection, where they had been bribed to say his disciples had stolen the body.

> Now as they were going lo! *Certain of the guard [Temple captains] went into the city and reported unto the high-priests all the things that had come to pass*; and being gathered together with the Elders and taking counsel *sufficient pieces of silver gave they unto the soldiers [Temple captains]*—saying—say ye his disciples coming by night stole him while we were sleeping; and *if this be reported unto the governor [Herod Antipas, who held the same Roman position as Pilate] we will persuade him, and will make you free from care*. And they taking the pieces of silver did as they were instructed (Matt. 28:11-15).

First and foremost, the Roman soldiers would *not* have reported to the high priests; they would have reported only to Pilate! Secondly, a Roman soldier would have been too afraid of Pilate, their own governor, to desert. Furthermore, any Roman deserter, should he be caught, would have been stripped of his citizenship. Since Rome was the ruler of the world, these soldiers would have had few places to hide, nor would they have wanted to give up their place in society because of an allegiance to these Jewish priests. Although bribes between the priesthood and the Roman *authorities* were not uncommon, the priesthood would not have tried to bribe Roman *soldiers* for fear that Pilate might hear of it and retaliate. As we have learned, he resented their power, and many times, he thwarted their designs. Herod, however, as the second Roman governor, might be persuaded not to act harshly against the Temple captains.

Christian tradition places the resurrection on "the third day", and this must be more exactly examined. Actually, Jesus arose on the "eighth" day of Passover. His body remained in the tomb for "three days" as reckoned by Jewish calculation. In an earlier part of this book we have discussed the importance of understanding the Hebrew calendar, and this is perhaps one of those instances in which it becomes extremely important. There have been major objections and misunderstandings concerning the length of time Jesus was entombed prior to his resurrection. Scholars have debated the day on which Jesus was executed simply because they were unable to count three days and nights in the tomb. The answer, again, is quite simple. Remember, if an event occurs on any part of a day (even if it is just for a few minutes), that short time is considered a whole day. Thus when Jesus was taken down from the tree it was Friday afternoon about 3:00 p.m. He was clad in grave clothes and hurriedly deposited in the tomb. From 3:00 until 6:00 is just three hours, but it is considered *a whole day*! From 6:00 p.m. on Friday to 6:00 p.m. on Saturday is yet another day (the second day). The last portion of the "three days" is from 6:00 p.m. on Saturday until just about midnight, *the third day*! Jesus arose from the grave sometime between midnight and 4:00 a.m. on what we would call Sunday morning. This is the reason it was "yet dark" (John

20:1) when the women appeared at the tomb, yet it was "after the Sabbath". The important thing to notice, however, is that three Hebrew days were completed. The Temple guards had certainly been surprised sometime during the night because they reported to the chief priests "all the things that were done" (Matt. 28:11-13). It was these Temple captains who had the privilege of being the first to witness the resurrection of Jesus. They had probably seen the messenger roll away the stone from the door of the tomb. Perhaps they had even seen Jesus emerge from it. Whatever they saw, they had been so overcome by the sight that they passed out from shock (Matt. 28:1-4). When they had returned to the high priests, they told them what they had witnessed, certainly something the priesthood hadn't expected. The Messiah had arisen!

Epilogue

THE TIME HAD COME for "filling up the measure" (17 Nisan, the first day of the Feast of Weeks). Jesus had walked in the paths of righteousness for the sake of YHWH. He had suffered the atrocities of a Jewish execution, and he had been buried in a tomb that would not hold him. Today, his teachings are echoed throughout the world. This Jew, this Hebrew Messiah, this Jesus who all hearts yearn for is alive! Since the first century, this world has not been the same. He is revealed by his Father, YHWH, and YHWH is revealed through Jesus. Throughout the centuries those who have ears to hear have been hearing the true message of Jesus: Worship YHWH! Honor His Son! The measure is almost full. One day soon Jesus will return as Emmanuel, the Prince of the World To Come, the World Without End, and when he does, we shall have our Sabbath rest. In the meantime, we must continue to follow our Master. Let us not confuse the witness of Jesus, what he told us of our Father YHWH, with the teachings of man's tradition; instead, let us work out our own salvation, let us follow his paths, "let us be going forth unto him *outside the camp*, his reproach bearing" (Heb. 13:13).

Finis

Appendix A

ENTRAPMENT

Matthew 12:24

21:46
22:15
22:35
26:3-4
26:59

Mark 2:7

3:2
3:6
3:22
8:11
11:18
11:27-28
12:12
12:13
12:18
14:12

Luke 6:7

10:25
11:15-16
11:53-54
14:1

16:14
19:39
19:47
20:1-2
20:19
20:20
20:27

John 5:16

5:18
7:11-12
7:19
7:25
7:30
7:32
7:44-47
8:20
8:48
10:33
10:39
11:8
11:53
11:57
12:10-11

Appendix B

LEADING THE NATION ASTRAY

Matthew 10:57

21:15
21:23
21:46

Mark 7:12

11:19

Luke 4:28-29

23:2
23:5
23:14

John 7:11-12

7:44-47
10:31
11:47-49
11:50-53

Bibliography

Aiyar, S. Srinivasa. *The Legality of the Trial of Jesus*, New Orleans. LA: Chas. E. George, 1914.
Alexander, David and Pat Alexander, eds. *Eerdmans' Handbook to the Bible*. Grand Rapids, Michigan: William B. Eerdmans Publishing Company, 1973.
All About the Bible. Westwood, New Jersey: Barbour and Company, Inc., 1989.
Allegro, John Marco. *The Mystery of the Dead Sea Scrolls Revealed*. New York: Gramercy Publishing Company, 1981.
———. *The Treasure of the Copper Scroll*. Garden City, N.Y.: Doubleday & Company, Inc., 1960.
The Apocrypha, KJV. Iowa Falls, Iowa: World Bible Publishers, Inc., n.d.
Avi-Yonah, Michael. *Ancient Scrolls*. London: Cassell & Company LTD, 1973.
Baigent, Michael and Richard Leigh. *The Dead Sea Scroll Deception*, New York: Summit Books, 1991.
Baltsan, Hayim. *Webster's New World Hebrew Dictionary*. New York: Simon & Schuster, Inc., 1992.
Barclay, William. *The Mind of Jesus*. New York: HarperSanFrancisco, 1976.
Barnstone, Willis, ed. *The New Covenant Commonly Called the New Testament, Volume I, The Four Gospels and Apocalypse*. New York: Riverhead Books, 2002.
———. *The Other Bible*, San Francisco: Harper & Row, Publishers, 1984.
Ben-David, Yirmiyahu. *The N'tzarim Reconstruction of Matiytyahu*. 2 Vols., Ra'anana, Israel: Schueller House, 1994.
Bentley, James. *Secrets of Mount Sinai, The Story of the Codex Sinaiticus*. London: Orbis, 1985.
Ben-Sasson, H. H., ed. *A History of the Jewish People*. Cambridge, Massachusetts: Harvard University Press, 1976.
Bialik, Hayim Nahman and Yehoshua Hana Ravnitzky, eds. *The Book of Legends, Sefer Ha-Aggadah*. New York: Schocken Books, 1992.
Blaiklock, E. M. *The Archaeology of the New Testament*. Nashville: Thomas Nelson Publishers, 1984.
———. *The Compact Handbook of New Testament Life*. Minneapolis, Minnesota: Bethany House Publishers, 1979.
Blech, Benjamin. *The Secrets of Hebrew Words*. Northvale, New Jersey: Jason Aronson, Inc., 1991.
———. *More Secrets of Hebrew Words*. Northvale, New Jersey: Jason Aronson, Inc., 1993.
Block, Abraham P. *The Biblical and Historical Background of Jewish Customs and Ceremonies*. New York: KTAV Publishing House, Inc., 1980.
Blomberg, Craig. *The Historical Reliability of the Gospels*. England: Inter-Varsity Press, 1987.
Bowker, John. *Jesus and the Pharisees*. New York, N.Y.: Cambridge University Press, 1973.
Brenton, Sir Lancelot C. L. *The Septuagint with Apocrypha: Greek and English*. Peabody, Massachusetts: Hendrickson Publishers, 2003.
Brown, Raymond E. *The Death of the Messiah, From Gethsemane to the Grave: A Commentary on the Passion Narratives in the Four Gospels*. Vols. 1–2, New York: The Anchor Bible Reference Library, a Division of Doubleday, 1998.
Brown, Robert K. and Philip W. Comfort, trans.; J. D. Douglas, ed. *The New Greek-English Interlinear New Testament*. Wheaton, Illinois: Tyndale House Publishers, Inc., 1990.
Bruce, F. F. *Peter, Stephen, James & John, Studies in Non-Pauline Christianity*. Grand Rapids: William B. Eerdman's Publishing Company, 1979.
Buckingham, Jamie. *A Way Through the Wilderness*. Old Tappan, New Jersey: Chosen Books, 1986.

Bibliography

Budge, E. A. Wallis. *Osiris and The Egyptian Resurrection*. New York: Dover Publications, Inc., 2 vols., 1973.
Bullinger, E. W. *Number in Scripture*. Grand Rapids, Michigan: Kregel Publications, 1967.
Bush, L. Russ, ed. *Classical Readings in Christian Apologetics*. Grand Rapids, Michigan: Academie Books, Zondervan Publishing House, 1983.
Butz, Jeffrey J. *The Brother of Jesus and the Lost Teachings of Christianity*. Rochester, Vermont: Inner Traditions, 2005.
Chadwick, Henry. *Origen, Contra Celsum*. Cambridge: Cambridge University Press, 1953.
———. *The Early Church*. New York: Dorset Press, 1967.
Clouse, Robert G., Richard V. Pierard, and Edwin M. Yamauchi. *Two Kingdoms, The Church and Culture Through the Ages*. Chicago: Moody Press, 1993.
Cohen, A. *Everyman's Talmud*. New York: Schocken Books, 1975.
Cohn, Haim. *The Trial and Death of Jesus*. New York: KTAV Publishing House, Inc., 1977.
———. *Jewish Law in Ancient and Modern Israel*. New York: KTAV Publishing House, 1971.
The Companion Bible: The Authorized Version of 1611 with the Structures and Critical, Explanatory, and Suggestive Notes and with 198 Appendixes. Grand Rapids, Michigan: Kregel Publications, 1990.
Cornell, Tim and John Matthews. *Atlas of the Roman World*. New York: Facts on File Publications, 1982.
Craveri, Marcello. *The Life of Jesus*. New York: Grove Press, Inc., 1967.
Crossan, John Dominic. *The Historical Jesus, The Life of a Mediterranean Peasant*. New York: HarperSanFrancisco, 1992.
———. *Who Killed Jesus?* San Francisco: HarperSanFrancisco, 1995.
———. *The Birth of Christianity, Discovering What Happened in the Years Immediately After the Execution of Jesus*. New York: HarperSanFrancisco, 1999.
Dalman, G. H. *Die Worte Jesu* (English Translation: *The Words of Jesus*). Edinburgh: Clark, 1902.
Danby, Herbert. Translated by Herbert Danby. *Tractate Sanhedrin, Mishnah and Tosefta*, New York: The Macmillan Company, 1919.
The Dead Sea Scrolls Bible: The Oldest Known Bible Translated for the First Time into English. Translated by Abegg, Martin, Jr.; Peter Flint, and Eugene Ulrich, New York: HarperCollins Publishers, 1999.
DeWitt, Roy Lee. *Teaching From the Tabernacle*. Grand Rapids, Michigan: Baker Book House, 1986.
Dimont, Max I. *Jews, God and History*. New York: New American Library, 1962.
Donin, Rabbi Hayim Halevy. *To Be A Jew*. United States: BasicBooks, A Division of HarperCollins Publishers, 1972.
———. *To Pray As A Jew*, United States: BasicBooks, 1980.
Douglas, J. D., ed.; Robert K. Brown and Philip W. Comfort, trans. *The Greek-English Interlinear New Testament*. Wheaton, Illinois: Tyndale House Publishers, Inc., 1990.
Edersheim, Alfred. *Old Testament Bible History*. Grand Rapids, Michigan: Wm. B. Eerdmans Publishing Co., 1971.
———. *The Life and Times of Jesus the Messiah*. Grand Rapids, Michigan: Wm. B. Eerdmans Publishing Co., 1971.
———. *Old Testament Bible History*. Grand Rapids, Michigan: William B. Eerdmans Publishing Company, 1982.
———. *Sketches of Jewish Social Life in the Days of Christ*. Grand Rapids, Michigan: Wm. B. Eerdmans Publishing Company, 1990.
———. *The Temple*. Grand Rapids, Michigan: Wm. B. Eerdmans Publishing Company, reprint 1990.
Eisenman Robert and Michael Wise. *The Dead Sea Scrolls Uncovered*. New York: Barnes & Noble, 1994.
Epstein, Rabbi Dr., BA. *The Babylonian Talmud*. London: Soncino Press, 1936, 1938, 1987.
Eusebius, Pamphilus. *The Ecclesiastical History of Eusebius Pamphilus*. Grand Rapids, Michigan: Baker Book House Company, 1991.
Foreman, Dale. *Crucify Him*. Grand Rapids, Michigan: Zondervan Publishing House, 1990.
Fosdick, Harry Emerson. *The Man From Nazareth As His Contemporaries Saw Him*. New York: Harper & Brothers, 1949.
Frankel, Ellen and Betsy Platkin Teutsch. *The Encyclopedia of Jewish Symbols*. Northvale, New Jersey: Jason Aronson, Inc., 1992.
Fredricksen, Paula. *From Jesus to Christ, The Origins of New Testament Images of Christ*. New Haven and London: Yale University Press, 2000.

―――. *Jesus of Nazareth, King of the Jews, A Jewish Life and the Emergence of Christianity*. New York: Alfred A. Knoph, a Division of Random House, Inc.
Freedman, David Noel, ed. *The Anchor Bible Dictionary*. New York: Doubleday, 1992.
Friedman, Richard Elliott. *Commentary on the Torah With a New English Translation*. New York: HarperSanFrancisco, 2003.
Fruchtenbaum, Dr. Arnold G. *Hebrew Christianity: Its Theology, History, & Philosophy*. Tustin, California: Ariel Ministries Press, 1992.
Frydland, Rachmiel. *What the Rabbis Know About the Messiah*. Cincinnati, Ohio: Messianic Publishing Company, 1993.
Fujita, Neil S. *A Crack in the Jar*. New York/Mahwah: Paulist Press, 1986.
Gersh, Harry, *The Sacred Books of the Jews*. New York: Stein and Day, 1968.
Ginzberg, Louis. *Legends of the Bible*. U.S.A.: Jewish Publication Society of America and Barnes & Noble Books, 1956.
Glatzer, Nahum N. *The Passover Haggadah*. New York: Schocken Books, 1981.
Goldin, Judah, trans. *Mishnah, Avot. The Living Talmud: The Wisdom of the Fathers and its Classical Commentaries*. New York: The Heritage Press, 1957.
Grant, Michael. *Jesus*. London: Rigel Publications, A Division of Orion Publishing Group, Ltd., 1977.
―――. *Jesus, An Historian's Review of the Gospels*. New York: Charles Scribner's Sons, 1977.
Green, Jay P., Sr., ed. and trans. *The Interlinear Bible, Hebrew-Greek-English*. Peabody, Massachusetts, Hendrickson Publishers, 1986.
Gundry, Robert H. *A Survey of the New Testament*. Grand Rapids, Michigan: Academie Books, Zondervan Publishing House, 1981.
Halpern, Baruch. *The First Historians, The Hebrew Bible and History*. San Francisco: Harper & Row, Publishers, 1988.
Hammer, Reuven, trans. *The Classic Midrash*. New York-Mahwah: Paulist Press, 1995.
Hengel, Martin; William Klassen, trans. *Was Jesus a Revolutionist?* Philadelphia: Fortress Press, 1971.
Herford, R. Travers. *Christianity in Talmud and Midrash*. London: Williams & Norgate, 1903.
Hislop, Rev. Alexander. *The Two Babylons*. Neptune, New Jersey: Loizeaux Brothers, 1959.
Holtz, Barry W., ed. *Back to the Sources, Reading the Classic Jewish Texts*. New York: Summit Books, 1984.
The Holy Bible, New International Version. Grand Rapids, Michigan: Zondervan Publishing House, 1984.
The Holy Bible, Old and New Testaments in the King James Version. Nashville, Tennessee: Thomas Nelson, Inc., 1976.
Hurlbut, Cornelius S. Jr., Ph.D. and George S. Switzer, Ph.D. *Gemology*. New York: John Wiley & Sons, Inc., 1979.
Hutchings, N. W. *Petra in History & Prophecy*. Oklahoma City, OK: Hearthstone Publishing Ltd., 1991.
Hynes, Arleen. *The Passover Meal*. New York: Paulist Press, 1972.
Ice, Thomas and Randall Price. *Ready to Rebuild*. Eugene, Oregon: Harvest House Publishers, 1992.
Idinopulos, Thomas A. *Jerusalem Blessed, Jerusalem Cursed*. Chicago: Ivan R. Dee, 1991.
James, E. O. *The Cult of the Mother-Goddess*. New York: Barnes & Noble, 1994.
The Jewish Encyclopedia. "Accusatory and Inquisitorial Procedure". New York: Funk and Wagnalls Company, 1901.
―――. "Anathema". New York: Funk and Wagnalls Company, 1901.
―――. "Bethphage". New York: Funk and Wagnalls Company, 1901.
―――. "Caiaphas-Caiaphas, Joseph". New York: Funk and Wagnalls Company, 1901.
―――. "Calendar". New York: Funk and Wagnalls Company, 1901.
―――. "Capital Punishment". New York: Funk and Wagnalls Company, 1901.
―――. "Crime". New York: Funk and Wagnalls Company, 1901.
―――. "Excommunication". New York: Funk and Wagnalls Company, 1901.
―――. "Jerusalem". New York: Funk and Wagnalls Company, 1901.
―――. "Miphkad". New York: Funk and Wagnalls Company, 1901.
―――. "Passover". New York: Funk and Wagnalls Company, 1901.
―――. "Passover Sacrifice". New York: Funk and Wagnalls Company, 1901.
―――. "Plan of the Second Temple". New York: Funk and Wagnalls Company, 1901, http://www.jewishencyclopedia.com/articles/14307-temple-plan-of-second.
―――. "Sanhedrin". New York: Funk and Wagnalls Company, 1901.

Bibliography

———. "Wachnacht". New York: Funk and Wagnalls Company, 1901.

———. "Xystus". New York: Funk and Wagnalls Company, 1901.

Johnson, Luke Timothy. *The Real Jesus: The Misguided Quest for the Historical Jesus and the Truth of the Traditional Gospels*. New York, NY: Harper SanFrancisco, 1996.

Kaplan, Rabbi Aryeh, trans. *The Living Torah, A New Translation Based on Traditional Jewish Sources*. New York/Jerusalem: Maznaim Publishing Corporation, 1981.

Keller, Werner; William Neil, trans. *The Bible as History*. New York: Bantam Books, 1956.

Kiehl, Erich H. *The Passion of Our Lord*. Grand Rapids, Michigan: Baker Book House, 1990.

Kolatch, Alfred J. *The Jewish Book of Why*. Middle Village, NY: Jonathan David Publishers, 1981.

———. *This is the Torah*, Middle Village, NY: Jonathan David Publishers, Inc., 1988.

Lapide, Pinchas E. *Hebrew in the Church, The Foundations of Jewish-Christian Dialogue*. Grand Rapids, Michigan: William B. Eerdmans Publishing Company, 1984.

Lamsa, George M., trans. *Holy Bible from the Ancient Eastern Text*. San Francisco: HarperSanFrancisco, 1933.

Levinas, Emmanuel, Annette Aronowicz, trans. *Nine Talmudic Readings*. Bloomington & Indianapolis: Indiana University Press, 1990.

Lewis, Jack P. *The English Bible from KJV to NIV*. Grand Rapids, Michigan: Baker Book House, 1991.

Lightfoot, John. *A Commentary on the New Testament from the Talmud and Hebraica*. 4 Vol., Peabody, Massachusetts: Hendrickson Publishers, 1997.

The Lost Books of the Bible and The Forgotten Books of Eden. United States: Alpha House, Inc., 1926.

McKinsey, C. Dennis. *The Encyclopedia of Biblical Errancy*. Amherst, New York: Prometheius Books, 1995.

Mack, Burton L. *Who Wrote the New Testament? The Making of the Christian Myth*. San Francisco: HarperSanFrancisco, 1995.

———. *The Lost Gospel, The Book of Q & Christian Origins*. San Francisco: HarperSanFrancisco, 1993.

Mahan, Rev. W. D. *The Archaeological and the Historical Writings of the Sanhedrin and Talmuds of the Jews*. Chicago, Ill.: The de Laurence Company, 1923.

Maimonides, Moses. *The Guide For the Perplexed*. Translated by M. Friedlander, Forgotten Books, 2008.

Mare, W. Harold. *The Archaeology of the Jerusalem Area*. Grand Rapids, Michigan: Baker Book House, 1987.

Martin, Dr. Ernest L. *The Original Bible Restored*. Portland, Oregon: ASK Publications, 1991.

———. *The Place of the New Third Temple*. Portland, Oregon: ASK Publications, 1994.

———. *The Secrets of Golgotha*. Alhambra, California: ASK Publications, 1988.

Mazar, Benjamin. *The Mountain of the Lord*. Garden City, New York: Doubleday & Company, 1975.

Meier, John P. *A Marginal Jew*. New York: Doubleday, 1991.

Mellinkoff, Ruth. *The Mark of Cain*. Berkeley: University of California Press, 1981.

Metzger, Bruce M. and Michael D. Coogan. *The Oxford Companion to the Bible*, New York and Oxford: Oxford University Press, 1993.

Michas, Peter A., Robert Vander Maten, and Christie D. Michas. *God's Master Plan From Aleph to Tav*. Troy, IL: Messengers of Messiah International Ministries, 1994.

Miller, Robert J. and Funk, Robert W., eds. *The Complete Gospels, Annotated Scholars Version*, Sonoma, CA.: Polebridge Press, 1994.

Nelson-Pallmeyer, Jack. *Jesus Against Christianity, Reclaiming the Missing Jesus*. Harrisburg, Pennsylvania: Trinity Press International, 2001.

Neusner, Jacob. *Judaism and the Interpretation of Scripture, Introduction to the Rabbinic Midrash*. Peabody, Massachusetts: Hendrickson Publishers, LLC, 2004.

———. *Judaism When Christianity Began, A Survey of Belief and Practice*. Louisville•London: Westminster John Knox Press, 2002.

———. *Rabbinic Literature and the New Testament*. Valley Forge, Pennsylvania: Trinity Press International, 1994.

———, ed. *The Mishnah, A New Translation*. New Haven and London: Yale University Press, 1988.

Newman, Louis I. *The Talmudic Anthology, Tales & Teachings of the Rabbis*. West Orange, New Jersey: Behrman House, Inc., 1945.

Nolan, Albert. *Jesus Before Christianity*. Maryknoll, New York: Orbis Books, 1995.

Ogg, Oscar. *The 26 Letters*. New York: Thomas Y. Crowell Company, 1961.

Palmer, Earl M. *The Intimate Gospel, Studies in John*. Word Books, 1978.
Parrinder, Geoffrey, ed. *World Religions From Ancient History to the Present*. New York, New York: Facts on File Publications, 1971.
Patai, Raphael. *The Messiah Texts*. New York, New York: Avon Books, 1979.
Paulus. *Das Leben Jesu* (1934 Goguel / Binswanger), book (German ed.).
Phillips, John. *Exploring the World of the Jew*. Chicago: Moody Press, 1988.
Potok, Chaim. *Wanderings*. Fawcett Crest, New York: Ballantine Books, 1978.
Powell, Evan. *The Unfinished Gospel*. Westlake Village, California: Symposium Books, 1994.
The Practical Bible Dictionary & Atlas. Nashville: Thomas Nelson Publishers, 1952.
Price, Reynolds. *Three Gospels*. New York: Scribner, 1996.
Rasmussen, Carl G. *NIV Atlas of the Bible*. Grand Rapids, Michigan: Regency Reference Library, Zondervan Publishing House, 1989.
The Restoration of Original Sacred Name Bible. Emory, Texas: Missionary Dispensary Bible Research, 1976.
Richards, Hon. John E. *The Illegality of the Trial of Jesus*. New Orleans, LA: Chas. E. George, 1914.
Richardson, Peter. *Herod, King of the Jews and Friend of the Romans*. Columbia, South Carolina: University of South Carolina Press, 1996.
Riedel, Eunice, Thomas Tracy and Barbra D. Moskowitz. *The Book of the Bible*. Toronto: Bantam Books, 1981.
Robinson, James M., ed. *The Nag Hammadi Library in English*. San Francisco: Harper & Row, Publishers, 1978.
Romer, John. *Testament*. New York: Henry Holt and Company, 1988.
Rosenberg, David, ed. *Congregation, Contemporary Writers Read the Jewish Bible*. San Diego: Harcourt Brace Jovanovich, Publishers, 1987.
Rotherham, Joseph Bryant. trans. *Rotherham's Emphasized Bible*. Grand Rapids, Michigan: Kregel Publications, 1994.
Rubenstein, Richard E. *When Jesus Became God, The Struggle to Define Christianity during the Last Days of Rome*. San Diego, New York, and London: Harcourt, Inc., 1999.
Ryrie, Charles Caldwell. *A Survey of Bible Doctrine*. Chicago: Moody Press, 1972.
Salderini, Anthony J. *Pharisees, Scribes and Sadducees in Palestinian Society*. Grand Rapids, Michigan: William B. Eerdmans Publishing Company, 2001.
Saller, Sylvester J. and Emmanuele Testa. *The Archaeological Setting of the Shrine of Bethphage*. Jerusalem: Franciscan Press, 1961.
Sanders, E. P. *The Historical Figure of Jesus*. New York: Penguin Press, 1993.
Schauss, Hayyim. *The Jewish Festivals from Their Beginnings to Our Own Day*. New York: Union of American Hebrew Congregations, 1958.
Scherman and Meir Zlotowitz, Rabbis, ed., *History of the Jewish People, The Second Temple Era*. New York: Artscroll History Series with Mesora Publications, 1982.
Schmidt, Werner H. *Old Testament Introduction*. New York: Crossroad, 1984.
Schonfield, Hugh J. *The Original New Testament*. San Francisco: Harper & Row, Publishers, 1985.
———. *According to the Hebrews, A new translation of the Jewish Life of Jesus (the Toldoth Jeshu), With an inquiry into the nature of its source and special relationship to the lost Gospel according to the Hebrews*. London: Duckworth.
The Scriptures. Republic of South Africa: Institute for Scripture Research.
Shanks, Hershel. *Understanding the Dead Sea Scrolls*. New York: Random House, 1992.
——— and Ben Witherington III. *The Brother of Jesus, The Dramatic Story & Meaning of the First Archaeological Link to Jesus & His Family*. New York: HarperSanFrancisco, 2003.
Silberman, Neil Asher. *Digging for God and Country*. New York: Alfred A. Knoph, 1982.
Smith, William. *Smith's Bible Dictionary*. New York: Family Library, 1975.
Soltau, Henry W. *The Tabernacle, The Priesthood and the Offerings*. Grand Rapids, Michigan: Kregel Publications, 1972.
Spier, Arthur. *The Comprehensive Hebrew Calendar*. Jerusalem/New York: Feldheim Publishers, 1986.
Spong, John Shelby. *Resurrection: Myth or Reality?* San Francisco: HarperSanFrancisco, 1994.
Stedman's Medical Dictionary. 23rd Edition. Baltimore/London: Williams & Wilkins, 1976.

Bibliography

Stern, David H., trans. *The Jewish New Testament*. Jerusalem, Israel: Jewish New Testament Publications, 1989.
Steinsaltz, Adin and Chaya Galai, trans. *The Essential Talmud*. New York: Basic Books, Inc., Publishers, 1976.
Stewart, Don and Chuck Missler. *The Coming Temple*. Orange, California: Dart Press, 1991.
Strom, Mark. *The Symphony of Scripture*. Downers Grove, Illinois: InterVarsity Press, 1990.
Strong, James. *The New Strong's Exhaustive Concordance of the Bible*. Nashville: Thomas Nelson Publishers, 1990.
Strong, James. *The Tabernacle of Israel, Its Structure and Symbolism*. Grand Rapids, Michigan: Kregel Publications, 1987.
Tanakh, The Holy Scriptures, JPS translation. Philadelphia: The Jewish Publication Society, 5748–1988.
Thayer, Joseph Henry, D. D. *The New Thayer's Greek-English Lexicon of the New Testament*. Peabody, Massachusetts: Hendrickson Publishers, 1981.
Thiede, Carsten Peter and Matthew D'Ancona. *Eyewitness to Jesus*, New York: Doubleday, 1996.
Throckmorton, Burton H., Jr., ed. *Gospel Parallels, A Synopsis of the First Three Gospels*. Nashville: Thomas Nelson Publishers, 1979.
Ulpianus, *Digest XLVIII. 20, 6* and *On the Duties of Proconsul, IX* in *The Civil Law, Including the Twelve Tables, The Institutes of Gaius, The Rules of Ulpian, The Opinions of Paulus, The Enactments of Justinian, and The Constitutions of Leo*. Translated by Samuel P. Scott: Cinncinnati The Central Trust Company, Executor of the Estate Samuel P. Scott, Deceased, Publishers; http://www.constitution.org/sps/sps11.htm.
VanderKam, James C. *From Joshua to Caiaphas, High Priests after the Exile*. Minneapolis, MN: Augsburg Fortress Press, 2004.
Vermes, G. *Jesus in His Jewish Context*. Minneapolis: Fortress Press, 2003.
———. *The Dead Sea Scrolls in English*. London, England: Penguin Books, 1987.
Vos, Howard F. *Archaeology in Bible Lands*. Chicago: Moody Press, 1977.
Waite, Charles B., A. M. *History of the Christian Religion to the Year Two Hundred*. Chicago: C. V. Waite & Co., 1900.
Watson, Alan. *The Trial of Jesus*. Athens & London: The University of Georgia Press, 1995.
Webster's Ninth New Collegiate Dictionary. Springfield, Massachusetts: Merriam-Webster, Inc., Publishers, 1986.
Whiston, William, trans. *The Works of Flavius Josephus*. 4 Vols., Grand Rapids, Michigan: Baker Book House, 1974.
White, L. Michael. *From Jesus to Christianity: How Four Generations of Visionaries & Storytellers Created the New Testament and Christian Faith*. New York: HarperSanFrancisco, 2004.
Wiesel, Elie. *Sages and Dreamers*. New York: Touchstone, Simon & Schuster, 1991.
Wight, Fred H. *Manners and Customs of Bible Lands*. Chicago: Moody Press, 1953.
Wilson, A.N. *Jesus, A Life*. New York: W. W. Norton & Company, 1992.
Wilson, Ian. *Jesus, The Evidence*. New York: Harper & Row, Publishers, 1984.
Wilson, William. *Wilson's Old Testament Word Studies*. McLean, Va.: MacDonald Publishing Co., n.d.
Wilson, Colonel R. E., ed. *Picturesque Palestine, Sinai and Egypt*. Palestine Exploration Society, New York: D. Appleton and Company, 1881.
Winter, Paul. *On the Trial of Jesus*. Berlin: Walter De Gruyter & Co., 1961.
Wylen, Stephen M. *The Jews in the Time of Jesus, An Introduction*. New York/Mahwah, N. J.: Paulist Press, 1996.
Yonge, C. D., ed. *The Works of Philo*. Peabody, Massachusetts: Hendrickson Publishers, 1993.
Young, Brad. *Jesus, the Jewish Theologian*, Peabody, Massachusetts: Hendrickson Publishers, Inc., 2004.
Young, Robert. *Young's Literal Translation of the Holy Bible*. Grand Rapids, Michigan: Baker Book House, 1898, Revised Ed.
Zeitlin, Irving M. *Jesus and the Judaism of His Time*. Cambridge: Polity Press, 1994.

JOURNALS AND MAGAZINES

Bahat, Dan, "Jerusalem Down Under". *Biblical Archaeology Review*, Volume 21, Number 6, November/December 1995, pp. 30–47.

Bibliography

Fine, Steven, "Did the Synagogues Replace the Temple?" *Bible Review*, Vol. XII, No. 2, April 1996, pp. 18–26, 41.

Jones, Vendyl. Vendyl Jones Research Institute Researcher, December, 1995, pp. 10–11.

Martin, Dr. Ernest L. "Where Did Solomon Build His Temple? *A.S.K.* Report #00078.

Pritz, Ray. "The Divine Name in the Hebrew New Testament", *Jerusalem Perspective*, Volume 4, Number 2, March/April 1991, pp. 10–12.

Qimron, Elisha and John Strugnell. "MMT", *Biblical Archaeological Review*, Volume 20, Number 6, November/December 1994, pp. 56–61.

Ritmeyer, Leen. "Locating the Original Temple Mount", *Biblical Archaeology Review*, March/April 1992, Volume 18, Number 2, pp. 24–45.

Sefrai, Shmuel. "Literary Languages in the Time of Jesus", *Jerusalem Perspective*, Volume 4, Number 2, March/April, 1991, pp. 3–9.